Business Entities:
A Practical Guide

AUSTRALIA
LBC Information Services, Sydney

CANADA & USA
Carswell, Toronto

NEW ZEALAND
Brooker's, Auckland

SINGAPORE & MALAYSIA
Thomson Information (SE Asia), Singapore

Business Entities: A Practical Guide

by

Andrew Clarke LL.M.

London · Sweet & Maxwell · 1996

Published in 1996 by Sweet & Maxwell Limited
100 Avenue Road, Swiss Cottage,
London NW3 3PF

Typeset by Wyvern Typesetting, Bristol
Printed by Clays Ltd, St Ives plc

No natural forests were destroyed to make this product;
only farmed timber was used and replanted.

The index was prepared by Robert Spicer, Barrister

A CIP catalogue record for this book is available from the British Library.

ISBN 0 421 50490 0

Acknowledgments

Many thanks to the following people: Professor Alan Bensted, Dr Adrian Chandler, Steve Frost, Julie Endicott, Karen Eastwood, Vicki Bradford, Joyce Green, Trudi Parker, James Newman and William Hull for their assistance with this project. And to Dr Stella Swain for her invaluable support and advice.

The authors wish to acknowledge and thank Jordan's Publishing for allowing the publication within this guide of the following documents and materials that are Jordan's copyright and are reproduced from *Company Law Materials*:

Table A, articles of association
Type A, B, C, transfer articles
Amendments and additions to table A
Forms G10 and G12
Stock Transfer form

Andrew Clarke is the author of all chapters of this book save for Chapters 14, 15 and 17 which were written by Steven Dinning.

Contents

1. Introduction to, and Overview of, Business Entities

Sole Traders

2. Overview of Sole Traders

Partnerships

3. Overview of Partnerships

4. Partnerships and Specific Legal Issues

Miscellaneous Issues: Sole Traders and Partnerships

5. Personal Insolvency

6. Taxation of Sole Traders and Partnerships

7. Business Names

Companies

8. Overview of Companies

9. Companies—General Matters and Incorporation

10. The Constituent Documents of a Company

11. Shares and Shareholders

12. Directors and Other Company Officers

13. Company Procedure

14. Basic Company Finance and Maintenance of Share Capital

15. Corporate Insolvency

16. Company Taxation

17. A Common Commercial Transaction: Sale and Purchase of a Private Limited Company

18. Specialist Topics

19. International Business Transactions

20. The European Community and European Community Law

21. Competition Law

22. Joint Ventures

Appendices

Appendix 1: Sole Traders

Appendix 2: Partnerships

Appendix 3: Companies

Appendix 4: Tax and Insolvency

Appendix 5: Glossary

Appendix 6: Ready Reckoner Regarding Fees, Percentages and Sterling Amounts Referred to in this Guide

Table of Cases

Table of Statutes

Table of Statutory Instruments

Table of E.C. Treaties

Table of E.C. Legislation

1. Introduction to, and Overview of, Business Entities

A. Background

1. TYPES OF BUSINESS ENTITIES

There are three main types of business entities or means of running a business:

    (a) sole trader;
    (b) partnership; and
    (c) company.

1.1

These business entities refer to businesses run from home or small shops (likely to be sole traders); professional and trading partnerships (*e.g.* lawyers and accountants) and companies (which can range from small, private operations to huge, publicly owned, international businesses).

This guide aims to examine each of these business entities and point out some of their practical and legal characteristics, their advantages and disadvantages.

What then are the sorts of matters that a solicitor or business adviser should be aware of when advising a client in relation to these business entities? The adviser must focus on the client's needs and recognise that there may be many situations in which legal advice is sought. For example:

    (a) on establishing a business, *e.g.* advising the founders of a company;
    (b) on expansion of the business, *e.g.* a company increasing its share capital;
    (c) on a change in the method of doing business, *e.g.* a sole trader forming a company; or
    (d) on a client leaving a business, *e.g.* advising on the ways of avoiding removal as a company director.

Flexibility of approach is required from the legal adviser. No two situations will be the same. How does a lawyer get around this? By having an organised approach; by being familiar with the principles pertaining to the business entities. One way of developing these traits is to use checklists, especially in the early days of training. These ensure thoroughness of approach. Checklists are a matter of individual choice, but a suggested checklist is given later in this chapter as the basis, at least, for advising a client in relation to establishing a business. There will, of course, be other checklists relevant to business entities. The "establishment of business entities" checklist will be developed in this guide in relation to sole traders, partnerships and companies.

Before setting out the checklist, it is helpful to have a "broad picture" of the three business entities.

2. AN OVERVIEW OF THE BUSINESS ENTITIES

1.2

Sole traders

    (a) these are one person businesses;

    (b) the person who manages the business, owns the business and keeps the profits.

Partnerships

    (a) these are businesses involving two or more people carrying on a business and intending to make a profit;

    (b) the two or more people own and manage the business. An important consequence is that the two people or more (the partners) bear unlimited personal liability for the debts of the business. They cannot simply say that, "it is a business debt, it has nothing to do with me personally";

    (c) risk and liability are, therefore, vital matters when someone is contemplating going into partnership.

Companies

    (a) the key difference between companies and the other two entities is that a company is a separate legal entity in its own right;

    (b) a company is a separate "legal being" from those people who own the company (the shareholders) and those people who manage the affairs of the company (the directors);

    (c) a key difference then between companies and the other entities is that a shareholder can, in general terms, say that "this is a company debt, it is for the company to pay and it has nothing to do with me."

Note These very general points made by way of overview are subject to exceptions and variations.

3. CONNECTIONS BETWEEN THE BUSINESS ENTITIES

1.3

Each of the business entities may be sold, expand in size and contract in size and may change form. For example, a sole trader may decide to "incorporate" the business, *i.e.* form a company in which he owns shares and may be a director.

Alternatively, a partnership may be dissolved when a partner leaves, leaving only one remaining partner who would then (after a certain period of time) be deemed to be a sole trader.

A company may be purchased by another company by the transfer of assets or shares such as to enable control of the business.

Again, these varied circumstances should alert a trainee to the fact that there are a number of situations in which legal advice will be sought.

B. The Solicitor's Business Checklist: Establishing a Business

In advising a client who is commencing a business enterprise, a checklist of matters will enable you to give the appropriate legal advice to a client who is then left to decide on the commercial risk-taking aspects of the venture. This divide between legal–professional advice on the one hand, and commercial risk-taking on the other, should be borne in mind from the outset of the solicitor–client relationship and maintained throughout. A suggested solicitor's checklist of advice to a person setting up a business, whatever the type, is given below.

1.4

1. SOLICITOR'S BUSINESS CHECKLIST OF INITIAL ADVICE

1. Type of enterprise/entity,
2. Choice of business name,
3. Formalities,
4. Constitution/rules,
5. Ownership,
6. Management,
7. Business premises and other assets,
8. Publicity,
9. Miscellaneous matters:

   (a) VAT,
   (b) Letterhead,
   (c) Choice of bankers, accountants, auditors,
   (d) National Insurance,
   (e) Insurance,
   (f) Licences,
   (g) Intellectual Property

1.5

Future management, finance and trading

10. Decision-making,
11. Expansion plans,
12. Reporting,
13. Borrowing:

    (a) secured or unsecured debts?
    (b) long- or short-term debts?

14. Taxation treatment,
15. Contractual arrangements,
16. Employees,

1.6

Other matters

17. Disputes,
18. Bankruptcy, insolvency and liquidation,
19. Confirmation of choice.

1.7

There may well be other matters to add to this checklist. The list should be able to provide the basis of the legal advice to be given to the client in respect of establishing business as:

(a) a sole trader;
(b) by way of a partnership; or
(c) by way of a company.

This guide will use such a checklist as a basis for discussing each of these business entities.

C. The Client Interview

1.8　It may be that a new client has made an appointment to come in to the office and all that you have been told is "Ms Smith—setting up a business." What do you do if it is the first time you are interviewing a client in respect of such a matter? You would probably devise some sort of checklist of the key points that you would wish to get instructions on and on which you would want to be able to give some sort of advice. No doubt the checklist will be refined and adapted if you have several similar instructions in respect of a new business. It is a question of finessing an approach that suits you.

The initial client interview is vital. This is when the solicitor presents the "human face" of the law firm. It is the point at which the client will gain a first impression, and decide whether or not to return for further advice or work. It is vital that the solicitor, therefore, makes a good, professional impression. This involves being organised, knowledgable, well-prepared, diligent and (increasingly) cost-effective.

The client's instructions and concerns may be confused. It is a solicitor's task to sort them out; to locate the *key concerns* and provide legal advice that takes account of the particular context and requirements of the client.

There is no right or absolute way for a solicitor to do this. There may, however, be issues of "good practice" that can be developed and enhanced at the expense of certain things that could be characterised as "bad practice" and which are the opposite of the "good practice."

In taking of instructions, the legal adviser should bear in mind the following points:

1. "Open" and "closed" questions —"open" questions may be a good idea at the start of the interview, *e.g.* "what can I do for you?" "Closed" questions are useful for obtaining details from the client.
2. Key points—try to determine the key concerns and worries of the client. Essentially, the client will want to "transfer" these concerns to you and get sound advice in return.
3. Advice versus risk—the lawyer advises but does not make the commercial decisions. It is the client who makes the commercial choices and takes on the "risk."
4. Fact and law—the client gives his "story" (the facts). The lawyer puts those facts in a legal context and points out the legal reference points (the law). It is a question of sifting through those facts and extracting

the legally significant ones and then advising in a context appropriate to the client's needs and instructions.

5. Interview location—an orderly desk and office, or better still, a client interviewing room creates a "professional ambience."
6. Scepticism/empathy—it may be that you sometimes need to adopt a "critical distance" from your client, *e.g.* as regards to the question of fault in a motor vehicle accident. At other times you may want to develop a co-operative approach and establish a rapport with the client. Empathy may sometimes be required, *e.g.* as regards taking probate instructions. Try to determine whether the client has a "hidden agenda."
7. Practical advice—the legal advice given should be practical and tailored to the client's objectives, *i.e.* it is advice that appreciates the wider commercial context.
8. The next steps—take the initiative. Explain to the client what you will do following the interview and when, and what you expect of the client. Be precise. Confirm the outcome in a letter.
9. Techniques of professionalism—confirm that you will look at an issue or consult someone if you do not know the answer. Do not bluff.
10. Be timely—try and complete a given task on or before the date you have told the client.

D. Legal Written Skills

1. ATTENDANCE NOTES AND FILE MEMORANDA

The purpose of the file note or memorandum is that it is an accurate summary of an event, relevant to the client's file, that will act as a memory and organisational aid. For example, a file note may be useful in constructing a letter of advice to the client, or providing a clear account for somebody else looking at the file at a later date. It is a common occurrence, for example, that the files of a solicitor on leave will be handled by another solicitor. Alternatively you may "inherit" a file when you move into a new department of the firm. There are any number of reasons why a file note (or memorandum to file) will be prepared and there are, similarly, any number of reasons why such a note will be important at a later date.

1.9

For example, a file note may well clarify events, *e.g.* in the unfortunate event of a negligence claim against the firm several years later. Obviously a solicitor handling several hundred files will have difficulty remembering matters on all the files in his care on any one day, let alone over a longer period. Therefore the file note is a vitally important "memory jog" and management tool.

The most common occasions requiring the preparation of a file note will be:

(a) to summarise a telephone call;
(b) to summarise a meeting with a client or the other side;
(c) to note some other event to do with a file.

A file note may simply comprise a few words dashed down, *e.g.* "X rang to say no offer at this stage.'' It may, on the other hand, run to a document several pages long, dictated and typed up. Whatever the type and subject matter, file notes should be constructed with a view to helping with the management and orderly conduct of the file. Once prepared they should be placed on the file in date order. There is no point having a whole pile of file notes that are not dated and do not identify the file to which they relate. All the good work done in preparing the file notes will be undone in the laborious and time consuming task of having to sort them out.

In the preparation of file notes, you should bear in mind the following points.

File notes checklist

1.10 1. The client's name and the identify of the file.
2. The date of the event or incident being referred to. If you leave the preparation of a file note for too many days events will become blurred. Prepare them as soon as possible afterwards, *e.g.* dictate a note straight after the phone call or meeting.
3. An accurate summary of the relevant facts.
4. The relevant legal issues.
5. Plain English—avoid legal expressions unless you explain them or you know that the client will understand them. If the file note is an ''in house'' communiqué it can contain reference to technical legal matters, *i.e.* the audience for it will be another solicitor within the firm, rather than a client, so the question of whether it contains ''legalese'' should not be relevant. Check your file note and amend if it is unclear. (If you fell under the ''Clapham Omnibus'' tomorrow could the person in the office next door get a clear view of the state of the file from your file note?)

2. LETTERS OF ADVICE TO CLIENTS

1.11 Writing letters of advice involves a specialised means of communication—principally trying to communicate legal principles in such a way that a client, no matter what his or her circumstances, can understand and be assisted by.

The first point to note is that your client relationship may be conducted largely by telephone. Secondly, that a great many letters emanating from a lawyer's office are of a mundane character, for instance, confirming a court hearing date or enclosing documents for perusal, and contain little or no reference to legal issues, points of law, case law, statute and the like.

The ''letter of advice'' refers to a letter in which you give a client legal advice. It may be that you wish to write more of these, but that little opportunity arises for you to display your legal knowledge. The client is not going to be very interested in the fact that you got the Torts prize or were the mooting champion at law school. They are not going to want a four-page letter on director's fiduciary duties unless they can afford the several hours research, redrafting and *angst* you have gone through in getting your letter past the partner in charge of the file. It should be relevant to their circumstances and provide a practical approach.

Letters of advice involving weighty legal topics may be few and far between. Their regularity will depend on many factors:

(a) the department in which you are working; and
(b) the type of client you are dealing with.

For example, you could be in a large London firm, working in the banking department, where your typical client is a qualified professional employee of a bank. If that is the case you will be communicating at a fairly sophisticated level and any letter of advice will reflect that specialisation and sophistication.

Alternatively, you may work in the family law section of a small firm with many legally aided clients. A lengthy letter of advice on the latest custody case will not be appropriate unless the circumstances are of particular relevance to the state of the file, for example, on the verge of an appeal to court.

Letters of advice and indeed any communiqués to clients should display the following hallmarks:

(a) they should have in mind the particular reader to whom they are addressed, *e.g.* an accountant or in-house lawyer as opposed to a client dealing with a lawyer for the first time;
(b) they should be clearly expressed;
(c) they avoid jargon or legalese (or if they include reference to them, they contain a clear explanation);
(d) they should be no longer than they need to be (long letters mean time, which means money for a client);
(e) the relevant legal issues should be clearly stated so that the client can understand them;
(f) the law having been stated, the client should be advised by way of the law being applied to the facts at hand in a practical manner.

In this sense, letters of advice are like law exams involving fact scenarios. There is a three-stage process involved in most cases:

(a) the law is stated accurately and relevantly;
(b) the relevant facts are selected; and
(c) there is a process of "application", *i.e.* facts to law and vice versa.

E. Commerciality

Increasingly business clients expect their legal advisers to be "commercial". It is assumed that the legal adviser gets the law right. Being "commercial" involves an extra element that includes:

1.12

(a) empathising constantly with the particular requirements of the client and the transaction at hand;
(b) appreciating the wider context of the situation.

This means having an understanding of the sorts of issues against which the legal advice will be provided, *e.g.* financial and economic conditions; practical problems such as "administrative hassle" with, for example, a licence application; delays; unexpected costs or obstacle;

(c) bearing in mind the worst-case scenario, because after all it is the client who is assuming the risk. This would, for example, involve explaining in practical terms the potential unlimited liability of a would-be partner or personal liability of a director on the dissolution of the business entity; and

(d) taking a "global approach" to the legal problem and being prepared to be flexible in terms of approach.

2.   Overview of Sole Traders

A. Introduction

As the name suggests, a sole trader involves one person commencing a business operation on his own account.   **2.1**

The key point is that there is no divide between the ownership and the management of the business. The two roles are merged in the one person, *i.e.* the person and the business are a single, indistinguishable business entity. This point is critical because, as we shall see, companies of whatever type are a separate legal entity, separate and distinct from the owners/shareholders and managers/directors.

Sole traders will typically be small businesses, *e.g.* street shops or businesses run from home. The title "sole trader" is not necessarily descriptive of the work of the business. Nor does it imply that a "sole trader" business cannot expand into another type of business entity or, alternatively, be sold or transferred and change its nature.   **2.2**

B. The Solicitor's Business Checklist as Applied to Sole Traders

1. TYPE OF ENTERPRISE/ENTITY

Obviously, as far as choice of business is concerned, a client will be advised as to sole trader, partnership and company. It will quickly be apparent if a sole trading entity is appropriate. The owner of the business will want to retain the management and control of the business.   **2.3**

2. CHOICE OF BUSINESS NAMES

This apparently simple business decision requires legal advice because of the restrictions on the use of certain names, as set out by the Business Names Act 1985. The provisions of the Business Names Act also apply to partnerships and companies in their use of business names. Chapter 7 of this guide sets out the relevant matters and restrictions in the Business Names Act, as that act applies to each of the three entities.   **2.4**

3. FORMALITIES

The key point for most clients will be whether there will be a lot of form-filling and setting-up costs involved in establishing the business. Obviously, the client will need to be informed as to the likely legal costs involved and these will reflect time spent on the matter.   **2.5**

A sole trading entity is informal in the sense that there is no requirement to have:

(a) a governing document or set of rules; or
(b) reporting requirements to an outside body

as there is with companies.

4. CONSTITUTION/RULES

2.6   As stated in paragraph 2.5, sole traders are "self-governing" because of the unity of ownership and management in the one person; hence, there is no requirement for a constitution.

5. OWNERSHIP

2.7   The sole trader is the only owner of the business. As such he can make decisions concerning the business without consulting with or requiring the approval of others.

6. MANAGEMENT

2.8   The sole trader is both the only owner and the only manager of the business. He has complete control over the running of the business in respect of all matters, *i.e.* the day-to-day administration, strategy, longer-term goals, etc.

7. BUSINESS PREMISES

2.9   The choice of business premises will be of significance, for several reasons, including:

(a) it will probably be the key initial asset of the business;
(b) it will be an asset that will potentially increase in value and, therefore, attract capital gains tax;
(c) if nominated as the "place of business" it will be there the business records are kept and where documents in court proceedings should be served.

8. PUBLICITY

2.10   As there are no formal reporting requirements, either of a financial or other nature other than the lodging of tax returns the sole trader's business is a "private affair". This is in contrast to companies, whatever their type, that are required to report several types of matters in accordance with the Companies Act 1985.

9. MISCELLANEOUS MATTERS

Value Added Tax (VAT)

2.11   Under the Value Added Tax Act 1983, a "taxable person", which expression includes a sole trader, partnership or company, is required to be registered if:

(a) he is involved in a business that supplies goods or services; and
(b) the value of the goods or services supplied (exclusive of VAT) exceeds £46,000 either:
  (i) in the preceding 12-month period; or
  (ii) is expected to do so in the next 30 days.

The standard rate of VAT is 17.5 per cent; however, many items, such as books and newspapers, are "zero rated", *i.e.* taxed at zero percent.

VAT is collected from the customer and paid to H.M. Customs and Excise. If a sole trader or other "taxable person" fails to comply with the Value Added Tax Act, both civil and criminal penalties may apply.

Letterhead, stationery, etc.

By section 4 of the Business Names Act 1985, a sole trader, irrespective of whether or not he uses a business name, has to disclose his own name and an address for service of documents (in the event of legal proceedings being commenced against the business) on all: **2.12**

(a) business letters,
(b) written orders for goods or services to be supplied to the business,
(c) invoices and receipts,
(d) written demands for payment issued by the business.

The sole trader's name and address also has to be displayed "in a prominent position" at the place of business.

There are both civil and criminal penalties if the Act is not complied with within this respect.

Choice of bankers, accountants and auditors

Many small businesses will not appoint an accountant or an auditor but instead prepare their own accounts. The larger and more complex a business, the greater the need for financial specialists. The auditor's role, should one be appointed, is to verify the accuracy of the accounts of the business.   **2.13**

National Insurance

A sole trader as a self-employed taxpayer pays class 4 National Insurance contributions under section 617(5) of the Income and Corporation Taxes Act 1988. One half of the contributions made are deductible from income profits.   **2.14**

Insurance

Obviously policies of insurance for premises and effects should be taken out as soon as possible to cover replacement value and accidental damage. Such insurances will often be a requirement of a lender or a lessor.   **2.15**

Licences

Regard should be had to the permits, licences and authorities that may be required for a business, *e.g.* liquor licence for a hotel.   **2.16**

Applications should be made as soon as possible.

Intellectual property

There may be intellectual property issues depending on the type of business. There may be matters concerning copyright, patents, registered designs,   **2.17** trade marks and the like. The client should be directed to an expert in these fields.

10. DECISION-MAKING

2.18   Because the sole trader owns all the assets of the businesses, he has the right to make all decisions related or incidental to the operation of the busines without having to refer to others or get the approval or consent of others. This situation is obviously subject to the sole trader complying with the various relevant statutory provisions, such as the Value Added Tax Act 1983, Business Names Act 1985, various taxing acts, etc.

11. EXPANSION PLANS

2.19   It follows from the nature of sole traders that the expansion of the business depends on the wishes of the owner/sole trader and, of course, trading conditions, etc. As with decision-making, the sole trader does not need to seek the approval of others in relation to such plans.

12. REPORTING

2.20   Apart from registration requirements under the Business Names Act 1985, the Value Added Tax Act 1983 and the lodging of taxation returns, the sole trader is not required to report matters pertaining to the business to an outside party. This is in contrast to companies which are required under the Companies Act 1985 to report many matters to the Registrar of Companies.

13. BORROWING

2.21   The sole trader may borrow money:

  (a) on an *unsecured basis* involving a simple contractual promise to repay the debt; or
  (b) on a *secured basis* so that assets in the business are mortgaged by the lender. The effect of the security is that, in addition to the contractual promise to repay the debt, the lender can have recourse to the assets secured in order to ensure repayment of the debt.

14. TAX TREATMENT

2.22   The sole trader's tax return will include the income profits from the business, together with other sources of income. Profits from a "trade" are taxed under Schedule D, Case I, and this schedule will be the main one applicable to sole traders.

15. CONTRACTUAL AGREEMENTS

2.23   It is the sole trader as owner of the business assets who enters into contracts with suppliers and others. The effect of this is that the sole trader is:

(a) personally liable to debtors of the business; and

(b) able to sue, and be sued by creditors of the business, in his name.

16. EMPLOYEES

When a business takes on an employee, the increasingly sophisticated and **2.24** statute-based area of employment law comes into play. With an accompanying specialisation among lawyers, it may well be that, unless you have some expertise in this area, the client will need to consult an expert in the area in regard to detailed advice as to employment law, pensions, etc.

Preliminary advice regarding the taking on by a business of an employee would include reference to the following matters:

Recruitment of employees

In advertising, interviewing and offering employment, a prospective **2.25** employer must be aware of the following statutes:

(a) the Sex Discrimination Act 1975,

(b) the Race Relations Act 1976,

(c) the Trades Union and Labour Relations (Consolidation) Act 1992 that outlaw discrimination—direct or indirect—on the grounds of:

  (i) sex,

  (ii) race,

  (iii) marital status,

  (iv) trade union membership.

An employer's breach of these statutes could result in a compensation award being made by a Tribunal.

The contract of employment

There is no specified form for a contract of employment, *i.e.* it may be oral, **2.26** in writing, or a combination of both.

However, by the Trades Union Reform and Employment Rights Act 1993, the employer must, within two months of the employee commencing work, provide the employee with a written statement that includes the following information:

(a) identity of employer and employee,

(b) the commencement date of the employment,

(c) the pay scales and how often the employee is paid,

(d) the hours of work,

(e) any provisions concerning:

  (i) holidays,

  (ii) sickness,

  (iii) pensions,

(f) the notice period required to end the contract,

(g) the finishing date for a fixed-term contract,

(h) the place(s) of work,

(i) disciplinary rules,

(j) grievance procedure.

There are other terms that are beyond the scope of this review. Any change in the terms has to be notified to the employee within one month of the change.

The Equal Pay Act 1970 provides that employees doing the same, or substantially the same, work must receive equal pay.

Income Tax and National Insurance

2.27 Employees will pay income tax in accordance with the "Pay As You Earn" (PAYE) system.

The PAYE system obliges the employer to deduct:

(a) income tax; and
(b) National Insurance contributions

from an employee and give the employee the net amount and pay the deductions withheld to the Revenue.

Insurance matters

2.28 An employer must take out a policy of workers' compensation insurance to cover employees:

(a) injured at work; or
(b) contracting a disease at work, or as the result of work.

The insurance certificate has to be displayed in the workplace.

The requirement for valid insurance to be carried by the employer does not affect the duties placed on the employer by the common law and by statute (Health & Safety at Work Act 1974) to guard against negligence with respect to:

(a) the actions of employees, *e.g.* training supervision, etc.,
(b) the system of work, *e.g.* guard-railings; protective clothing, etc.,
(c) the plant and equipment, *e.g.* maintenance, age of it; proper instructions followed.

Under common law, an employer found liable in negligence would be subject to pay monetary compensation; under the Health & Safety at Work Act 1974 criminal penalties prevail.

Terminating employment

2.29 An employer cannot simply dismiss an employee in any manner he wishes to. There are several potential avenues open potentially, to a dismissed employee:

(a) Wrongful dismissal: A dismissal that does not correspond with the terms of the contract of employment and, in particular, the statutory notice periods set down by the Employment Protection (Consolidation) Act 1978.

(b) Unfair dismissal: This applies to employees who have been in their employment for at least two years. Such an employee is an "eligible" employee, protected under section 54 of the Employment Protection (Consolidation) Act 1978.

The onus of proof is with the employer to show that the dismissal is "fair". A dismissal is "fair" if it falls within one of the five reasons set out in section 57 of the Employment Protection (Consolidation) Act 1978. Those reasons can be summarised as follows:

(a) the employee's capabilities or qualifications;
(b) the employee's conduct;
(c) the redundancy of the employee;
(d) the employee's continuation would involve the contravention of a statute;
(e) there was a "substantial reason" to justify dismissal.

Redundancy
(See of the grounds in section 57 above.)

If an employee is made redundant after two years' employment, the employer will be obliged to make a redundancy payment based on age, length of service and a "week's pay" and, as determined by a formula set out in the Schedule to the Employment Protection (Consolidation) Act 1978. **2.30**

Discrimination
As has already been noted, an employer cannot discriminate on the basis of sex, race or marital status in relation to taking on employees. The same considerations apply to promotion and day-to-day treatment of employees and to the dismissal of employees. An employee discriminated against in any of these respects could seek compensation from the employer. **2.31**

17. DISPUTES

A sole trader can make all decisions affecting the business without consulting others. **2.32**

The sole trader may have disputes, however, with suppliers, creditors, debtors, etc., of the business.

There will be three methods of solving such disputes:

(a) *"Self-help"'*—the sole trader and other party resolve the matter among themselves by letter, phone, a meeting, etc., without outside help. This method has the advantages of being quick and cheap.
(b) *Legal proceedings being issued*—this may follow "self-help" methods that have failed. A sole trader should be carefully advised as to the expected cost and delays involved in taking such action.
(c) *Arbitration proceedings*—in place of legal proceedings being issued—the sole trader should be advised of the possibility of using an independent arbitrator to resolve a dispute. The arbitrator can be chosen on the basis of a particular, relevant expertise. The arbitration process may turn out to be less formal; more flexible; cheaper and quicker than resolving the matter through the courts. Resorting to arbitration usually requires the consent of both parties. This is in contrast to litigation where one party unilaterally decides to commence legal proceedings. Another advantage of arbitration is that

the arbitrator's decision can be both final and binding on the parties. There is no forum of appeal as there is with litigation.

Each dispute needs to be seen in light of the particular circumstances surrounding it. Only then will the best method for resolving it come to light.

18. BANKRUPTCY

2.33   A sole trader can be bankrupted if he fails to satisfy a statutory demand from a creditor(s) for an unsecured amount in excess of £750 for a period of 21 days or more.

If a sole trader is bankrupted the assets of the sole trader, including those used in the business, will vest, on the making of the bankruptcy order by the court, in the trustee in bankruptcy. The only property that the bankrupt is able to keep is personal effects such as tools of the trade, clothes and the like.

19. CONFIRMATION OF CHOICE

2.34   At the end of the day, it is the client's choice as to the best entity for their business purposes to operate a business. The legal adviser can only present the options and try to highlight the legal pitfalls and advantages of each option. The ultimate ''commercial risk'' lies with the client.

3. Overview of Partnerships

A. Introduction

3.1

A partnership is a business carried on by two or more people, aimed at making a profit. The assets of the business are owned by the partners individually or on a shared basis. The liabilities and debts of the partnership are shared between the partners on what is known as a "joint" basis or "joint and several" basis. Liability is joint in respect of the partnership's contractual obligations (*i.e.* judgment against one party is binding on all others) and joint and several in respect of partnership torts (*i.e.* judgment against one party does not prevent successive actions being brought against any or all of the others).

The distinction between "joint" and "joint and several" liability is of little practical importance because the Civil Liability (Contribution) Act 1978 allows successive actions to be brought against parties who are jointly liable notwithstanding an earlier judgment against one of them. Of more importance is the principle that, notwithstanding the precise nature of liability, all partners are liable without limit for the debts and obligations of the partnership. The concept of unlimited liability means that, where a partnership is liable to a third party in contract or tort and a judgment has been obtained on the relevant "joint" or "joint and several" basis, enforcement is possible in certain circumstances against the personal assets of any particular partner without limit. For example, it may be that the partnership concerned has insufficient assets to satisfy judgment but that one particular partner has personal assets to do just that. Of course, the partner suffering enforcement will look to his right of contribution from his fellow partners but whether or not he is successful in obtaining a contribution will depend on their abilities to pay at the relevant time.

Whilst unlimited liability may be seen as a risk for partners going into a partnership business, a partnership business offers privacy from public scrutiny in that accounts and returns do not have to be lodged with a central body (as in the case for companies) and there is a relative lack of administrative cost (again compared to companies).

The shared liability nature of partnerships means that prospective partners should know each other quite well and "trust" one another in financial and other business matters. A partner's relationship with the other partners is covered by the latin expression *uberrimae fidae*, *i.e.* one of utmost trust and confidence. This is also reinforced by the fact that the partners owe "fiduciary duties" to each other. These fiduciary duties include a duty to account; not to compete with the partnership business, etc., are spelt out in sections 28, 29 and 30 of the Partnership Act 1890.

As with advising a client in respect to setting up as a sole trader the ultimate choice (the risk element of the decision) is the client's and not the solicitor's. As a legal adviser all you can properly do is to point out the advantages and disadvantages of each entity as they apply to the client's particular circumstances and requirements.

B. The Solicitor's Business Checklist as Applied to Partnerships

3.2   The points on the solicitor's business checklist will be dealt with in turn as they apply to partnerships.

1. TYPE OF ENTERPRISE/ENTITY

3.3   The choice of business entity for two or more people wishing to establish a business will be either a partnership or a company. The appropriate choice in each case will depend on the particular circumstances and requirements of the client. For instance, a client's concern about unlimited liability might mean that a company structure is preferred. Alternatively, the client's key priority may be privacy of business affairs, so that a partnership is appropriate. It is a question of balancing various issues.

2. CHOICE OF BUSINESS NAMES

3.4   See Chapter 7 on the Business Names Act 1985. Unless a partnership business simply adopts a business name that includes each of the names of the partners, there are various restrictions which will apply.

3. FORMALITIES

3.5   There may be registration requirements under the Business Names Act 1985 (see Chapter 7) or the need to register for VAT purposes, but there is certainly not the same degree of paperwork involved as there is in establishing a company. The partners do not have to enter into a written partnership agreement. If no written agreement is entered into, their dealings with each other and the outside world will be governed in accordance with the Partnership Act 1890. However, the terms of the Partnership Act 1890 are not always appropriate—for example, they may be seen as inflexible, insufficiently commercial, or not tailored to the specific needs of the business—so that many partnerships choose to regulate their affairs by specifically drafted agreements.

4. CONSTITUTION/RULES

3.6   As stated the partners are not required to have a partnership agreement or set of rules (see paragraph 3.5 above). If they do enter into one it need not be in writing. It could be oral or partly oral, partly written. Alternatively the partners could rely on the Partnership Act 1890 (again see paragraph 3.5 above).

5. OWNERSHIP

3.7   The partners themselves own the partnership business. They own each of the assets that go to making up the partnership business. They may own those assets jointly or particular partners may own particular assets. There is not a separate body or entity (as there is with companies) that owns assets in its own name and similarly incurs liabilities.

6. MANAGEMENT

The partners usually manage the business. It may be that an individual partner (or small number of partners) is delegated the responsibility of the day-to-day management of the business—the "managing partner". There is *not* a separate entity known as "the partnership" that is separate and distinct from the partners. Compare this situation with companies where "the company" is a distinct entity from the owners (the shareholders) and the managers (the directors).

3.8

7. BUSINESS PREMISES

The partnership business may buy or lease premises from which the business is conducted. The location of the premises will be an important feature of the business and in particular in helping to build "goodwill" or reputation. See the comments on business premises for sole traders.

3.9

8. PUBLICITY

A lack of publicity (and hence a degree of privacy) is a facet of partnership business. They do not need to report to a public body on a regular basis as companies do.

3.10

9. MISCELLANEOUS MATTERS

Value Added Tax
See the comments for sole traders.

3.11

Letterhead, stationery, etc.
In most cases, the partners' names have to be displayed on stationery, etc., irrespective of the choice of business name. See Chapter 7 on the Business Names Act 1985.

3.12

Choice of bankers, accountants and auditors
These matters will normally be addressed by the Partnership Agreement if there is one.

3.13

National Insurance
Contributions of National Insurance paid by an employer in respect of an employee are deductible from income profits.

3.14

10. DECISION-MAKING

Usually all the partners will be involved in the major management issues of the partnership; for example, the direction or type of business; admitting a

3.15

new partner; expelling an existing partner. These types of decisions and how they are taken may be specifically dealt with by the Partnership Agreement. It may be that the day-to-day administration of the business rests with one partner known as the managing partner.

The partners, as they also own the business, do not need to obtain the consent or approval of others to business decisions (whereas in the case of companies, directors or managers may have to seek the consent or approval of the shareholders prior to undertaking certain transactions).

The management structure of a partnership will depend on the size of the business and the requirements of the partners involved.

11. EXPANSION PLANS

3.16 As with sole traders, the partners can decide (after financial and other advice if necessary) on plans to expand the business.

12. FINANCIAL REPORTING

3.17 The lack of reporting, relative to companies, is an advantage of partnerships. Apart from disclosure requirements when using a business name, VAT, income tax arrangements and the like, the affairs of the partnership are private. There is no requirement to:

    (a) publish financial reports; or

    (b) report certain information, such as a partner leaving, as there is with a company.

13. BORROWING

3.18 The decision whether to borrow will depend on the partners, as will the amount to be borrowed.

The partners can provide a lender with security for the borrowing by mortgaging various assets that are owned by the partners and classified as partnership property. One important restriction on a partnership's ability to borrow money, compared to a company, is that a partnership cannot give a "floating charge" that secures the assets and undertakings of the partnership, because the partnership is not a separate entity that owns assets. Security must therefore be taken over particular assets, which assets are owned by and in the names of the partners.

14. TAX TREATMENT

3.19 The tax treatment of partnerships is at present in a period of transition. Schedule D, under which most income of partnerships and sole traders is taxed operates on what is known as a "preceding year" basis. What this effectively means is that there is a delay between the generating of income and the payment of income tax on that income.

All of the other income schedules operate on a "current year" basis, *i.e.* income is earned and tax is paid in the same year, there is no gap or delay as there is with the preceding year basis. The reason for the changes to partnership tax treatment is because Schedule D is being brought into line with the other Schedules, *i.e.* it will operate on a "current year" basis. The changes are being phased in gradually. The phase-in period commenced on April 6, 1994 and will end in the tax year 1997–98 when all businesses will be taxed on a current year basis.

In the meantime, there are different taxation rules to consider, depending on the date that the business was established:

(a) a business in existence before April 6, 1994 will be taxed on a preceding year basis until tax year 1997–98; and

(b) a business established after April 6, 1994 will be taxed on "transitional rules" (see Chapters 6 and 16).

15. CONTRACTUAL ARRANGEMENTS

As with sole traders, the partners enter supply, distribution and lease arrangements in their names and are liable to third parties in accordance with the Partnership Act 1890.

3.20

16. EMPLOYEES

See paragraphs 2.24–2.31 for detailed comments.

3.21

17. DISPUTES

Disagreements and disputes amongst the partners will hopefully be rare, given that their relationship is a fiduciary one.

3.22

There may be "internal disputes" (as between partners) or disputes with third parties or disputes that contain both elements, *e.g.* a debt owed to a third party that also involves questions concerning a partner's authority to bind the firm.

How a dispute involving the partners is solved will be set out in the Partnership Agreement or if there is no Partnership Agreement or the agreement does not cover the point, by the Partnership Act 1890.

18. BANKRUPTCY

A partner, just as any other individual, can be made bankrupt if he owes to a creditor an unsecured amount of more than £750. A bankruptcy order can be made by the court following a statutory demand being unpaid for 21 days or a judgment obtained by a creditor is not able to be executed.

3.23

Under the Partnership Act 1890, the death or bankruptcy of a partner automatically dissolves the partnership (section 33). Therefore, it is important that in drafting a Partnership Agreement that the client is advised on this point and the appropriate steps are taken (usually to delete section 33's effect). Whatever the case, it is important to obtain specific instructions on this point.

19. CONFIRMATION OF CHOICE

3.24   As with the other business entities, the ultimate commercial risk is the client's. The legal adviser should always bear in mind the distinction between legal advice and commercial decision-making. Obviously legal advice that is commercially minded and tailored to meet the client's needs is apposite.

4. Partnerships and Specific Legal Issues

A. Introduction

1. PARTNERSHIP AGREEMENT

Partnerships are governed by either:

4.1

(a) the terms of the particular Partnership Agreement or Deed that has been specifically drafted for the purposes of the business; or

(b) if no Partnership Agreement has been drafted, the provisions of the Partnership Act 1890.

It is therefore important when drafting a Partnership Agreement for a client that the terms of the Partnership Act 1890 are understood and borne in mind and where appropriate, specifically excluded. The results of not doing so may be drastic. For example, section 32(c) of the Partnership Act provides that a partnership entered into for an undefined time *may* be dissolved on the giving of notice to that effect (*i.e.* immediately!) by a partner to the other partner(s). Even if a Partnership Agreement has been drafted but is silent on a particular provision contained within the Partnership Act, the provision in the Partnership Act will be deemed to apply and were a court asked to interpret the matter it would decide the matter by reference to the Act. A partnership relationship without a partnership agreement is a very fragile arrangement, without any certainty as far as the day-to-day operations of the business, the plans of the partners and the direction of the business.

Even if there is a Partnership Agreement in place, section 19 of the Partnership Act provides that the rights and duties of the partners may be "varied by the consent of all the partners, and such consent may be either express or inferred from a course of dealing." It is important therefore that the partners:

(a) comply with the terms of the Agreement; and

(b) regularly update the Agreement so that it complies with the course of dealings.

Section 19 of the Partnership Act is referred to as the "parol evidence" section because a partner could give oral evidence of a course of a dealing, the result of which could be to overturn the written terms.

The Partnership Act, or the Partnership Agreement, or a combination of both is equivalent to the Articles and Memorandum of Association for Companies, *i.e.* they regulate the partnership's activities internally and the dealings with third parties.

The Partnership Act is now over 100 years old and may not be as commercial a document as is required in the specific circumstances of a particular partnership business.

The aims of putting in place a partnership agreement are as follows:

(a) it is tailor-made to meet the commercial and personal requirements of the partners and the business;

(b) it allows for the efficient management of the business;

(c) it regulates the working relationship between the partners and between the business and the outside world, and

(d) it prevents certain provisions contained in the Partnership Act 1890 from applying to the business.

2. The Legal Nature of a Partnership

4.2   Section 1 of the Partnership Act 1890 provides the definition of a partnership and contains three elements, namely:

(a) that there are two or more people;

(b) carrying on a "business" (which is defined by section 45 of the Partnership Act to *include* every "trade, occupation or profession" and by section 1(2) of the Partnership Act to *exclude* companies);

(c) with a view (*i.e.* an intention if not an actual realisation) of making a profit.

All elements of section 1 of the Partnership Act need to be satisfied before it can be said that a partnership exists in law. Whether a partnership exists in a particular case will be determined by reference to the requirements of section 1 of the Partnership Act and will be a question of fact. This situation is in contrast to companies whose creation is evidenced by the issue of a Certificate of Incorporation following the lodging of the necessary documentation with the Registrar of Companies.

3. Partnerships as a Separate Legal Entity

4.3   A partnership is not a separate legal entity from the individuals who together form and comprise the partnership. A partnership is, however, treated as a separate entity to a limited extent. Those instances are:

(a) for litigation purposes Order 81 Rules of Supreme Court provides that instead of having to issue legal proceedings against each of the individuals partners, proceedings may be commenced against "the partnership" and that similarly "the partnership" may issue proceedings against a third party; and

(b) for taxation of partnerships in existence before April 6, 1994, which are continuing, a partnership return is filed and the individual partners file their own tax returns.

For new partnerships, *i.e.* those in existence after April 6, 1994, the partnership is not treated as a separate entity. There is no partnership return or joint liability for tax. Instead each partner deals with the Revenue separately. This is dealt with in more detail in Chapter 6.

For these two purposes only, a partnership is recognised as being independent of the individual members.

4. The Number of Partners in a Partnership

Under section 716 of the Companies Act 1985, "trading" or "business associations" must be limited to 20 partners unless they are "professional partnerships".

Professional partnerships such as firms of solicitors and accountants, or stock-broking firms who are members of the Stock Exchange, may have more than 20 partners in accordance with section 716(2).

4.4

5. The Nature and Liability of Partners

Unless it is a *limited* partnership, the liability of the partners is unlimited:

4.5

    (a) it is joint and several for tortious liability (see Partnership Act 1890, s. 12); and

    (b) it is joint for contractual liability (see Partnership Act 1890, s. 9).

Different statutory provisions apply to limited partnerships. Limited partnerships are those formed pursuant to the Limited Partnership Act 1907. Such partnerships are characterised by the following matters:

    (a) the liability of the partnership business to its creditors is unlimited (see s. 4);

    (b) they can have no more than 20 partners (see s. 4(2));

    (c) some individual partners will have limited liability and are to be referred to as "limited partners" (see s. 4(2));

    (d) other partners will have unlimited liability and are referred to as "general partners". It is a requirement of the Limited Partnership Act 1907 that at least one partner has unlimited liability for the debts of the business (see s. 4(2));

    (e) details of the liability situation of each of the partners and the status of the business as having limited liability must be recorded with the Registrar (see s. 5). If not, by section 5 of the Limited Partnership Act 1907, it shall be deemed to be a general partnership governed by the Partnership Act 1890.

6. The Partnership Name

For detailed comments, see Chapter 7.

4.6

Business Names Act 1985

    (a) if the firm name is simply comprised of the name of the partners— no approvals for or registration of the name is required (Business Names Act 1985, s.1);

    (b) if the firm name is comprised of words/names other than the names of the partners, consultation of the Regulations published by the Secretary of State is necessary. The Regulations are referred to in section 6 of the Business Names Act 1985. They comprise a list of words and expressions. The purpose of the list is that if a word or expression contained in the list is proposed to be used as a business name (or as part of a business name) the use of the word or expression will require the prior written approval of the Secretary of State or both the Secretary of State and a specified organisation.

The appropriate procedure for the approval of a proposed business name, which contains words referred to in the Regulations list, is:

(a) to write to the relevant government body or other relevant body asking if they object to the use of the name; and
(b) then provided that there is no objection, apply to the Secretary of State for approval for the use of the name.

The disclosures requirements are set out in section 4 of the Business Names Act 1985. The proprietors of the business, *i.e.* the partners need to disclose:

(a) the name of each partner; and
(b) an address for service of writs on the partnership *on every*:
   (i) business letter,
   (ii) order for goods and service,
   (iii) invoice,
   (iv) receipt,
   (v) written demand for payment of a debt.

7. THE DURATION OF THE PARTNERSHIP

4.7 So far as the duration of a partnership is concerned, reference needs to be made to the Partnership Act 1890 or the provisions of the Partnership Deed (if there is one is existence) or both. The Partnership Act has certain provisions referring to the duration of a partnership. These provisions will apply if:

(a) there is no Partnership Agreement; or
(b) there is a Partnership Agreement but it is silent or does not cover the particular provisions set out in the Partnership Act.

Alternatively, the Partnership Agreement may contain its own duration provisions and exclude the effect of the Partnership Act.

As far as the Partnership Act 1890 is concerned sections 26 and 32(c) of the Partnership Act 1890 enable one partner to dissolve the partnership business simply by giving notice of such dissolution to the other partners. Unless otherwise stated in the notice, dissolution is effective immediately. These provisions could prove disastrous to a partnership for they theoretically allow one partner to say to the others "the partnership is at an end" without specifying a period of notice or without taking into account whether it is a sound decision commercially.

A partnership agreement would ordinarily, unless there are particular circumstances applying, exclude the operation of sections 26 or 32(c) of the Partnership Act 1890, and substitute its own specific provision concerning duration.

A fixed-term partnership generally cannot be dissolved by notice being given by one or more partners but must run for the duration of the period or term agreed by the partners in accordance with section 27 of the Partnership Act 1890.

8. DRAFTING A PARTNERSHIP AGREEMENT

There is no statutory obligation set out in the Partnership Act 1890 or elsewhere requiring the partners to have a Partnership Agreement to govern the affairs of the partnership (compare the requirement under the Companies Act 1985 that every company has or is deemed to have Memorandum of Association and Articles of Association). The Partnership Act provisions will apply unless the Partnership Agreement provides to the contrary or excludes its operation. **4.8**

Whether or not there is a partnership in existence is a question of fact, *i.e.* the fact that there is a Partnership Agreement is not conclusive of there being a partnership in existence. The key benefit of having a partnership agreement is that it promotes certainty between partners and in their dealings with third parties.

B. Setting up and Expanding the Partnership

1. INTRODUCTION

The sources of "finance" (*i.e.* cash or other assets) available to a partnership will comprise: **4.9**

(a) "capital", *i.e.* the permanent investment by a partner in the partnership usually made at the beginning of the partnership by the founding partners or when an incoming partner joins the partnership;
(b) borrowings from either:
(i) a partner, *i.e.* an "advance" made to the partnership; or
(ii) from a third party, *e.g.* bank;
(c) once established and trading, the retained profits of the partnership business.

In addition to facilitating the growth of the partnership business, the categories of capital, borrowings and profits are significant in two other respects. First, they regulate to a significant extent the financial rights and duties of the partners during the life of the partnership, and second, on the dissolution of the partnership.

Under section 24(1) of the Partnership Act 1890, both capital invested in the partnership business, profits generated by that business and any losses are shared equally between the partners unless there is an agreement to the contrary.

On the dissolution of the partnership business, section 44 of the Partnership Act 1890 specifies the following order of payment:

(a) debts owed to third parties are repaid first (in full);
(b) advances (debts owed to partners) are repaid next (in full);

(c) capital contributions are returned to partners (in full);

(d) any remaining profits are shared by the partners according to the profit-sharing ratios agreed.

The provisions of the Partnership Act referred to above may be varied by the Partnership Agreement drafted in respect of a particular partnership business.

If section 44 of the Partnership Act 1890 is adopted unamended, the following points should be borne in mind:

(a) in advising a third party lender to a partnership, in relation to security for repayment of the loan arranging a fixed charge against a specific partnership asset(s) would be a prudent course of action (remember a floating charge would not be available);

(b) in advising a partner who has made an ''advance'' to a partnership, that such advance should be clearly documented and distinguished from a capital contribution or from a retention by the partnership of profit, because, in particular, the advance is repaid ahead of capital and profit on dissolution of the partnership;

(c) in advising a partner making a capital contribution, that it is a ''risk'' investment to the extent that it is unsecured and there is no guarantee of recouping any or all of the capital investment, depending on the performance of the partnership business. The risk nature of the capital investment is exacerbated by the fact that capital is repaid, only *after* third party debt and advances have been repaid in full. The capital contribution is not a readily ''realisable'' investment in the sense that it will not be recouped:

  (i) in relation to a particular partner unless that partner ''leaves'' the partnership (*i.e.* retirement, expulsion, death, bankruptcy); or

  (ii) in relation to all of the partners, until the dissolution of the partnership business;

(d) in advising a partner on profit sharing that if there is no agreement to the contrary the Partnership Act, s. 24(1) provides, as with capital, that it is divided equally between the partners. A particular matter to be aware of is that if profit is not distributed to a partner in accordance with his entitlement, *i.e.* undrawn profit, that matter is documented and the partner concerned does not prejudice his entitlement to receive such profit at a later time.

2. DISTINGUISHING PARTNERSHIP PROPERTY FROM PERSONAL PROPERTY

4.10   ''Partnership property'' is property used by, belonging to and available to the partnership business. On the other hand ''personal property'' in relation to a partner is that property that does not fall under the umbrella of the partnership business. A partner is free to deal with his personal property as he likes: property that is ''partnership property'' is subject to the Partnership Act provisions or the Partnership Agreement in place.

For practical purposes, the critical difference between classifying property as partnership property is that it will be distributed on a winding up (in accordance with the Partnership Act 1890, s. 44 or the Partnership's

Agreement) whereas personal property will remain the property of an individual partner and only exposed to meet the debts of the business after partnership property has been exhausted.

3. PARTNERSHIP PROPERTY

Section 20 of the Partnership Act 1890 provides that all property brought in to the partnership business or acquired for the purposes of the partnership business is presumed to be partnership property. However, the presumption can be overturned by the intention of the parties and the particular facts that apply.

4.11

Example: Determining partnership property (Miles v. Clarke [1953] 1 All E.R. 779)

Facts: This case involved a two-partner photographic business. The premises used by the business was subject to a lease in the name of one of the partners, Clarke. He had held the premises lease in his own name before going into partnership and whilst in partnership it remained in his sole name. The only arrangement between the partners was that they would split the profits on an equal basis, apart from that, as the judge put it, the business "just drifted on". When the business came to an end, the question in issue was whether the premises lease in Clarke's name had become partnership property or did it remain his personal property?

Held: The judge decided that his task was a minimal one, that was, merely to give "business efficacy" to what had gone on. In the absence of any agreement as to the running of the business other than the splitting of profits, he ruled that whilst stock in trade (such as photographic film) had become partnership property, the premises lease remained Clarke's personal property.

Section 21 of the Partnership Act 1890 provides that unless a "contrary intention appears" property bought with partnership money is deemed to be the partnership's property. Hence, monies drawn from the partnership's account to purchase an asset will ordinarily mean that the asset in question is deemed to be partnership property.

4. GOODWILL

Goodwill is the reputation or standing of the partnership and may be attributable to several factors including;

4.12

(a) particular areas of expertise of the partners, *e.g.* doctors;
(b) a particular partner's expertise, *e.g.* a tax specialist in a legal practice;
(c) the location of the partnership business.

Goodwill is an asset of the business that will be of nominal value at the commencement of the business but will grow in value as the business grows.

This raises the question on the sale of business: how should goodwill be valued?

A commonly adopted but arbitrary method is that the net profits for a particular year as determined usually by the previous year's audited accounts will be multiplied by a figure of two or three. In order to protect goodwill after the sale of the business (*i.e.* goodwill will be dissipated if custom is lost to the new owner after the sale) a restraint of trade clause is commonly used to prevent the former partner from setting up in a competing business within a certain vicinity, *e.g.* a five-mile radius and within a certain time period, *e.g.* three years.

A restraint of trade clause is liable to be struck down by a court unless it is reasonable in three respects:

    (a) time,
    (b) distance; and
    (c) the business interest being protected.

C. Relationships between Partners

1. BACKGROUND

4.13   The relationships between partners is governed by principles of equity and in particular the application of the standard concerning "fiduciaries". A fiduciary is one who owes a duty of trust and confidence to another. For example, solicitor to client, doctor to patient, director to company, trustee to beneficiary. The list of fiduciary relationships is not closed. Partners stand in a fiduciary position to one another, each owing reciprocal duties of trust, honesty and confidence so that the partnership business can be conducted in an environment where there is trust and mutual respect between the partners concerning in particular the financial affairs of the business.

2. DUTY OF GOOD FAITH

4.14   In general terms there is an overriding duty of good faith between partners, *i.e.* there are a number of limits imposed on the majority of partners being able to bind the whole firm:

    (a) the partners are under a fiduciary duty to each other to exercise their powers for the benefit of the firm as a whole;
    (b) the majority must consult the minority before imposing their views;
    (c) certain provisions of the Partnership Act 1890 limit the exercise of majority rule over the minority, *e.g.* section 24(8) of the Partnership Act requires unanimity for there to be a change in the nature of the partnership business whilst section 24(7) does so on the issue of admitting a new partner to the business.

3. UTMOST GOOD FAITH

4.15   The fiduciary relationship between partners is said to be one of *uberrimae fidae* (utmost good faith) as between the partners. The particular elements of the *uberrimae fidae* notion are set out in sections 28–30 of the Partnership Act 1890

True accounts and full information (Partnership Act 1890, s. 28)
Partners are bound by general duty of disclosure to each other. A partner is required to disclose all relevant information, *i.e.* that which affects or may affect the business, in his possession to his partners.

> *Example: A partner's duty of disclosure (Law v. Law [1905] 1 Ch. 140)*
> (a) One partner offered to buy the partnership share of the other.
> (b) The proposing purchaser did not disclose facts to the would-be vendor–partner (facts which made the vendor's partnership share more valuable)
> (c) Rescission of the sale by the would-be vendor partner was granted by the court, *i.e.* the sale was set aside on the basis of a failure to disclose.

Secret profits (Partnership Act 1890, s. 29)
There is a duty on every partner to account (*i.e.* return) to the partnership any profit made by a partner arising out of the partnership business. Such profit is held on constructive trust for the benefit of the partnership as a whole.

4.16

Competing in the same business (Partnership Act 1890. s. 30)
There is a duty of non-competition on each partner. This means a partner cannot set up in business against the partnership or be involved in a competing business whilst a partner and he is under a duty to account to his fellow partners for any profits derived from a business of the same nature.

4.17

A quite narrow test has been applied to determine whether a particular competing business is a "business of the same nature".

Section 30 has been held to apply to a partner working on both a morning and an evening newspaper in that were competition with one another.

Section 30 has been held *not* to apply to a partner working with ship-brokers in competition with a firm of ship-builders.

4. Relationship Between Partners

The relationship between partners is governed by:

4.18

(a) the terms of the Partnership Agreement; or
(b) the terms of any oral agreement or understanding between the partners; or
(c) if there is no Partnership or other Agreement, by the terms of the Partnership Act 1890.

5. Key Provisions of the Partnership Act 1890

Indemnity
Section 24(2) of the Partnership Act 1890 provides that a partner is indemnified by the partnership for payments made or for personal liabilities incurred by a partner in:

4.19

(a) the ordinary and proper conduct of the partnership business; or

(b) for the preservation of the partnership's business or property.

Conducting partnership business

Section 24(8) of the Partnership Act 1890 provides that "ordinary matters" connected with the partnership are decided by a simple majority of the partners. There is no casting vote provided by the Partnership Act as there is with Table A in relation to companies (see paragraph 10.8 below).

Section 24(7) of the Partnership Act 1890 provides that a unanimous vote is required for a new partner to be admitted to the business and section 24(8) provides likewise if there is to be a change in the nature of the business.

Section 24(5) of the Partnership Act 1890 provides that every partner is entitled to take part in the management of the business. Obviously with large partnerships the management tasks will be delegated to a sub-committee or managing partner.

D. Partners' Liability to Third Parties: Authority

1. BACKGROUND

4.20   Under section 9 of the Partnership Act 1890, the partners have joint liability for the partnership's contractual debts and liabilities, such as monies owed to a supplier for the supply of goods to the business. In practice, a partner sued under section 9 will seek a right of contribution from the other partners, *i.e.* he will join the other partners as defendants to the legal proceedings.

Partners have joint and several liability for tortious liability (Partnership Act 1890, s. 12), such as when a partnership is sued for negligence.

Under section 17(1) an incoming partner is not liable for debts of the partnership incurred before he joined the partnership. However, there may be a novation of contracts with creditors so that liability is assumed by the incoming partner.

Novation involves drawing up a new contract on the same terms as the original contract between the creditor and the partnership (which will now include the new partner)

Whilst it may appear unusual or even imprudent that a newly admitted partner assumes liability for debts incurred by the partnership before he joined the partnership, such an arrangement may be part of the package arranged for the partner to buy into the business. As such, it may suit his personal financial position. The key issue for the incoming partner will be to ascertain the exact nature and amount of liability to be assumed under a novated contract.

A partner's authority to bind the firm

4.21   Agency principles are relevant to partnerships.

In particular, partners are agents of the firm who can bind it to contractual and other obligations. This is similar to the role played by directors in relation to companies.

Whether or not an act done by a partner binds the firm depends on the nature and extent of the instructions and authority that has been actually given to (or is implied) by the other partners.

If an act done by a partner is in some way authorised by the partners, the partnership will be liable for it. So for example, if a partner, Bob, is authorised to negotiate an extension of lease, the partnership will be bound by whatever is negotiated on its behalf by Bob.

However, if an act done by a partner is in no way authorised by the partnership but is simply a "frolic of his own", the partnership will not be liable and the partner will be personally responsible for the act.

In practice, it may often be difficult to decide whether an act done is:

(a) an individual act independent of the partnership business; or
(b) an act done as an agent of the partnership business.

Determining whether a partner is personally responsible for a particular act (and is therefore personally liable) or whether the partnership business is responsible, may require an examination of the following matters:

(a) the source of the particular partner's authority;
(b) the nature and extent of that authority;
(c) the particular act or event in question; and
(d) the knowledge of the third party dealing with the business.

Each of these elements will be examined below in the context of the different types of authority on which a partner may be relying namely, express authority, implied authority and apparent authority.

Express authority (Partnership Act 1890, s. 6) and implied authority
Section 6 of the Partnership Act 1890 provides that a partnership is liable   **4.22**
for any act done in the firm's name by any person who is authorised to do it. The source of the authority may be:

(a) set out in a partnership agreement, a service contract or orally provided. This is referred to as actual express authority; or
(b) it may be authority which is implied by reference to the actual express authority. This is referred to as actual implied authority.

Apparent authority
A third party, *e.g.* a bank or trade supplier dealing with a partner, is generally   **4.23**
able to assume that the partner has the relevant authority known as apparent or ostensible authority to be able to authorise the transaction as part of the business of the partnership and thereby bind the partnership contractually.

The scope of the apparent or ostensible authority of a partner is not easy to establish and will depend on the surrounding facts in each case.

Section 5 of the Partnership Act 1890 attempts to define apparent authority. It has several elements, namely:

(a) the type of partnership business;
(b) the usual way of running that type of partnership business; and
(c) the knowledge of the third party concerning the partner's authority.

A partnership will be bound by those acts which represent a usual way of carrying out the particular type of partnership business in question *unless* the third party knows that the partner concerned did not have authority or does not know or believe that the person with whom they have been dealing was a partner at all.

Example: the type of partnership business (Mercantile Credit Co. Ltd v. Garrod [1962] 3 All E.R. 1103)

Facts: This case concerned the scope of the apparent authority of a partner in a garage business. The partner was prohibited from buying and selling vehicles. In contravention of the prohibition, he sold a vehicle to a third party.

Held: that the partnership was liable because the act of selling the vehicle was within the scope of what outsiders would expect of a garage business.

Example: the usual way of conducting a partnership business (Niemann v. Niemann (1890) 43 Ch.D. 198)

Facts: A debt which was owed by a third party to the partnership was proposed to be satisfied not by the payment of cash but by the issuing of shares in a company. One of the partners of the firm sought to accept such form of payment and this was challenged by his fellow partners.

Held: The partnership business was not bound to accept this form of payment because it represented an unusual manner of seeking to satisfy a debt.

2. Holding Out

4.24   The term "holding out" refers to the situation when former partners of the business are unwittingly or otherwise represented to the outside world as continuing partners. The most common example of this is when a departed partner's name remains on the firm's letterhead. Section 14 of the Partnership Act 1890 provides that a former partner may be liable as if he were still a partner. In order to be liable under this provision the following matters must be satisfied.

   (a) the third party dealing with the firm extended credit to the firm on the basis of the holding out (the term "credit" is widely interpreted to include goods as well as cash);
   (b) the partner in question must be shown to have contributed (whether through negligence or deliberately) in some way to the representation and the subsequent misunderstanding of the third party. It was held in *Tower Cabinet Co. Ltd v. Ingram* [1949] 2 K.B. 397 that a partner who had specifically instructed that firm letterhead bearing his name should be destroyed on his departure (but which was not) was not liable under section 14.

3. Partnership Businesses as Separate Entities

4.25   As already noted a partnership unlike a company is not a separate legal entity. However, for tax and litigation purposes, it is treated as separate.

Order 81 of the Rules of the Supreme Court allows the firm to be sued in the name of the partnership so that all partners at the date that the cause of action accrued are parties to the action:
The writ may be served on:

(a) any partner;
(b) anyone having control at the principal place of business of the partnership; or
(c) by post sent to the principal place of business.

Suing a partner for personal debts
Section 23 of the Partnership Act 1890 provides that a third party who has obtained a judgment against a partner in a personal capacity may enforce judgment against that partner's share of the partnership property by obtaining a separate charging order from the court.

E. Dispute within a Partnership

1. BACKGROUND

When drafting a Partnership Agreement it is essential to provide for the resolution of disagreements or disputes as between the partners. Disputes can be about practically any matter of business ranging from, for example, the holiday entitlements of the partners or use of the partnership letterhead, through to serious matters such as the misuse of partnership moneys. Just as the Partnership Agreement is designed to regulate the orderly affairs of the partnership, it must also provide mechanisms for the settlement of disputes of all kinds.   **4.26**

2. MEANS OF SETTLEMENT OF PARTNERSHIP DISPUTES

There are various means by which disputes may be resolved and they include: **4.27**

(a) self-help;
(b) inclusion of an arbitration clause in the Partnership Agreement;
(c) the retirement of one of the partner(s) in dispute and the purchase by the continuing partner(s) of his share of the partnership;
(d) the expulsion of a partner(s) by the continuing partner(s) and purchase of his share of the business; or
(e) most drastically of all, dissolution of the partnership.

Self-help
Self-help will obviously be the preferred option for resolving a partnership dispute. Self-help means that the partners settle differences between themselves without the involvement of outsiders.   **4.28**

Self-help will be an attractive option because it should settle the matter quickly, cheaply and provide that the dispute remains confidential from the outside world.

Arbitration

4.29   It is essential that there is a clause in the partnership agreement providing for arbitration or if there is no partnership agreement that the partners must agree between themselves to refer the dispute to arbitration.

The main advantages of arbitration are that:

(a) it will hopefully provide a quick, cost-effective settlement of a dispute;

(b) the arbitrator's decision is usually final and binding on the parties, *i.e.* there are no rights of appeal; and

(c) that the appointed arbitrator may possess some particular expertise in respect of the subject matter of the dispute.

Retirement

4.30   In order to resolve a partnership dispute it may prove necessary or politic that a partner or partners retire from the partnership, *i.e.* that they cease their involvement in the business.

Retirement will usually involve the continuing partners purchasing the out-going partner's share of the partnership business.

The retirement of a partner may or may not lead to a dissolution of the partnership (it depends on the terms of the partnership agreement or whether the Partnership Act 1890 applies). If the Partnership Act 1890 applies, a notice given by a partner that he is to retire from the firm is, in effect, a notice of dissolution of the partnership (in accordance with sections 26 and 32 of the Partnership Act 1890). In practice therefore, any partnership agreement adopted by the business should provide that a partner's notice of retirement does not end the business but merely terminates the involvement of the retiring partner in the business.

Expulsion

4.31   Expulsion is the most drastic means of settling a partnership dispute because it involves a partner being ousted from the partnership against his will (in that way it is the partnership equivalent to section 303 of the Companies Act 1985 for company directors, see paragraph 12.5 below).

Because of its draconian nature, three factors need to be borne in mind by the partnership in exercising the expulsion of a partner:

(a) there needs to be an express term/power contained in the partnership agreement (Partnership Act 1890, s. 25);

(b) there needs to be compliance with the precise terms of the power in the partnership agreement;

(c) it must be exercised in a bona fide manner, *i.e.* a manner that is honest and within the spirit of the power provided in the partnership agreement.

Expulsion involves a partner being dismissed from the partnership business against his will. Expulsion may arise as the result of:

(a) a serious one-off breach of a partner's obligations (for example, dishonesty involving partnership funds or other financial impropriety); or

    (b) persistent breaches of a partner's obligations (for example, failing to attend partners' meetings or taking time away from the business without notifying the other partners).

Dissolution of the partnership

Under the terms of the Partnership Act 1890, the partnership business may be dissolved in several ways, including: **4.32**

    (a) by notice to that effect being given by one partner if it is a partnership at will Partnership Act 1890, ss. 26 and 32(c);

    (b) by expiration of a fixed term of duration Partnership Act 1890, s. 32(a);

    (c) automatically, for example on the death of a partner Partnership Act 1890, s. 33;

    (d) by the occurrence of an event which renders the business unlawful, for example an export business which breaches government regulations Partnership Act 1890, s. 34;

    (e) by a court order, Partnership Act 1890, s. 35.

F. A Partner Leaving the Partnership

There are several reasons for and ways in which a partner will leave the business.   **4.33**

    These include consensual arrangements, such as:

    (a) retiring for reasons of ill health or age; or

    (b) joining another business.

These also include non-consensual arrangements, such as:

    (c) the expulsion of a partner pursuant to Partnership Act 1890, s. 25 or in accordance with a partnership agreement; or

    (d) the bankruptcy or mental illness of a partner pursuant to Partnership Act 1890, s. 33.

1. PURCHASING AN OUTGOING PARTNER'S SHARE OF THE BUSINESS

Whatever the circumstances of the partner's departure, the Partnership Agreement should provide that the continuing partners have the right to purchase the outgoing partner's share of the business. This right should be on a pre-emptive basis, *i.e.* a right to buy the share given to the partners in preference to third parties. Alternatively, it may be that the partners wish to dissolve the business if they are not willing to purchase the share. This may well be the case if it is a small business comprising few partners, without the ability to raise the necessary finance to buy out the departing partner.   **4.34**

    Any option to purchase the share of the outgoing partner should be included in the partnership agreement (see generally Partnership Act 1890, s. 42). As to the purchase of a departing partner's share of the business, the partnership agreement should address the following points:

(a) *Departing event.* The "departing event" or similar should be a defined term. For example, will it include both consensual and non-consensual types of departure?

(b) *Option to purchase.* An option to purchase clause should give the partners a pre-emption—*i.e.* a first right of refusal to purchase the share. Other ancillary matters to be addressed might include:

    (i) how long do the partners have to exercise their option?

    (ii) is it exercised by written notice?

    (iii) when, if at all, do third parties get a chance to purchase the share if the partners fail to exercise their pre-emption right?

    (iv) is the business to be dissolved if no one takes up the right to purchase?

(c) *A "garden leave" clause.* This involves consideration of the role to be played by the departing partner between the:

    (i) the date on which the notice period for the departure has been notified; and

    (ii) the date of departure itself.

For example, do the continuing partners want the departing partner to remain active in the business or would they rather he stays away, continues to be paid, has no contact with the clients and notionally at least, "cuts the lawn" at home? Such a provision is aimed at protecting the goodwill of the business and causing a minimum of disruption to the continuing partners and the business.

(d) *Valuation of the departing partner's share.* What is the mechanism for valuing the share? If the partners cannot agree a value as between themselves, they may want to refer the matter to an accountant or auditor.

(e) *Arbitration.* The principal purpose of such a clause would be to settle the valuation referred to above if, for example, the accountant or auditor cannot do so to the satisfaction of the parties.

(f) *Payment to the partner.* Will payment be a one-off payment or payable over time? This will depend on the cash-flow of the business and the ability to raise funds. If there is a delay and section 42 of the Partnership Act 1890 applies, the outgoing partner can seek the greater of:

    (i) interest on the amount owed at the rate of five per cent per year; or

    (ii) the profits attributable to his share of the business for the period of delay.

(g) *Restraint of trade clause.* This clause is designed to protect the business and its goodwill. It will prevent the partner, so far as it is reasonable, from setting up a competing business within a certain distance from the business premises and within a certain time period from the departure date. It may also provide that the departing partner cannot contact or solicit custom from the partnership's customers.

(h) *Indemnity clause.* Under section 17(2) of the Partnership Act 1890, a departing partner remains liable for debts incurred whilst he was a partner.

Section 17(3) of the Partnership Act 1890 provides that a retiring partner may be released from his existing partnership liabilities by a specific agreement to that effect between:

(i) himself;

(ii) the firm as newly constituted without him; and

(iii) each of the creditors in relation to the particular debts.

Unless it is a business with only a few creditors it will be impractical to obtain individual releases.

Alternatively, such an agreement can be inferred by examining the course of dealing between the creditors and the new firm. However, rather than relying on an actual or inferred release, the usual practical solution is that the departing partner will negotiate to be indemnified for existing debts by the continuing partners and that such indemnity will form part of the consideration paid for his share of the business, *i.e.* the partner's share will be calculated by determining his share of the partnership's assets less liabilities and in return he is indemnified in respect of those liabilities. The indemnity provision could then be invoked if a creditor attempted to sue the departed partner for payment of a partnership debt. The crucial point for the continuing partners is that the indemnity only covers those debts and liabilities actually disclosed by the departing partner. It is often the case that the continuing partners would require a cross-indemnity from the departing partner holding them harmless to liabilities which come to light after his departure, but which he did not disclose. A schedule of disclosed debts should be form part of the document evidencing the arrangement between the parties so as to avoid uncertainty.

(i) *Holding out*. Where a partner leaves the partnership, he may be at risk of incurring liability for debts and obligations incurred after he leaves. For example, he may be "held out" to the world as a partner pursuant to section 14 of the Partnership Act 1890, and, therefore, may still be liable as if he were a partner. The holding out can be words, writing or both. A common example is the fact that a partner's name remains on the letterhead. Accordingly, a departing partner should ensure that his name is removed from the letterhead. The legal adviser should also bear in mind section 36 of the Partnership Act 1890. Clients of the firm are entitled to assume that those partners with whom they have been dealing are partners of the firm until they are notified otherwise. Hence, existing clients should be advised in writing on the departure of a partner. Potential clients of the business should be advised under section 36(2) of the Partnership Act 1890 by an advertisement placed in the *London Gazette*.

2. THE DEATH OR BANKRUPTCY OF A PARTNER

Section 33(1) of the Partnership Act 1890 provides that unless the partnership agreement states otherwise, either the death or bankruptcy of a partner results in the automatic dissolution of the partnership.

4.35

To counter the effect of this, a provision is commonly inserted in a partnership agreement will provide that the:

(a) partnership business will continue despite a partner's death or bankruptcy; and
(b) that the deceased or bankrupt partner's share of the business will be purchased by the ongoing partners.

Section 36(3) of the Partnership Act 1890 provides that the estate of a partner who dies or who becomes bankrupt will not be liable for debts of the firm contracted after he dies or is bankrupted.

Delay in the payment for a deceased or bankrupt partner's share in the partnership is covered by section 42 of the Partnership Act 1890. In that case, his estate or representative is entitled to:

(a) five per cent interest on the amount of his share of the partnership assets; or
(b) *profits* made for the period from death to the date of payment attributable to the partner's share of partnership assets will be charged in *addition* to the price agreed to be paid for the share.

Tax
See Chapter 6.

G. Dissolution of the Partnership

1. BACKGROUND

4.36   Dissolution of the partnership business involves the:

(a) gathering in of partnership assets and monies owed by debtors to the partnership;
(b) the payment of partnership creditors; and
(c) the distribution of capital and partnership profits to the partners in accordance with the partnership agreement or, if in the absence of a partnership agreement, in accordance with the terms of the Partnership Act 1890.

Dissolution by notice (Partnership Act 1890, ss. 26, 32(c))

4.37   Under section 32(c) of the Partnership Act 1890 a partnership at will can be dissolved immediately by means of a notice given by one of the partners to the others. This may have disastrous financial and trading consequences.

It is important therefore to cancel the effect of sections 26 and 32 of the Partnership Act 1890 in the Partnership Agreement which states that the partnership business will not cease on notice to retire being given by one partner to the others, but that the business continues and the only effect of the notice is that it triggers the process that allows the continuing partners to purchase the retiring partner's share of the business.

Dissolution by death or bankruptcy (Partnership Act 1890, s. 33)
As has already been discussed, section 33 of the Partnership Act 1890 pro-   **4.38**
vides that unless the partners agree otherwise, the death or bankruptcy of a
partner will automatically dissolve the partnership business.

If there is a partnership agreement adopted, the usual practice is to treat:

(a) the death of a partner in the same way as the retirement of a partner,
    except that the partnership share will be purchased by dealing with
    the deceased partner's Personal Representative, and

(b) the bankruptcy of a partner as a matter giving rise to the expulsion
    of the partner concerned, and for the negotiations for the purchase
    of the partner's share of the business to be conducted with the
    Trustee in Bankruptcy.

Dissolution by the Court (Partnership Act 1890, s. 35)
On the application of a partner, the court may decree a dissolution of the   **4.39**
business in, amongst others, the following cases:

(a) the permanent incapacity of a partner, *e.g.* a long illness of a per-
    manent nature;

(b) the prejudicial conduct of a partner, *e.g.* a partner with dishonesty
    conviction;

(c) wilful or persistent breaches of the partnership agreement;

(d) if the business is a loss-making business (there is a practical imposs-
    ibility of making a profit), *i.e.* the application is made to stem the
    flow of losses—if there is delay in dissolving the partnership, more
    moneys will be lost;

2. REALISATION OF THE PARTNERSHIP'S ASSETS

On the dissolution of a partnership business: **4.40**

(a) partnership property is used to pay the partnership's debts; and then

(b) the surplus property, if any, is distributed to partners as it is due to
    them (see Partnership Act 1890, s. 39).

3. DISTRIBUTION OF THE PARTNERSHIP'S ASSETS

Subject to the terms of any partnership agreement, the partnership assets   **4.41**
are applied in the following manner by section 44 of the Partnership Act
1890:

(a) creditors, *i.e.* banks and other third party creditors are repaid first;

(b) advances (loans) by partners to the partnership are repaid next;

(c) capital (*i.e.* the "permanent investments" of partners to the
    business) are paid back to each partner next; and

(d) the residue, if any, is distributed to the partners in accordance with
    the profit sharing ratios contained in the partnership agreement.

H. A Partnership Agreement Overview

4.42   A Partnership Agreement or deed (an agreement under seal) is usually comprised of the following sections:

(a) *The Parties. i.e.* the people who will be bound by the agreement. Their names and addresses and how they will be referred to throughout the document.

(b) *Recitals*. The purpose of recitals is to "set the scene" for the "operative" provisions that follow. The recitals give a brief background to the legal arrangement that is documented in the operative part. The recitals are not normally legally binding on the parties whereas the operative provisions are.

(c) *Definitions*. Definitions refer to those words, phrases, statutes and the like that may be referred to several times throughout the document. Rather than "clogging up" the operative part of the document with definitions, they can be put in the definitions section. This also helps to ensure that a particular word or term is referred to in a consistent fashion, *e.g.* if the term "precedent partner" is defined, it should be referred to in the document in this particular format and with the same intended meaning each time.

(d) *Operative parts*. The legal part of the document that creates binding and enforceable rights and duties between the parties. Compare the recitals that are not usually legally enforceable.

(e) *Schedules*. If there are any further documents to be attached or documents to which the operative part refers, these may go in the appendices. Another example might be lists of chattels or furniture, etc., in a lease agreement. In a partnership, the partners might wish to clarify "partnership property" by actually listing it in an appendix or schedule.

(f) *Execution clauses*. The signing provisions where the parties or their authorised representatives sign the document.

An example of a partnership agreement and a summary of its terms is contained in Appendices 2.2.1 and 2.2.2 respectively.

5.   Personal Insolvency

A. Legislation

The Insolvency Act 1986 contains provisions concerning both: **5.1**

  (a) personal bankruptcy (relevant to individuals, including sole traders and partners in a partnership); and

  (b) company insolvency and winding-up.

For these purposes the Insolvency Act 1986 incorporates and consolidates the provisions of:

  (a) the Bankruptcy Act 1914;

  (b) the Insolvency Act 1985; and

  (c) the Companies Act 1985 (insofar as it relates to insolvency and bankruptcy).

B. Background

Bankruptcy is dealt with in Part Two of the Insolvency Act 1986. The general **5.2** provisions in Part Three of the Act apply to both individuals and companies.

Bankruptcy affects individuals. They may or may not be involved in a business. If they are involved in a business, irrespective of their title or role within the business, they may be exposed to bankruptcy. In so far as the three main business entities are concerned, the following people may be exposed to bankruptcy:

  (a) a sole trader;

  (b) a partner in a partnership business;

  (c) a director, shareholder, shadow director, creditor or debtor of a company; or

  (d) an employee of any of the above.

As far as providing legal advice, it may be prudent to advise a client about bankruptcy in certain preliminary instances, such as:

  (a) when a sole trader is setting up in business;

  (b) when a person is joining a partnership business; or

  (c) if a company director is being asked to provide a personal guarantee for a company debt.

However, for most practical purposes, the client requiring bankruptcy advice will be experiencing financial difficulty. "Financial difficulty" is not a term defined by the Insolvency Act 1986, but it may involve one or more of the following matters:

(a) that the client cannot pay his debts as they fall due;
(b) that on a balance sheet test, assets are outweighed by liabilities;
(c) that there are cash flow problems in the short term because money is tied up in assets which cannot be quickly realised; or
(d) that one or more creditors are threatening legal proceedings or other action.

It may be that such financial difficulty is short-lived and is solved through financial planning and other steps such as asset sales or the renegotiation of payment arrangements with creditors. If financial difficulties persist however, the individual concerned is exposed to the following outcomes:

(a) they may be made bankrupt. This involves the court making a formal order to that effect. The practical consequences are drastic. In addition to the stigma, the bankrupt loses all but a few of their assets and their estate is controlled by the Official Receiver, a Court appointed official. Thereafter, raising money or being able to be involved in business at all becomes problematic for the individual concerned. For example, a person cannot be a company director if they are subject to a bankruptcy order. In the usual course, a bankruptcy order applies for a three-year period. Bankruptcy is discussed in more detail below in section D.
(b) alternative to the formal procedure of bankruptcy, there are two informal processes available. They are as follows:
   (i) for a scheme or arrangement to be put into effect under the Deeds of Arrangements Act 1914; or,
   (ii) since 1986 and the introduction of the Insolvency Act, an individual voluntary arrangement (IVA) which is essentially an arrangement between an individual and his creditors which is sanctioned by the court.

The advantages of informal arrangements are that they avoid the court making a bankruptcy order. They may also provide greater flexibility to the particular business situation such as, for instance, allowing the person to remain as a company director.

Overview of Bankruptcy and Informal Arrangements

Financial Difficulty for the Individual Concerned

—cannot pay debts as they fall due;
—fails a balance sheet test; or
—lenders causing difficulty for the business

Formal Arrangements (a Bankruptcy Order is made by the Court)	**Informal Arrangements**
(a) statutory demand not satisfied within 21 days.	(a) Deed of Arrangement—problems of binding creditors;
(b) judgment obtained but not satisfied.	*or*

Bankruptcy Order—inability to pay   (b) Individual Voluntary
debts as they fall due.   Arrangement (IVA)
Vesting of Property in Trustee in
Bankruptcy.
Duration of Bankruptcy—3 years
ordinarily.

C. Informal Arrangements

1. INTRODUCTION

As mentioned above, there are two informal arrangements available to a   **5.3**
person in financial difficulty (and his creditors). As mentioned, the scheme
of arrangement provided under the Deeds of Arrangement Act 1914 have
rarely been used because they only bind those creditors who actually consent
to their terms. This has meant that any non-consenting creditors could press
for a bankruptcy order against the debtor against the debtor if they were not
satisfied with the terms of the scheme.

Hence the creation of Individual Voluntary Arrangements under the Insolvency Act 1986.

An Individual Voluntary Arrangement (known as an IVA) is an alternative
to formal bankruptcy proceedings. They were introduced by the Insolvency
Act 1986. An IVA may be used in a situation where the creditors decide not
to force the debtor into bankruptcy proceedings, which involve the court
making a formal bankruptcy order against the debtor under Part 9 of the
Insolvency Act 1986.

Under an IVA, the creditors of the person in financial difficulty will probably receive less than 100 pence in the pound, but they may receive payment
more quickly than if formal court proceedings were commenced.

Whilst under section 259 of the Insolvency Act 1986, the terms of the
IVA are reported to the court, it does not require the court's approval as to
its content or objectives.

Approximately one in every eight personal insolvencies is now dealt with
by way of an IVA. An IVA has the following features:

(a) the person is not subjected to a formal bankruptcy order;
(b) the person is not therefore disqualified from acting as a director of
    a company—this may be crucial if the company and director's fin-
    ances are closely linked—nor is the person under the legal disabili-
    ties suffered by bankrupts including the vesting of their property in
    the Trustee in Bankruptcy;
(c) the court can stay all other current legal proceedings and prevent
    new proceedings from being commenced against the person the sub-
    ject of the IVA;
(d) they are as flexible as the debtor and creditors will allow them to
    be and may include phased payments whereby the debtor pays his
    creditors over a period of time for example;
(e) they are private;

(f) the costs should be lower than for a formal bankruptcy.

The first practical step a person in financial difficulty will take in relation to an individual voluntary arrangement will be to approach a person known as a licensed insolvency practitioner. The phrase "to act as an insolvency practitioner" is defined in section 388 of the Insolvency Act 1986 in different capacities, depending on whether the term is used in relation to an individual or company.

It includes the following capacities in relation to an individual:

(a) acting as the supervisor of a voluntary arrangement (as is the case with an IVA);
(b) acting as a trustee in bankruptcy (as in the case with a formal bankruptcy order being made by the court); and
(c) acting as the administrator of a deceased person's estate.

2. Qualifications for Insolvency Practitioners

5.4   Section 389 of the Insolvency Act 1986 provides that it is an offence for a person to act as an insolvency practitioner without being duly qualified.

An insolvency practitioner must be a member of a "recognised professional body" that is listed in regulations published by the Secretary of State for Trade and Industry pursuant to section 391 of the Insolvency Act 1986. Generally, insolvency practitioners are qualified accountants although some are qualified as lawyers.

The order of events with an IVA
The steps involved in setting up an IVA are as follows:

(a) A qualified insolvency practitioner is approached by the debtor.
(b) The insolvency practitioner seeks a stay in respect of those proceedings which have already been commenced against the debtor. This is the first court hearing (see Insolvency Act 1986, ss. 252–254).
(c) The debtor and insolvency practitioner prepare a financial "proposal" that will be put before the creditors for their approval (Insolvency Act 1986, ss. 252–254).
(d) The second court hearing involves the proposal being submitted to the court (Insolvency Act 1986, s. 259)
(e) A meeting of creditors is then held between 14 and 28 days after the second court hearing. The proposal that has been prepared by the debtor and the licensed insolvency practitioner must then be approved by 75 per cent in money value of the creditors.

3. Effect of the Individual Voluntary Arrangement

5.5   The IVA will bind all the creditors of the person in financial difficulty except for the:

(a) non-assenting preferred creditors, *i.e.* those creditors who are owed preferred debts, including VAT, employee wages, taxation liabilities and pension contributions, etc. Preferred debts are defined in section 386 of the Insolvency Act 1986; and

(b) non-assenting secured creditors as they can pursue the debtor in accordance with the rights in their security documentation. Secured creditors are defined in section 248 of the Insolvency Act 1986.

D. The Bankruptcy Petition (Insolvency Act 1986, ss. 264–275)

1. BACKGROUND

A bankruptcy order made by the court will only be made as the result of a petition being presented to the court.   **5.6**

A petition is a written application that complies with the requirements set out in the Insolvency Act 1986. The petition may be presented to the court by:

(a) one or more of the creditors of the business, known as a *creditor's petition* (dealt with in paragraph 5.7–5.8 below);

(b) the debtor himself, known as a *debtor's petition* (dealt with in paragraph 5.9 below);

(c) the Insolvency Practitioner who is in involved in overseeing a voluntary scheme or arrangement between the debtor and his creditors or by a person bound by such a scheme. In either case, the leave of the court will be required. The grounds set out in the petition will relate to the debtor failing to comply with the scheme itself or with the directions of the Insolvency Practitioner or the fact that the debtor has provided false or misleading information wich has had a bearing on the scheme; or

(d) the Director of Public Prosecutions, in limited circumstances, under the Power of Criminal Courts Act 1973.

The creditor's petition
In order to lodge a bankruptcy petition, a creditor must have the necessary *locus standi*. The term *locus standi* is more commonly used in administrative law. It questions whether the creditor has "standing", *i.e.* the ability to commence bankruptcy proceedings against the debtor? The threshold test for establishing *locus standi* is that the creditor must be owed an unsecured debt (or debts) amounting to £750 pursuant to section 276(4) of the Insolvency Act 1986. The debt does not need to be a judgment debt, *i.e.* court proceedings need not have been commenced or completed in respect of the debt.   **5.7**

The reference to *locus standi* refers to unsecured debts only because the holder of a secured debt (a secured creditor) may take recourse against the secured assets if the debtor fails to repay any monies owed. Such an option is not available to an unsecured creditor.

If a secured creditor takes action under the security documentation and yet is still owed money once the security element has been exhausted, he can present a creditor's petition for the outstanding amount (if the threshold £750 test is met for that balance that is in effect unsecured because it has not been covered by the security document).

Example: A secured creditor issuing a creditor's petition. Jack's Trading owes a debt of £10,000 to the First National Bank. The loan is secured against Jack's motor vehicle worth £8,000.

Jack's Trading defaults on repayments of the loan. The vehicle is seized, leaving a £2,000 debt outstanding. This debt is unsecured as the security element (the car) has been "exhausted". The bank can lodge a creditor's petition in respect to the £2,000 debt outstanding.

The contents of the creditor's petition

5.8   The creditor's petition alleges that the debtor is:

    (a) unable to pay; or
    (b) has no reasonable prospect of paying the debt(s), details of which are set out in the petition.

The matters alleged in the petition are deemed to be proved if the debtor fails to comply with a "statutory demand" within three weeks (or a lesser period, if there is a "serious possibility" that the debtor's property, or its value, will be diminished to a significant extent if the three-week period were allowed to elapse).

The matters alleged in the petition are also deemed to be proved if the execution or other process issued in respect of a judgment debt has not been satisfied in whole or in part.

A "statutory demand" is a demand in a form that complies with Rule 6.1 of the Insolvency Rules 1986 made pursuant to the Insolvency Act 1986.

Statutory demands are defined in section 268 of the Insolvency Act 1986 to include:

    (a) a liquidated sum (a certain rather than simply an approximate amount) that is payable immediately by the debtor;
    (b) a liquidated sum payable by the debtor pursuant to a judgment or other order of the court; and
    (c) a liquidated sum that is payable at some future date.

The creditor's petition will be dismissed by the court if the statutory demand that has been served on the debtor, has been complied with in full within the 21-day or other period as specified by the court.

The debtor's petition

5.9   It may be that the debtor himself files a petition with the court. With such a petition, there are two requirements under section 265 of the Insolvency Act 1986 that have to be met:

    (a) the debtor has a sufficient "connection" with England and or Wales; and
    (b) is unable to pay his debts.

When presenting the petition to the court, the debtor also lodges a "statement of affairs" which contains full details of his:

(a) assets;
(b) liabilities; and
(c) the amounts owed to the creditors.

Once the petition has been presented to the court, it can only be withdrawn with the leave (permission) of the court.

2. THE COURT HEARING

Generally the court will either: **5.10**

(a) make the bankruptcy order (if the conditions set out above have been satisfied); or
(b) will make an interim order so that the debtor can devise a scheme of arrangement, *i.e.* an IVA.

In the case of the debtor's own petition, the bankruptcy order will not be made by the court if all four of the following criteria under section 273 of the Insolvency Act 1986 are met:

(a) the unsecured debts of the debtor are less than the small bankruptcy level, which is currently £2,000;
(b) the debtors total assets' value is more than the minimum amount of £2,000;
(c) the debtor has not been bankrupt or the subject of a scheme of arrangement in the previous five years; and
(d) it is appropriate in the court's opinion that a report be obtained from a licensed insolvency practitioner. This process is aimed at avoiding a formal bankruptcy and heading the debtor instead towards an IVA because it will normally be far less expensive to administer and less costly to the debtor.

E. The Trustee in Bankruptcy

On the court making the bankruptcy order, all property belonging to the   **5.11**
bankrupt vests automatically by operation of law in the Trustee in Bankruptcy. This means that there is a "deemed" transfer of the bankrupt's property such that the usual requirements of transfer such as delivery, the signing of documentation, etc., do not have to be gone through first.

1. THE OFFICIAL RECEIVER

Immediately the bankruptcy order is made, the Official Receiver becomes the receiver and manager of the bankrupt's estate.

The Official Receiver's powers include:

(a) selling any goods (including perishables good) whose value is liable to diminish;
(b) to take such steps as are necessary to protect the property of the bankrupt; and

(c) any other powers given to a receiver appointed by the High Court.

The official receiver's *duties* include:

(a) investigating the affairs of the bankrupt person; and
(b) making a report in those affairs for the court.

The official receiver will, generally within 12 weeks of his appointment, call a meeting of creditors of the bankrupt for the purpose of appointing a trustee in bankruptcy. The official receiver is usually therefore an interim appointee for a limited period of time.

A statement of affairs must be prepared by the bankrupt within 21 days of the bankruptcy order being made by the court pursuant to section 288 of the Insolvency Act 1986.

This requirement can be dispensed with by the official receiver or the 21-day time-limit can be extended by the official receiver.

The statement of affairs includes details of the bankrupt's creditors, the assets, debts and creditors and any other matters specified in regulations to the Insolvency Act 1986.

2. APPOINTMENT OF THE TRUSTEE IN BANKRUPTCY

5.12   The appointment of the trustee in bankruptcy will take place either at:

(a) the time the bankruptcy order is made by the court, *i.e.* the trustee in bankruptcy immediately replaces the Official Receiver; or
(b) by the creditors at a meeting of creditors called by the official receiver.

If a meeting of creditors is not held, the official receiver automatically becomes the trustee in bankruptcy. If the official receiver decides not to call a meeting of creditors, he can be compelled to do so by one-quarter by value of the creditors.

The meeting of creditors appoints the trustee in bankruptcy by passing by a simple majority resolution.

If a trustee in bankruptcy is not appointed, the official receiver will continue in his capacity as trustee in bankruptcy.

The trustee's role (or the official receiver if a trustee is not appointed), in broad terms, is as follows:

(a) to collect in the assets and estate of the bankrupt person;
(b) to convert, where possible, the estate to cash;
(c) to establish the identity of the creditors and the debts they are owed, referred to in section 322 of the Insolvency Act 1986 as proof of debts; and
(d) to distribute, in cash or kind, the estate to the creditors of the bankrupt in the order set out in section 328 of the Insolvency Act 1986.

F. Effect of Bankruptcy Order

5.13   The making of a bankruptcy order will be a traumatic event for most people. It may well involve the stigma of adverse publicity. It will have serious practical ramifications. For example the bankrupt:

(a) loses control of his property because, subject to limited exceptions, it vests in the trustee in bankruptcy and is thereafter controlled by the trustee;

(b) will not be able to be a company director (including shadow director) or promoter of a company without the leave of the court, otherwise he will be guilty of an offence under section 11 of the Company Directors Disqualification Act 1986;

(c) will be subject to inquiry, as far as his dealings or property is concerned, by the court on the application of the trustee or official receiver under section 366 of the Insolvency Act 1986.

The Insolvency Act 1986 contains an extensive number of further restrictions and sanctions of which the legal adviser to a bankrupt may need to advise, some of which are dealt with below.

1. THE VESTING OF THE BANKRUPT'S PROPERTY AND INCOME

On the making of the bankruptcy order, the bankrupt's estate immediately vests in the trustee in bankruptcy in accordance with section 306 of the Insolvency Act 1986. The "estate" of the bankrupt is very broadly defined in section 283(1) of the Act to include virtually all of the bankrupt's property except for property specifically excluded such as

(a) provisions for "basic domestic needs" for the bankrupt and his family (s. 283(2));

(b) property held on trust by the bankrupt (s. 283(3)); or

(c) property disclaimed by the trustee, for example on the basis that it could not be sold for more than its replacement value (s. 308(1)(b)).

As for the bankrupt's income, it does not automatically vest in the trustee in bankruptcy but the trustee in bankruptcy may also seek what is known as an "income payments order" under section 310(1) of the Insolvency Act 1986 which requires the bankrupt person to pay to the trustee so much of his income as the court believes is excess to the "reasonable domestic needs" of the bankrupt and his family.

"Income" is broadly defined in section 310(7) to include every "payment in the nature of income" from any business, office or employment.

2. PERSONAL CONSEQUENCES OF BANKRUPTCY

Once the bankruptcy order has been made, the bankrupt is subject to many restrictions. Such restrictions are too numerous to mention in detail. The bankrupt may be committing an offence if he breaches these restrictions. Such restrictions include the following:

5.14

(a) under Chapter 6 of the Insolvency Act 1986, entitled "Bankruptcy Offences", for example, he:

    (i) cannot obtain credit over a certain prescribed amount (currently £250) without disclosing his status as a bankrupt person (s. 360(1)); and

    (ii) cannot engage indirectly or otherwise in a business other than the one relevant to the bankruptcy, without making

disclosure to all people with whom he is dealing (s. 360(2)).
(b) under section 11 of the Company Directors' Disqualification Act 1986, he cannot be a promoter, director or shadow director of a company.

3. PROPERTY WHICH DOES NOT VEST IN THE TRUSTEE IN BANKRUPTCY

5.15   The following categories of property do not vest in the trustee in bankruptcy on the making of the bankruptcy order by the court.

(a) Property held on trust, by the bankrupt, *i.e.* the bankrupt holds the legal interest only in the property whilst the beneficial interest vests in a beneficiary (see Insolvency Act 1986, s. 283(3)(a)).
(b) Goods subject to retention of title (or "Romalpa") clauses. Romalpa clauses arise when the vendor third party retains title goods until they are paid for in full by the purchaser (bankrupt). For example, a supplier Marx Bros supplying computers to Bob's Trading has supplied 10 computer screens subject to payment terms over 10 months by equal instalments. The contract specifies a Romalpa clause. If Bob is made bankrupt within the 10-month period, the computer screens will not vest in the trustee in bankruptcy but will instead remain the property of Marx Bros until payment is complete.
(c) Such tools, books, vehicles and other items of equipment necessary to the bankrupt for use personally by him in his business, vocation or employment (see Insolvency Act 1986, s. 283(2)(a)).
(d) Clothing, bedding, furniture, household equipment and provisions necessary to satisfy the "basic domestic needs" of the bankrupt and his family (see Insolvency Act 1986, s. 283(2)(b)).

4. THE BANKRUPTCY'S MATRIMONIAL HOME (INSOLVENCY ACT 1986, ss. 336–338)

5.16   The Insolvency Act 1986 contains provisions safeguarding the interests of the bankrupt's spouse and dependent children (under 18) if they are living in the house at the time of the presentation of the bankruptcy petition and when the bankruptcy order is made. The manner of so doing is to create a charge in favour of such persons which the trustee in bankruptcy must apply to the court to have set aside.

(a) If the home is in bankrupt's sole name the spouse has a right of occupation that is treated as a charge on the property. As such, the trustee in bankruptcy will require a court order before being able to sell the property.
(b) If the home is in joint names the trustee in bankruptcy will require a court order to be able to sell and realise the bankrupt's interest in it under section 30 of the Law of Property Act 1925.

The following matters must, pursuant to section 336(4) of the Act, be considered by the court in deciding whether to set aside the charge:

(a) the creditor's interests;

(b) the needs and resources of the bankrupt's spouse;
(c) the needs of the bankrupt's children;
(d) the spouse's conduct and, in particular, whether it contributed to the bankruptcy; and
(e) all other relevant circumstances.

In the case of minor children living in the home, the bankrupt himself has a right of occupation as do the children under section 337, which requires the leave of the court before they can be evicted or excluded from the home. The court will consider similar criteria to those above.

The above considerations provided in relation to the family home do not last indefinitely. The rationale of the Act is to provide short-term relief from eviction, etc. Section 336(5) of the Insolvency Act 1986 provides that after 12 months from the date of vesting of the bankrupt's property in the trustee, the court shall assume, "unless the circumstances of the case are exceptional, that the interests of the bankrupt's creditors outweigh all other considerations."

G. Rules for Preserving and Increasing the Bankrupt's Assets

1. DISCLAIMER FOR ONEROUS PROPERTY (INSOLVENCY ACT 1986, ss. 315–321)

Whilst the property of the bankrupt (subject to limited exceptions) vests in the trustee in bankruptcy on the making of the bankruptcy order, it may be that the trustee in bankruptcy will not want to lay claim to all property belonging to the bankrupt and thereby responsible for it. Such property may simply be more "trouble than it's worth". The Insolvency Act 1986, by section 315, refers to this category of property as "onerous property" and it is this property that the trustee in bankruptcy will disclaim after reviewing the property portfolio that has vested in him.

5.17

Onerous property might, depending on the circumstances, include the following items:

(a) unprofitable contracts entered into by the bankrupt, *e.g.* stock-in trade contracted to be purchased at high prices;
(b) not readily saleable property, *e.g.* old premises or a leasehold interest close to expiry; or
(c) property giving rise to liabilities and onerous obligations, *e.g.* the maintenance of property which may be time-consuming and expensive.

The trustee in bankruptcy is discharged from any personal liability in relation to onerous property once he disclaims it (Insolvency Act 1986, s. 315(3)).

2. Distress (Insolvency Act 1986, s. 347)

5.18   Distress is a form of remedy available to a landlord against a tenant when the tenant fails to pay rent. If a bankrupt, in his capacity as a tenant, has failed to pay rent, the landlord can commence distress proceeding in which he seeks possession of the bankrupt's goods and effects so as to sell them and thereby satisfy the unpaid rent.

A landlord can distrain against the bankrupt's goods for no more than six months' rent accrued before the making of the bankruptcy order. The distress proceedings can be commenced after the making of the bankruptcy order. Section 347 contains specific provisions curtailing the powers of landlords in such circumstances. There are only two exceptions to the rule against proceedings being commenced after the making of the bankruptcy order:

    (a) a secured creditor who can take action under the security documents; and

    (b) a landlord for distress proceedings.

3. Execution of Judgments (Insolvency Act 1986, s. 346)

5.19   As a consequence of the fact that a bankrupt's property vests in the trustee in bankruptcy on the making of the bankruptcy order, it is generally the case that no new legal proceedings can be commenced against the bankrupt after that date.

For legal proceedings which were commenced before the making of the bankruptcy order, the proceedings will be stayed by reason of the commencement of the bankruptcy—see Insolvency Act 1986, s. 285.

For legal proceedings in which judgment has been obtained against the bankrupt before the commencement of the bankruptcy, section 346 of the Insolvency Act 1986 provides, in general, that the judgment creditor must obtain any judgment sum or benefit before the commencement of the bankruptcy if they fail to do comply with section 346 they will stand in the queue of creditors of the bankrupt and their right to payment will be determined by reference to the Insolvency Act 1986.

H. Disposals and Payments Made after the Bankruptcy Petition

5.20   Between the date of:

    (a) presentation of the petition to the court; and

    (b) bankruptcy order itself, at which time the estate of the bankrupt vests in the trustee in bankruptcy,

any dispositions made by the bankrupt in this period will be void unless approved by the Court beforehand or subsequently ratified by the court (see Insolvency Act 1986, s. 284(1)).

An exception to this is section 284(4) which provides that a person acquiring property or payment from the bankrupt within this period is not bound by section 284(1), *i.e.* so that the transaction in question will stand, so long as that person:

(a) was acting in good faith;
(b) provided consideration, *i.e.* acted for value; and
(c) did not have notice that the bankruptcy petition had been presented.

1. UNDERVALUE TRANSACTION (INSOLVENCY ACT 1986, S. 339) AND PREFERENCES (INSOLVENCY ACT 1986, S. 340)

Both undervalue transactions and preferences are voidable at the option of the trustee in bankruptcy. Both involve dealings that the bankrupt will have made before the court made the bankruptcy order. In practice, the trustee in bankruptcy will examine the business affairs of the bankrupt with a view to determining whether any transaction possibly coming within the terms of sections 339, 340 or 423–425 of the Insolvency Act 1986 took place. If they did, the trustee will apply to the court to have them set aside and the transaction effectively can be cancelled, so that the property the subject of the transaction is returned to the pool of assets that vests in the trustee.

5.21

Undervalue transactions

For undervalue transactions, the relevant period of inquiry is up to five years before the bankruptcy order is made by the court (Insolvency Act 1986 s. 341(a)). An undervalue transaction is one in which the bankrupt has dealt with his property such that:

5.22

(a) he effectively gave it away, *i.e.* he did not receive any consideration for it; or
(b) he sold it for less than its market value. The test is whether he sold it for "significantly less consideration" than it is worth.

It is an objective matter for the trustee in bankruptcy or liquidator to prove. No element of fraud is required to be proved.

Example: An undervalue transaction. The matrimonial home which is owned by the bankrupt in his sole name is given to his spouse as a gift (*i.e.* where there is no consideration paid) one year before the bankruptcy order is made. Depending on the circumstances, this might also constitute a fraudulent transaction under section 423(1)(a)(see paragraph 5.24 below).

Preferences

Transactions classified as "preferences" involve the debtor (bankrupt) paying one of his creditors to the advantage of that creditor and to the disadvantage of the other creditors, *i.e.* one creditor is being favoured, or put in a better position than he is entitled to under the Insolvency Act 1986. The debtor needs to be influenced in his course of action by the fact that he is favouring one creditor over the others, *i.e.* the debtor must have a prerequisite element of knowledge.

5.23

The period of inquiry for a preference under section 341(2) of the Insolvency Act 1986 is:

(a) six months before the bankruptcy order if the creditor who has been favoured is an arm's length client; or

(b) two years before the bankruptcy order, if the creditor who has been preferred is an "associate" of the bankrupt. An "associate" includes a spouse, sibling, child, aunt, uncle, etc. For details, see Insolvency Act 1986, s. 435.

A further requirement with both undervalue transactions and preferences is that the bankrupt normally is either insolvent at the time of the transaction or becomes insolvent as a result of the transaction being set aside (s. 341(2)).

Example: An undervalue transaction. The matrimonial home which is in the bankrupt's sole name is given to the bankrupt's spouse one year before the bankruptcy order, this might also be a *fraudulent transaction, i.e.* alternative grounds of invalidating the transaction exist.

Example: A preference. Paying an unsecured debt when the debtor is insolvent (*i.e.* allowing one creditor to "jump" the creditor's queue) and there is no sound commercial reason for doing so by which the bankrupt can justify the transaction.

2. Transaction Defrauding Creditors (Insolvency Act 1986, ss. 423–425)

5.24   Such transactions can be set aside at anytime. There is no time-limit or relation back period as there is with preferences or undervalue transactions.

Application to set aside transactions can be made by the following persons in the following circumstances:

(a) where the debtor has been made bankrupt, by the Official Receiver or Trustee in Bankruptcy, or with leave of the court, a victim of the transaction in question (Insolvency Act 1986, s. 424(1)).

(b) where the debtor is subject to an individual voluntary arrangement (IVA), by the supervisor of the scheme or a victim of the fraud, whether bound by the scheme or not (Insolvency Act 1986, s. 424(1)(b)); or

(c) in any other case, by a victim of the transaction (Insolvency Act 1986, s. 424(1)(c)). Section 423(1) includes reference to undervalue transactions. For a transaction to be classed as fraudulent, the applicant must show that the purpose was either:

(i) to put assets beyond the reach of creditors (s. 423(3)(a)); or

(ii) prejudicing the interests of the creditors (s. 423(3)(b)).

Example: Fraudulent transactions. A debtor not disclosing the existence of stock-in-trade to an existing lender (who holds a floating charge) in order to secure further monies from a new lender.

As already noted, fraudulent transactions are not restricted to cases of winding-up or administration orders, *i.e.* undervalue fraudulent transactions can be set aside whenever they were made.

Creditors can apply to set aside fraudulent transactions before the bankruptcy order is made. Once the order is made, only the trustee in bankruptcy can apply to the Court.

I. Distribution of Assets

Secured creditors will be afforded protection by virtue of the rights set out in the security documentation. Usually their remedy will be to seize and sell assets or appoint a receiver and manager to a business.   **5.25**

For unsecured creditors they must look to the Insolvency Act 1986 for their protection. This sets out an order of entitlement for creditors of a bankrupt. Whether a creditor gets paid (if at all) will depend on:

(a) what type of debt he is owed;
(b) the available assets of the bankrupt; and
(c) the amount of the debts in each class of creditor.

ORDER OF ENTITLEMENT

The order of payment of the creditors under the Insolvency Act 1986 is as follows:

(a) Administration costs of the bankruptcy, *i.e.* the official receiver and   **5.26**
    trustee in bankruptcy's cost, professional advisers, etc.
(b) Sums paid by masters to apprentices.
(c) Preferential debts for an individual debtor are the same as for a company in liquidation and are defined in section 386 of the Insolvency Act 1986. Each of the periods referred to below, refer to periods before the bankruptcy order is made.

Wages	(4 months)
VAT	(6 months)
National Insurance contribution and PAYE	(12 months)
Holiday pay	(all arrears)

(d) Ordinary *unsecured* creditors, *e.g.* trade creditors.
(e) *Postponed* creditors, *e.g.* loans between *spouses*.
(f) Any surplus will go to the bankrupt.

As with companies in liquidation, the following rules set out in section 328 of the Insolvency Act 1986 apply to payment:

(a) each class of creditor must be paid in full before the next class receives anything; and
(b) if the assets are insufficient to meet the debts owed to the creditors of the class, they are paid rateably, according to the value of the debts owed to them respectively.

J. Discharge of the Bankruptcy Order

On discharge from bankruptcy, the bankrupt receives a certificate of discharge from the court.   **5.27**

The bankruptcy then:

(a) commences on the day the bankruptcy order is made by the court;
(b) and ceases when the bankrupt obtains a certificate discharge from the court (Insolvency Act 1986, s. 278).

Most bankruptcies under the Insolvency Act 1986 are automatically discharged after three years.

If the particular circumstances justify it, there will not be a three-year automatic discharge pursuant to section 279(2) of the Insolvency Act 1986. For example, "criminal bankruptcies" are only discharged after five years, and then only with a separate order from the court. An example of a criminal bankruptcy might be one in which the bankrupt was found guilt of carrying out a fraudulent transaction.

A court order will also be required to discharge a bankruptcy order against a bankrupt who has been bankrupted in the previous 15 years under section 279(1) of the Insolvency Act.

The official receiver may oppose an automatic discharge of bankruptcy. For example, if obligations have not been fulfilled by the bankrupt.

EFFECT OF DISCHARGE OF BANKRUPTCY ORDER (INSOLVENCY ACT 1986, s. 281)

5.28 Generally, once the bankruptcy order has been discharged, the bankrupt is free from:

(a) the disqualifications suffered by an undischarged bankrupt; and
(b) continuing liability to meet his bankruptcy debts.

However, the bankrupt remains obliged to assist the trustee in bankruptcy to get in, sell and/or distribute the bankrupt's former property, if such matters remain outstanding, pursuant to section 281 of the Bankruptcy Act 1986. Section 281(2) of the Act provides that the discharge from bankruptcy does not affect the rights of a secured creditor to enforce their security.

Once discharged from the bankruptcy order, the bankrupt is still, however, required under section 281 of the Insolvency Act 1986 to pay the following sums:

(a) fines payable to the Crown;
(b) provable debts where money liability:
    (i) is based on fraud or a fraudulent breach of trust;
    (ii) is for personal injuries caused by: negligence, nuisance, breach of contract, etc.; or
    (iii) is in respect of any family law proceedings including an affiliation order or a maintenance order.

6. Taxation of Sole Traders and Partnerships

A. Introduction

1. Providing Legal Advice

The legal adviser to a business may be called on to provide advice on a range of issues involving several different types of tax. With the proliferation of tax relevant legislation, and the detailed changes to such legislation which take place on a regular basis (as well as the need to be up to date on aids to interpretation such as Statements of Practice issued by the Commissioner), the provision of tax advice is becoming increasingly specialised and will usually be provided by a specialist within the firm. The lawyer's role in terms of general tax advice is to:

6.1

- (a) identify the tax problems or potential problems;
- (b) identify the business tax reliefs that may be available;
- (c) identify possible changes to the business. An example might be that the accounting period that has been adopted can be changed so as to provide a better tax planning system; and
- (d) trying to appreciate the commercial and other constraints faced by the business.

2. Aims of this Chapter

The primary aim of this chapter is to provide an overview of the different types of tax and to highlight some of the practical tax concepts applying to businesses such partnerships and self-employed taxpayers, *i.e.* sole traders and partners. There are three types of tax to which reference will be made in this chapter:

6.2

Income Tax
Income tax is the tax payable on assessable income profits by the following:

- (a) individuals, *i.e.* sole traders, partners (and as is discussed in Chapter 16, directors and employees in general);
- (b) partnerships, *i.e.* the business is subject to a joint assessment and each partner is required to settle his own tax assessment comprising part of the joint assessment;
- (c) the personal representative of a deceased estate; and
- (d) trustees of a trust.

We will concentrate on the first two categories.

The main statute dealing with income tax is the Income and Corporation Taxes Act 1988. Under this Act income received by a business is taxed according to its source or nature and nominally allocated to one of the schedules set up under the Act. For the self-employed taxpayer or partnership business, Schedule D is most relevant.

Schedule D, Case I deals with the income of a trade whereas Case II deals with the income derived from a profession.

Capital gains tax

Capital gains tax involves assessing to tax, certain gains over and above inflation (and subject to certain deductions) made when the taxpayer disposes of so-called "chargeable assets." For practical purposes, the assessable capital gains made by a self-employed taxpayer will be added to the pool of assessable income.

The main statute dealing with capital gains tax (CGT) is the Taxation of Chargeable Gains Act 1992. The Capital Allowances Act 1990 will also be considered.

Inheritance tax

The arrangements made by an individual who has been involved in a business before or at the time of his death will also be considered. Inheritance in general terms taxes certain "chargeable transfers" the effect of which is to reduce the size of the deceased's estate. The primary legislation is the Inheritance Taxes Act 1984.

3. OVERVIEW OF THE ASSESSMENT OF THE SELF-EMPLOYED TAXPAYER

6.3   The starting point is that, in general terms, the income profits generated by a business (whether it is a sole trader's business or a partnership business) are subject to the payment of income tax.

Income profits are classified according to the various schedules specified under the Income and Corporation Taxes Act 1988. For example, Schedule D, Case I, deals with profits from a trade. A group of partners running a retailing business would be subject to this Schedule. On the other hand, a professional partnership such as a firm of solicitors or accountants is taxed under Schedule D, Case II (income profits from a profession).

In the case of a sole trader as the owner of the business who is, it will be the sole trader assessed to income tax and is liable to pay such assessment, *i.e.* the income profits generated by the business will be disclosed on the sole trader's taxation return. In the case of a partnership, it will be the individual partners who are assessed and liable to pay income tax in accordance with the profit-sharing ratios as set out in the partnership agreement, or on an equal basis under the Partnership Act 1890 if there is no agreement.

B. Key Concepts in the Tax Assessment of Business

1. INCOME AS OPPOSED TO CAPITAL

The word "income" is not defined anywhere in the taxation legislation.

6.4

The receipts of a business may, in general terms, be either of an "income" nature or a "capital" nature.

The determination of the nature of the receipt will depend on the facts in each case and the particular rules applicable under the legislation.

The *general* rules are that:

    (a) income receipts are subject to the payment of income tax; and
    (b) capital receipts are subject to the payment of capital gains tax.

2. TAXABLE INCOME PROFITS

The self-employed taxpayer will pay income tax by reference to the taxable income profits made by the business. The starting point is to determine the gross income or revenues made by the business. From this will be deducted those expense incurred in making such income. In broad terms the gross revenue less the deductible expenses (see section 5 below) will provide the profit figure. This profit figure may be further reduced by other items such as:

6.5

    (a) charges on income (see section 6 below);
    (b) personal allowances (see section 7 below)
    (c) capital allowances (see section 8 below); and
    (d) losses made in, for example, previous years of the business (see section G of this chapter).

3. THE TAX YEAR

The income Tax Year for sole traders and partnership (which is otherwise referred to as the "year of assessment" or "tax year") runs from April 6 of one year to the following April 5. The reason for this is historical, as April 5 was the end of what was known as a period of account. Note, however, that the Corporation Tax Year (discussed in paragraph 16.8) runs from April 1, of one year to March 31, of the following year.

6.6

4. THE INCOME SCHEDULES

As already stated, income profits are categorised according to the source of the income. The income Schedules list the various sources of income.

6.7

Each Schedule has its own rules for determining:

    (a) the amount of income profits; and
    (b) the available deductions (if any).

As the term "income" is not defined in the taxation legislation, in practice it refers to all the sums calculated under the Schedules, *i.e.* if a receipt is not "income" it will usually be "capital". However, some capital items, *e.g.* "golden handshakes" (which are payments made on the termination of employment that fall outside the employee's contractual entitlements) are *deemed* to be income and are taxed as such.

Schedule	Source	Basis of assessment
A	Rents and other receipts from land in U.K.	Rents receivable less outgoings of the current year of assessment
C	Public revenue	Income of the current year of assessment
D		
Case I	Profits of a trade in U.K.	
Case II	Profits of a profession or vocation in U.K.	
Case III	Interest, annuities and other payments	Traditionally on a preceding year basis but now being brought into line with the other schedules so as to operate on a current year basis.
Case IV	Securities out of the U.K. not charged under Schedule C	
Case V	Possessions out of the U.K. not charged under Schedule C (but excluding foreign employment)	
Case VI	Annual profits or gains not falling under Cases I–V and not charged by virtue of any other Schedule; and certain income directed to be so charged.	
E		
Cases I, II and III	Offices, employments and pensions (both "home" and foreign). Also, chargeable benefits under the social security legislation.	Income in the year of receipt.

F	Dividends and certain other distribution by companies	Income of the current year of assessment.

5. DEDUCTIBLE EXPENSES

Deductible expenses are those amounts that are: **6.8**

    (a) not prohibited by statute;
    (b) usually of an income rather than capital nature; and
    (c) incurred wholly and exclusively for the purpose of the trade.

For example, travel expenses incurred during the course of the working day but not the expense of travelling to and from the place of work.

6. CHARGES ON INCOME

Charges on income are, in general terms, those amounts which a taxpayer is   **6.9**
obliged contractually to pay to a third party. They are defined in section 338 of the Income and Corporation Taxes Act 1988. The main charge on income for present purposes is the payment of interest by the individual or business in respect of borrowings. Charges on income reduce the assessable income profits.

7. PERSONAL ALLOWANCES

There are various personal allowances which depend on the particular indi-   **6.10**
vidual's circumstances. For example, the personal allowance, the married couple's allowance, and the blind person's allowance. They have the effect of reducing the taxable income of the individual concerned.

For example, the personal allowance is currently £3,765. In effect this means that the first £3,765 earned is free from tax.

8. CAPITAL ALLOWANCES

Capital allowances are governed by the Capital Allowances Act 1990. The   **6.11**
term refers to the notional depreciation (or "writing down" in terms of the book value) of certain capital assets which are owned and used by the sole trader or partnership business. Claiming capital allowances enables the business to reduce its taxable income profits.

The term "capital assets" refers to items intended to assist the running of the business such as plant and machinery, and the premises. They are of a semi-permanent or permanent nature so far as the business is concerned, in contrast to stock in trade, which is intended to be bought and sold on a daily or regular basis.

In general, capital allowances are an exception to the usual position that there is no income tax relief for expenditure on *capital* items.

For plant and machinery, a capital allowance of up to 25 per cent of the qualifying expenditure on a reducing balance basis is available. This means that fixed plant and machinery purchased for say £100,000 may be written down by £25,000 in the first year. In the second year it will by written down by £17,750 (*i.e.* 1/4 of £75,000) to £57,250 and so on until the asset is sold or written off.

For industrial buildings purchased by a business—for example, a mill, factory or similar premises; a building used for the storage of manufactured goods or raw materials; a workers' canteen but not normally a retail shop, a house, a showroom or office premises—a capital allowance of 4 per cent per annum on a straight-line basis of the original cost is allowed, *i.e.* such assets will take 25 years to "write off" to a nil book value.

C. An Example of the Tax Assessment of a Self-employed Individual

6.12   Assume Alan Griffiths Electronics, a sole tradership records the following income, etc., in the 1996–97 tax year. Griffiths is not married.

Total Income from the business £100,000
Deductible expenses £50,000
Charges on income £5,000
During the tax year he sold a business asset and made a net capital gain of £10,000.

Step one: ascertain the statutory income which is the total income less the deducible expenses, *i.e.* £100,000 less £50,000 leaving £50,000;
Step two: deduct the charges on income, *i.e.* £50,000 less £5,000 leaving £45,000
Step three: add the capital gain subject to the annual relief for CGT which is presently £6,300, *i.e.* the total capital gain of £10,000 is reduced to a taxable capital gain of £3,700 bringing taxable income to £48,700.
Step four: deduct the personal allowance of £3,765 giving a taxable assessable income of £44,935.

Income tax will be charged as follows for the tax year April 6, 1996 to April 5, 1997 on the sum:

    (a) from 0 to £3,765 zero, *i.e.* the personal allowance;
    (b) from £3,766 to £7,665 at 20 per cent (the lower rate);
    (c) from £7,666 to £29,265 at 24 per cent (the basic rate); and
    (d) over £29,265 at 40 per cent (the higher rate).

The marginal rate refers to an individual's highest rate of tax. In this case, Alan Griffith's marginal rate is 40 per cent.

D. An Overview of Schedule D

6.13   As noted already, Schedule D, Case I deals with the profits from a trade and Case II the profits from a profession.

Schedule D has traditionally operated on what is referred to a preceding year basis. What this has meant, in practical terms, is that there has been a delay between the generation of income by a business and the payment of income tax in respect of that income. This has allowed business planning advantages to Schedule D taxpayers, primarily by allowing them to make provision over a period of time to meet the tax liabilities of the business.

The other income Schedules in the Income and Corporation Taxes Act 1988 are operated on a current year basis so that the income is both generated and subject to tax within the same tax year without an invervening delay.

The preceding year basis of assessment which has operated under Schedule D is as follows:

—to ascertain the relevant income profits for a particular tax year (call it year three for our purposes), go to the previous tax year (*i.e.* year two for our purposes) and determine the accounting period that ends in that previous tax year (*i.e.* in year two). The profits for that accounting period are then attributed to year three.

E. Change of the Preceding Year Basis for Schedule D

The Finance Act 1994 has introduced measures that will eventually change the preceding year basis of assessment under Schedule D to that of a current year basis so as to bring Schedule D into line with the other income Schedules.

6.14

By the tax year commencing April 6, 1997 and ending on April 5, 1998, all Schedule D income will be taxed on a current basis.

Until then, there will be different systems of assessment depending on whether a business came into existence before April 6, 1994 or on or after that date.

1. Businesses in Existence Before April 6, 1994

The following transitional scheme will apply to businesses that existed before April 6, 1994:

6.15

- (a) Tax Year 1994–95: the preceding year basis of assessment applies;
- (b) Tax Year 1995–96: the preceding year basis of assessment applies;
- (c) Tax Year 1996–97: a transitional position—tax will be based on the average of profits for the two-year accounting period ending in the tax year 1996–97, *i.e.* an averaging application of the preceding year rule;
- (d) Tax Year 1997–1998: the new current-year basis of assessment applies. For example, if the accounting period is January 1, 1997 to December 31, 1997, the profits for that period will be subject to tax in the 1997–98 tax year which runs from April 6, 1997 to April 5, 1998 (as well as the 1996–97 tax year).

2. Businesses in Existence after April 6, 1994

The new current year rules for Schedule D will apply immediately to businesses which came into existence after April 6, 1994.

6.16

3. BUSINESSES IN EXISTENCE BEFORE APRIL 6, 1994 BUT WHICH ARE DEEMED TO CEASE AFTER APRIL 6, 1994

By virtue of section 113(1) of the Income and Corporation Taxes Act 1988, there is a deemed *cessation* of the business whenever a partner leaves, the business, irrespective of whether that partner is replaced or not. The partnership, as constituted immediately after the partner leaves, is then treated as if it had just come into existence once the change has taken place.

So far as the changes to the preceding year rules are concerned, businesses caught by the deeming provisions of section 113(1) Income and Corporation Taxes Act 1988 after April 6, 1988 will be treated as if they were new businesses and will be subject to the current-year rules, from the moment of creation.

Due to the overhaul of Schedule D it is necessary to examine the rules briefly with respect to:

(a) pre-April 6, 1994 partnerships (''old partnerships'') that are taxed on a preceding year basis; and
(b) post-April 6, 1994 partnerships (''new partnerships'') that are taxed on a current-year basis.

F. The Taxation of Pre-April 6, 1994 Businesses

1. METHOD OF PAYMENT OF SCHEDULE D INCOME TAX

6.17   There are two instalments for the payment of Schedule D income tax.

Examples: Payments of Schedule D tax. If the tax year runs from April 6, 1994 to April 5, 1995 payments of instalments of tax will be January 1, 1995 and July 1, 1995.

An important feature of the ''preceding-year'' basis of taxation and the method of payment of tax is that there is a delay between:

(a) the business increasing its profits; and
(b) the Revenue increasing the amount of tax collected from the business to reflect the increase in profits.

Example: Preceding-year basis of assessment. Beth's Trading has an accounting period that runs from January 1 to December 31:

(a) The tax year runs from April 6 to the following April 5.
(b) As Beth's Tradings accounting period runs from January there is an overlap between that tax year and accounting period.
(c) For the tax year April 1993 to April 1994, Beth's Trading will pay tax on the income derived in the accounting period that ended in the 1992–93 tax year.
(d) The tax paid is therefore considerably delayed from the time when the income profits in respect of it were actually made.
(e) The payment of income tax will be in two instalments. The first

instalment will be January 1, 1994 and the second instalment on July 1, 1994.

The Opening Year Rules for pre-April 6, 1994 businesses (Income and Corporation Taxes Act 1988, ss. 61, 62)
The opening years of pre-April 6, 1994 businesses are taxed in the following way:

6.18

(a) 1st tax year: the actual profits (on a straight-line apportionment) to April 5;
(b) 2nd tax year: the actual profits of the first 12 months of trading;
(c) 3rd tax year: the "normal basis", *i.e.* preceding-year basis of assessment of income applies.

In effect, the first 12 months' profits are used as the basis of the income-tax assessment for the first three years of the business.

Example: The old opening year rules. Zaworski's Restaurant began trading on 6 January, 1991 and made the following profits:

January 6, 1991–January 5, 1992—£12,000
January 6, 1992–January 5, 1993—£24,000
January 6, 1993–January 5, 1994—£36,000

The business would be taxed as follows:

(a) for the period April 6, 1990–April 5, 1991 the taxable income profits will be £3,000 (*i.e.* 1/4 (or three months) of the first year's profits of £12,000 apportioned on a straight-line basis);
(b) for the period April 6, 1991–April 5, 1992 the taxable income profits will be £12,000 (*i.e.* the profits of the first 12 months' trading);
(c) for the period April 6, 1992–April 5, 1993 the taxable income profits will be £12,000 (*i.e.* the preceding-year basis).

The opening years election for pre-April 6, 1994 businesses
If the profits in the first accounting year are high (resulting in correspondingly high assessments to tax under the opening year rules) the taxpayer can instead elect to have the year two and year three income taxed on the basis of the *actual profits* made in those years rather than on the basis of the first 12 months' profits. The election covers both the second and third taxation years. The election is made by the taxpayer in writing to the Revenue, under section 62 of the Income and Corporation Taxes Act 1988. If the election is not made, the first 12 months' profit will be used as the basis of the income-tax liability for, in effect, the first three years of the business.

6.19

2. THE CLOSING-YEAR RULES

The closing-year rules for pre-April 6, 1994 businesses
In the final year of the business, the "closing-year assessment" will cover the period from April 6 to the date of termination of the business on a straight line apportionment. For example if a business terminated on December 31,

6.20

1993, the taxable profits for 1992–93 would be 3/4, *i.e.* nine months of the profits in the accounting period January 1, 1992 to December 31, 1993.

In each of the two years before the final year, the business is taxed on a "normal" or preceding-year basis under Schedule D. The result of the application of the preceding-year rules is that the income profits of the second last year of the business escaped being assessed. In order to remedy this the Revenue can elect via section 63 of the Income and Corporation Taxes Act 1988 to tax these years on the *actual profits* made. The revenue is likely to make its election therefore if the second last year of the business has high profits.

G. The Taxation of Business Commencing on or after April 6, 1994

1. TAX ELECTIONS FOR NEW BUSINESSES

6.21   As we have seen, old partnerships, tax affairs and planning were characterised by various elections:

> (a) the opening-years election under section 62 of the Income and Corporation Taxes Act 1988 made by a partnership business or sole trader when the first-year profits were high and then followed by a drop in profit in years two and three; and
> (b) the closing-years election under section 63 of the Income and Corporation Taxes Act 1988 by the *Revenue* when the profits are rising towards the end of the business.

With new businesses, these elections are redundant. Hence, the tax-planning opportunities available are reduced.

A new business can claim "overlap relief" for tax paid twice on the same income. This may occur:

> (a) if the tax year and the accounting period do not correspond; and
> (b) at the end of the business on the basis of the closing-year rules for new businesses.

2. CHANGES IN THE COMPOSITION OF THE NEW PARTNERSHIP

6.22   As we have seen with old partnerships, the effect of section 113(1) of the Income and Corporation Taxes Act 1988 was to deem partnerships as at an end for tax purposes if there was any change in partners whatsoever.

For new partnerships section 113(2) is amended such that the "deeming element" is removed. Now in order to be treated for tax purposes as discontinued there must be an *actual* discontinuance of the business:

> (a) *all* the partners leave, *i.e.* there is no continuity of ownership;
> (b) a sole trader dies; or
> (c) the partners dissolve the business.

Hence there is no longer any need when drafting a partnership agreement to include an election provision under section 113(2) of the Income and Corporation Taxes Act 1988 whereby each of the partners and their personal representatives and trustees in bankruptcy elect to treat the partnership as continuing for tax purposes.

3. THE OPENING-YEAR RULES FOR BUSINESSES COMMENCING ON OR AFTER APRIL 6, 1994

The *current* basis of assessment under Schedule D will apply to businesses commencing on or after April 6, 1994:

    6.23

    (a) "old" businesses, *e.g.* from April 6, 1997 for the tax year April 6, 1997–April 5, 1998;

    (b) "old" businesses who do *not* make a continuing election under section 113(2) of the Income and Corporation Taxes Act 1988, if there is a deemed discontinuance. If no election is made the business will be treated as commencing from the date of the deemed discontinuance.

The current-year basis differs from the preceding-year basis in the following respects:

    (a) there is no delay between earning income and paying tax on that income;

    (b) profits taxed equal profits earned. If they do not, the tax payer is entitled to "overlap" relief for the extra tax paid. Overlap relief may be claimable by the tax payer from the Revenue when the business' accounting period is other than April 6 to the following April 5.

The "new" opening-year rules affect the first two years of the business and are as follows:

Year of commencement:	Tax is based on the profits made in the period from the date of commencement of the business to the following April 5.
Second year:	Tax is based on the profits made in the first 12 months of trade, *i.e.* from the date of commencement to the following equivalent day. This is the current-year basis.
Third year:	Tax is based on the profits made in the current tax year.
Subsequent years:	As with the third year, *i.e.* on a current-year basis.

4. THE CLOSING-YEAR RULES FOR BUSINESSES COMMENCING ON OR AFTER APRIL 6, 1994

In the final tax year of the business, the taxable income profits will be those for the period commencing from the end of the accounting period in the second last year to end of the business.

    6.24

Example: New closing-year assessment. Max Mex Bros has an accounting period July 1 to June 30. The business finishes on December 31, 1995. Therefore:

    (a) The last tax year is April 6, 1995–April 5, 1996.

    (b) The second last tax year is April 6, 1994–April 5, 1995.

    (c) The accounting period that ends in the second last year is that which ends June 30, 1994.

    (d) Therefore, the last tax year will be attributed with the income profits for the period commencing July 1, 1994 and going through 18 months to December 31, 1995.

    (e) Max Mex Bros would be entitled to overlap relief for any income in this period that is taxed twice.

H. Tax Relief for the Trading Losses of a Business

6.25   A trading loss occurs when the sole trader or partnership's deductible expenses and outgoings are greater than the income profits generated by the business.

    Loss relief is dealt with in several ways under the taxation legislation. For example:

    (a) In the year following "the loss year" there will be a nil tax assessment on the basis of normal (preceding-year) assessment under section 380 of the Income and Corporation Taxes Act 1988: the loss may alternatively be "carried across", *i.e.* set off against the traders' or partnerships' other schedule income for that tax year.

    (b) unabsorbed capital allowances may also be carried across against other schedule income.

1. Losses "Carried Forward" (Income and Corporation Taxes Act 1988, s. 385)

6.26   Section 385 provides that losses may be carried forward to the next accounting period that records a profit until exhausted.

    Examples: Losses carried forward. Bob's Trading makes a loss of £10,000. In the next three years it made profits of £3,000 per year and in year four a £1,000 profit.

    The £10,000 loss can be carried forward and offset against those four years of income, producing and assessments.

2. Losses "Carried Back" (Income and Corporation Taxes Act 1988, s. 388)

6.27   Section 388 of the Income and Corporation Taxes Act 1988 provides that in the final 12 months of the business (a) a loss or (b) unused capital allowances may be carried back to three years before the final year of the business.

3. Losses Carried Back (Income and Corporation Taxes Act 1988, s. 381)

6.28   Section 381 of the Income and Corporation Taxes Act 1988 provides that losses made in the opening four years of the business may be carried back three years before the loss-making year. Relief is set off against the most recent years first. This form of relief is to assist new businesses.

3. LOSSES UNDER INCORPORATION RELIEF (INCOME AND CORPORATION TAXES ACT 1988, s. 386)

Section 386 of the Income and Corporation Taxes Act 1988 provides that on the transfer of an unincorporated business to a company, and when the consideration paid for the business is wholly or mainly by way of shares in the company to the former owners of the business, the owner of the business may set off unabsorbed *losses* incurred before the sale of the business against income received from the company. This form of relief, known as "incorporation relief", is available while the person owns shares in the company.   **6.29**

The loss can be set off against the shareholder's income from the company including:

(a) dividends received on shares; and
(b) salary paid by the company

whilst the person is a shareholder in the newly formed company.

Example: Incorporation relief. Bob sells his business and receives 10,000 shares in ABC Ltd. The business made a loss of £2,000 in the year before he sold it. The loss of £2,000 can be set off by Bob against any dividend income he receives in respect of the ABC Ltd shares or salary or fees he receives from the company.

I. Specific Provisions Affecting Trading Partnerships

For the purpose of the collection of and assessment to tax a partnership is treated as a separate legal entity: **6.30**

(a) Trading partnerships are taxed under Schedule D, Case I.
(b) Professional partnerships are taxed under Schedule D, Case II.

1. THE METHOD OF TAXING PARTNERSHIPS

The Finance Act 1994 has affected the manner in which partnerships are taxed. Again, it is necessary to distinguish between partnerships: **6.31**

(a) in existence before April 6, 1994;
(b) in existence after April 6, 1994.

2. THE METHODS OF TAXING PARTNERSHIPS IN EXISTENCE BEFORE APRIL 6, 1994

With professional and trading partnerships in existence before April 6, 1994, the precedent partner (*i.e.* the senior or first named partner in the partnership agreement) must file a return of partnership income. Each partner files his own tax return in which he claims personal allowances.   **6.32**

The Revenue then makes a *joint* assessment to tax in the partnership's name (*i.e.* the aggregate amount of tax for which each partner is liable). Liability for payment of the tax assessment of the partnership is joint, and not several.

The joint assessment is based upon:

(a) each partner's profit-share for the current tax year, *i.e.* as set out in the Partnership Agreement (the partnership's profits are taxed on the preceding-year basis in accordance with current-year profit-share ratios set out in the Partnership Agreement); and

(b) takes into account each partner's:

(i) *Personal reliefs.* For example the first £3,765 slice of income is exempt from the payment of income tax in the tax year 1996–97; and

(ii) *Charges on income.* For example, 50 per cent of National Insurance Contribution (NIC) is a charge on income profits.

The Revenue will supply information to the precedent partner setting out the apportionment between the partners, in relation to the partnership tax return.

3. The Taxation of Partnerships in Existence after April 6, 1994

6.33   For partnerships that commence after April 6, 1994, each partner will be individually assessed to tax rather than all the partners being jointly and severely liable for the payment of the partnership's tax bill in respect of the partnership's income.

Each partner will:

(a) include partnership income in his personal tax return; and

(b) be solely liable to pay the taxation liability in respect of his share of partnership profit.

A partnership return will still have to be lodged for the purpose of showing:

(a) the total taxable profit of the partnership, and

(b) the allocation between the partners.

Partnerships in existence before April 6, 1994, will be bound by this scheme from the tax year 1997–98.

J. Deductions by the Partnership

6.34   Salary paid to partners and interest paid to partners in respect of their capital contributions are treated as a means of distributing or allocating profits of the partnership and are not deductible as "expenses" by the partnership. The partnership's accounts must show salary for each partner separately in the allocation of profits. Both salary and profit are treated sharing as profit sharing by the Revenue.

K. The Taxation of Interest Payments Made by the Business

If the partnership or the sole trader borrows money for one or more of the purposes set out below, the interest, if paid by the business, is a deductible business expense for the partnership itself or the sole trader, *i.e.* it is an amount deductible from income profits.

6.35

If interest is paid by the partner, it is a *charge on income*, *i.e.* it reduces the income of that partner.

There may be several purposes for the borrowing:

(a) contribution of capital, *i.e.* permanent investment;
(b) a share in the partnership;
(c) to make a loan to the partnership wholly and exclusively for the purposes of the partnership business;
(d) machinery and plant (for which capital allowances apply) that is made in the partnership.

L. Retirement Provisions

Further reference to pensions is made in Chapter 16.

1. PERSONAL PENSIONS

Schedule D taxpayers, such as partners and sole traders, can deduct the contributions they make to personal pensions schemes on a sliding scale ranging from 17.5 per cent to 40 per cent of their income, depending on their age.

6.36

The pension itself is a tax-free fund. This means that as it accrues in value, it is not subject to the imposition of tax.

There are two ways of taking the pension sum on retirement, namely:

(a) by way of an annuity (an annual amount) which is taxed as earned income when received; or
(b) by a lump sum (approximately 25 per cent of the total amount of the lump sum is tax free).

2. STATE RETIREMENT PENSIONS

The state retirement pension is a state-run scheme funded by National Insurance contributions. An employee is required to contribute for a 90 per cent period of his working life in order to be entitled to receive the full amount of the benefit.

6.37

It is taxed as earned income in the hands of the recipient.

3. NATIONAL INSURANCE CONTRIBUTIONS

Under section 617(5) of the Income and Corporation Taxes Act 1988, half of a sole trader or a partner's National Insurance contributions are tax deductible (as a charge on income), from income profits.

6.38

M. The Taxation of Capital Gains for Businesses

1. GENERAL PRINCIPLES

6.39   The rules on capital gains tax are primarily found in the Taxation of Chargeable Gains Act 1992. Under the Act a liability to pay capital gains tax (CGT) arises when a chargeable person disposes of a chargeable asset at a price in excess of the inflationary price increase of the asset.

In order to compute the CGT liability it is necessary to determine the following matters:

    (a) the acquisition price of the asset including associated expenses and fees;

    (b) the disposal price including associated fees and expenses;

    (c) the inflationary increase in the price by reference to the indexation allowance;

    (d) expenditure to improve the value of the property or to defend title to the asset will be deducted from the disposal price.

The taxpayer will pay CGT at his marginal rate on the chargeable gain. Each taxpayer receive an annual CGT exemption of £6,000.

A taxpayer's primary place of residence is exempt from CGT. Second homes are not. In general the disposal of business assets will be subject to the payment of CGT but various business reliefs may be claimed.

6.40   *Example: General CGT calculation.* Simon sells a holiday flat in 1996 for £120,000 which he purchased for £40,000 in 1985. He spent £300 on the survey and £500 on legal fees in purchasing. His expenses on sale were £2,500. He spent £10,000 renovating and improving the cottage. The indexation allowance reveals that the inflation price of the flat is £80,000, *i.e.* its price should have risen by £40,000 on account of inflation. He is a 40 per cent taxpayer.

The CGT payable is calculated as follows:

Disposal Price:	£120,000
Less:	
Purchase price in total	£40,800
Improvement cost:	£10,000
Disposal costs:	£2,500
Total:	£53,300

The disposal price of £120,000 less the sum of £53,300 is the total gain on the sale, *i.e.* £66,700.

The price the property should have rise on account of inflation is £40,000. It appears therefore that Simon has made a chargeable gain of £26,700. Simon therefore has to pay CGT on the sum of £26,700, the first £6,300 of which will be exempt and the balance which will be taxable at 40 per cent.

2. Capital Gains Tax on Death

On the death of a sole trader or partner, there is no capital gains tax payable **6.41** by personal representative of the estate or the beneficiary of an asset of the estate. The assets are however ascribed a new value for ongoing capital gains tax calculations. In effect the capital gains which accrued during the deceased taxpayer's life will be ignored but the beneficiary will be deemed to have acquired the asset in question for the purpose of CGT calculations. This means that when the beneficiary disposes of the asset, he will be liable to pay CGT.

3. Capital Gains Tax in the Business Context

The chargeable capital gains made by partners and sole traders are subject **6.42** to the normal rules applying to capital gains.

Partners are deemed to be connected in relation to the acquisition and disposal of partnership assets. Bona fide or arm's length transactions are those where the full consideration or "market value" is paid by the purchaser. In dealings between partners, the partners have to satisfy the Revenue that the price paid for the particular asset or interest in the business is the same as that which would be paid by a stranger. If the Revenue is not satisfied on this point, it would deem a market price to apply to the transaction in question.

Example: A "connected" transaction. Ian, Ron and David run a partner- **6.43** ship business that sails yachts in the Greek Islands. Ian departs the business and his third share of the business is purchased by Ron and David for £500,000 representing a chargeable capital gain of £300,000. The Revenue will need to be satisfied that the price paid (£500,000) is a price that would be paid by a "stranger" as Ron and David are "connected" as partners to Ian.

4. Statements of Practice

Statement of Practice are issued periodically by the Inland Revenue and deal **6.44** with the interpretation of taxing statutes. They deal with specific provisions and should be treated with a degree of caution, as they simply represent the Revenue's view of the law, and do not have the force of law.

Statement of Practice number D12 of 1975 deals with taxation concerning partnerships. It has been added to by Statement of Practice number 1 of 1979 and Statement of Practice of number 1 of 1989.

N. Capital Gains Tax (CGT) and Business Reliefs

1. Overview

When a partnership business or sole trader sells a "chargeable asset", a **6.45** liability to CGT is triggered. In the case of a partnership, the disposal by the partnership is treated, for CGT purposes, as being a disposal made by each of the individual partners.

Although the tax return is made by the firm, the assessment to CGT is made for each of the individual partners in the proportions that they own the *partnership assets* and is determined primarily by reference to the terms of the partnership agreement, *i.e.* each partner is treated as owning a fractional share of each chargeable asset in the partnership.

A partner who retires, or is expelled from the partnership, is treated for CGT purposes as making a disposal of his fractional part of each chargeable asset in the partnership.

This leads to the important practical point in when advising a business client of the question of "business reliefs". Business reliefs are designed to *reduce* or *delay* the payment of CGT or inheritance tax (collectively referred to as "capital taxes").

6.46   Business reliefs may apply in relation to several business transactions. These include:

(a) a sole trader or partnership selling a "business asset" and using the proceeds of sale to purchase a replacement business asset. If there is a taxable capital gain made on the sale of the asset and the proceeds are used to purchase a replacement asset, the capital gain may be deferred or delayed until such time as the replacement asset is sold and not replaced by a "business asset". This *delay* in the payment of CGT is referred to as "rollover" or "replacement of business assets" relief. See section 2 below.

(b) a sole trader or partner retiring from a business, *i.e.* having no further active involvement in the business. This form of relief is known as retirement relief and various conditions as to length of ownership of assets, age of the claimant and type of asset have to be met before the Revenue will grant relief. Retirement relief acts to *reduce* the CGT liability of a sole trader or partner. See section 3 below.

(c) a sole trader or partnership business becoming an incorporated business, *i.e.* a company and the consideration or payment for the transfer of assets being paid in the form of shares in the company. This is known as incorporation relief. It acts to *reduce* the capital gains tax liability on the sale of the unincorporated business. See section 4 below.

(d) a sole trader or partner making a gift of business assets to someone (the donee). Such a transaction can "hold over" or delay the payment of CGT if the donor and donee make an election to do so. The business assets can be given away by the donee thereby further delaying CGT. CGT will be payable if the donee sells rather than gives away the assets in question. See section 5 below;

(e) inheritance tax which is dealt with in section N of this chapter.

2. REPLACEMENT OF BUSINESS ASSETS RELIEF

6.47   Replacement of business assets relief (otherwise referred to rollover relief and referred in section 155 of the Taxation of Capital Gains Act 1992 is a form of taxation relief incurred on the sale of particular business assets that are then replaced by certain other business assets of either the same type or falling within a list of assets under the Act. For example, land, buildings, goodwill, fixed plant and machinery. The application of rollover relief is similar for companies, sole traders and partnerships.

Replacement of business assets relief postpones the payment of CGT. The relief works by rolling the capital gain made on the sale of an asset into the purchase price of the replacement asset thereby reducing the deemed acquisition price of the replacement asset. Capital gains tax will be paid when the replacement asset is sold and not replaced. The rationale for the relief is to encourage the investment by businesses in business assets.

Rollover relief can also be claimed by individuals where they own one of the nominated business assets which is used by the business. The relief is then available to the individual rather than the business, *i.e.* the individual must purchase the replacement asset.

The conditions that have to be met in order to claim rollover relief are as follows: **6.48**

(a) *Who can claim rollover relief*: either the business or an individual who owns the asset which is used by the business;

(b) *Type of asset*: see Taxation of Chargeable Gains Act 1992, s. 155. The list includes buildings, fixed plant and machinery, land and goodwill;

(c) *Time of purchase of replacement asset*: the replacement asset must be purchased within three years of the sale of the old asset or can be purchased no more than one year before the sale of the old asset, *i.e.* the old and replacement asset can both be owned at the same time for up to one year.

Example: Rollover relief. Sam owns land which is used by the partnership business of which he is a partner. He sells the land for a capital gain of £100,000 and purchases replacement land at a price of £250,000.

If rollover relief is applied the gain on the sale of the old asset will be rolled into the purchase of the replacement asset giving it a deemed acquisition price of £150,000, *i.e.* £250,000 less the £100,000 rolled into it.

3. RETIREMENT RELIEF

Retirement relief is referred to in sections 163 and 164 of the Taxation of Capital Gains Act 1992 and Schedule 6 to that Act. The conditions that have to be met by a sole trader or partner to be eligible for retirement relief are as follows: **6.49**

Age: either 50 years of age at the date of disposal of the asset (although he need not retire from the business altogether), or to have been forced to retire before 50 years (*i.e.* "early") on the grounds of ill health; and
Length of ownership: has owned the property for at least one year prior to the disposal. The full amount of retirement relief is obtained after 10 years ownership. The retirement relief claimable increases by 10 per cent per year on a straight line basis. Thus whilst ownership for two years gives 20 per cent relief, ownership for eight years gives 80 per cent relief; and

Disposal: the claimant must make a "material disposal" or other "qualifying disposal" of defined business assets. This includes a disposal or sale of:

(a) a business, or a part of a business, *i.e.* a sole trader who sells his business, or a partner who sells his share in the partnership assets will qualify;

(b) specific assets used for the purpose of the business when the business ceased trading—generally the business must have been owned by the sole trader or a partnership of which she was a member.

The conditions must be satisfied at the date when the business ceased (*i.e.* either 55 years of age, or retired due to ill health, and have owned the asset for at least one year);

The disposal may take place within a "permitted period" after the cessation of the business (one year) unless the Revenue allows a longer period.

Business assets: the disposal must be of chargeable *business* assets, *i.e.* gains on other assets, for example, private investments will not get the relief, *e.g.* land held for private purposes.

Examples: Eligibility for retirement relief

6.50   Situation 1: Amanda has owned her sole trader business for 21 years. She is 63 years of age and retires from the business. She is entitled to full retirement relief.

Situation 2: Simone is 41 years of age and retires from the business. She is not entitled to retirement relief unless she can prove to the Revenue that she retired on the grounds of ill health.

Situation 3: Brenda is 70 years of age and has owned the business for only 6 months. She is not entitled to any retirement relief as she has not been able to satisfy the one-year ownership test.

Amount of retirement relief available

Retirement relief exempts from charge to CGT the following amounts:

100 per cent of capital gains of up to and including £250,000; and
50 per cent of capital gains between £250,000 and £1,000,000.

The maximum amount of retirement relief claimable is available on disposals or associated disposals involving capital gains in excess of £1,000,000. The relief applicable in such situations is £625,000 calculated as follows:

(a) £250,000, *i.e.* 100 per cent of £250,000, plus
(b) £375,000, *i.e.* 50 per cent of the £750,000 balance up to £1,000,000.

With full retirement relief therefore, a capital gain of £1,000,000 can be reduced to a taxable gain of £375,000.

Example: Computation of retirement relief. Amanda from situation 1 above sells her business for a capital gain of £600,000. She is entitled to the following retirement relief:

£250,000 (being 100 per cent of the first £250,000 capital gains); *plus* £175,000 (being 50 per cent of the gain between £250,000 and £600,000). The total retirement relief available to Amanda is therefore £425,000.

Claiming retirement relief

Retirement relief applies automatically when a person is 50 years of age and retires from the business.

6.51

If a person retires before 50 years of age due to ill health, he can make a claim for retirement relief within a period of two years from the date of his retirement. Such relief is claimed by written application to the Revenue together with supporting medical evidence of ill health.

4. INCORPORATION RELIEF (TAXATION OF CAPITAL GAINS ACT 1992, s.162)

When an unincorporated business is incorporated, *i.e.* a sole tradership or partnership business becomes a private limited company, a specialised form of CGT relief known as incorporation relief may be available to the seller of the unincorporated business.

6.52

Incorporation relief is a postponement rather than an exemption from the payment of CGT.

Incorporation relief can be claimed when an unincorporated business (whether run by a sole trader, partnership or trustees) is sold to a company and the purchase price paid for the business is wholly or partly paid for in return for shares in the purchasing company.

Incorporation relief applies when:

(a) the unincorporated business is sold at a capital gain;
(b) shares are received as consideration for the sale;
(c) the capital gain is deducted from the value of the shares received, *i.e.* it is "rolled into" the share purchase price;
(d) the shares are then purchased at the lower acquisition base for CGT calculation;
(e) this means when the shares are eventually sold the CGT postponed will be paid.

Example: Incorporation relief. Bob sells his sole tradership to ABC Ltd at a capital gain of £20,000. He receives shares worth £50,000 in ABC Ltd.

6.53

The incorporation relief will apply as follows:
the £20,000 gain will be rolled into the actual acquisition price of the shares which is £50,000 giving the shares a deemed acquisition price of £30,000. When Bob sells the shares in ABC Ltd, subject to other reliefs, he will pay CGT based on the share's deemed acquisition price of £30,000.

Where the company provides only part of the consideration payable for the unincorporated business by way of shares in the company (*i.e.* the rest is paid for in the form of cash or debentures, etc.), only a corresponding part of the capital gain can be rolled forward and deducted from the value of the shares.

The relevant formula is as follows—the capital gain rolled forward equals the total capital gain multiplied by the market value of the shares in the company divided by the total price paid for the unincorporated business.

Example: Computing incorporation relief. If Bob, from the previous example, received £25,000 worth of shares and £25,000 cash he could only roll one-half of the £20,000 capital gain (*i.e.* £10,000) into the shares giving them a base value of £40,000.

5. HOLDOVER RELIEF

6.54   Holdover relief acts to delay the payment of capital gains tax. It is governed by the Taxation of Chargeable Gains Act 1992. It covers:

(a) transfers between spouses (s. 58); and
(b) the gift or undervalue sales (*i.e.* where less than market value is paid) of business assets (s. 165). In this situation the donee and donor can make a joint election to hold over the capital gain. When the donee *sells* the asset in question he will be liable to pay:
   (i) his own capital gains tax for the period of his ownership; plus
   (ii) the capital gains tax for the period relating to the donor's period of ownership.

The conditions which have to be met to claim holdover relief under section 165 of the Taxation of Chargeable Gains Act 1992 are as follows:

(a) *Type of asset*: an asset which is used for the purpose of a trade, profession or vocation (see s. 165(2));
(b) *Conditions*: a joint election to hold over the capital gain is made by the donor and donee to the Revenue in respect of a gift of under-value sale of a business asset.

O. Inheritance Tax for Businesses

1. INHERITANCE TAX GENERALLY

6.55   Inheritance tax is payable on certain transfers ("chargeable transfers") of property comprised in the estate made under a will or prior to the taxpayer's death. Chargeable transfers are those transactions which have the effect of diminishing the value of the estate of the individual concerned. Chargeable transfers are defined under sections 1 and 2 of the Inheritance Tax Act 1984. They are transfers:

(a) of value, *i.e.* they diminish the value of the transferor's estate;
(b) made by an individual; and
(c) which are not exempt under the Act.

The charge to tax may arise as follows:

(a) on certain life-time transfers, immediately at the time the transaction is made;

(b) on certain life-time transfers the liability may arise at any time if the transferor dies at any time within seven years from the date of the transfer. Such transfers are known as potentially exempt transfers (PETs). If the transferor survives more than three years from the time of making the chargeable transfer, tapering relief is available as follows depending on the amount of time of the transfer before the taxpayer's death:

    (i) 3 to 4 years before death—80 per cent of the death charge is payable;

    (ii) 4 to 5 years before death—60 per cent of the death charge is payable;

    (iii) 5 to 6 years before death—40 per cent of the death charge is payable;

    (iv) 6 to 7 years before death—20 per cent of the death charge is payable; or

(c) on a transfer occurring on the death of the taxpayer.

"Chargeable transfers" include:

(a) gifts, *i.e.* where no consideration is payable; and

(b) undervalue transactions which include a gratuitous element or gift component, *i.e.* less than the market (or arm's length) price has been paid to the taxpayer or his estate.

Other general points to note are the following:

(a) if a taxpayer has made no chargeable transfers within seven years before death, the rate of tax payable on the first £200,000 of the estate is nil; and

(b) in respect of lifetime gifts, a taxpayer has an annual exemption of £3,000 that can be rolled over once, *i.e.* a gift of cash of up to £6,000 can be made free from inheritance tax.

2. INHERITANCE TAX IN THE BUSINESS CONTEXT

As has been noted, transactions where the market price has been paid will not be chargeable transfers. In the case of a partnership business, the partnership interest of a partner who dies or retires will usually be sold on a pre-emption basis to the continuing partners. **6.56**

Inheritance tax should not be payable if the Revenue is satisfied that the market price has been paid. The Revenue will investigate that the price paid is the market one where the sale of the interest is to a "connected person".

A "connected person" includes the taxpayer's family members and fellow partners (see Taxation of Chargeable Gains Act 1984, s. 286).

Transactions involving connected persons will need to establish that the market price was in fact paid, *i.e.* that there was no gratuitous element involved. The onus of proof is on the taxpayer.

Example: Inheritance tax liability. Bob sells his house valued at £100,000 to Ian, his business partner, for £50,000. Bob faces a potential IHT liability on the £50,000 loss to his estate unless he can prove that the price paid is the market price.

3. INHERITANCE TAX BUSINESS PROPERTY RELIEF

6.57   The purpose of business property relief (BPR) is to prevent a business from having to be sold in order to pay the IHT liability.

In addition to any BPR, any IHT amount that is payable, after allowing for business property relief, may often be paid by way of interest-free instalments under section 227 of the Inheritance Tax Act 1984.

The relief works by reducing the loss to the donor's estate that has been caused by the transfer or settlement in the will of "relevant business property."

The definition of "relevant business property" includes:

(a) the business of a sole trader;
(b) an interest in a partnership business including land, whether freehold or leasehold.

100 per cent relief from inheritance tax assessment is available in both cases. The rationale for the relief is to encourage the turnover of business assets so as to enable the continuation of the business.

Where the relevant business property is the subject of a binding contract at the date of death of a partner, the IHT business property relief will not be available, *i.e.* the partnership agreement should avoid imposing an obligation on the ongoing partners to purchase the outgoing partner's share; instead, the partnership agreement should provide an option to purchase the deceased partner's share in the partnership.

There is a requirement of ownership for two-year period before death for IHT business property relief to apply.

If IHT business property relief is not available, payment by instalments of the IHT liability is generally available.

As has already been noted, full consideration and commercial transaction transfers should not give rise to an IHT liability because there is no loss to the partner or sole trader's estate.

7.   Business Names

A. Introduction

Assume that a professional partnership such as a law or accounting firm is comprised of 100 partners. It would be ludicrous for the firm to be called "Smith, Brown . . ." and so on down to the hundredth partner's name. Instead, such partnership businesses adopt a business name, which may or may not include the names of some, or perhaps none, of the present partners. The choice of business name will depend on:

(a) the number of partners in the business;
(b) the age of the partnership business. For example, a law firm established for 200 years may still carry the name of the original founding partners. The name will be well known and a valuable asset of the partnership;
(c) the goodwill associated with a name, *e.g.* recognisability as in (b) above, which will be useful for advertising purposes, etc.;
(d) the type of partnership activity.

Each of the three main business entities—sole trader, partnership and company—can adopt a business name if they wish to do so. However, before they can be adopted and used by a business, certain business names require approval from the Secretary of State for Trade and Industry or, depending on the circumstances, another specified organisation or both.

B. The Business Names Act 1985

The use of business names is governed by the Business Names Act 1985. The first point to note is that Business Names Act 1985 does *not* apply to all business names (section 1). The Business Names Act does not apply to the following categories of business names:

(a) A partnership whose business name consists of the names (both forenames and surnames) of the partners or with the addition only of the letter "s" at the end of the surname;
(b) A sole trader on the same basis as a partnership;
(c) A company that uses a corporate (rather than business) name, *e.g.* ABC Limited trades under that name.

The Business Names Act 1985 applies to all other business names. The business names to which the Act applies can be divided into several categories.

1. BUSINESS NAMES ACT 1985, S. 4—DISCLOSURE REQUIREMENTS

7.3   Section 4 of the Business Names Act 1985 applies to business names that contain words that are additional to those set out in section 1 of the Act referred to above. Section 4 sets out certain requirements that apply to such business names. An example would be "Amanda Perez Bakery"—such a business name is required to show the individual's name and a business address on all:

(a) business letters,
(b) written orders for goods or services,
(c) invoices/receipts,
(d) written demands for payment issued; and
(e) at the place where the business is carried on.

Section 4(2) of the Business Names Act 1985 requires that the address of the business and name of the proprietor of the business is supplied in writing to those dealing with the business or when requested.

Section 4(3) of the Business Names Act 1985 provides that partnerships comprising of more than 20 partners—*i.e.* professional partnerships—need not comply with listing all of the partners' names on the documents referred above, so long as it keeps such a list at its principal place of business.

Breach of section 4 of the Business Names Act 1985

7.4   By section 5 of the Business Names Act 1985, if a business is in breach of section 4 of the Act, a civil action in contract brought by the business against a third party can be dismissed by the court if the third party can show:

(a) he had a claim against the business that could not be pursued because of the breach by the business of section 4; or
(b) he suffered some financial loss because of the breach of section 4.

2. SECRETARY OF STATE APPROVAL

7.5   Sections 2(1) and 3(1)(a) of the Business Names Act 1985 refer to business names containing words and expressions that require the approval of the Secretary of State for Trade and Industry before they can be used. Such words and expressions are set out in regulations to the Business Names Act 1985 and are referred in the Companies House brochures as "sensitive words and expressions". They include the following categories:

(a) Words that imply national or international pre-eminence, *e.g.* International, National, United Kingdom, Great Britain, England, English, Scotland, Scottish, Wales, Welsh, etc.
(b) Words that imply governmental patronage or sponsorship, *e.g.* Authority, Board, Council.
(c) Words that imply business pre-eminence or representative status, *e.g.* Association, Federation, Society, Institute.
(d) Words that imply specific objects or functions, *e.g.* Assurance, Charity, Insurer, Chamber of Trade, Post Office, Trust, Register, Sheffield, Stock Exchange.

3. "Relevant Body" Approval

Section 3(1)(b) of the Business Names Act 1985 refers to specific words **7.6** requiring the approval of a particular organisation or "relevant body" in *addition* to the Secretary of State's approval.

The procedure is as follows:

    (a) Write to the relevant body.
    (b) Obtain a letter of approval from the relevant body in order to use the business name.
    (c) Send a copy of the letter of approval to the Secretary of State as well as seeking the Secretary of State's approval.

Examples

    (a) The use of the words "Dental" or "Dentistry" requires the approval of the Registrar of the General Dental Council.
    (b) The use of the expression "special school" requires the approval of the Department of Education.

4. Connection with the Government

Section 2(1)(a) of the Business Names Act 1985 requires the Secretary of **7.7** State's approval for business names that "would be likely to give the impression that the business is connected with Her Majesty's Government or with any local authority."

Most of these words are covered by the "sensitive words and expressions" list, but section 2(1)(a) would cover words not on the list but meeting the "likely connection" test set out above.

5. Names that might Constitute a Criminal Offence

In the list of sensitive words and expressions published are words whose use **7.8** "*might* constitute a criminal offence" without approval.

Example

    (a) The use of the word "Architect" requires the prior approval of the Architects' Registration Council of the United Kingdom.
    (b) The use of the word "Bank" requires the prior approval of the Bank of England.

C. Breaches of the Business Names Act 1985

By section 7 of the Act, a breach of the Act may constitute an offence punish- **7.9** able on summary conviction, and by fine.

8. Overview of Companies

A. Introduction

8.1 The third common type of business entity is the company. Companies are dealt with in Chapters 8 to 17 inclusive. The term "company" encompasses all types and sizes of company from the one person business to the multinational conglomerate. A feature of all companies is the separation between:

(a) the owners of the company (the shareholders); and
(b) the company itself, whose affairs are managed by the directors.

The separate existence of the company allows, in theory:

(a) a shareholder to claim that the extent of his liabilities are determined by the amount payable on his shares; and
(b) a director to be indemnified by the company for actions taken on the company's behalf.

Companies provide an investor with the means of limiting his liability or potential loss to the amount unpaid on the shares he holds if the company fails financially. Companies are separate and distinct legal entities. That is, they exist independently of the shareholders (members); the directors; the employees; the debtors and the creditors. The company can adopt contracts (through the agency of the directors). The company can therefore assume liabilities. It can sue in its own name and be sued in its own name. In addition to contractual liability, the company can be liable in tort (negligence).

The Companies Act 1985 now refers to one-person companies. Section 24 provides that *private* companies need only have one member or shareholder. This amendment brought the Act into line with European regulations. Formerly, a private company required two or more members. Public companies are unaffected by these amendments. They require two members.

Because the company is a distinct entity, its survival or continuation is quite distinct from its directors and members who are involved with it. The company is said to have "perpetual succession", it survives, even if a particular member or director leaves. Compare this situation with partnerships where under the Partnership Act 1890, if a partner leaves the firm, for whatever reason, the business is automatically dissolved.

Whilst the limitation of a member's liability may be an advantage enjoyed by a company, this advantage will, in practice, often be curtailed in the case of small private companies because lenders to the company will require personal guarantees from the directors (who are usually also the shareholders) securing the repayment of loans made by the company. Personal guarantees put a director's personal assets, *e.g.* house, etc., at risk in the event of the company being unable to repay the loan. Hence directors who give personal guarantees of this kind are in much the same sort of potential liability situation as partners. Hence in advising people setting up such companies, the issues of mutual trust and confidence as between directors and shareholders is vitally important. All companies are established by a process of incorporation or registration which involves certain documents, including constituent documents, being lodged with the Registrar of Companies. Companies may be expensive to establish. It depends on the speed of operation required. For example an expedited registration of documents costs £200 (for same-day registration) compared to the usual £20 fee. Another cost factor will concern the degree of "individuality" given to the constituent documents—the memorandum of association and the articles of association.

There will be associated periodical reporting costs as well. For example, lodgment of the annual accounts with the companies registrar. There will also be matters reported to the registrar that affect the affairs of the company. For example, when a director or the company secretary leaves the company. These and other matters are, therefore, part of the company's "public record" or history that any member of the public can, on the payment of a search fee obtain from Companies House in Cardiff.

As with the other business entities, there is no right or wrong answer as to choice. It will be a question of ascertaining a client's requirements and offering legal advice which reflects the commercial considerations.

B. The Solicitor's Business Checklist as Applied to Companies

The points on the solicitor's business checklist established in Chapter 1 will be dealt with in turn as they apply to companies.

1. TYPE OF ENTERPRISE/ENTITY

A private company need only have one member (Companies Act 1985, s. 24). As we have seen the great advantage of limited liability may be offset by the giving of a personal guarantee. It is a question of trying to ascertain the key requirements and concerns of the client. It may be that the client wants the borrowing advantages offered to a company as opposed to a partnership, *i.e.* because the company is a separate entity, it can borrow funds in its own name and secure the loan by, for example, a mortgage debenture.

8.2

2. CHOICE OF BUSINESS NAMES

Companies can and often do adopt business names under which they trade and by which they are known. Such names need to be registered under the Business Names Act 1985 at Companies House. Some business names require the approval of:

(a) the Secretary of State for Industry;
(b) a particular body or organisation; or
(c) both (a) and (b).

For further details, see Chapter 7 dealing with the Business Names Act 1985.

8.3

Company names

8.4   As far as the name of the company is concerned, the legal adviser needs to bear in mind sections 25, 26, 29 and 349 of the Companies Act 1985. These matters are discussed in Chapter 10.

3. FORMALITIES

8.5   Of the three business entities, companies are the most formal. Documents must be lodged with Companies House in order to "create" a company; a process known as incorporation or registration. There is no choice as to whether to have documents, as there is with the partners deciding whether to adopt a partnership agreement. When a company is incorporated it will have constituent documents—the memorandum of association, which sets out key details such as type of company, name, number of shares created, etc.— and the articles of association, which is the company's set of rules that bind each of the members one to the other or *inter se* and the company to each member.

Technically, a shareholder can take the company to court if the company does not comply with the Articles insofar as they concern membership rights. The other documents required on incorporation are details of the first director, secretary (the Form G10) and the Form G12 (the solicitor's statutory declaration of compliance to affirm that the incorporation accords with the legislative requirement of the Companies Act 1985). The standard incorporation fee (payable to the Registrar of Companies) is £50 or £200 if the incorporation is urgent.

Shelf v. tailor-made companies

Those people responsible for establishing a company, known alternatively as founders, promoters, or subscribers can either:

(a) purchase a company (from law stationers or solicitors) which is already incorporated. These are known as "shelf" or "off the peg" companies; or

(b) set one up specifically for their purposes. These are known as "tailor-made" companies.

8.6   *(a) Shelf companies.* As such companies have already been incorporated, they will have a memorandum (including a company name), articles, and director(s) and secretary appointed. It is a non-active company waiting to be purchased.

Obviously the purchaser(s) of the shelf company will want to become members and to appoint new directors and also change the name of the company. These matters can be achieved quite quickly because the work involved in actually incorporating the company has already been done. It is simply a question of adapting the shelf company to meet the particular requirements of the people purchasing it and of lodging amending documents.

There are different types of shelf companies available and the differences will focus on matters in the memorandum and articles, *e.g.* the amount of share capital, the type of company as far as shareholder liability is concerned; the form of the articles may well vary also.

For example, a shelf company may have:

(a) articles in the form of table A, unamended;
(b) articles in the form of table A but with (standard) amendments or otherwise; or
(c) articles in some form other than table A.

The type of memorandum and articles will reflect the concerns of the purchasers. Obviously the purchasers are able to vary the memorandum and articles once they have purchased the shelf company, in accordance with the requirements of the Companies Act 1985.

The advantages of buying a shelf company, assuming it meets the needs of the purchaser(s) without much amendment, are (a) speed; and (b) reduced cost.

(b) Tailor-made companies. The second type of company is one started **8.7** from scratch, *i.e.* the memorandum and articles are drafted based on the client's specific instructions and circumstances. The company will be incorporated in due course when the documentation meets these criteria.

The advantage of tailor-made companies is that they will meet the particular requirements of the client.

The disadvantages may be:

(a) delay, depending on the drafting of the documents; and
(b) cost, *i.e.* solicitor's fees involved in the drafting and advice process.

4. CONSTITUTION/RULES

Every company, whatever the type, will have a set of constitutional docu- **8.8** ments. By constitutional documents, we refer to the set of rules and regulations governing the company, *i.e.* governing the relationship between shareholders; between each shareholder and the company; and governing what the company can and cannot do. The two constituent documents are the Memorandum and Articles of Association.

The Memorandum of Association

Every company will have a memorandum of association. By section 1(1) of **8.9** the Companies Act 1985, it will be signed and lodged with the registrar of companies, before a company can be incorporated.

The Articles of Association

Section 7(1) of the Companies Act 1985 provides that the subscribers of a **8.10** company limited by shares *may* register a set of articles of association with the registrar of companies.

Section 8(2) of the Companies Act 1985 states that if articles are not registered or do not exclude or modify table A then table A articles will apply or will fill in any "gaps" in the articles have been registered, *i.e.* table A will apply by implication. Table A is simply an example or model set of articles of association which may be used unamended or amended to suit the company's requirements.

The subscribers of a company limited by guarantee or which is unlimited *shall* register a set of articles with the registrar of companies.

By section 8(4) of the Companies Act 1985, table C, D and E type articles of association are relevant to companies limited by guarantee and unlimited companies.

5. OWNERSHIP

8.11   The ownership of the company vests in the shareholders. There is a chain of ownership: the company as a separate entity owns assets; the unit of ownership in the company is the shares, which are themselves owned by the shareholders. The value of the shares will increase and decrease as a reflection of the change in the underlying value of the company's assets, *e.g.* land, premises, fixed plant and machinery, stock in trade, goodwill (reputation), profit, cash, etc., less liabilities such as borrowings, trader creditors, etc. That is why, at the end of the day, share ownership is a risk investment.

The shares may be owned by:

(a) an individual or company as beneficial owner; or
(b) an individual or company in the capacity of trustee or nominee; that is, they hold the legal title and the beneficial interest vests in a third party.

For the purpose of ascertaining membership of the company, it is the individual or business entity whose name and address is shown in the Register of Members at the company's registered office who is treated as if they were a member. For example, they will be entitled to receive notices of shareholders' meetings.

Shares can only be issued or sold to the "public" by "public companies" (that is those companies who comply with Part 3 of the Companies Act 1985). Hence, the market for the issue or sale of shares in private companies is restricted to present members and their families and "word of mouth" third parties. Private companies cannot advertise the issue or sale of shares.

6. MANAGEMENT

8.12   The management of the company, that is the day-to-day running, administration and the longer-term decision making, rests principally with the directors. Usually this will be made clear by the articles.

As noted, article 70 of table A delegates the general management of the company to the directors.

It is the case, however, that the directors can delegate some, but not all, of their powers.

Example: Delegation by the Board of Directors
  (a) the appointment of a managing director to look after day-do-day matters;
  (b) the appointment of committees to investigate or administer specific matters;
  (c) the appointment of alternative directors;
  (d) the appointment of specialists, *e.g.* auditors and marketing analysts.

7. BUSINESS PREMISES AND OTHER ASSETS

As set out in paragraph 8.11, the assets of the company are owned by the company as a separate entity. If the company buys freehold premises for use as the registered office, it will be the company which is the registered owner. (It may be the case with small, private limited companies that an individual shareholder(s) owns the premises and leases them to the company.)   **8.13**

The shares held by the shareholders will reflect the value of the assets owned by the company. It will be the company, as owner, that pays any Capital Gains Tax payable, if it sells assets that are subject to the CGT legislation.

The choice of a company's business premises is important for several reasons:

  (a) it is the recorded office address of the company for public purposes, *i.e.* it is a matter of record at Companies House;
  (b) it is the place at which certain records must be kept in accordance with the requirements of the Companies Act 1985;
  (c) it is the place at which those records can be inspected by shareholders;
  (d) it is the place at which the service of litigation documents is made in respect to court proceedings commenced against the company; and
  (e) it will be an important asset of the business in terms of image, location and the "goodwill" or reputation of the company.

The main assets of a company will be:

  (a) the premises,
  (b) leasehold or freehold property,
  (c) factory/offices,
  (d) fixed plant and machinery,
  (e) stock in trade,
  (f) cash,
  (g) debtors, and
  (h) goodwill.

The main liabilities will be:

  (a) borrowings:
       (i) secured
       (ii) unsecured
  (b) trade creditors;
  (c) other creditors.

8. PUBLICITY

8.14   Companies, whatever their type, are the most "public" of the three business entities in that they are required to lodge documents with a central body (Companies House) and copies of those documents are then available to members of the public for a fee (the companies search).

There is no "central registration of documents" equivalent for either sole traders or partnerships.

9. MISCELLANEOUS MATTERS

Value Added Tax (VAT)
8.15   See paragraph 2.11 above.

Letterhead, stationery, etc.
8.16   See Chapter 7. Section 349(2) of the Companies Act 1985 provides that a company's name must appear on:

(a) all business letters,
(b) notices and official publications,
(c) cheques, money order, etc., and
(d) parcels, invoices, receipts and letters of credit.

Breach of section 349(1) may result in a fine (Companies Act 1985, s. 349(2)) and also possible personal liability on the director or officer involved (Companies Act 1985, s. 349(4)).

Choice of bankers, accountants and auditors
8.17   Every company whatever the type, is required pursuant to the Companies Act 1985, s. 384 to appoint an auditor in accordance with Chapter 5 of the Companies Act 1985, unless coming within the terms of the Companies Act 1985, s. 388A.

National Insurance contributions
8.18   Contributions paid by the company as an employer are a deductible business expense. A company employee cannot deduct such contributions from his income profits. They are paid out of the gross salary.

10. DECISION-MAKING

8.19   As stated, the directors will usually be empowered with the general management and conduct of the company's affairs.

They will usually *initiate* the decision-making process. For example, a change of direction of company business; a major acquisition or sale by the company; or a change of director.

There are many matters of company business that the directors can both initiate and complete. However, there are several items of business, which by the Companies Act 1985, require the approval of the shareholders at a general meeting before they can be completed. For example, the change of the company's name. The specific rules concerning who decides particular matters are set out in the Companies Act 1985.

The Companies Act 1985 also gives the shareholders certain opportunities to initiate the company's decision-making process. For example:

(a) with the removal of a director under section 303 of the Act; or
(b) to call a meeting of shareholders (if they hold sufficient shares and votes); or
(c) to have a matter discussed at a meeting of shareholders.

11. EXPANSION PLANS

As with those matters discussed in paragraph 8.19, expansion plans will *usu-ally* be initiated by the directors and approved by the shareholders. **8.20**

The great advantage with a company is that it can raise money by issuing to its existing or new shareholders, shares in the company in exchange for cash, assets or both. The company then has a "pool" of investors.

Another advantage enjoyed by companies is the ability to raise money by borrowing from a bank or other lenders. Part of the security a company can give to a lender in respect of repayment is what is referred to as a "floating charge"—that is, a mortgage over all of the "assets" and undertaking of the company (apart from certain specific assets (such as land) that will be the subject of a "fixed charge"). The floating charge hovers over the assets of the company until default is made in repayment. Those assets are then subject to the floating charge documentation. For further details, see Chapter 14.

12. REPORTING

There are several strands to the notion of "reporting" relevant to companies: **8.21**

(a) as we have seen in paragraph 8.14, companies, usually through the company secretary, must report various matters, *e.g.* the appointment of a director; annual accounts, etc., to the Registrar of Companies (this does not happen with partnerships and sole traders).
(b) a director is under an obligation to report certain matters to his board of directors or the shareholders. For example, if he has a *personal* interest in a contract in which the company is the one of the contracting parties he must disclose it (Companies Act 1985, s. 317).
(c) the directors owe a general duty of good faith to the company and they must have regard to the interests of the members and employees. The board of directors must report certain matters to the members as required by the Companies Act 1985.

13. BORROWING

For a full discussion, see Chapter 14. **8.22**

As discussed in paragraph 8.20, a company has a ready "pool" of finance—the shareholders.

The company may also wish to raise short-term finance from the shareholders by issuing what are known as "redeemable" shares to its shareholders, *i.e.* the company issues the shares in exchange for cash and then buys back the shares when it is in a position to repay the shareholders. The shareholders in small, private, limited companies may often also be the directors of the company. They will usually hold on to their shares for the duration of the business. They are also free to sell their shares (although they cannot advertise their sale as this would fall within the definition of a sale to "the public"). A public company has a ready market for its shares—the public—and can avail itself of advertising and an organised public, trading system.

All companies have access to their own shareholders for the purpose of raising funds by the sale of shares. If the company borrows from shareholders it will usually be by way of the specialised type of share mentioned above—the "redeemable" share. The major source of borrowing however, will be via third parties, *i.e.* banks, building societies and other lenders.

The type of borrowing will be:

(a) unsecured, *i.e.* a debenture document involving a promise to repay monies. The lender's remedy against the company in the event of default would branch off the contract

(b) secured, *i.e.* a debenture document including a promise to repay *and* a charge or mortgage element.

The lender's remedies are two-fold. One lies in contract; the second to enforce the "security aspect" usually by appointing a receiver to step into the company in the place of the directors and ensure repayment of the amount borrowed, plus costs and interest and then to "return" the company to the directors.

These types of borrowing may be short or long term. In practice, a lender would be more prepared to give a long-term loan on a secured rather than unsecured basis.

The expression "gearing" refers to the amount of money borrowed in relation to the asset basis of the company. Usually a lender will require that an asset base is several times larger (say three to one) the size of the amount lent.

14. TAX TREATMENT

8.23   The company because it is a separate legal entity incurs tax liabilities for the payment of Corporation Tax (CT) and Capital Gains Tax (CGT).

The company's tax liabilities are quite separately incurred and paid from those incurred by directors, shareholders and employees of the company. Directors and employees come under the definition of "officer" for tax purposes and the income they receive falls under Schedule E.

Shareholders may receive dividends (that is a payment per share out of company profits on a yearly basis) from the company and fall under Schedule F as income received.

The company's income profits may fall under any or all of the Income

Schedules and the income will be aggregated, just as it would be for an individual.

The company's corporation tax liability is known as Mainstream Corporation Tax (MCT). MCT is paid annually. Payments of advanced corporation tax will also be paid by the company throughout the year when the company pays a dividend to the shareholders. Advance Corporation Tax (ACT) is simply a pre-payment—an early payment—of part of the MCT liability.

Small, private, limited companies, where the directors and members are the same people, may often use property (by means of a term of licence arrangement) that is actually the property of the individuals. The consequence of this is that the individual who owns the asset is liable to pay CGT when the asset is sold (and is able to keep the proceeds of sale).

When a company sells an asset it owns and a capital gains is made, the company pays the CGT. In effect capital gains made by companies are taxed twice:

(a) the company pays on the sale of the *asset* (referred to under then legislation as a "chargeable asset"); and
(b) the shareholder pays on the sale of his *shares* in the company, which in turn are a reflection of the increase in the value of the company's underlying assets.

15. CONTRACTUAL ARRANGEMENTS

As companies are separate and distinct from their shareholders, they have contractual capacity. The company, acting through its directors, can in its own name enter into contracts of all types—to purchase land, to borrow moneys, to sell stock in trade, etc. As a consequence, companies have the capacity to sue and be sued.

8.24

Companies are, however, also governed by their constituent documents which provide them with their objects and powers. The issue to resolve is where do companies stand contractually if they act beyond the scope of their memorandum or constitution?

Under the *ultra vires* principle the answer would generally have been that such an act was void. Now, however, regard must be had to sections 35, 35A and 35B of the Companies Act 1985. (See paragraph 12.21).

16. EMPLOYEES

As part of its contractual capacity, a company can enter into contracts with individuals (variously under service agreements or contracts of employment) who are classified as employees. These are typically directors, company secretary and other employees.

8.25

The company may also use the service of independent contractors, *i.e.* consultants, auditors, etc., who are not employees of the company. The significance of the distinction between "employees" and "independent contractors" includes the fact that policies of workers' compensation insurance taken out by the company cover employees but not independent contractors.

The taking on or letting go of employees is usually a matter for the directors, falling within the general ambit of article 70, table A (see paragraph 8.12 above or its equivalent provision when table A is not adopted). One significant exception to this is when the company takes on a director under a service agreement of more than five years' duration that:

(a) cannot be terminated by the company by notice; or
(b) can only be terminated by the company in "specified circumstances".

Service agreements for more than five years, are dealt with by section 319 of the Companies Act 1985 and require the approval of the shareholders (by a majority vote) in general meeting to the suggested term before the term becomes a part of the service agreement. If the members' approval is not obtained, the term inferred in the service agreement is void and the agreement can be terminated by the company by giving "reasonable notice" (Companies Act 1985, s. 319(6)).

17. DISPUTES

8.26   The directors as agents of the company (and charged with managing its affairs), play a key role in avoiding disputes and settling matters on its behalf. They have the power to bind the company in such matters. As with other business entities, the means of settling disputes involving companies as a party, are as follows:

(a) self-help involving negotiation as between the parties;
(b) arbitration where an independent, expert settles the matter; or
(c) the issuing of legal proceedings.

In any proceedings it will be the company that is a party to the proceedings and referred to by its corporate name. The company's evidence will be provided by its directors and employees amongst others.

18. BANKRUPTCY, INSOLVENCY AND LIQUIDATION

8.27   Whilst an individual shareholder or director of a company may be declared bankrupt this will not ordinarily affect the financial position of the company. As the company is a separate legal entity, its financial situation—healthy or otherwise—will be separate from these groups. It may be that a small limited company is so closely financially linked with its shareholders or directors that the two do impact on each other.

Example: Small companies and shareholders. ABC Ltd has three shareholders—Ken with 29,999; Vera with one and Bob with one share. As well as putting in the share capital, Ken has lent the company money under a mortgage debenture. In this situation, Ken's finances are obviously closely linked with that of ABC Ltd.

(a) If a company is in financial difficulty, there are several courses of events that may take place depending on the particular circumstances.

(b) It may be that financial situation is hopeless, *i.e.* there are cash flow difficulties and the assets of the company are outweighed by the company's combined liabilities. This is a situation of insolvency and it may well be that the creditors appoint a liquidator to:
  (i) get in the assets;
  (ii) pay the company's debt off;
  (iii) distribute any surplus to shareholders; and
  (iv) wind-up the company so that the company is eventually struck off the public register of companies.

(c) Alternatively, it may be that a secured creditor holding a mortgage debenture over the company's assets has not received an interest payment due to be paid by the company. The typical remedy provided by the mortgage debenture is that the secured creditor can appoint a receiver who effectively:
  (i) replaces the directors;
  (ii) runs the company as a going-concern;
  (iii) ensures the secured creditor is paid all money owed under the mortgage debenture by selling company assets if necessary; and
  (iv) hands the company back to the directors.
It may well be that there is little left of the company's assets after the receiver hands the company back to the directors and it may well slip into insolvent liquidation as described in paragraph (i) above.

(d) A third option is that the company makes a "voluntary arrangement" with its creditors, *i.e.* a financial plan is devised to pay off creditors (possibly overtime and at reduced rates to avoid the expense and publicity of a former insolvent liquidation.)

Alternatively to the matters set out above, which are dictated by the company's financial problems, it may be that the shareholders have voluntarily decided to wind up the company through choice. This procedure is referred to as a solvent liquidation, on the basis that assets outweigh liabilities in the company's balance sheet. As with an insolvent liquidation, the liquidator's tasks will include:

(a) getting in the assets;
(b) paying off any debts;
(c) distributing the excess cash or assets to the shareholders (there will be an excess of cash or assets as it is a solvent company).

19. CONFIRMATION OF CHOICE

As has been stressed already, it will be for the client to decide the ultimate commercial viability of any venture that is being contemplated. For the lawyer, it is a matter of providing legal advice that bears in mind the general commercial considerations and, the client's particular requirements.

8.28

9. Companies—General Matters and Incorporation

A. Statutes Concerning Companies

9.1   In this chapter, the following statutes will be referred to:

The Companies Act 1985 (which includes amendments, principally under the Companies Act 1989)
The Company Director's Disqualification Act 1986
The Insolvency Act 1986

B. Introduction

9.2   British companies evolved out of the international shipping trade that developed in the fifteenth century between Britain and the Far East.
   The first companies were known as "chartered companies" because they were set up by authority of royal charter. The characteristics of these companies quickly became:

(a) the concept of "joint stock", *i.e.* members contributed capital to the company—they were the owners in effect of the company;
(b) the company was managed by directors appointed by the investor-members.

There was therefore a division between ownership and management and a ready means of raising capital, depending on the number of, and resources available to, investors.
   By the 1850s companies were established under the control of parliament rather than the Crown and this is predominantly the case now, although there are a few companies (*e.g.* some charities, etc.) still established by "Royal Charter".
   Nowadays, companies are an extremely popular and flexible means of running a business ranging in size from a corner shop to an international conglomerate. The popularity of them can be put down to the following factors:

9.3   *(a) Limited liability.* Limited liability refers to the liability of the shareholders of the company. With companies limited by shares, a shareholder's liability is determined by reference to:

(a) the number of shares they own; and
(b) the amount outstanding in respect of those shares.

With companies limited by guarantee, the shareholder's liability is limited by reference to a guarantee document.

The great majority of limited liability companies are those limited by shares. A shareholder owning shares in such a company will be liable to pay the par or face value of the shares (denoted on the share certificate) to the company. The par value is the amount per share set out in the authorised share capital clause in the memorandum of association. The shareholder's liability to the company may arise in two instances:

(a) from time to time when "calls" are made by the directors seeking payment on those shares which are nil paid (*i.e.* none of the par value has been paid) or partly-paid (some of the par value has been paid); or

(b) by the liquidator if the company goes into liquidation and a shareholder has not fully paid the par value of their shares.

If a shareholder's shares have been "fully paid", *i.e.* the whole of their par value has been forwarded by the shareholder to the company, that is the extent of the shareholder's liability.

(b) Separate entity status. The company is a separate legal person, *i.e.* it is separate and distinct from its members and its managers (the directors). This, in essence, means the company may sue and be sued in a court in its own name, rather than in the names of the members. **9.4**

Example: *The company as a separate entity.* Peter and Sue set up "Hangliders Ltd" and become its first two directors. Hangliders Ltd prepays for £1,000 worth of material for the manufacture of hangliders from the supplier, Airborne Bros. The material is not delivered by Airborne Bros as per the order contract. Who sues Airborne Bros? The company "Hangliders Ltd" does.

Likewise, if Airborne Bros delivered material to Hangliders Ltd and was not paid, it would sue the company Hangliders Ltd.

Another consequence of being a separate legal entity is that a company files its own taxation returns and pays what is known as corporation taxation.

(c) Raising share capital. A company may have many owners or shareholders and thereby raise money ("capital") by issuing shares and expanding in size.

C. Sources of Company Law

Irrespective of the classification or type of companies, they are governed by and required to comply with the Companies Act 1985. This Act is a consolidating act that brings together a great deal of statute and common law relating to companies. Since 1985 there has been a major amending act in 1989. **9.5**

The major sources of law for a company are:

(a) the Companies Act 1985 as amended by the Companies Act 1989;

(b) the Insolvency Act 1986;

(c) common (or judge-made) law; and

(d) the company's own internal regulations, which are known as the company's Articles of Association and its main constituent document, the Memorandum of Association.

D. Registration and Incorporation

9.6   The Companies Act 1985 provides for the creation of companies by a system known as incorporation or registration. A company is said to be incorporated when the Registrar of Companies (*i.e.* the person responsible for administering the Act) issues a certificate of incorporation.

In summary, the founders of the company (also called "the promoters" or "subscribers") sign a document known as the Memorandum of Association and lodge it together with other documents with the Registrar of Companies at Companies House in Cardiff (where all the public records of English and Welsh companies are kept). The first of these documents and records will be:

(a) the documents lodged to facilitate incorporation (the process of registration);

(b) the Certificate of Incorporation issued by the Registrar of Companies (the process of incorporation).

The incorporation documents lodged with the Registrar are the following:

(a) *Memorandum of Association*. This is the main constituent document setting out basic information much as company name, type, number of shares created, objects, etc.

The founders of the company sign the memorandum of association. In signing the memorandum, they agree to subscribe for (take) at least one share each in the company. The founders are therefore the first two members of the company and the shares that they are issued with as a result of signing the memorandum are known as "subscriber shares".

(b) *Articles of Association*. This is the second constituent document. The internal regulations of the company governing the rights and duties of the following relationships:

   (i) each member to every other member; and

   (ii) each member to the company as a separate entity. (See Appendix 3.2.)

(c) *Form G10* (duly completed). This is a document setting out the relevant details including occupation and other directorships held, of the company's first directors and secretary. The directors' secretary signs the Form G10 and consent to act in the nominated capacities as set out. The Form G10 also includes the registered office address of the company. (See Appendix 3.3.1)

If any of the information in the Form G10 is amended, the following documents are lodged with the registrar of companies:

   (i) change of registered office—Form 287;

   (ii) change of director, secretary or particulars—Form 288.

(d) *Form G12* (duly completed). This is a statutory declaration sworn by the solicitor or person responsible for registering the incorporation documents with the Registrar and in particular, confirming that any requirements pertaining to registration set out under the Companies Act 1985 have been compiled with. (See Appendix 3.3.1)

(e) *Registration fee.* This is payable to the Registrar of Companies. The incorporation fee is £20 normally (and takes between seven and 10 working days) or, if incorporation is required on a same-day basis, a fee of £200 is payable.

The Registrar will—usually within a couple of weeks of the lodgment of the incorporation documents—issue the Certificate of Incorporation which officially creates the company. The Certificate of Incorporation will be dated so that it can be said that a particular company was incorporated on a particular date.

E. Pre-Incorporation Contracts

Pre-incorporation contracts are those agreements, contracts and the like actually entered into by the subscribers of the company and purportedly on the company's behalf before the company is incorporated, *i.e.* before a certificate of incorporation has been issued. Such contacts are intended to bind a contractual party—the "company"—even though it does not yet exist. Hence, pre-incorporation contracts present special problems. For instance: **9.7**

(a) What happens if the company is never incorporated and yet a third party has supplied goods to it? Who will be liable to pay for the goods?

(b) What happens if the company is incorporated but the pre-incorporation contract is not one that the members want to take up ("ratify") and fulfil in the company's name?

In order to deal with these situations, the subscribers of the company need to be advised of the provisions set out in section 36C of the Companies Act 1985, which deals specifically with the pre-incorporation contracts.

Section 36C of the Companies Act 1985 deals with "contracts, deeds and obligations." It would include supply and distribution agreements; purchase orders; sales orders, etc.

Section 36C(1) of the Act provides that a contract is purported to be made by or on behalf of a company when the company has not been formed "has effect, subject to any agreement to the contrary, as one made with the person purporting to act for the company or as agent for it, and he is personally liable on the contract accordingly".

Hence, a contract signed "for and on behalf of" an unformed company or a contract signed by someone as a director of an unformed company will be caught by section 36C of the Companies Act 1985 and the person signing will be personally liable unless the company adopts the contract at a later date, when it is incorporated. Unless the company is prepared to adopt the contract when it is incorporated through the shareholders ratifying it in general meeting, the person signing on the company's behalf must ensure that there is a specific "agreement" that he is not to be held liable on the contract and that this is specifically acknowledged by the third party, *i.e.* the third party would need to agree to novate the contract when the company is incorporated.

There are therefore several risks to which a client should be alerted, if contemplating entering a pre-incorporation contract. A person entering a pre-incorporation contract should consider the following:

(a) not signing the contract at all—simply to have a draft contract in place that will be signed by the company when it is incorporated; or

(b) if the contract is signed, sign it in the capacity of agent, *i.e.* "for and on behalf of" the company, and obtain a specific written acknowledgement from the other party that:

(i) the client will not be personally liable; and

(ii) the company will be liable in due course.

However, if the company is never incorporated, or there is a falling out between the promoters or if the third party refuses to accept return of the goods, etc., it may be difficult to avoid the application of section 36C of the Companies Act 1985.

F. Types of Companies

9.8   There are two methods of classifying companies and they have some degree of overlap with each other.

First, companies may be "public" or "private". This classification system is based on the ownership of the shares of a company. In other words, are they owned by "the public" or are they owned by a "select" group of people who do not meet the definition of "the public"?

The meaning and extent of the term "the public" becomes crucial in determining the difference, for it is only public companies who may offer for sale, shares to "the public".

The second method of classification that builds on the public-private classification system is, having established an answer to the primary question as to the ownership of the shares question, *i.e.* public as opposed to private, how is the liability of individual shareholders determined and what is its extent? Is that liability limited in any way, or is it potentially unlimited in much the same way as the liability of a partner in a partnership?

There are, on this basis, three types of company structure to consider:

1. LIABILITY LIMITED BY SHARES

9.9   As mentioned earlier, the great majority of companies, whether public or private, are "limited by shares". The essential feature is that shareholder's liability is limited by the reference to the amount of monies payable in relation to the shares held by the member.

The amount payable by a shareholder for each share held will depend on the following factors:

(a) the par or face value of the share, *i.e.* what is the share's value as set out in the company's constitution (usually the memorandum of association); or

(b) the amount paid for that share by the shareholder. For example, has only part of the par value been paid? (a partly-paid share) or has all of the par value been paid (a fully-paid share)?

Example 1: Shareholder liability limited by shares. Sue has been issued with 100 shares of £1 each in Hangliders Ltd. She has partly-paid 50p for each of the 100 shares. Hence, the shares are partly paid to 50p.

Sue's potential future liability as a shareholder in Hangliders Ltd is 50p per share, or £50 in total, *i.e.* 50p multiplied by 100 shares.

The liability will arise in two possible situations:

(a) when the directors of Hangliders Ltd make "a call" or "calls" on the shareholders. A call is a request in writing that accords with the terms and conditions on which the shares were taken by a share-holder, seeking a payment in respect of the shares. Calls can be made until the shares are fully paid; and

(b) in the event of Hangliders Ltd going into insolvent liquidation, the liquidator would seek the unpaid balance (if any) on the shares held by shareholders.

Example 2: Shareholder liability. Cheryl, Beryl and Meryl operate a pri-vate company, which is limited by shares. It is an after-school child-minding service trading as "ABC Pick-ups", a registered business name. Each of them is a director. The Company has an authorised share capital of £100,000 comprised of 100,000 shares of £1 each. 10,000 shares have been issued and allotted to each of the directors (*i.e.* a total of 30,000 shares have been issued, leaving a total of 70,000 shares that have not).

Cheryl has paid £1 on each of her shares (*i.e.* they are fully paid)
Beryl has paid 50p on each of her shares (*i.e.* they are partly paid to 50p.)
Meryl has paid 1p on each on her shares (*i.e.* they are partly paid to 1p.)

As to their respective liabilities as shareholders:

Cheryl has no further liability on her shares.
Beryl has liability of £5,000, *i.e.* 50p on 10,000 shares.
Meryl has liability of £9,900, *i.e.* 99p on 10,000 shares.

2. LIABILITY LIMITED BY GUARANTEE

These companies fix a member's liability by reference to a specific monetary amount, rather than by reference to the shares, *i.e.* Carol and Alice incorpor-ate a company in which they each guarantee to meet £50,000 of the com- **9.10** pany's debts should the company fail and be "wound-up" (*i.e.* go into insolvent liquidation). There are only a small percentage of companies of this type and we do not consider them in any detail in this book.

3. UNLIMITED LIABILITY COMPANIES

9.11   The third type of company is said to be unlimited. This means that, rather than a member's liability being limited by reference to either shares or a specific guaranteed amount, the member's liability on a "winding-up" or "liquidation" is potentially unlimited. Hence, their disadvantage to members and their similarities to partnerships so far as potential liability is concerned. One advantage, however, is that such companies do not need to file accounts with the Registrar at the companies office. Such companies are not dealt with in this book.

G. Public Companies

Both public and private companies are defined in the Companies Act 1985. Basically, a private company is pursuant to section 1(3) of the Act, a company other than a public company. The main differences between a public and private company are as follows:

9.12   *(a) The amount of authorised share capital.* Authorised share capital is the amount of share that the company may issue and it one of the matters set out in the Memorandum of Association.

Example: Authorised share capital. An example might be: "The company has an authorised share capital of £100,000 divided into 200,000 shares of 50p each."
     The key to a public company is that the *minimum amount* of authorised share capital established in the authorised share capital class in the Memorandum of Association has to be at least £50,000. It can be comprised of any number of shares having any nominal value so long as the number of shares multiplied by the par value equals at least £50,000. This could comprise:

> 100,000 shares of 50p each
> 200,000 shares of 25p each
> 500,000 shares of 10p each

Example: Authorised share capital—public companies. A private company can have a share capital clause of £2, or some other nominal amount on the other hand, but this will obviously restrict the private company from being able to issue many shares if it only has two shares of £1 each. For the sake of being able to issue shares in the future to members (shareholders), a small, private company might typically commence with an authorised share capital of, say, £2,000 being 2,000 shares of £1 each.

So whilst the authorised share capital is set out in the Memorandum of

Association, the shares are said to be "issued" to members (shareholders) by the company. A company cannot issue more shares than are created by its authorised share capital clause in the Memorandum of Association. If it does, it has to first increase its authorised share capital clause by amending its Memorandum of Association.

Example: Increasing the authorised share capital. If Dave and Pete, founders of Mexican Gorilla Catchers Ltd have issued 5,000 shares of £1 each (*i.e.* they each hold 2,500 shares) and the authorised share capital clause in the Memorandum of Association is £5,000, being comprised of 5,000 shares of £1 each, in order to issue *more* shares to either of themselves, Dave and Pete would need to increase the authorised share capital clause in the Memorandum of Association, which would involve an amendment to the company's Memorandum of Association (this is referred to as an "increase in the authorised share capital").

(b) The value of paid up share capital. A public company is required to have at least 25 per cent of the par (or "nominal") value of its initial authorised share capital paid up by members.

9.13

Example: Paid up capital. Cosmology Ltd has issued 300,000 shares of 40p each to its three members—Pluto, Sun and Moon, the three Californian founders. Each has 100,000 shares. In order to satisfy the public company requirements, each of them is required to have contributed at least 10p (25 per cent of 40p) on each of the share held by them, *i.e.* each of them has contributed £10,000 to what is called the Company's paid-up share capital.

(c) The issue of shares or debenture to the public. As noted already, a share is a unit of ownership in a company.

9.14

A debenture is a document that acknowledges indebtedness. If a company issues a debenture to a member, the member will have contributed monies to the company and, in return, the company will have given the member a document acknowledging that the company owes the member monies. It is simply another means of a company raising money on a short- or long-term basis, *i.e.* Strapped Ltd issues a debentures to J. Paul Gatsby, Jnr for £1,000,000.

The key point is that only a public company can issue shares or debentures to "the public". The phrase "the public" can be difficult to define. If the shares were advertised for sale in the newspaper, that would be an example of an attempt to sell shares to the public. It would be illegal for a private company to do so.

(d) The name of the company. A public company must end with "Public Limited Company", "PLC" or the Welsh "CCC".

9.15

Private companies must include the word "Limited" in their name, *e.g.* P. Gascoigne Knee Reconstructions Ltd.

(e) The numbers of directors. Public companies must have at least two

directors. Private companies need only have one. (However, a sole director of a private company cannot also be the company secretary).

H. Quoted Companies

9.16   Some public companies are also said to be "quoted companies". This means that the shares of the company are "quoted" on a stock exchange. In order to become quoted, a public company must meet the rigorous requirements of the Stock Exchange rules. The "FTSE 100 Index" is an index based on the share prices of certain of the quoted companies at the London Stock Exchange.

I. The Private Company Limited by Shares

9.17   As already referred to, this is the most common form of company.

They may often involve family or friends setting up "small" companies (small in terms of the authorised share capital clause in the Memorandum of Association or the number of shareholders), in which the shareholders (members, owners) will often also be the directors (*i.e.* responsible for the running of the company and its dealings with third parties). Such companies are characterised by the following characteristics:

(a) that the personnel comprising the Directors (collectively referred to as the Board of Directors) remain "stable", *i.e.* stay with the company for a lengthy period and remain on good working terms with one another;

(b) that the directors and/or shareholders have equal "power" and "control" over the company's day-to-day affairs and decision-making, and its future direction;

(c) that the "investment", whether it be money, time, expertise or whatever its form, is equal as between members/shareholders, so that they are equally committed to the success of the company;

(d) that as set out above, the directors who manage the company will often also be the owners (shareholders) of the company.

FEATURES OF THE PRIVATE LIMITED COMPANY

9.18   A private company limited by shares has the following features:

(a) it is defined by section 1(3) of the Companies Act 1985 as one that is not a public company;

(b) it is prohibited from offering of shares or debentures to the public;

(c) it must have at least one director;

(d) it must have two members—the second member will be secretary as the sole director cannot be both director and secretary;

(e) the first two members will be the subscribers (or founders), *i.e.* the people who set up the company;

(f) it is a separate legal entity, *i.e.* separate and distinct from its members;

(g) it may sue and be sued in its own name;

(h) it has its own contractual capacity;

(i) as with other companies, the court will sometimes look behind the theory of the company as being a separate and distinct entity and examine the "reality" of the situation and impose personal liability on the members/directors, in certain circumstances. For instances:

    (i) fraudulent trading under section 213 of the Insolvency Act 1986 when, for example, there is actual dishonesty;

    (ii) wrongful trading under section 214 of the Insolvency Act 1986 when the company continues to trade even though it is in a situation where the balance sheet reveals that liabilities outweigh assets.

10. The Constituent Documents of a Company

A. Introduction

10.1 The two documents together form a company's constitution are the:

(a) Memorandum of association; and
(b) Articles of association.

B. The Memorandum of Association

The memorandum of association contains the following pieces of information about a company:

1. THE NAME OF THE COMPANY

10.2 A solicitor intending to set up (incorporate) a company for a client who has chosen a tentative name for the company should first conduct an index search at Companies House. The index will indicate whether the name is already in use and therefore not available.

Regard must also be had to sections 25 and 26 of the Companies Act 1985, and the regulations made pursuant to section 29 of the Companies Act 1985. Section 26 of the Companies Act 1985 provides that a company name cannot be:

(a) offensive;
(b) criminal;
(c) connected with the government; or
(d) misleading to the public (this could lead to a passing off action brought by another company who believes there is confusion in the public's mind and, as a result, a loss of business has affected that rival company or business).

Section 29 of the Companies Act 1985 provides that regulations can be made by the Secretary of State for Trade and Industry containing words which require the prior approval of:

(a) the Secretary of State; or
(b) a norminated body

before their use as part of a corporate name.

Section 349 of the Act requires that the company's full name is placed on all letterheads, invoices and other business documents as well as at the place of business.

If a company adopts a business name, the terms of the Business Names Act 1985 must be complied with.

2. THE COMPANY'S OBJECT(S)

In the context of the company's constitutional documents, the term "objects" refers to the company's chief activities, as distinct from its "powers" which are ancillary matters enabling the attainment of the objects. So whilst cattle breeding would be an object, the capacity to borrow for that purpose would be a power.

10.3

Traditionally, companies were required to list their objects and powers in their memorandum and articles and to comply with the limitations set out. If a company acted beyond those written terms, the act in question was void. This was the basis of the *ultra vires* doctrine. The effect of the *ultra vires* doctrine has been greatly reduced by provisions contained in the Companies Act 1985:

(a) section 3A provides that if a company adopts as its general object of the formula "general commercial company" then it is able to conduct any type of trade or business (subject of course to the Companies Act 1985) without being limited by the terms of its constituent documents. Most companies incorporated pursuant to the 1985 Act have adopted this formula as have many pre-1985 companies by amending their constitutions. As a matter of both caution and habit, many companies still set out their objects and powers in full in addition to adopting the wording of section 3A;

(b) sections 35, 35A, 35B and section 322A have largely removed the problems of *ultra vires* so far as third parties dealing with the company are concerned. (See paragraph 12.21 below).

3. THE COMPANY'S REGISTERED OFFICE ADDRESS.

A company must keep a copy of certain of its documents at its registered office. See paragraph 8.13.

10.4

4. THE TYPE OF COMPANY

Information concerning whether the company is public or private and the type of liability of the shareholders. See paragraph 9.8.

10.5

5. THE COMPANY'S AUTHORISED SHARE CAPITAL

This refers to the number and par (or nominal) value of the shares created on paper in the memorandum.

10.6

Example: Authorised share capital. ABC Ltd's share capital clause may state that "ABC Ltd has share capital of £100,000, comprised of 100,000 shares each having a par value of £1."

Hence:

(a) the authorised share capital is £100,000;
(b) the par value of each share is £1;
(c) the company can issue 100,000 shares before it needs to increase its authorised share capital clause by altering its memorandum of association.

C. Tailor-Made and Shelf Companies

10.7   A client wishing to use a company as a trading entity has a choice of:

(a) an "off-the-shelf" company which is already incorporated with its own constituent documents. The clients can become members and shareholders and make such amendments as they wish. The advantages of the shelf company are speed and cost;
(b) alternatively, the client may require a tailor made company where there are particular provisions to go into the constituent documents and the like.

(See paragraph 8.6 above).

D. The Articles of Association

10.8   Articles are a set of rules or regulations governing the relationship as between members and as between the company and the members. They also govern matters of procedure, for example concerning the holding of directors' and shareholders' meetings.

Private limited companies will either have:

(a) their own specifically drafted set of articles of association, designed to meet the particular requirements of the business; or
(b) table A articles of association together with minor variations or additions that are suited to the particular operation.

SOURCE OF TABLE A

10.9   Table A is a model set of articles of association (internal regulations of a company), being in accordance with section 14(1) of the Companies Act 1985, that is, a contract:

(a) between the company and each member; and
(b) between the members *inter se* or, as between themselves

for use by a private company limited by shares.

Case law has established that the contractual nature of the articles is limited to those matters concerning the activities of shareholders in their capacity as shareholders. Determining "membership matters" as distinct from "other matters" is a crucial part of the legal advice to a shareholder seeking to enforce a matter in accordance with the articles.

Section 8(2) of the Companies Act 1985 provides that table A, articles of association, will apply if:

(a) a company has not registered a set of articles of association with the companies registrar; or
(b) if the articles of association, which have been registered, do not:
    (i) exclude; or
    (ii) modify table A.

Table A is contained in the Regulations to the Companies Act 1985 made by the Secretary of State.

Table B, also contained in the Regulations to the Companies Act 1985, provides a model of a memorandum of association for a private company limited by shares.

E. Typical Amendments to Table A for Private Limited Companies

The articles of association of a company are amended by following the procedure set out in section 9 of the Companies Act 1985. This provides that the articles can only be amended by way of a special resolution passed by the shareholders of the company in general meeting. For details of special resolutions, see paragraph 13.12. **10.10**

Table A is usually adapted to the particular needs of the client. The alterations will depend on the facts of each case.

Listed below are some of the more common alterations that appear in the standard amendment document in Appendix 3.2.1.

2. TRANSFER OF SHARES—ARTICLE 24

Article 24 of table A gives the directors a partial control over the transfer of shares. The directors are able to block the transfer of shares that are partly paid or on which the company has a possessory interest known as a "lien". A lien may arise when a call has been made on shares but which has not been paid by a shareholder in accordance with his contract of allotment. **10.11**

There are several variations of article 24 most of which are designed to increase the directors' control over the transfer and ownership of the shares. This is obviously an important issue for small, private limited companies where there has to be a degree of trust and co-operation between the participants.

The main variations on article 24 are types A, B, and C transfer articles discussed later in this chapter and which are included in Appendix 3.2.3. Another variation is the "absolute discretion" provision that enables directors to block all share transfers whatsoever. An example is provided in the typical amendments to table A also included in the Appendix 3.2.3.

2. CASTING VOTES—ARTICLES 50 AND 88

The chair of a directors' meeting gets an extra or casting vote under article 88 in the event of an equality of votes. Similarly under article 50 the chair **10.12** of a shareholders' meeting gets a casting vote on an equality of votes, whether taken on a show of hands or on a poll. See paragraph 13.10.

In order to provide for equality as between shareholders and as between directors, such casting votes will often be deleted from the articles. This is especially the case with small, private limited companies where co-operation is important. In effect, there must be agreement on matters without the need to resort to a casting vote.

3. RETIREMENT OF DIRECTORS BY ROTATION—ARTICLE 73

10.13   Article 73 of table A requires that one-third of the number of directors retires at each annual general meeting (AGM) of shareholders and that the first appointed directors retire before later appointed directors.

Such a provision will obviously be inappropriate if there are only two directors. For small, private limited companies the provision will often be inappropriate because it does not allow for a long standing, and therefore stable, management team. As a consequence, the rotation provision will often be deleted as part of the standard amendments made to table A.

4. DIRECTORS' INTEREST IN CONTRACTS—ARTICLE 94

10.14   Article 94 provides that a director cannot vote at either a directors' or shareholders' meeting on a contract in which he has a personal interest. Such contracts include his own service agreement, substantial property transactions and loans made by the company.

With small, private limited companies, the fact that a director cannot vote on certain contracts will mean that he may not participate fully in the affairs of the company. With two-person companies this will affect the quorum, which is two for both directors' and shareholders' meetings under article 40 and 89 respectively. Hence, article 94 will often be deleted so that a director can vote on a contract in which he has an interest.

Whether or not a company has deleted article 94 does not affect the requirement under section 317 of the Companies Act 1985 that the director *disclose* his interest in the contract in question, at either:

(a) the first Board meeting at which it is discussed; or
(b) the next Board Meeting after which the interest becomes apparent.

Alternatively to deleting article 94 altogether, it may be suspended or relaxed on a one-off basis under article 96.

5. QUORUM PROVISIONS—ARTICLES 40 AND 64

10.15   As discussed, table A provides shareholders, for quota of two for both directors' and shareholders' meetings. It may be that these numbers are reduced to one for certain private companies.

6. VOTES PER SHARE—ARTICLE 54

Article 54 provides that a shareholder gets one vote per share on a vote by **10.16** poll taken at a shareholders' meeting. This can be increased or "weighted" in respect of a particular issue or issues in respect of a particular shareholder or group of shareholders. The most common example of a weighting of votes is for a director to be given extra votes to be able to avoid being removed against his will as a director by the shareholders under section 303 of the Companies Act 1985.

F. Articles Added to Table A

Table A may also be added to by way of standard additional articles. Key **10.17** amongst these is the power of directors to issue shares.

THE ISSUE OF SHARES BY DIRECTORS

As will be discussed, table A does not give authority to the directors to **10.18** issue shares. This authority must be given by an additional article or by the shareholders in a general meeting. The authority to issue shares is provided by section 80 of the Companies Act 1985 and an example of such a power is included in the amendment document.

In the case of a tailor-made company it will usually be the case that authority is given to the directors to issue shares up to the authorised share capital amount pursuant to section 80 of the Companies Act 1985. See paragraph 11.8.

G. Optional Transfer Articles

As has been discussed, article 24 gives the directors a partial discretion to **10.19** refuse to register the transfer of partly paid shares or shares on which the company has a lien.

There are several variations of article 24 available including:

(a) an absolute discretion provision—for example "the directors may, in their absolute discretion and without assigning any reason therefore, declined to register the transfer of a share, whether or not it is a fully paid share, and the first sentence of Clause 24 in Table A shall not apply to the company" (see Appendix 3.2.2);

(b) type A transfer article give rights to:
  (i) a member of the family of a shareholder, or deceased shareholder; and
  (ii) the trustee of a trust created by a member.
  Other than these two groups, directors have a discretion to refuse to register the transfer of shares to a shareholder of whom they do not approve (see Appendix 3.2.3).

(c) type B transfer article (see Appendix 3.2.3) gives a pre-emption right given to existing members. There are several steps involved that can be summarised as follows:

   (i)   A member wanting to transfer shares gives a transfer notice to the company. The company becomes the agent of the shareholder for the purpose of selling the shares;

  (ii)   within seven days of receiving the transfer notice, the company issues an offer notice to members. The closing date for acceptances in relation to the offer notice is at least 21 days and not more than 42 days afterwards (referred to as the offer period);

 (iii)   within eight days of receiving an offer notice, an intending purchaser can ask the company auditor to certify the "fair value" of the shares;

 (iv)   at the close of the offer period, if all the shares on offer have been applied for, the company notifies the proposing transferor of the shares by issuing a sale notice;

  (v)   if no sale notice is issued by the company, the proposing transferor can sell *all or any of the shares* referred to in the transfer notice to any person at any price;

 (vi)   however, the directors have an absolute discretion to refuse to register the transfer of shares to a shareholder of whom they do not approve;

(d) Type C transfer article is an amalgam of transfer articles types A and B (see Appendix 3.2.3).

H. Amending the Company's Constitution

10.20   As we have noted, every company, whatever its type or size, is required to have a memorandum of association and articles of association. These are collectively referred to as the constituent documents.

These documents together reflect the present organisation and structure of the company and the future plans of that company. It may well be that there is a facet or facets of either of the constituent documents that requires amendment to better reflect a change in the circumstances or plans for the company.

There will be many reasons for changes to constituent documents. For example, a shelf company name may be changed to something with more commercial appeal and better able to generate goodwill, *e.g.* 123 Ltd, a shelf company, changes its name to Brown Computers Ltd.

Another change to the memorandum may reflect the company's ambition to raise capital from the shareholders by increasing its share capital clause, *e.g.* Smith Ltd has authorised capital comprising 10,000 £1 shares that have all been issued. The directors have proposed the creation of a further 80,000 £1 shares, making the authorised share capital £100,000 comprising shares of £1 each.

Likewise, with the Articles of Association. For example, the direction may wish to have further control over the transfer of shares by altering Article 24. Article 24 can be characterised as a "partial discretion" provision. It allows the directors to block the transfer of partly paid shares (those with moneys still to be paid in respect of the par value) and shares on which the company has a "lien" or possessing interest (for example, if a call is made by the directors and not met on the due date by the shareholders.

As noted in paragraph 10.19, article 24 maybe varied by several means including:

(a) making the discretion "absolute", *i.e.* so that it applies to *all* shares; or

(b) providing some form of pre-emption right so that members, their family or some other specified group such as employees get a first right to purchase the shares.

I. Amending the Memorandum of Association

Each of the five pieces of information set out in the memorandum of associ-   **10.21**
ation the name of the company, registered office, authorised share capital, type of liability and the objects of the company, may be altered only to the extent and the manner provided by section 2(7) of the Companies Act 1985. The Companies Act 1985 provides both:

(a) the authority for; and

(b) the method of changing any aspect of the memorandum of association.

The changes to the memorandum of association and authorising sections can be summarised, as follows:

Item in Memorandum of Association (Companies Act 1985)	Authority to amend Memorandum and Procedure (Companies Act 1985)
1. Company Name (s.2(1)(a))	Change of name (s.28)—special resolution
2. Registered office (s.2(1)(b)) England and Wales or Scotland	Registered office to be: in *Wales*— s.2(2)—special resolution. For other cases s.2(2)—special resolution. There is no power to change the country in which the registered office is situated
3. Type of liability (ss.2(3), (4))	s.49 re-registration of a limited company as unlimited—directors' statutory declaration required s.51 re-registration of unlimited company as limited special resolution required

4. Objects clause (s.2(1)(c))	s.4—special resolution— extraordinary general meeting (EGM) s.5—objection procedure given to 15% in nominal value of the shareholders)
5. Share capital (s.2(5))	*Increase of share capital* (s.121) There needs to be a power contained in the articles: If so by (ordinary resolution). *Reductions of capital* (s.135) requires the approval of the Court *and* a special resolution and consent of creditors.

Finally, in relation to altering the memorandum of association, it is worth noting that any term in the memorandum that *could* have been included in the articles (*i.e.* any provision falling outside section 2 of the Companies Act 1985) can, by section 17 section of the Act be changed by special resolution, unless the memorandum of association provides otherwise.

J. Amending the Articles of Association

10.22   Section 9(1) of the Companies Act 1985 of the Act provides that a company can alter its articles of association by special resolution. Section 9(2) provides that an alteration made to the articles is:

(a) valid as if it had been originally part of them; and
(b) is itself also subject to alteration by special resolution.

A special resolution is defined by section 378(2) of the Act to be a resolution passed at a general meeting of shareholders, held on 21 days' notice, at which three-quarters of the votes cast are in favour of the resolution.

However, it has been held that in limited and particular circumstances, a special resolution is not required. Such an example is provided where, despite "neither a meeting nor a resolution in writing," there is "an expression of the unanimous will of all the corporation acting together and being intra vires the company." This principle was established in the case *Cane v. Jones* [1980] 1 W.L.R. 1451. In *Cane v. Jones*, a written agreement between the shareholders constituted "an expression of the unanimous will".

The power to amend the article whilst it can be expanded beyond the strict holding of section 9 of the Companies Act cannot, however, be restricted or contracted out of, *i.e.* the section 9 power to amend the Articles is always available to the company.

K. Members' Rights Regarding Amendment of the Company's Constitution

Section 16 of the Companies Act 1985 provides some limitations on the   **10.23**
binding nature of the amendment of the company's constitution.
   A member is not bound by an amendment if it means:

(a) having to subscribe for more shares; or
(b) an increased liability to contribute to share capital or otherwise to pay money to the company *unless* by section 17(2) of the Companies Act he agrees to be bound.

L. Shareholders' Agreements

Shareholders' agreements (also referred to as "behind the curtain"   **10.24**
agreements) are used for the purpose of supplementing:

(a) the articles of association; or
(b) the service agreement between the company and a director or other employee.

The aim behind a specific contract of employment or a shareholders' agreement, is that they provide certainty of terms between the parties.
   The advantages of a shareholders' agreement are as follows:

(a) they are *not* public documents that have to be lodged at Companies House—compare this to the constituent documents;
(b) they may be fuller in content than the constituent documents; and
(c) they may clarify the nature of the contractual matters binding upon the shareholders. This is because the articles are only binding on shareholders in so far as they affect their rights as and in their capacity as shareholders. Shareholders' agreements will be binding without such a limitation.

   An illustrative case of a situation where a shareholders' agreement would have been of great use in clarifying a matter of importance affecting the management of a company was provided by the *Read* case.

Example: Requirement for a shareholders' agreement (*Read v. Astoria Garage (Streatham) Ltd* (1952) Ch. 637) illustrates where a drafted service agreement or shareholders' agreement should have covered a matter of great importance. A director's service contract did not contain a "length of office" clause. There was no shareholder's agreement in place. In this situation what was the termination provision that would be applied? It was held that there was an *implied* application of the articles of association in the absence of a provision in the service agreement.

11. Shares and Shareholders

A. Background

11.1 Shares are units of ownership in a company and are owned by the share-holders. A company's shares are "created on paper" in the authorised share capital clause in the memorandum of association. Shares are an intangible form of property. Ownership of them is evidenced by a share certificate in favour of the shareholder and the fact that the shareholder's name is entered in the Register of Members. Shares are transferred not by delivery (as with stock in trade, plant and equipment and the like) but by means of a transfer document (the stock transfer form—see Appendix 3.3.2).

B. Types of Shares

11.2 The two most common types of shares are:

(a) ordinary shares; and
(b) preference shares.

The two terms are not terms of art (nor are they defined in the Companies Act 1985) and the rights and obligations attaching to ordinary and preference shares may vary from company to company.

The setting out of the rights and obligations attaching to shares is to be found in:

(a) the company's articles of association; and
(b) the contract of allotment that specifically describes the shares and the rights and liabilities attaching.

In general terms, the main differences concerning ordinary and preference lie in the following areas:

(a) the voting rights attaching to the shares;
(b) the right (if any) to dividends;
(c) the rights on winding-up the company.

Each of these three areas will be briefly discussed below.

1. Voting Rights

11.3 The usual situation is that ordinary shares have attached to them the right to vote at shareholders' meetings. The holder of an ordinary share will get one vote at a shareholders' meeting on a vote taken by a "show of hands" and one vote for every share held on a vote by way of a poll.

By contrast, preference shares do not normally carry a right to vote at shareholders' meetings unless the company has fallen behind in the payment of dividends that it has earlier declared as payable (see paragraph 11.4 below).

2. DIVIDENDS

Preference shares usually provide a specific right to the shareholder to receive a dividend, which is preferential to any right to a dividend payable on ordinary shares.

11.4

The right to a dividend can never be automatic in any event, because the payment of a dividend requires the following matters to take place:

(a) that the company makes a profit;
(b) that the directors recommend a figure be paid out of profit in respect of shares, *i.e.* a dividend is declared at say 20p per share; and
(c) that the shareholders approve the directors' recommendation (or a sum less than the recommendation; they cannot increase the directors' recommendation).

It is only after these matters have occurred that a shareholder's right to a dividend will arise. The right must also be one of the matters addressed in the articles of association or the contract of allotment.

The owner of preference shares will generally be entitled to receive a dividend before the ordinary shareholder.

3. ENTITLEMENTS ON A WINDING-UP

On a winding-up of the company, whether on a solvent or insolvent basis, the holder of preference shares will usually rank as a creditor ahead of the holder of ordinary shares.

11.5

As a category of "creditor" on a winding-up of a company, shareholders rank last after all other creditors. Within the group of shareholders though, the preference shareholders will be paid ahead of the ordinary shareholders. In this sense the holders of ordinary shares bear the ultimate risk of losing their investment in a company.

C. Shareholders

The members of a company are:

11.6

(a) The subscribers (signatories) to the memorandum, whose names are the first entered in the company's register of members after incorporation pursuant to section 22(1) of the Companies Act 1985; and
(b) all others who agree to become members *and* whose names are entered on the company's register of members pursuant to section 22(2) of the Companies Act 1985.
This second group of members incudes those who hold shares:
(i) by way of issue and allotment, *i.e.* shares are issued and allotted from the company's authorised share capital to shareholder Ann;

(ii) by transfer, *i.e.* the transfer of already issued and allotted shares from shareholder Ann to shareholder Beth;

(iii) by transmission, *i.e.* on the death of shareholder Ann her personal representative Bill may elect to have his name entered in the register of members or to transmit the shares to the person named in the will;

(iv) vesting by operation of law, *i.e.* on the bankruptcy of a shareholder, his property including his shareholding vests by operation of law (without the completion of transfer documents) in the trustee in bankruptcy;

(v) to satisfy a qualification test, *e.g.* a director may be required to hold a certain number of "qualification" shares in the company before he can be appointed a director. Such a requirement may be found in the articles, the service contract or a shareholder's agreement;

(vi) by virtue of some other reason, *e.g.* employees of the company have a share scheme under which, for instance, they may participate in rights issues made by the company.

D. Duties of Shareholders

11.7   Unlike directors, shareholders are not ordinarily in a position of trust in relation to the company, *i.e.* they are not fiduciaries. As a result, they can usually cast a vote at a shareholders' meeting in any way they wish. They can put their personal interests ahead of the company and the other shareholders. They can vote to approve contracts in which they have a personal interest (compare article 94 table A for the contrasting position regarding directors). They do not have to disclose whether or not they have a personal interest (compare the situation set out in Companies Act 1985, s. 317 for directors). All of these points are in contrast to directors who owe strict duties of confidence and trust to the company.

These general statements of principle in relation to shareholders are, however, subject to exceptions. For example:

(a) if in a company, a shareholder is also a director, he will be bound in two capacities—one as a shareholder, the other as a director. The strict duties applying to directors will therefore apply and the person cannot simply rely on his capacity as a shareholder to ignore the stricter duties. The "double-capacity" situation will arise in family-run or small, limited companies or close companies.

(b) a *majority* shareholder (*i.e.* the holder of more than 50 per cent of the shares carrying voting rights) is not able to simply vote in any way he likes, if this is unfair or inequitable as regards the interests of the minority shareholders. This principle was established in *Clemens v. Clemens Bros Ltd* [1976] 2 All E.R. 268.

E. The Issue and Allotment of Shares

Every memorandum of association contains an authorised share capital clause. For example "the authorised capital of the company is £10,000 being comprised of 10,000 shares of £1 each."

11.8

Shares are "created" on paper in the authorised share capital clause of the memorandum of association. All the shares that have been created in the memorandum can theoretically be issued to shareholders. If more shares than have been created are to be issued, the authorised share capital clause must be increased and thus, more shares created.

1. THE ISSUE OF SHARES

The general process of a company getting shares to a shareholder from the authorised share capital is known as the "issue" of shares. It is the beginning of the process that is completed by the "allotment". The phrase to "issue and allot" is therefore a composite one.

11.9

2. THE ALLOTMENT OF SHARES

The allotment takes place after the issue of shares. It occurs when a person has an unconditional right for their name to be entered in the company's register of members. When this right occurs will depend on the contract of allotment between the company and the shareholder.

11.10

3. ISSUE OF SHARE CERTIFICATES

Pursuant to section 185 of the Companies Act 1985 the share certificate has to be sent by the directors to a shareholder within two months of allotment or within two months of a lodgement of a transfer of shares.

11.11

4. RETURN OF ALLOTMENTS

The company, within one month of making an allotment of shares, must in accordance with section 88 of the Companies Act 1985 make a return of allotments to the Registrar of companies stating:

11.12

(a) the name and address of the allottee, *i.e.* the shareholder; and
(b) the number of shares allotted to the shareholder.

5. THE POWER TO ISSUE SHARES (COMPANIES ACT 1985, S. 80)

Shares are issued and allotted by the directors of a company. The power to issue shares is governed by section 80 of the Companies Act 1985. The power under this section does not arise automatically, but must be given to the directors either by:

11.13

(a) the terms of the articles of association. As has been noted, article 70 of table A provides a general management power to the directors, but table A does not contain a specific power to issue shares; or

(b) if no power is contained in the articles of association, the directors must be given such a power by the shareholders in general meeting. Article 2 of table A gives the *company* the ability to issue shares and to attach rights to the shares in the contract of allotment. It does not, however, give the *directors* such a power.

Therefore, with articles in the form of table A, the *directors* do not have the power to issue shares and must be given the power by the members at an extraordinary general meeting (EGM).

Three meetings are required in order to provide this power to issue shares:

(a) a directors' meeting at which they revolve to call an EGM to give a section 80 power;

(b) an EGM of shareholders at which a section 80 EGM resolution is passed; and

(c) a second directors' meeting is convened at which the issue and allotment of shares takes place.

6. Power to Issue Shares—Ordinary Resolution (Companies Act 1985, s. 80(8))

11.14 Although the articles are altered by a company adopting a resolution under section 80(1) power to issue shares, it is achieved by way of an ordinary resolution, as set out in section 80(8) of the Companies Act 1985, rather than the normal situation, which is by special resolution required under section 9 of the Act.

7. Limitation Period (Companies Act 1985, s. 80(4))

11.15 The directors' authority to issue shares is limited to a period of five years.

8. Extension of Limitation Period (Companies Act 1985, s. 80A)

11.16 By an elective resolution—that is a resolution agreed by all the shareholders of the company—it may be provided that the authority given to the directors to issue shares can be made indefinite, *i.e.* the period of five years specified in section 80(4) of the Act may be extended.

F. Pre-emption Rights or "Rights of First Refusal"

1. General Background

11.17 A pre-emption right is a right of first refusal given to the members of the company or a specified group before third parties get an opportunity to purchase shares or participate in a particular transaction, such as the issue of shares from the company's authorised share capital.

The purpose of pre-emption rights is to allow the current shareholders an opportunity to retain control of the ownership of the company. As we have seen, pre-emption rights will often also be given to partners in a partnership, in particular, in relation to purchasing the interest of a partner who is leaving or has left the partnership business. If the pre-emption right is not taken up within a certain time, the partnership may be dissolved, or a third party may purchase the interest or some other event may take place.

Pre-emption rights are an important feature of private limited companies for the following reasons:

(a) there will usually be only a few shareholders and they will want to retain control of the company, both in its day-to-day operation and its future direction;

(b) the shareholders will often also be the directors and they will want stability of management and ownership;

(c) there needs to be close co-operation between members of the company, including certainty of planning and control;

(d) there is a limited market for the shares and it is difficult, in any event, to determine their market price.

For all these reasons, pre-emption rights will need to be borne in mind by the legal adviser in relation to:

(a) the issue and allotment of shares from the issued share capital to existing shareholders ahead of outsiders or third parties. This is dealt with by section 89 of the Companies Act 1985; and

(b) the transfer of shares (which will have already been issued and allotted) from one shareholder to another shareholder of the company before outsiders get an opportunity to purchase such shares. This is usually dealt with by the articles of association—usually variations on article 24 table A.

G. Pre-emption Rights on the Issue of Shares (Companies Act 1985, s. 89)

Section 89 of the Companies Act 1985 provides that, when a company issues and allots "equity securities" from its authorised share capital, it has to offer them to each of the existing shareholders in a proportion "which is as nearly as practicable equal to the proportion in nominal value" of those equity securities which they already hold.

11.18

"Equity securities" are defined by section 94 of the Companies Act 1985 to include shares and rights to subscribe for shares.

Section 89 of the Act affords a measure of protection to existing shareholders. It means that their power and influence cannot be diminished by the directors resorting to issuing and allotting shares to new shareholders without *first* offering them to the existing shareholders in proportion to their existing shareholdings.

Example: Pre-emption rights on the allotment of shares. ABC Ltd have four shareholders—Mary, Jo and Barbara, each holding 10,000 shares of £1 each and Wendy, who holds 20,000 shares of £1 each.

On the issue and allotment of a further 10,000 shares of £1 each, in order to comply with section 89 of the Companies Act 1985, the shareholders would be entitled to be offered, on a first right of refusal basis, the following shares:

	Number of shares
Mary	2,000
Jo	2,000
Barbara	2,000
Wendy	4,000
Total:	10,000

MATTERS AFFECTING THE OPERATION OF SECTION 89 OF THE COMPANIES ACT 1985

There are several matters that need to be considered in relation to the scope of section 89:

Cash consideration

11.19   Section 89(4) provides that the pre-emption provision of section 89(1) only applies to the allotment of equity securities that are wholly for cash consideration. If the shares are allotted for consideration which is in whole, or in part, other than in cash, the pre-emption provision of section 89(1) will not apply.

Example: Pre-emption on allotment of shares. If the issue and allotment by ABC Ltd will be paid for by Mary by her giving her motor vehicle to ABC Ltd as consideration for the 2,000 shares she will receive, the pre-emption provision will not apply to any of the 10,000 shares being issued and allotted, *i.e.* if any part of the issue whatsoever is to he paid for, other than by cash, section 89(2) will not apply.

Exclusion of Companies Act 1985, s. 89

11.20   Section 91 of the Act allows a *private* company to exclude section 89's pre-emption provision by stating as such in its memorandum or articles of association.

Section 95 of the Act also allows *any* company to disapply section 89(1) by a provision in its articles of association or by a special resolution passed at a shareholders' meeting.

A shareholder not taking up pre-emption rights

11.21   As already noted, section 89(1) of the Companies Act 1985 provides that the existing shareholders are given a pre-emption right to take up shares issued in the company in proportion to their existing shareholdings. It does not guarantee that a particular shareholder will be able to take up their rights in a particular case; that will depend on a shareholder's financial and other circumstances.

Example: Pre-emption and shareholders rights. If Wendy, the shareholder in ABC Ltd, who has been offered by way of section 89(1) of the Companies

Act 1985, 4,000 shares of £1 to be paid for immediately, and she cannot afford to pay the £4,000 cash required, she will not be protected by section 89(1) and it may well be that the 4,000 shares are offered to the other or new shareholders. This situation, of course, would need to be seen in the light of the particular circumstances of the case and taking into account Mary's possible remedies under, for example section 459 of the Act, where she could argue a case of "unfair prejudice" if it had been the case that the issue of shares was made with the specific knowledge of her inability to pay for the shares on issue and to dilute her shareholding from its present 40 per cent, *i.e.* 20,000 shares of 50,000 down to 33.3 per cent, *i.e.* 20.000 shares out of 60,000 in total now issued.

H. The Transfer of Shares

Sections 182–189 of the Companies Act 1985 deal with the transfer of shares in a company. **11.22**

Section 182(1)(b) of the Act provides that the transfer has to be:

(a) in a manner consistent with the company's articles of association; and
(b) subject to the Stock Transfer Act 1963.

For a company with articles of association in the form of table A, article 24 deals with the transfer of shares.

If the articles are in a form, other than table A unamended, the relevant transfer article will need to be complied with.

The chief relevance of the Stock Transfer Act 1963 is that it provides the form of instrument of transfer of the shares—a document known as the stock transfer form. The stock transfer form is the key document in the transfer of shares process. See Appendix 3.3.2.

The main information that is included in the stock transfer form is:

(a) the company in which the transferor holds shares;
(b) the number and type of the transferor's shares;
(c) the names of both transferor and transferee; and
(d) the consideration paid for the shares.

The transfer of shares will be subject to stamp duty unless it falls within one of the exemptions listed on the reverse of the stock transfer form.

A distinction needs to be made between the procedures for transferring: **11.23**

(a) all of a shareholder's shares, *i.e.* all the shares referred to in the shareholder's share certificate; and
(b) less than all of a shareholder's shares, *i.e.* a partial transfer where a shareholder will retain some shares after the transfer.

Example: Procedure on the transfer of all of a shareholder's shares. Assume that the transferor Amanda is transferring all 100 of her shares in XYZ Ltd to transferee Ben. They are worth £10 each.

The steps to be taken will be as follows:

(a) Amanda will complete the Stock Transfer Form.
(b) Amanda will then send:
    (i) the completed stock transfer form; and
    (ii) the share certificate
    to Ben (and receive the £1,000 consideration).
(c) Ben will arrange for the stock transfer form to be stamped (stamp duty is currently 0.5 per cent of the value transferred, rounded up to the nearest 50p). Stamp duty will be £5.
(d) Once stamped, Ben will send the stamped stock transfer form and share certificate to XYZ Ltd requiring the directors to consider article 24, table A, or its equivalent. Assuming that the directors of XYZ Ltd are, having regard to the transfer article in the articles of association, willing to allow Ben to become a shareholder, they will:
    (i) delete Amanda's name from the register of members;
    (ii) insert Ben's name in the register of members; and
    (iii) issue a new share certificate in Ben's name.
(e) Ben is now a holder of 100 shares in XYZ Ltd. Amanda is no longer a shareholder, having received £1,000 for her shares.

Example: Procedure on a partial transfer of shares. Assume that Amanda is transferring 50 of her 100 shares in XYZ Ltd to Ben.

The procedure differs in two respects from a transfer of all shareholders' shares (*i.e.* as in the example above):

(a) Instead of Amanda sending the stock transfer form and share certificate to Ben they will be sent to the company. Why?
    Essentially, to protect Amanda's interests because Amanda does not want to ''arm'' Ben with apparent title to all 100 shares. So, the company receives the stock transfer form and the share certificate and stamps the stock transfer form ''certified lodged.'' The company then passes the stock transfer form to Ben to arrange for stamping. The company, in the meantime, holds on to the share certificate.
(b) The second difference is that, at the end of the transfer process, two share certificates will be issued:
    (i) one to Ben for Ben's 50 shares; and
    (ii) a fresh one to Amanda for the 50 shares retained by Amanda.

Both Ben and Amanda will be shown as members of the company in the register of members.

I. Pre-emption Rights on the Transfer of Shares

11.24   As discussed in section F above, a pre-emption right or right of first refusal on the transfer of a share gives existing members of the company (or other specifies classes, *e.g.* the member of a family of a member) a first right to purchase such shares, so that only if that specified group declines to purchase will a third party get the opportunity to purchase.

Article 24, table A does not contain a pre-emption right. However, type

B optional transfer article (which varies article 24 and is contained in Appendix 3.2.3) does contain a pre-emption right in the following terms:

> "(b) the shares comprised in any transfer notice shall be offered to the Members . . . as nearly as may be in proportion to the number of shares held by them."

J. Matters to be Considered as part of a Transfer of Shares

1. THE TERMS OF THE COMPANY'S ARTICLES AND THE ROLE OF THE DIRECTORS

If a company has articles of association in the form of table A, article 24 **11.25** provides only limited power to the directors to refuse to register the transfer of shares, *i.e.* article 24 applies only to partly paid shares or shares on which company has a lien. See also paragraph 10.19.

Article 24 of table A provides the directors with a "partial discretion." There are several alternatives to article 24. The two main alternatives are:

(a) an absolute discretion article, *i.e.* the directors are given an "absolute discretion" (subject to them exercising their power of refusal bona fide in the interests of the company's asset, set out below), to refuse to register the transfer of *any* shares in the company); or
(b) a pre-emption right provision, *i.e.* the articles provides that existing members or their families get a first right of refusal over shares in the company if it is proposed that they are to be transferred.

It is important, therefore, to review the transfer article in each case.

It is the articles of association, (as the company's internal regulations), which will determine the directors' discretion and powers in relation to the refusal to register the transfer of shares (and thereby complete the new owner's title to the shares).

The usual position (*unless* the articles state otherwise) is:

(a) a shareholder has a right to transfer shares; and
(b) the transferee has a right to be registered in the register of members.

Example: Directors' discretion under article 24, table A.

(a) If Amanda has 100 fully paid shares in XYZ Ltd, which has table A articles, the directors cannot refuse to register the transfer to Ben by reference to table A.
(b) If, on the other hand, Chris has 100 *partly paid* shares in XYZ Ltd, which has table A articles, the directors could refuse to register the transfer to David by reference to article 24.

The refusal to register the new member's name is a decision taken by the directors. The power is a fiduciary one to be exercised by the directors. The directors in exercising their decision must have regard to those facts and matters set out in the company's constituent documents.

The case of *Percival v. Wright* (1902) 2 Ch. 421 establishes the principle that a director's duties generally are owed to the company as a separate legal entity and not to individual shareholders. The directors must therefore exercise the power to refuse to register a potential shareholder's name in a bona fide manner, in the interests of the company. This principle was established by *Re Smith and Fawcett Ltd* (1942) 1 Ch. 304:

(a) the test of what was "bona fide" was applied subjectively in *Re Smith and Fawcett, i.e.* the question for the court to resolve, was the directors' view bona fide and in the interests of the company;

(b) a *mala fides* intention referred to in *Re Smith and Fawcett* case, will depend on the evidence in each case. The burden of proof for establishing a *mala fides* intention lies with the person making the allegation.

11.26   Three further related points are established by the case *Tett v. Phoenix Property & Investment Co. Ltd* (1986) B.C.L.C. 149:

(a) the courts are reluctant to overturn the board of directors' view as to what is bona fide in the company's interests;

(b) if the director's discretion to refuse to enter a potential member's name in the register of members is unfettered and not limited to specific grounds of refusal, the court will not compel the directors to give reasons for their refusal; and

(c) if there is a pre-emption provision in respect of a transfer of shares, directors are under a duty to refuse to register the transfer of shares where a member has breached the company's articles of association pre-emption provision by not offering the shares to other members first.

Other case law has also established that:

(a) after a period of two months, beginning from the lodging of the stock transfer form by the transferee and a request to be registered as a member, there is deemed to be a refusal to register by the directors;

(b) the directors must positively adopt a resolution to refuse to register the transfer, *i.e.* they cannot simply fail to take action;

(c) if the directors do not take any action, court proceedings can be commenced to:

    (i) rectify the register of members; and

    (ii) issue a share certificate,

i.e. the transferee has a prima facie right to be registered in the register of members unless *actually* refused by the directors.

2. PAYMENT FOR SHARES

11.27   Consideration or payment provided by a shareholder for the shares issued and allotted by the company may be in the form of:

(a) *Cash.* See section 89 of the Companies Act 1985—pre-emption rights apply only to shares issued for wholly cash consideration unless extended by the company to shares issued other than for cash. The return of allotments will follow the format set out in section 88(2)(a) of the Act.

(b) *Non-cash*. The return of allotments will follow the format set out in section 88(3) of the Act.

If shares are issued at a premium, *i.e.* above their par or nominal value, the excess will be placed in an account known as the share premium account. This account forms part of the company's share capital and can only be reduced in accordance with the procedure set out in section 135 of the Company's Act 1985.

Example: Share premium account. If shares of £1 nominal value are issued for £1.30, the 30p per share goes in the *share premium account* (Companies Act 1985, s. 130).

Shares can not be issued at a discount because it amounts to a quasi reduction of share capital that requires approval under section 135 of the Companies Act 1985, *i.e.* a company cannot issue £1 shares for 70p.

3. STAMP DUTY

Stamp duty is a tax on documents imposed by the Stamp Act 1891. The stock transfer form which effects the transfer of shares is liable to duty. The rate of stamp duty presently payable on a share transfer is 0.5 per cent of the market value of the transfer. It may be difficult to ascertain market value for shares transferred in a private company. The market value for the shares will generally be set by reference to the latest set of accounts. **11.28**

4. THE VALUATION OF SHARES IN A PRIVATE LIMITED COMPANY

When shares are sold at a profit, there may be capital gains payable. The application of Capital Gains Tax rules obviously relies on being able to value shares in question. How can the shares be valued in a private company when the shares are not listed on a stock exchange (*i.e.* so that the price of the shares are not able to be readily determined). Private companies are prohibited by section 81 of the Companies Act 1985 from offering shares to "the public." Many private companies have restrictions in their articles on the right of a member to transfer shares. **11.29**

The market price or fair value, if it cannot be agreed between buyer and seller, may have to be determined by a third party such as the company's auditor.

K. The Death of a Shareholder

Article 31 of table A provides that on the death of a shareholder, his shares vest automatically by operation of law in his personal representative. The personal representative is entitled to receive the following items: **11.30**

(a) dividends payable on the shares; and

(b) notices of meetings of members.

The personal representative does not get a right to vote at a shareholders' meeting until his name has been registered by the directors in the register of members pursuant to article 31 table A. It may be that an important shareholders' meeting is forthcoming and the personal representative may, for the purpose of being able to vote, apply to the directors to be registered as a member. Ordinarily, however, the personal representative will not become a member of the company. The personal representative has a right to transfer the shares to the beneficiary named under the will.

Article 30 of table A provides that on a death or bankruptcy of a shareholder, the personal representative or trustee in bankruptcy has two choices:

(a) he may elect to become the registered holder of the shares by giving written notice to that effect to the company, *i.e.* by a letter application to the directors; or

(b) he may elect to have some person nominated by him as the transferee of the shares. This will usually be the beneficiary named under the will. If he elects in this manner, he must execute an instrument of transfer of the shares, *i.e.* a stock transfer form, in favour of that person.

L. Amendment of Company's Records on a Shareholder's Departure

11.31   On the departure of a shareholder for whatever reason, the company secretary attends to amendment of the following records kept at the company's registered office:

(a) the register of members is amended by deleting the shareholder's name, and including the new shareholder's name;

(b) the register of directors (required by section 288 of the Companies Act 1985) if the shareholder was also a director. Any change in directors also requires notifying the registrar. With small private companies, directors will often also be members and run the company;

(c) the register of directors' interests in shares and debentures is required to be maintained in accordance with sections 324–325 of the Companies Act 1985. The director is obliged to notify the company, in writing, within five working days of obtaining any interest in shares or debentures of the company. This requirement also applies to interests held by the director's spouse or children. This requirement is, in addition to the director's duty of disclosure, under section 317 of the Act in relation to:

(i) contracts; or

(ii) proposed contracts.

There will be overlap, of course, if a contract or proposed contract relates to an interest in or purchase of shares in the company.

COMPANIES HOUSE RECORDS

A change in directors must be notified to the registrar of companies within   **11.32**
14 days of the change pursuant to section 288(2) of the Companies Act 1985.

As far as a change in shareholders is concerned, a return of allotments
must be made by the directors within one month of the allotment of shares
under section 88 of the Act. As such, the annual return is a static record from
year to year of the shareholders in the company. However, on the transfer of
shares no records are kept by the companies registrar except for the annual
return, which will show the shareholders from year to year.

M. Company Disputes

The general principle is that if a wrong is done to the company, it is the   **11.33**
shareholders in general meeting who decide to take action and it is the company who is the plaintiff. This principle was established in *Foss v. Harbottle*
(1843) 2 Hare 461. An individual shareholder is not usually permitted to sue
for a wrong done to the company of which he is a member. It is up to the
majority in general meeting to decide such matters.

There are three principles established by *Foss v. Harbottle*, namely:

   (a) If a wrong is done to a company (as an entity distinct from its
       members) then, only the company may sue for redress, *i.e. the
       proper plaintiff principle.*
   (b) The court will not interfere with the internal management of com-
       panies acting within the powers set out in the constituent documents,
       i.e. the internal management principle.
   (c) A member cannot sue to rectify a mere informality or irregularity
       if the act, when done, would be within the powers of the company
       and if the intention of the majority of members is clear, *i.e. the
       irregularity princi_l*

1. SUMMARY OF *FOSS V. HARBOTTLE* (1843) 2 Hare 461

Foss was a minority shareholder. Foss and another member brought an action   **11.34**
against Harbottle and other directors and shareholders of the company, claiming that they had unlawfully sold land to the company at an exorbitant price
so that the company made a loss:

   (a) it was held by the court that Foss's court action failed;
   (b) the sale by the defendants could have been ratified by the majority
       of the shareholders (as there was no fraud) but they had chosen not
       to do so; and
   (c) it was up to the majority shareholders to bring an action in the
       company's name, if they wished to do so, and if they did not wish
       to act, the minority shareholders (subject to exceptions), were
       powerless to prevent the sale or to obtain redress.

There are two justifications for the proper plaintiff principle:

   (a) a company is a separate legal entity, *i.e.* separate and distinct from its members. Therefore, the company is the proper plaintiff in the legal action when a wrong is done to the company; and

(b) the decision whether or not the company should take legal action is taken either by:
  (i) the directors; or
  (ii) the members in general meeting.

In general, the court do not want to interfere with these internal decisions

2. EXCEPTIONS TO THE RULE IN *FOSS V. HARBOTTLE*

11.35   Several exceptions to the "proper plaintiff principle" have been developed so that a shareholder can bring an action where the company will not. One such exception is where there has been fraud on the minority. For example, where the majority shareholders have received a better price for their shares than the minority shareholders. Another example is section 459 of the Companies Act 1985—where a member has a right to petition the court for relief if his interests as a shareholder have been "unfairly prejudiced" by the way in which the company's affairs are being conducted.

3. UNFAIR PREJUDICE (COMPANIES ACT 1985, s. 459)

11.36   Section 459(1) of the Companies Act 1985 allows a member of a company to apply to the court by petition for an order that: "the company's affairs are being, or have been, conducted in a manner which is unfairly prejudicial to the interests of its members generally, or of some part of its membership" (which has to include the member petitioning the court).

Once an order has been made under section 459 of the Act, *i.e.* that the affairs of the company are, or have been, conducted in an unfair and prejudicial way, the court can then go on to make further orders under section 461 of the Act.

The phrase "unfair prejudice" has been given a broad definition by the courts. It may be specific or general. It may result from:

(a) *An act.* For example, the directors issuing shares on a pre-emption basis to existing shareholders when they know that a particular shareholder will be unable to pay for his entitlement and, as a result, his shareholding as a percentage of issued shares will be reduced; or

(b) *An omission.* For example, the directors fail to offer shares to a company member when they offer them to other company members.

In order to commence an action under section 459 of the Act, the plaintiff must ordinarily be a shareholder of the company. Section 459(2) provides that a section 459 petition may also be bought by a person who, though not a member, has had shares transmitted to him or by operation of law, *i.e.* a trustee in bankruptcy in the case of the bankruptcy of a shareholder and a personal representative in the case of the death of a shareholder and to those to whom shares have been transferred, although their names are not in the register of members.

In *R. A. Noble & Sons (Clothing) Ltd* (1983) B.C.L.C. 273 it was established that a member of the company can bring his action within the terms of section 459 if he can show:

(a) the value of his shareholding in the company has been *seriously diminished*;
(b) or at least *seriously jeopardised*

by reason of a course of conduct on the part of those persons who have had *de facto* control of the company, *i.e.* the scope of section 459 includes shadow directors and such persons have acted in the conscious knowledge that this was unfair to the member or that they were acting in bad faith.

The test applied in the *Noble* case was whether a reasonable bystander observing the consequences of the conduct, would regard it as having unfairly prejudiced the petitioner's interests.

In *Re a Company* (1987) B.C.L.C. 141 it was established that there must be some financial harm or prejudice done to a shareholder. The concept of unfairness involves resort to very broad concept. It was held that there was to be no "gloss" to limit the expression "unfair prejudice"

Example: (Companies Act 1985, s. 459) Unfair prejudice. In *Re Cumana Ltd* (1986) B.C.L.C. 430, C.A., a rights issue made under section 89 of the Companies Act 1985 was on apparently favourable terms to all the shareholders. However, it could not be taken up by one minority shareholder because of his financial position and would have had the desired effect of reducing his shareholding, and therefore his influence, in the company.

It was held that such action amounted to "unfair prejudice" under section 459 of the Act.

4. REMEDIES AVAILABLE UNDER SECTION 461 OF THE COMPANIES ACT 1985

Section 461 of the Companies Act 1985 provides several broad-based reme-   **11.37**
dies for the court to consider under an application brought within section 459 of the Act. By section 461(2), the court may make such order as it thinks fit, including:

(a) regulating the future conduct of the company's affairs;
(b) requiring the company to act or refrain from acting;
(c) authorising civil proceedings to be brought in the name and on behalf of the company as the court directs (this is a specific statutory exception to the rule in *Foss v. Harbottle*); or
(d) providing for a disgruntled member's shares to be purchased by other members or by the company itself.

5. THE JUST AND EQUITABLE WINDING-UP OF A COMPANY

Section 122(1) of the Insolvency Act 1986 provides the bases on which a   **11.38**
court will order the winding-up of a company. A company will be wound-up if, on the evidence, it is "just and equitable" to do so. The "just and equitable" ground is simply one of the seven grounds for the winding-up of a company set out in section 122(1).

The various grounds for winding-up a company under section 122(1) of the Act are:

(a) the company passes a special resolution that the company be wound-up by the court ("voluntary liquidation");

(b) concerns a public company not being issued with a certificate under section 117 of the Companies Act 1985;

(c) concerns an "old" public company within the meaning of the Consequential Provisions Act;

(d) if the company:
   (i) does not commence business within one year of its incorporation; or
   (ii) suspends its business for a whole year;

(e) the number of members in a public company is reduced below two (refer to section 24 of the Companies Act 1985);

(f) the company is unable to pay its debts ("insolvent liquidation"); or

(g) the court is of the opinion that it is *just and equitable* that the company should be wound up.

11.39   The matters relevant to the court making a winding up order under section 122(1)(g) of the Insolvency Act 1986 are that:

(a) the member who presents the petition to the court must have a "tangible interest" in the winding-up, *e.g.* a tangible interest is an entitlement to payment on a winding-up; and

(b) other remedies, (other than the drastic section 122(1)(g) just and equitable winding-up, will be considered by the court;
Example: Solutions considered by the courts other than a winding-up order. An application under sections 459 and 461 of the Companies Act 1985, may allow, for example, consideration of a reasonable offer by the other members of the company to buy the petitioner's interests.

(c) the words "just and equitable" enable the court to recognise rights, expectations and obligations of members *inter se* and to wind-up a company where:
   (i) rights or obligations have been thwarted; or
   (ii) obligations have simply not been observed.

That is, even if what is being done is strictly within the law, the court may still impose the nebulous concept of "equitable considerations" to the relationships in the company.

Example: Equitable considerations applied to companies. In the case *Ebrahimi v. Westbourne Galleries* [1973] A.C. 360 certain principles were established by the House of Lords in relation to the just and equitable winding-up of a company that was intended to be run along partnership lines. Lord Wilberforce commented that the association between the members was not a "purely commercial one", *i.e.* it contained an extra element of trust, and as such the articles of association did not "exhaust" the parameters of the relationship. Such companies are referred to as "quasi-partnership" companies. As such, the members and shareholders have even higher duties of mutual trust and confidence than is normally expected in companies.

It was held in *Ebrahimi* that grounds for dissolution of a quasi-partnership company may exist where there is no mutual confidence between members and between directors.

The effect of *Ebrahimi's* case is that the concept of good faith applied to the dealings between partners has been applied to dealings between members and directors in small private limited companies. The court held that there are circumstances where the exercise of legal rights in such companies is subject to equitable considerations that might make it unjust for a member to insist on the exercise of the express rights or their exercise in a particular way.

Factors, which may be relevant to whether the *Ebrahimi* principle will be applied in a particular case, include the following: **11.40**

(a) whether an association has been formed on the basis of a personal relationship, involving mutual confidence, for example, as in *Ebrahimi's* case where a partnership became a limited company, but nevertheless remained run on partnership lines;

(b) an agreement that all, or some, of the shareholders shall participate in the conduct of the business;

(c) where there are restrictions on a member's right to transfer his interest in the company. For example, if the member is removed from management he may not be able to sell his shares and reclaim his investment.

12.   Directors and Other Company Officers

A. Background

12.1   A company, as an artificial legal person, can only act through the people who make up the company, *i.e.* the directors and shareholders. The directors, in their capacity as the managers and administrators of the company, are the main group through which the company acts.

The term "director" may cover a number of different types of people ranging from full-time managers (usually referred to as executive directors) to occasional directors ("non-executive" directors) to those people not actually listed as directors but performing that task from "behind the scenes" and known as shadow directors. (See section M below.)

Directors are in a fiduciary position in relation to the company. That is, they owe duties of trust, honesty and confidence to the company. They also owe a duty of care (or competence) to the company by whom they are employed. As we will see, the fiduciary duties are more onerously applied to directors than the duty of care. Case law has established that the directors owe their principal duties to the company. Section 309 of the Companies Act 1985 provides that the directors must also have regard to the interests of the members and the employees. The Insolvency Act 1986 also provides that the directors must bear in mind the interests of creditors to whom the company owes money.

12.2   What is involved in the concept of managing the affairs of the company? In general terms, it can be divided into three areas:

(a) *Day-to-day administration*. For example, ordering stationery; employing staff; monitoring office expenses, etc.

(b) *Longer-term strategies and planning*. For example, entering supply contracts; deciding on the location of the office; the purchase of plant and equipment; borrowings made by the company; deciding whether to establish the business overseas.

(c) *Liaising with and keeping the shareholders contented*. The shareholders are the owners of the business. In investing in shares they have contributed "risk capital". They may lose their investment but that is the risk they take. Shareholders are primarily concerned about the profitability of the business from which they may receive dividends. Dividends, therefore, are *income* for shareholders in respect of their investment.

Shareholders will also be concerned about maintaining and improving the value of the company's assets.

Under the Companies Act 1985 the shareholders get certain "opportunities" to check on the performance of directors. In particular, a majority of shareholders have the ability to remove a director against his will from the board of the company. See section D below.

The details of a particular director's role will be found in:

(a) the company's constituent documents, *i.e.* the articles or memorandum of association;
(b) the director's contract of employment ("service agreement") with the company;
(c) a shareholder's agreement (if there is one); and
(d) in relevant legislation, primarily the Companies Act 1985 and the Insolvency Act 1986.

B. The Appointment of Directors

Directors are regulated under table A by articles 64–98.　　　　　**12.3**

(a) The first director(s) are appointed on incorporation of the company and the director's details are set out in the Form G10. The first directors are usually the subscriber(s) who sign the memorandum of association.
(b) The articles of association will usually contain details as to the appointment of subsequent directors. The method of appointment for such directors under table A is set out in articles 76–79. The retirement of directors is also dealt with by articles 73–80.

　　Appointment of a director under article 76, table A requires the recommendation of the directors and the approval by an ordinary resolution, *i.e.* a majority of votes at a shareholders' meeting.

　　Article 79 allows the directors to appoint a person to fill a vacancy or to appoint an additional director, so long as such appointment is confirmed at the next Annual General Meeting (AGM) and so long as it does not cause the number of directors to go beyond the number specified in the articles.

　　Article 73 requires that one-third of the number of directors retire at each AGM. This is known as retirement by rotation. The first appointed directors retire first. As has been pointed out in paragraph 10.13 dealing with the amendment of articles, article 73 is often deleted with small, private limited companies.

(c) The register of directors must be regularly and accurately updated both:
　　(i) at the company's registered office; and
　　(ii) with the registrar of companies (Companies Act 1985, s. 288)
(d) Article 64 of table A provides that a private company limited by shares must not have less than two directors. Under section 282 of the Act a private company may now have one director.
(e) Directors do not have to hold shares, unless the articles specify that the directors must hold "qualification shares".

Table A does not contain a requirement that directors hold qualification shares.

If the articles of association specify that a director is to hold
qualification shares, the allotment and issue of a share certificate
must occur within two months of the director's appointment (*i.e.*
within 14 days of a change of director).

C. Directors' Contracts of Employment

12.4   Directors, as employees of the company, will usually be subject to terms and
conditions set out in service agreements with the company, in addition to the
articles of association. Because the directors are in a fiduciary position in
relation to the company certain of the contracts of employment require the
approval of the shareholders in general meeting. Approval is required for a
director's contract of employment with a term of more than five years or a
term that cannot be terminated within five years except in specific circumstances. Section 319 of the Companies Act 1985 provides that copies of such
proposed contracts of employment must be available for inspection by the
shareholders for a period of 15 days prior to the approval meeting and that
they must be approved by an ordinary resolution (a majority of votes).

If article 94 table A applies, a director (who is also a shareholder) cannot
vote to approve the terms of his service agreement. Such a director must,
however, make a disclosure of his interest in the contract under section 317
of the Companies Act 1985.

If the approval of the members is not obtained in accordance with the
requirements of section 319 of the Act:

(a) the notice provision in the contract is void;
(b) the rest of the terms in the contract are unaffected; and
(c) the contract is terminable by the company by reasonable notice, *i.e.*
a "reasonable notice" provision is substituted for the actual clause
contained in the contract.

D. Removal of a Director by the Shareholders (Companies Act 1985, s. 303)

12.5   As the directors are the managers of the company its eyes and ears (so to
speak), it is important for the success of the company that they have a good
working relationship with each other and with the shareholders. However,
there may be disagreement and infighting, personality clashes and the like,
that lead to one or other director becoming the subject of removal proceedings
taken by the shareholders under section 303 of the Companies Act 1985.

Section 303 of the Act gives the shareholders the right to remove a director
from office against his will. Effectively, the director is being dismissed by
the owners of the company.

It may not be necessary to use the section 303 removal procedure if, for
example:

(a) the articles of association contain a retirement by rotation clause for the directors, *e.g* article 73 states that one-third of the directors are to retire annually, so that the director is contractually bound to retire anyway in a short time; or

(b) a director is coming to the end of a fixed-term contract that is not going to be renewed.

Section 303 gives the members in general meeting the right to remove a director by passing an ordinary resolution, *i.e.* a simple majority of 50 plus 1 per cent vote cast at the general meeting. See paragraph 13.19.

A written resolution (Companies Act 1985, s. 381A) cannot be used to remove a director or an auditor, *i.e.* a meeting of the members of the company must be held.

Obviously, the use of section 303 of the Act will arise where there has been a falling out in the company between directors and the "targeted director" will not resign of his own free will.

The courts have traditionally been reluctant to interfere in the internal affairs of the company; it is up to the shareholders to decide whether to utilise section 303 procedure.

Section 303 was introduced in 1948. The rule before 1948 was that, to be able to dismiss a director, power had to be given to members in the company's articles of association and, where such a power was given by the articles, it was usual to require a special resolution (*i.e.* a three-quarters majority of the votes cast). This made the provision in the 1948 Companies Act difficult for shareholders to implement against a director whom they wanted to replace.

The operation of section 303 is not restricted by anything contained in either the: **12.6**

(a) articles of association; or

(b) anything in an agreement between the director and the company, *i.e.* the service contract or a shareholder's agreement.

Section 303 of the Companies Act 1985 provides:

(a) for "special notice" to be given by the member to the company 28 days before the general meeting is held proposing the removal of the directors pursuant to section 379 of the Act; and

(b) an ordinary resolution to be passed at the general meeting approving the removal of the targeted director, *i.e.* a simple majority of votes.

There are two practical ways in which the effectiveness of section 303 of the Companies Act 1985 can be reduced:

(a) Although the members have the right to remove the director, the director is not deprived of any right to compensation or damages that may exist by reference to the terms of the director's service agreement with the company, or otherwise. This means that it may be expensive to remove a director. As a result, other methods of obtaining control, such as appointing additional directors (and diluting the authority of the "targeted director") may be preferable. The factors which may have a bearing on a director's compensation claim after removal from the company board include:

    (i) his length of service;

    (ii) his remuneration package:

    (iii) the term of the service agreement still to run;

    (iv) his level of performance; and

    (v) his treatment by the Board of Directors.

(b) Enhanced voting rights given to a director must be taken into account. This is also referred to as weighted votes. Article 54, table A provides that each shareholder gets one vote per share on a poll vote. Weighting the votes involves increasing the number of votes per share to more than one. This principle was established in *Bushell v. Faith* [1969] 2 Ch. 438. Weighted votes may be given to a director, either in respect of a particular circumstance, *e.g.* on a section 303 resolution to remove him; or so that he has enhanced voting rights on resolutions generally, in addition to a resolution to remove, *i.e.* a director has enhanced voting rights on all resolutions. This will depend on the particular negotiations concerning a particular service agreement. The key point is that weighted votes are taken into account (if a poll is requested) in determining whether or not there is a majority of votes to pass an ordinary resolution, as required by section 303.

Example: Weighting of votes (Companies Act, s. 303). Sue, a director of Cobblers Limited with table A articles, has 10 votes per share on a vote by poll in relation to a resolution to remove her as a director under section 303 of the Companies Act 1985.

Sue has 10,000 shares in Cobblers Limited. There are a total of 90,000 shares that have been issued to Dave, Mary and Peter, the other shareholders. Can the other shareholders remove Sue on a vote by poll?

The answer is that they cannot because they can only muster 90,000 votes against Sue's 100,000 votes, *i.e.* 10 votes multiplied by 10,000 shares on a vote by poll. The other shareholders therefore cannot achieve a majority of the votes cast and Sue cannot be removed as a director against her will. (Sue can request a vote by poll under article 46(c), table A as she has 10 per cent of the voting rights.)

E. Disqualification of Directors

12.7   The articles of association may provide for a director to vacate his office. Article 81, table A provides that the office of a director should be vacated if:

    (a) he is prohibited by law from being a director;

    (b) he becomes bankrupt;

    (c) he is, or may be, suffering from a mental disorder;

    (d) he resigns from office; or

    (e) he is absent for more than six months from directors' meetings and the directors resolve that his office be vacated.

1. COMPANY DIRECTORS' DISQUALIFICATION ACT 1986

Section 1 of the Company Directors Disqualification Act 1986 provides that a court may make a disqualification order against a person, which means in effect that the person cannot, without the leave of the court, act in any of the following capacities:

    (a) a director;
    (b) a liquidator;
    (c) a receiver or manager; or
    (d) a founder of the company.

Under the Company Directors' Disqualification Act 1986 the Court may make a disqualification order against a company director in several circumstances including:

    (a) following conviction for an indictable offence in connection with a company (s. 2);
    (b) for persistent breaches of companies legislation (s. 3);
    (c) for fraud or fraudulent trading (s. 4);
    (d) for being a director of an insolvent company *and* being deemed to be unfit to be involved in the management of a company; and
    (e) for wrongful trading (s. 10).

By section 11, an undischarged bankrupt cannot act as director.

The consequences for a director who breaches a disqualification order under the Act are that he:

    (a) commits a criminal offence (s. 13); and
    (b) may be personally liable for the company's debts (s. 5).

F. Directors' Powers

Management of the company is generally undertaken by the directors. Article 70 of table A provides that the "business of the company shall be managed by the directors who may exercise all the powers of the company".

12.8

The articles may delegate certain powers exercised by the directors to others. Article 71 of table A provides that the director can appoint "agents" to perform certain delegated tasks. Article 72 provides that the board of directors can delegate to:

    (a) a committee of directors consisting of one or more directors;
    (b) the managing director (article 84 provides that the managing director is not subject to retirement by rotation); or
    (c) to alternate directors who are dealt with by articles 65–69.

1. BOARD OF DIRECTORS' MEETINGS

The chairman gets one vote (article 88), plus one casting vote (article 91) in the event of there being an equality of votes at a board meeting.

12.9

The quorum refers to the number of directors required to be present to conduct a valid meeting (article 89 sets the number at two).

Article 93 provides that the directors may proceed with their meetings by written resolution; it is the same concept as written resolutions for members (Companies Act 1985, s. 381A), except copies of the directors' written resolutions do not have to go to the auditors for their approval.

G. Directors' Duties

12.10   Directors' duties are owed primarily to the company. This principle was established by the case *Percival v. Wright* (1902) 2 Ch. D. 421. The duties are imposed by case law and statute, primarily the Companies Act 1985.

As mentioned in paragraph 12.1, the nature of the director's duties are two-fold:

  (a) the relatively light duty of skill and care (*i.e.* a breach of which duty is likely to result in a negligence claim against the director); and
  (b) the extremely onerous fiduciary duties (*i.e.* trust and confidence the breach of which, depending on the circumstances may require the director to return monies to the company, *i.e* to account to the company; the disqualification of the director or the personal liability of the director for company debts).

By section 309 of the Companies Act 1985, the directors must also have regard to:

  (a) the interests of members; and
  (b) the interests of the employees in general.

The directors must also have regard to the interests of the creditors—see paragraph 12.33.

1. THE DUTIES OF CARE AND SKILL

12.11   The duties of skill and care refer to the degree of competence required from a director in relation to managing the affairs of the company including dealings with the other directors, the shareholders and third parties. A breach of these duties may result in a negligence action being brought against the director and that director being personally liable rather than relying on company funds. Generally, the courts have:

  (a) taken a "narrow view" of what the duties of directors are *i.e.* they have not applied stringent standards; and
  (b) not required any special "directorial" standard of skill and care from directors. This is in contrast to other professional groups such as doctors, accountants, solicitors and the like who are subject to higher standards of care and skill because of their expertise.

In the case of *Re City Equitable Fire Insurance Company Ltd.* [1925] Ch. 407 three broad propositions were set out by Romer L.J.:

  (a) *Degree of skill—particular knowledge and experience*. The degree of skill to be exercised by a director is not an objective standard, but is gauged by reference to the director's particular knowledge and experience. A director is not liable for an error of judgment. This was illustrated by the case of *Re Brazilian Rubber Plantations and Estates* (1911) 1 Ch. 425. It was held that no special qualification or expertise in respect of the company's particular business operation is required from a director. "He may undertake the management of a rubber company in complete ignorance of everything connected with rubber, without incurring responsibility for the mistakes which may result from such ignorance" (at page 437).

(b) *Need not give continuous attention to company's affairs.* The duties of a director are, in general terms, of an intermittent nature, *i.e.* attending board meetings; committee of board meetings. A director is not bound to attend all meetings but as many as can reasonably be managed. This standard will depend on whether a director is an executive or non-executive director and what is included in the particular articles or service agreement.

(c) *Delegation by the directors to others, so long as the circumstances are not suspicious.* The directors are able to delegate matters so long as there are no matters that would make it imprudent. An obvious matter of delegation would be preparation of the company accounts by the company accountant, which are then sent to the auditors. Delegation by the directors is inevitable in even a small limited company and is usually sanctioned by the articles (see, for example, articles 70 and 72 of table A), so long as there are not any "suspicious circumstances."

Section 13 of the Supply of Goods and Services Act 1982 provides that certain contracts for the supply of services" have implied in them that the services will be carried out with reasonable skill and care. Directors have been exempted from the application of section 13 by a statutory instrument, *i.e.* a director's service agreement will not be affected by section 13 of the Supply of Goods and Services Act.

2. FIDUCIARY DUTIES

As mentioned already, directors are fiduciaries in relation to the company. **12.12** They therefore owe fiduciary duties. Fiduciary duties are of a strict standard compared to the duties of skill and care. A breach of fiduciary duties may result in a fine, disqualification from being a director, imprisonment, having to return funds to the company and personal liability.

The term "fiduciary" refers to notions of trust and confidence. A fiduciary agrees to act for, or on behalf of, or in the interests of another person in the exercise of a power or discretion that will affect the interests of that other person in a legal or practical sense. This principle was confirmed by the High Court of Australia in *Hospital Products Ltd v. United States Surgical Corporation* [1984] 156 C.L.R. 41

There are numerous fiduciary relationships recognised by law. The categories are not closed and include:

(a) trustee to beneficiary,
(b) agent to principal,
(c) solicitor to client,
(d) director to company.

Directors owe their primary duty of allegiance to the company (as a separate legal entity) and not to the shareholders, creditors or fellow directors (Compounds Act 1985, s. 309(2), *Percival v. Wright* (1902) Ch. D. 421).

Section 309(1) of the Companies Act 1985 provides that, in the performance of their duties, the directors "are to have regard" to the interests of:

(a) the members; and
(b) the employees.

The substance of the fiduciary duties owed by a director to the company are to be found in:

(a) case law; and
(b) statute, primarily the Companies Act 1985, the Insolvency Act 1986 and the Company Directors Disqualification Act 1986. Several of the statutory provisions affecting directors are dealt with in section H below and Chapter 15.

Before looking in more detail at the content of the fiduciary position of directors, it is worth noting that some commentators have argued that the imposition of fiduciary duties on directors is inappropriate. This is based on the fact that the fiduciary concept is based on the role of the trustee. The roles of trustees as opposed to directors are seen as quite distinct. For example, in broad terms, the trustee's role is to preserve and carefully invest the trust's capital assets for the benefit of the beneficiaries. The hallmarks of their role are financial prudence and low risk-taking.

On the other hand, the director's role is to make business and investment decisions; and to act entrepeneurially and to take such risks as may be sanctioned by board or shareholder meetings.

In order to overcome these distinctive roles, the courts when dealing with director's fiduciary duties have taken the following two-fold approach:

(a) they will not generally interfere with commercial decisions taken by the directors; and
(b) they will concentrate on abuses of trust and confidence and the manner in which directors have exercised their discretionary powers.

The common law cases have developed many principles relating to the director's fiduciary position. A summary of some of these principles is set out below:

(a) they cannot make secret profits out of their position;
(b) if they were to make secret profit out of their position, they hold such profits as constructive trustees (the company being the beneficiary) and must account to the company for them *i.e.* return them;
(c) information they receive in relation to their positions is the company's property;

   (d) they may, depending on the circumstances have to disclose information to the shareholders;

   (e) they cannot compete with the business during their term of office;

   (f) after they depart the business, they are bound to comply with certain terms of departure including:

       (i) a reasonable restraints of trade clause and

      (ii) non-disclosure of trade secrets.

For further details concerning the content of a director's fiduciary duties, a specialst company law text should be consulted.

H. Statutory Provisions of the Companies Act 1985 Affecting Directors

1. ACCOUNTS (COMPANIES ACT 1985, ss. 227–247)

The directors must ensure that the accounts, primarily, the balance sheet (a **12.13** snapshot of the company's financial situation on a particular day) and the profit and loss statement (which is a summary over a period of time of the company's financial situation), are prepared for the accounting reference period of the company. These documents must be filed with the registrar of companies within 10 months of the end of the accounting reference period and put before a general meeting for approval, unless elective resolutions have been passed to dispense with this requirement.

2. INTERESTS IN CONTRACTS—DISCLOSURE PROVISIONS (COMPANIES ACT 1985, s. 317)

A director who is directly, or indirectly, interested in a contract involving **12.14** the company, as one of the contracting parties, must declare the nature of that interest to the board of directors pursuant to section 317 of the Companies Act 1985. Article 85 of table A also deals with a director disclosing the nature and extent of any material interest in a contract connected with the company.

Section 317 does not specify the form of the declaration, so it may be in written or oral form. It would be prudent if advising a client to stipulate that a section 317 disclosure be in written form to advance the best evidence principle, were the matter to become litigious.

Section 317(2) of the Companies Act 1985 deals with the timing of the disclosure and requires that the declaration of the interest is made:

   (a) at the first directors' meeting, at which the proposed contract is discussed; or

   (b) at the next meeting of directors, after the director became interested.

Failure to comply with this section can result in the director being fined (Companies Act 1985, s. 317(7).)

The section 317 declaration of interest provision is quite distinct from the article 94 prohibition against voting on a contract for a director who is "interested in it".

Whilst article 94 is often deleted by a company to enable a director to vote on all matters, including those in which he is interested, Section 317 cannot be varied or excluded, *i.e.* it overrides any provision to the contrary contained in the company's articles of association, or elsewhere.

3. DIRECTORS' SERVICE CONTRACTS (COMPANIES ACT 1985, S. 319)

12.15   Copies of the directors' service contracts are required to be kept at the registered company's office (Companies Act 1985, s. 318).

As noted in section C above, prior approval by the members by ordinary resolution is required for a service contract that exceeds five years and that cannot be determined by the company giving notice within that term (Companies Act 1985, s. 319).

If a potential service agreement for a director, which includes a term greater than five years, is not first approved at a shareholder's general meeting, the term of the service contract is deemed to be void and the contract is terminable by the company giving "reasonable notice." Reasonable notice will depend on the circumstances.

4. SUBSTANTIAL PROPERTY TRANSACTIONS (COMPANIES ACT 1985, S. 320)

12.16   Prior approval of the members by ordinary resolution passed at a general meeting is required if the company acquires an asset of requisite value from a director or disposes of such an asset to a director. "Requisite value" is equal to sums over £100,000 or over 10 per cent of the company's net assets. The net assets figure is, pursuant to section 320(2), determined by reference to the latest audited accounts or if no accounts have been prepared, *i.e.* it is a new company, by reference to the amount of share capital actually paid up. Assets worth less than £2,000 do not, in any event require approval from the shareholders.

Example: Substantial Property Transaction. Bob, who is both a director and shareholder of ABC Ltd, is intending to sell a piece of land worth £25,000 to the company. The net worth of the company is £150,000. Does this transaction need to be approved by the shareholders?

This transaction does have to be approved (under section 320) because it is over £2,000 in value and it is also in excess of 10 per cent of the company's net assets.

Bob will have to declare his interest in this contract under section 317 of the Companies Act 1985 and may not be able to vote at a shareholders' meeting to approve the contract if article 94 of table A is contained in the articles.

5. LOANS (COMPANIES ACT 1985, SS. 330–341)

12.17   It is forbidden by section 330 for a company to make a loan to a director, or provide a guarantee or security unless:

(a) pursuant to section 337 of the Companies Act 1985 it is to enable the director to carry out his directorial duties, or, it is for the purposes of the company. The prior approval of the shareholders is required at an EGM before the loan can be made and the loan is repayable within six months of the next AGM. The amount of the loan can be no more than £20,000; or

(b) if the loans are for other purposes than those set out above, sections 332 and 334 of the Act provides that the total loan(s) must not exceed £5,000. Section 335(1) of the Companies Act 1985 allows for loans up to £10,000 to be made by the company to a director so long as they are in the ordinary course of business and meet the conditions set out in section 335(2), which are principally that the value and terms of the transaction are the same as they would have been had the transacion involved someone unconnected with the company.

6. PUBLICITY

A register of directors and secretaries is required to be maintained at the company's registered office pursuant to section 288 of the Companies Act 1985. If there is a change of director or secretary, notice has to be provided to Companies House within 14 days of the change. Directors' interests in shares or debentures of the company includes the interest of a director's spouse and children (Companies Act 1985, ss. 324–325). Must be disclosed to the company (s. 324) and kept in a register maintained at the company's registered office pursuant to section 325 of the Act.   **12.18**

I. The Company Secretary

The company secretary is not required to hold any particular qualification.   **12.19**
The sole director cannot also be the secretary.
  The first company secretary is named in the Form G10.
  Subsequent secretaries are:

(a) appointed; and
(b) removed in accordance with the terms and conditions set out by the directors or articles of association.

  Primarily, the company secretary is the company's record keeper responsible for maintaining the internal records of the company, *e.g.* minutes of board and general meetings and the *external* records, *e.g.* matters filed with the registrar of companies.
  The Secretary's functions are threefold:

(a) record keeper;
(b) office manager; and
(c) administration of the company.

  An outsider (a third party) is entitled to rely on a company secretary's decision in relation to an administrative matter, even if it turns out that the company secretary did not have the authorisation of the board of directors.

Example: A company secretary's authority (Panorama Developments (Guildford) Ltd. v. Fidelis Furnishing Fabrics Ltd [1971] 2 Q.B. 711). In this case, a company was bound to pay for the use of hired motor cars, even though the company secretary had hired them for his personal use, it was held that the secretary had ostensible authority to make contracts relating to the administration of the company, such as the hiring of motor cars.

J. The Auditors

12.20   The role of the auditor is, in general, to confirm the accuracy of the company's accounts and to confirm that they represent a true and fair view of the company's financial position.

The qualification for a person to be appointed as an auditor of a company is membership of a body of accountants recognised by the Secretary of State (Companies Act 1985, s. 389).

Auditors are entitled to receive copies of written resolutions and such resolutions will not be effective until the auditors have had a period of seven days within which to object and call for the holding of a meeting of shareholders of the company (see paragraph 13.19). Auditors cannot be removed by written resolution (as is the same case with directors).

The company normally is required to reappoint the auditor at the AGM. However, the company can, by elective resolution resolve not to have to do this.

If the company's auditors are negligent in performing their work, it is the company who is ordinarily the proper plaintiff (in accordance with the principle in *Foss v. Harbottle* (see paragraph 11.33)) to sue for the loss, and not the members.

K. Liability of the Company to Third Parties

12.21   As was mentioned in paragraph 8.24, companies have their own contractual capacity. The source of that contractual capacity is the company's constituent documents, and the directors are the company's contractual agents with the necessary authority to bind the company to agreements, arrangements and the like with third parties. This raises the following enquiry: what is the effect of a company entering a contract which is beyond the scope of its constituent documents? Traditionally the answer provided by the *ultra vires* doctrine was that such an act, being beyond power was void. That position has now changed by virtue of sections 35, 35A, 35B and 322A of the Companies Act 1985.

(a) Section 35(2) of the Act provides just a member can stop an act that is beyond the scope of the memorandum of association, by bringing injunction proceedings *before* a binding legal obligation has been entered into by the company.

(b) Section 35(3) provides that the directors may be personally liable to the company for an act which "does not observe any limitation

on their powers flowing from the company's memorandum." However, the company may ratify such a contract and may also separately indemnify the directors, if they choose to do so.
  (c) Section 322A(2) provides that:
        (i) where a company enters into a transaction which is beyond
            its constitution; and
       (ii) one of the parties is a director or an associate of a director
            then, the transaction is voidable at the company's option.

In any case, section 322A(2) provides that the director or associate involved
must account to and indemnify the company for any resultant loss or damage.
Such a transaction can be ratified by the company in general meeting pursuant
to section 322A(5).
  These provisions are dealt with further in paragraph 12.24 below.

1. AGENCY (THE DIRECTORS' AUTHORITY TO CONTRACT ON BEHALF OF THE
COMPANY)

Article 70 of table A provides for the general delegation of the management   **12.22**
of the company to be given to the directors.
  The company is liable to third parties for the acts of their agents (including
directors) that are within the scope of that agency.
  As agents of the company, directors have *actual authority* for the purpose
of, or reasonably incidental to, attaining or pursuing the company's objects.
Actual authority can be defined as the authority conferred by the contract that
regulates the principal and agent relationship. The content of the authority is
usually found in:

  (a) the service agreement that has been negotiated between the director
      (as agent) and the company. Auditors, advertising agents, the man-
      aging director and the secretary, etc., may also be classified as
      agents; or
  (b) the memorandum or articles of association of the company in
      question.

  *Example: nature and scope of a directors actual authority (Freeman and
Lockyer v. Buckhurst Park Properties (Mangal) Ltd* [1964] 1 All E.R. 630).
It was held that the scope of a director's actual authority is to be found by
applying ordinary principles as to the constitution of contracts. Regard is to
be had to the express words and implied terms.

  Directors also have *ostensible authority*. Ostensible authority is difficult   **12.23**
to define. If a particular act is of a category that is *capable* of being performed
as *reasonably incidental* to the attainment or pursuit of the company's
objects, then it will generally be within the director's authority. If an act by
an agent of the company is outside the scope of the actual authority, it may
still bind the company as being within the apparent or ostensible authority.
Ostensible authority is wider than actual authority, *i.e.* it can be seen as a
second, larger circle existing outside actual authority.
  The practical test in relation to determining ostensible authority was enun-

ciated in *Rolled Steel Products (Holdings) Ltd v. British Steel Corporation* [1986] Ch. 246 *per* Slade L.J. where he said that unless the person or third party is *put on notice to the contrary*, a person or third party dealing in good faith with a company, which is carrying on an *intra vires* business (*i.e.* one within the objects of the company), is entitled to assume that its directors are properly exercising such powers for the purposes of the company, as set out in its memorandum of association. Correspondingly, a person in such circumstances, can hold the company liable to any such transaction of this nature.

The scope of a person's ostensible authority will be determined by virtue of:

(a) his status, for example his position as a director or managing director, etc.; or

(b) a representation made to the third party by someone with the *actual* authority to manage the business of the company, such as a director.

Example: A director acting beyond ostensible or apparent authority. (Biggerstaff v. Rowatt's Wharf Ltd [1896] 2 Ch. 93). The relevant facts of this case concerned the ostensible authority given to a Mr Davy, described as "the managing director" of the defendant company. The question to be determined was whether he had the ostensible authority to assign debts, that were owed to the company, to third parties.

It was held that as managing director, he *theoretically* could be given such a power by the articles of association. However, in the circumstances, it could not be said that he was acting within the limits of his apparent authority, *i.e.* this was an act beyond the authority deriving from his status of managing director.

Apparent authority will be difficult to define in general terms and requires resort to the particular service agreement and articles of association.

2. STATUTORY PROVISIONS CONCERNING OSTENSIBLE AUTHORITY

12.24   Sections 35A and 35B of the Companies Act 1985 add to the doctrine of ostensible authority developed by the common law. Both these sections assume that the board of directors can bind the company. This is the case with a company having articles in the form of table A, article 70, which states that "the company shall be managed by the directors who may exercise all the powers of the company."

Section 35A(1) of the Act provides that a third party dealing with a company in *good faith* can *assume* that directors are free from any limitation under the company's constitution (*i.e.* the good faith assumption provision).

Example: A limitation provided in the articles of association. A mortgage debenture has been arranged between XYZ Ltd and its bankers for the sum of £200,000. XYZ Ltd's articles state that for a loan of over £100,000, it needs first to be authorised and approved by an EGM of shareholders. No such approval is obtained. Can the bank enforce the loan?

Under the rule in section 35A(1) of the Companies Act 1985, the bank, if it has acted in good faith, can enforce all the obligations in the mortgage debenture against XYZ Ltd.

Section 35A(2) of the Companies Act 1985 provides clarification of the good faith provision contained in section 35(1); that is bad faith cannot be assumed only on the basis that the third party knew that an act was beyond the director's powers (*i.e.* there needs to be some element beyond mere knowledge of the fact that the act in question is beyond the scope of the memorandum of association and articles of association of the company concerned).

Example: good faith being shown by a third party in its dealing with the company (TCB Ltd v. Gray [1986] Ch. 621). In this case the company's articles provided that when the company's seal was affixed to documents it also had to be signed by a director. A floating charge was signed not by a director but by an attorney for a director, *i.e.* the signing by the attorney was an act that was beyond the terms of the company's articles. The issue to be resolved was whether the attorney's signature bound the company?

It was held that the company was bound on the basis of section 35A(1) and (2) of the Companies Act 1985, *i.e.* the third party was not acting in bad faith. There needed to be an element beyond mere knowledge, *i.e.* that the third party knew the directors were acting beyond the scope of the articles, was alone, not enough.

Section 35A(4) of the Companies Act 1985 provides that a *member* may prevent the company from doing an act that is beyond *the powers of the directors*, *i.e.* some form of injunctive relief is available; however, it must be *commenced* before the company incurs any *legal obligation*, *i.e.* before there is a binding contract. In *TCB v. Gray*, referred to above, a member would need to have brought injunction proceedings to stop the company before the floating charge had been signed.

Section 35B of the Companies Act 1985 provides that a third party dealing with the company is *not* under any *obligation* whether acting in good faith or not, to enquire into the powers of the directors.

L. Liability of the Directors to Third Parties

1. BREACH OF WARRANTY OF AUTHORITY

As already noted, a director is an agent of the company. If a director has either actual or ostensible authority for an act done on the company's behalf, he is not ordinarily personally liable (assuming that there has been no element of fraud).   **12.25**

If a director acts beyond his scope of actual or ostensible authority, he may be personally liable to the third party, *i.e.* an action for breach of warranty of authority could be brought by the third party against the director.

2. INSOLVENCY ACT PROVISIONS

Under the Insolvency Act 1986, directors may be personally liable on matters investigated by the liquidator on a winding-up. These matters are dealt with   **12.26** in Chapter 15. The provisions to which a solicitor should advise a director include fraudulent trading (section 213), wrongful trading (section 214) and misfeasance proceedings (section 212). See Chapter 15.

If found liable under any of these sections, a director *may* have to contribute from his personal assets towards the liabilities of the company. A legal adviser should therefore pay particular attention to the advice given to directors when the financial circumstances of the company deteriorate.

M. Other Types of Directors

12.27   There are several types of directors referred to in the Companies Act 1985 and table A articles of association. These include, in addition to "directors", alternate directors, shadow directors, additional directors and executive and non-executive directors. Each of these will be briefly considered.

1. ALTERNATE DIRECTORS

12.28   Alternate directors are referred to in articles 65–69 of table A provides that they may be appointed by a director and may act in the director's place when the director is not available.

2. SHADOW DIRECTORS

12.29   Section 741(2) of the Companies Act 1985 defined a shadow director as "any person in accordance with whose directions or instructions the directors of a company are accustomed to act." A person who simply gives professional advice to a company would not normally be a shadow director. Shadow directors are deemed to be directors of the company under some provisions of the Companies Act 1985 and the Insolvency Act 1986. For example, the Insolvency Act 1986, s. 214(7), provides that the wrongful trading provision (s. 214) apply to shadow directors as if they were directors, *i.e.* recorded on the register of directors at the company's registered office and at Company's House. Their names should be included in the section 288 of the Companies Act 1985 register of directors.

3. ADDITIONAL DIRECTORS

12.30   These are referred to in article 79 of table A. They may be appointed by the directors to fill a vacancy or to add a director to the board. Article 79 provides that the shareholders must approve the appointment at the next AGM or the person must resign.

4. EXECUTIVE AND NON-EXECUTIVE DIRECTORS

12.31   These are not terms of art but generally refer to full-time as opposed to part-time directors *i.e.* executive directors typically devote their full working time to the company and receive a salary whereas non-executive directors devote occasional time to the company and receive a relatively small director's fee.

5. MANAGING DIRECTORS AND ORDINARY DIRECTORS

Article 84 table A provides that subject to the Companies Act 1985, the directors may appoint a managing director who may provide the company with "services outside the scope of the ordinary duties of a director". Such services and duties will be included in an agreement or arrangement between the company and the managing director. Article 72 provides that the directors can delegate "any of their powers" to the managing director or a committee of one or more directors. Directors other than the managing director will generally be referred to as ordinary, non-managing directors.

N. Personal Financial Liability of Directors

The personal liability of directors may also be relevant in two respects: **12.32**

- (a) to the creditors in general under the Insolvency Act 1986; and
- (b) to a *secured creditor* in respect of a personal guarantee provided by the director for the company's debts.

1. COMPANIES IN FINANCIAL TROUBLE—INSOLVENCY ACT 1986

In addition to those matters set out in section G above, the directors must **12.33** also have regard to the interests of the company's creditors, especially if the company is in financial difficulty. Under the Insolvency Act 1986, the directors face several possible actions that may result in the Court making an order against the director for *personal liability* for the *company's debts*. Such proceedings will generally be commenced by the liquidator of a company once the company has gone into liquidation. For full details, refer to Chapter 15.

Such actions include:

- (a) section 212 "*misfeasance proceedings*". This involves the director breaching his fiduciary duties or trustee obligations;
- (b) section 213 "*fraudulent trading*".

This involves some actual element of dishonesty on the director's part. Conviction may also carry a fine.

- (c) section 214 "*wrongful trading*".

This involves a breach of the director's duty of care akin to negligence. Wrongful trading will typically involve a company that is in a poor financial situation. This may be as a result of out-of-date, inaccurate or poorly kept accounts. It may be as a result of excessive borrowings or poor sales or any other reason. Section 214 deals with the financial and managerial competence of the directors. The directors, if the company is in insolvent liquidation or has no reasonable prospect of avoiding such a fate, are required to take every step with a view to minimising the loss to the creditors. That is, they have to put in place effective steps to stem the flow of losses. The practical points concerning possible section 214 proceedings are that the directors:

(a) have not provided systems for the detection of such financial problems; or

(b) realising that such problems exist, they have not acted quickly or efficiently to monitor and alleviate the problem. Such steps might include:

    (i) holding regular board meetings;

    (ii) making sure the accounts are up to date;

    (iii) liaising with the auditor and obtaining expert finanical advice; and

    (iv) keeping the creditors informed of developments

Each of the provisions discussed above should be borne in mind by the financial adviser. They may be bought in the alternative by the liquidator.

2. Directors' Personal Guarantees

12.34 A director's personal guarantee provides that the director's own assets are given as security for loans taken out and other obligations entered into by the company. Personal guarantees are often required by the company's creditors, *e.g.* banks, especially in their dealings with small companies.

The effect of a director providing a guarantee is to negate the theory of the "limited liability" of directors and or shareholders.

If a director guarantees repayment of a loan taken out by a company, the company bears the primary liability for repaying the loan and only if and when this primary liability is exhausted will the guarantor be proceeded against. This is in contrast to the liability of a person providing an indemnity that is a primary liability ranking alongside the liability of the borrower.

O. Financial Protection Given to Directors

12.35 Apart from those matters set out in the director's service agreement, the company may provide some measure of financial protection in relation to potential litigation actions being commenced against the director or in respect of the broader issue of the director's personal liability for debts of the company.

Such financial protection might involve a policy of insurance or an indemnity in respect of legal costs, such as article 118 of table A.

1. Insurance Policies

12.36 Increasingly, companies, worried about the potential personal liability of their directors, are arranging specifically tailored insurance policies to protect them from liabilities and costs.

For example:

(a) protection from civil-law suits brought by disgruntled shareholders or creditors; or

(b) if they are dismissed (for example under section 303 of the Companies Act 1985), their legal fees will be paid to enable them to sue the company for compensation for wrongful dismissal, etc, depending on the circumstances.

Such policies have also been extended to non-executive (part-time) directors as well as executive (full-time) directors.

2. Table A Indemnity

Article 118 of table A provides that a director will be indemnified out of the assets of the company against any liability incurred by him in defending any proceedings, whether civil or criminal, in which judgment is given in his favour or in which he has been acquitted. This covers negligence claims, breach of duty, and breach of trust in relation to the affairs of the company. If the director is found liable in respect of one of these actions he would not be covered by the terms of article 118 and would have to pay his own legal costs as well as any fines imposed.

    The indemnity provided by article 118 may be expanded or reduced according to the requirements of the particular company.

12.37

13.   Company Procedure

A. Background

13.1   In this chapter we consider how a company conducts its business and how decisions are made by it. For instance, if a company wants to sell a piece of land; enter a marketing agreement; purchase goods from a director; change its name, etc., how does it do these things? Essentially, a company acts through its directors and shareholders.

Whilst a company is a legal entity, separate and distinct from its owners (the shareholders) and its managers (the directors), it cannot initiate or proceed with an action without the involvement of the directors or the shareholders, or both of these groups. The company deals with third parties principally through the agency of the directors.

The directors and shareholders for their part act and make decisions on the company's behalf through the medium of the meeting; hence the term "shareholders' meeting" and "directors' meeting." Decisions taken at such meetings are referred to as resolutions.

There may be several stages involved and meetings to be held in order to conclude a particular piece of company business. In general, the more important the item of business, the more likely it is that the directors will have to seek the approval of the shareholders at a shareholders' meeting. Less important issues can usually be resolved by the directors alone.

Of course, not every action taken by or on behalf of a company requires a directors' meeting to be held. The directors will be delegated with the responsibility of running the company and there will be many matters that fall under this general administrative category. This is the case with the managing director under table A.

In considering company procedure, whatever the type of meeting, several steps may be involved:

(a) *Administrative matters*. These can be decided by a director without the need for a meeting.

(b) *Directors' meetings*. These are also called board meetings. The directors meet and agree matters by majority vote. Each director gets one vote unless the chair gets an additional or casting vote in the event of an equality of votes. A shareholder's meeting will be resolved to be called if necessary or required by the articles or the Companies Act 1985. Article 70 of table A provides that the "business of the company shall be managed by the directors who may exercise all the powers of the company". Such a provision allows the directors to decide whether to commit the company to taking out a loan or giving security along with numerous other decisions about the business. However, if there is a wish to change the company's name, the directors

156

cannot decide that matter of business at a board meeting but must comply with the directions set out in section 28 of the Companies Act 1985.

(c) *Shareholders' meetings.* These will either be EGMs or AGMs. Notice is required to be given to each shareholder at the address specified in the register of members. Shareholders can attend and vote. They get one vote on a show of hands; they get votes according to the number of shares held on a vote by poll. Shareholders approve matters (or otherwise) as required by the Companies Act 1985. For example, if the company is to change its name, a special resolution is required to be passed at the EGM (see paragraph 13.12) in accordance with section 28 of the Companies Act 1985.

(d) *Reconvened directors' meetings.* These follow the shareholders' meetings and effect the business approved by the shareholders at the earlier shareholder meeting. The directors carry out "the mechanics" of a transaction. For example, with the change of name procedure under section 28 of the Companies Act 1985, the directors at the reconvened board meeting will amend the Memorandum of Association in readiness for the reporting requirements in paragraph (f) below.

(e) *Administrative follow-up.* The company secretary will complete minutes of meetings as required by the Companies Act 1985, and the rest of the statutory books.

(f) *Reporting requirements.* The company secretary will lodge with the companies registrar such documentation as is required under the Companies Act 1985. For example, if the company changes its name, the company secretary is required within 14 days of the EGM to lodge with the Registrar of Companies, a copy of the special resolution, a prescribed fee (currently £20) and an amended copy of the Memorandum of Association showing the change.

(g) *Completion matters.* In order to finalise a piece of company business, there may be certain matters which practically complete the process. For example, when a company changes its name, the Registrar of Companies issues an amended Certificate of Incorporation which records the date of name change. This certificate is sent to the company, thereby completing the process.

B. General Matters Concerning Meetings

Meetings, whether of the directors or shareholders, will be conducted by reference to the Companies Act 1985 and the articles of association. Table A provides the following rules in relation to the following issues:

13.2

(a) *Notice for meetings.* How much notice is required to be given to the people attending the meeting?

(b) *Calling meetings*. Who calls the meetings?

(c) *Contents of the notice of meeting*. What does the notice of meeting specify?

(d) *Quorum*. How many people must be present for the proceedings of meeting to be valid and the resolutions that have been passed, binding?

(e) *Proxies*. Do people have to attend in person or can they send a representative to vote on their behalf?

(f) *Agenda*. Who will decide the matters to be discussed at the meeting?

(g) *Voting*. How will votes be taken and counted? The two forms of voting are a show of hands, *i.e.* one vote per person present or poll vote that takes account of the number of shares held by a shareholder. Poll voting is only available at shareholder meetings and depends on the terms in the articles.

(h) *Chair's role*. Will there be a Chair to oversee the meeting and will the chair get a casting vote in the event of an equality of votes?

(i) *Passing resolutions*. Will matters be passed by a simple majority of votes or by some greater majority (such as three quarters of the votes)?

(j) *Minutes of meetings*. Who will prepare these and where will they be kept?

C. Directors' Meetings

13.3   Under article 70 of table A, the general power to manage the affairs of the company is delegated to the directors. Most sets of articles of association will include a provision similar to article 70. An important consequence of such a provision is that a meeting of the directors will be the usual point at which company business is initiated.

It may be that a particular matter of company business can be decided by the directors at a meeting (by a means of passing a directors' resolution) without the need to take the matter on a stage further to approval by a meeting of shareholders (either an EGM or AGM). Whether a matter can be decided by the directors alone, or whether it needs to go on to be approved by the shareholders, depends on:

(a) the requirements of the company's articles of association; and
(b) the requirements of the Companies Act 1985, and any other legislation relevant to the company's affairs.

1. DIRECTORS' MEETINGS—GENERAL MATTERS

13.4   In relation to the general matter concerning directors' meetings, table A provides as follows:

(a) *Notice for directors' meetings*. Article 88 provides that a director or secretary may call a meeting of directors. No notice period is specified. Essentially it is a matter for the directors to decide amongst themselves. Often the article will provide that the directors can conduct their meeting by telephone, video link-up or some other form of communication.

(b) *Calling directors' meetings*. Article 88 provides that a director of the company or the company secretary can call meetings.

(c) *Contents of the notice of directors' meetings*. This is not specified in table A. Article 88 provides that the directors may regulate their proceedings as they think fit.

(d) *Quorum for directors' meetings*. Article 89 specifies that two directors must be present (this can include an alternative director).

(e) *Proxies at directors' meetings*. Article 89 provides that alternate directors can be counted in the quorum.

(f) *Agenda*. The agenda will be informal in the sense that it will be the directors themselves who decide what is discussed.

(g) *Voting at directors' meetings*. Article 88 provides for resolutions to be passed by a majority of votes by a show of hands.

(h) *The chair' role at directors' meeting*. Article 88 provides that the chair gets a casting vote (in addition to his other vote) in the case of an equality of votes.

(i) *Passing resolutions at a directors' meeting*. Article 88 provides for a simple majority of votes.

(j) *Minutes of directors' meetings*. Article 100(b) provides that the company secretary prepares minutes of directors' meetings.

Example 1: Directors' resolutions. Examples of matters that can ordinarily be decided by the directors alone include:

(a) the taking on of staff (including the company secretary;
(b) the numerous day-to-day administrative tasks necessary to run the company;
(c) the decision for the company to borrow money, or to take out security for a loan.

These decisions can be justified by reference to article 70 of table A.

Example 2: Directors' resolutions plus members' approval. On the other hand, the Companies Act 1985 may specifically require the second-stage approval of the members (in addition to the first stage, *i.e.* the directors' approval) before a matter can be effective in law. An example of this is a decision to change the name of the company. Such a decision would ordinarily be initiated by the directors (article 70 of table A), but is then required by section 28(1) of the Companies Act 1985, to pass a special resolution at an EGM to that effect.

This procedure can be represented as follows:

(a) *First stage.* To initiate an item of company business a directors' meeting is held at which a resolution is passed (by majority) to agree to put the change of name resolution before a meeting of shareholders for their approval.

(b) *Second stage.* A shareholders' meeting is called by the directors by following the procedure set out in the articles of association. This will include details such as:

(i) who is entitled to receive notice
(ii) the amount of notice required

For table A purposes, these matters are set out in article 38. Approval and authorisation by the shareholders at the shareholders' meeting. This is effected by the passing of a special resolution to change the company's name pursuant to section 28(1) of the Companies Act 1985.

(c) *Third stage.* The directors reconvene and carry out the necessary documentation to change the name.

(d) *Fourth stage.* The change of name documentation (and a fee) is lodged with the registrar of companies who will in due course issue a new certificate of incorporation.

2. THE FIRST DIRCTORS' MEETING

13.5   The agenda for the first meeting of directors will report and confirm several administrative matters. Among these matters are the following:

(a) report the incorporation of the company,
(b) report as to the directors, secretary and registered office,
(c) to appoint a chair of the board of directors,
(d) to appoint auditors,
(e) to fix the accounting reference date,
(f) to appoint bankers,
(g) to allot shares,
(h) to seal share certificates,
(i) to register for the purposes of VAT,
(j) to notify of shares held by directors under section 324 of the Companies Act 1985,
(k) to provide notice of directors' interests in contracts under section 317 of the Companies Act 1985,
(l) to approve the costs of incorporation.

3. OTHER DIRECTORS' MEETINGS

Future directors' meetings will be held at the discretion of the directors in accordance with the articles. At those meetings the directors may also resolve to call meetings of shareholders for the purpose of passing resolutions pursuant to the Companies Act 1985.

13.6

Example: Directors' resolution to call an EGM. An example of the wording that might be adopted for a resolution is:

"It was resolved that an EGM of the company be convened and held on (date) to consider the following resolutions:

(a) that director Bob's service agreement with a fixed term of seven years be approved by ordinary resolution in accordance with section 319 of the Companies Act 1985. A copy of the proposed service agreement is available for inspection in accordance with section 319(5) of the Act.

(b) that the company's proposed transfer of land to Bob (such land being situated at 1 Smith St) be approved by ordinary resolution in accordance with section 320 of the Act, the land being in excess of 10 per cent of the company's net assets."

D. Shareholders' Meetings

The shareholders may meet at two types of meeting—the Annual General Meeting (AGM) and the Extraordinary General Meeting (EGM). The main purpose of the AGM is for the shareholders to be updated on the company's affairs and to be able to question the directors on those affairs. The company's accounts will also be presented to the shareholders.

13.7

EGMs are all other meetings of the shareholders. Generally they will be called by the directors but there are limited circumstances in which the shareholders themselves can call such meetings. The Court may also call such meetings in certain circumstances.

An annual general meeting may be dispensed with, for private companies, by adopting an elective resolution under the Companies Act 1985, s. 379A. See paragraph 13.14.

1. TYPES OF MEETING FOR MEMBERS

Table A provides for two types of general meeting under article 36, which provides that all general meetings other than AGMs shall be called EGMs.

Annual General Meetings

AGMs are held once every calendar year and not more than 15 months apart (except the first AGM, which must be held within 18 months of incorporation. Hence if a company is incorporated in December 1994 it must hold its first AGM before May 1996. It must hold its second AGM before August 1997.

13.8

The notice period required for an AGM specified by article 38 table A is 21 "clear days", defined in table A to exclude:

(a) the day on which the notice is sent; and

(b) the day which the meeting is held.

The specified notice period may be shortened if the company complies with section 369 of the Companies Act 1985 and/or article 38(b) table A.

A private company may pass an elective resolution (see section 379A of the Companies Act 1985) to dispense with the holding of AGMs as per section 366A.

Extraordinary General Meetings

13.9   EGMs are generally convened by the directors or they may be requisitioned by the members who hold that paid-up capital that carries 10 per cent of the votes under section 368 of the Companies Act 1985. This is also confirmed by article 37 of table A, which requires the meeting to be held not later than eight weeks after the company receives the requisition.

The Companies Act 1985 also provides two other avenues by which shareholders' meetings may be called, namely:

(a) Section 371—by the Court if for any reason it is impracticable to call a meeting on the application of a director or member or of its own motion; or

(b) Section 367—by the Secretary of State for Trade and Industry if a company does not hold an AGM in accordance with section 366.

The court also has limited powers to call shareholders meetings for specific and limited purposes such as to consider an arrangement sanctioned by the court under section 425 of the Act. The usual notice is 14 days, but 21 days' notice is required in the case of a special resolution, or one to appoint a director. Short notice is available, if agreed by a majority in number of the shareholders who hold 95 per cent in nominal value, or with a private company 90 per cent of the shareholders pursuant to section 369 of the Act and article 38(b) table A.

2. SHAREHOLDERS' MEETINGS—GENERAL MATTERS

13.10   In relation to the general matters concerning shareholders' meetings, table A provides as follows:

(a) *Notice for shareholders' meetings.* Article 38 provides 21 days' clear notice for a special resolution and at least 14 day's clear notice for an ordinary resolution. Article 38 also provides for short notice. Notice must be sent to all members and to the personal representative of a deceased shareholder and the trustee in bankruptcy of a bankrupt shareholder. Notice must also go to the directors and auditors under article 38.

(b) *Calling shareholders' meetings.* Article 37 provides that the directors will usually call them but as mentioned there is the ability for shareholders and the Courts to call them in specific circumstances.

(c) *Contents of the notice of shareholders' meetings.* Article 38 provides that the notice must specify time and place of meeting, nature of the business to be transacted, whether it is an AGM or EGM.

(d) *Quorum for shareholders' meetings.* Article 40 specifies a quorum of two people entitled to vote being present in order for the meeting to be valid.

(e) *Proxies at shareholders' meetings.* Articles 55–57 allow for the proxy to vote incase of the shareholder. Article 59 allows the proxy to vote on a poll vote.

(f) *Agenda.* The agenda will generally be established by the directors. However shareholders have opportunities to influence the matters discussed at meetings and in fact whether a shareholders' meeting is held. For example, as noted already:

(i) Section 376 of the Companies Act 1985 allows a shareholder with 5 per cent of the voting rights to request that a resolution is put before a shareholders' meeting. The shareholder can also circulate, at his own expense, a written statement of no more than a 1,000 words in support of the resolution; and

(ii) Section 368 of the Companies Act 1985 allows a shareholder with at least 10 per cent of the voting rights to request of the directors that they hold an EGM.

(g) *Voting at shareholders' meetings.* Covered by articles 54–63. Voting will either be on a show of hands, *i.e.* one vote per shareholder unless a poll is demanded. Article 54 provides that on a poll a member gets one vote per share. It may be that a shareholder has more than one vote per share, *i.e.* a *Bushell v. Faith* weighting of votes per share and these will be taken into account on a poll.

(h) *The chair's role at a shareholders' meeting.* Article 50 gives the chair a casting or extra vote whether it is on a show of hands or a poll, when there is an equality of votes.

(i) *Passing resolutions at a shareholders' meeting.* The number of votes required will depend on the type of resolution to be passed. The most common resolutions are ordinary resolutions requiring a majority of votes, *i.e.* 50 per cent plus one vote or special resolutions requiring 75 per cent of the votes.

(j) *Minutes of shareholders' meeting.* Article 100(b) requires that the company secretary prepare minutes of meeting.

E. Types of Shareholders' Resolutions

The following types of resolutions are generally adopted by companies and are subject to the following details (which may be varied depending on the company's articles):

1. ORDINARY RESOLUTIONS

13.11
(a) the notice required depends on the type of meeting and type of resolution. Fourteen days clear notice is usually required for ordinary resolutions to be passed at EGMs. Twenty-one days clear notice is usually required for AGMs. Short notice may be available (article 38 and section 369 of the Companies Act 1985);

(b) the exact wording of the proposed resolution is required in the notice of meeting;

(c) a majority of the votes cast is required. This would be a majority on a vote by a show of hands and 50 per cent *plus one vote* on a vote by poll.

2. SPECIAL RESOLUTIONS

13.12
(a) the notice required is 21 days (s. 378(2)) unless short notice has been adopted (s. 378(3));

(b) the specification of the proposed resolution as a special resolution together with the exact wording is required in the notice of meeting;

(c) the resolution is passed by a majority of not less than three quarters of members voting, whether on a show of hands or poll (s. 378(2));

(d) a copy of the resolution must be lodged with the Registrar of Companies within 15 days of it being passed pursuant to Companies Act 1985, s. 380.

3. EXTRAORDINARY RESOLUTIONS

13.13
(a) the notice required is 21 days (s. 378(2));

(b) the specification of the proposed resolution as an extraordinary resolution together with the exact wording is required in the notice of meeting;

(c) the resolution is passed by a majority of not less than three quarters of members voting, whether on a show of hands or poll (s. 378(1));

(d) a copy of the resolution must be lodged with the Registrar of Companies within 15 days of it being passed pursuant to Companies Act 1985, s. 380;

(e) extraordinary resolutions are required in specific circumstances under the Insolvency Act 1986. For example, section 84(1)(c) provides that a company may be wound up voluntarily if the company resolves by extraordinary resolution to the effect that it cannot by reason of its liabilities continue its business and that it is advisable to wind up.

4. ELECTIVE RESOLUTIONS

13.14
(a) the notice required is 21 days (s. 379A(2)) unless short notice has been adopted (s. 378(3));

(b) the specification of the proposed resolution as an elective resolution together with the exact wording is required in the notice of meeting (s. 379A(2)(a));

(c) the resolution is passed by all the members entitled to attend and vote at the meeting, whether in person or by proxy (s. 379A(2)(b));

(d) a copy of the resolution must be lodged with the Registrar of Companies within 15 days of it being passed pursuant to Companies Act 1985, s. 380;

(e) the elective resolution may be revoked by passing an ordinary resolution to that effect (s. 379A(3));

(f) elective resolutions are available to private companies for the purpose of:

(i) dispensing with certain procedural requirements under the Companies Act 1985; and

(ii) streamlining the management of the company.

The matters for which elective resolutions can be passed are set out in section 379A(1) and include:

(a) making indefinite the directors' authority to issue shares which is limited to five years under section 80 (see s. 80A);

(b) dispensing with the laying of accounts and reports before the annual general meeting as is usually required under section 241 (see s. 252);

(c) dispensing with the holding of AGMs as is usually required under section 366 (see s. 366A);

(d) amending the majority required to authorise short notice under section 369(3) (see ss. 369(4) and 378(3)); and

(e) dispensing with the annual appointment of auditors as is ususlly required under section 385 (see s. 386).

5. Filing of Resolutions

Printed copies of special, extraordinary and elective resolutions must be filed   **13.15**
with the registrar of companies within 15 days of being passed pursuant to section 380 of the Companies Act 1985. Ordinary resolutions must also be filed in the case of an increase of authorised share capital under section 123, and the authority to issue shares under section 80.

F. Advising a Shareholder

It is necessary when advising a shareholder to ascertain the following   **13.16**
information:

(a) What is the company's authorised share capital?, *i.e.* how many shares have been created in the company's memorandum of association?

(b) What is the company's issue and allotted share capital?, *i.e.* have all the shares been issued or if not, how many shares are there that can still theoretically be issued? This may be crucial if, for example, you are advising a shareholder about a rights issue of shares. It may be for instance that the shareholder cannot afford the shares, so will

      not be able to take up his entitlement and thereby have his parent
      shareholding reduced.

(c) Are the shares fully paid or partly paid?

(d) What are the voting rights if any attaching to the shares?

(e) Do the shares carry a right to receipt of a dividend, when one is
declared? If dividends have been consistently withheld by directors
and there is an element of ''unfair prejudice'' affecting the shareholder's interests, the shareholder may have grounds to commence
proceedings under section 459 of the Companies Act 1985, for
example.

(f) How many voting shares does the client have and what percentage
of the company's shares carrying a right to vote do they represent?
This last point is crucial because it will designate the rights and
duties applicable to the shareholder under:

     (i) the common law;

    (ii) the company's articles of association; and

   (iii) the Companies Act 1985.

13.17   The following table represents the various significant thresholds that establish the rights and duties of shareholders. It is important that these matters
are kept in mind when obtaining instructions from and advising shareholders.
The left-hand column deals with either the *number* of voting shares held *or*
the *percentage* of the total voting shares represented by that number. The
right-hand column deals with the significant matters to be borne in mind in
respect of the shares held.

Number of shares held or per-centage of total voting shares held by a member	Matters to bear in mind (Companies Act 1985)
1. 1 share held	1.1 s. 366 A(3) A member can request that an AGM be held if the company has adopted an elective res-olution to dispense with the holding of AGM's pursuant to s. 379A.
	1.2 s. 459 an unfair prejudice petition **Note** a ''member'' includes transferees and people taking shares by transmission s. 459(2).
	1.3 The right to vote at share-holders' meetings is depend-ent on the articles and the contract of allotment.

1.4 The right to appoint a proxy see arts. 59 and 60; also s. 37.

2.
(a) 5% of voting shares held

2.1 s. 376(2)(a)
Such members can have a *resolution* put on at an EGM.

(Note this right is also given to not less than 100 members who have paid up an average of £100 in respect of their shares, *i.e.* they represent a *paid up* share capital of at least £10,000 (s. 376(2)(b)).

(b) 5% in *number* of the members, where the "company does not have a share capital" *and* if the Articles are silent on the point.

(b) s. 370(3)
Such members may call a general meeting.

3.1 10% of the *voting* shares held or 10% of paid-up capital

3.1 s. 368(2)
Such members can requisition the directors to hold an EGM.

s. 368(4) if the directors ignore the requisition or refuse to convene the general meeting, such shareholders can convene it and seek from the company, the "reasonable" costs of doing so. (s. 368(6)).

3.2 10% of the *issued* share capital *and* if Articles are silent on the point.

3.2 s. 370(3) allows two ore more shareholders holding not less than one-tenth of the issued share capital to call an EGM.

4. 25% of the voting shares.

4.1 With 25% of the votes, a shareholder *cannot* block an *extraordinary* resolution (s. 378(1)).

4.2 With 25% of the votes, a shareholder *cannot* block a *special* resolution (s. 378(2)).

5.	25% plus 1 or more votes.		This is known as "negative control", *i.e.* it allows a shareholder(s) to block the passing of special and extra-ordinary resolutions. This is very significant because it means that the company's art-icles of association cannot be amended without the approval of such a share-holder or at least some of the shareholders comprising this group.
6.	50% of the voting shares.	6.1	Equal control with the other half of shareholder(s).
		6.2	Such a member does not have the ability to pass *ordinary* resolutions as they require a majority of votes.
7.	50% *plus* at least 1 vote.	7.1	A majority shareholding, *i.e.* the shareholder(s) can pass an ordinary resolution.
		7.2	A majority shareholder must have regard to "equitable considerations" (see *Clemens'* case at paragraph 11.7) in respect of how they exer-cise their vote, etc.
8.	75% of the voting shares.	8.1	Special resolutions can be passed by such share-holders (s. 378(2)) and extraordinary resolutions (s. 378(1)), *i.e.* virtually com-plete control of the company at general meeting including the ability to amend the articles.
		8.2	Regard must be had to *Clemens'* case.

G. Alternatives to Meetings

It may be the case that the directors and or shareholders require the flexibility **13.18** of not having to hold formal meetings because of the delays and difficulties that may be involved in actually getting people around a table in the one room. In practice therefore, the articles provide that the directors can conduct meetings by telephone, video-link or other means of communication.

Alternatively, the articles may provide for written resolutions that are "valid and effectual" as if passed at a meeting. Article 93 table A provides that resolutions in writing signed by all the directors entitled to received notice of a meeting are effective as if a board meeting had been held.

For the shareholders, a similar provision is set out in section 381A of the Companies Act 1985. This is discussed below.

H. Written Resolutions

Section 381A of the Companies Act 1985 allows *private companies* to dis- **13.19** pense with the holding of meetings. A written resolution may be passed by *all* members who would have been entitled to attend and vote at the meeting. The written resolution is prepared and then sent out to be signed by the members (the resolution may possibly be sent in counterparts if there are several members or if there is going to be a delay getting each one to sign it). Once it has been signed by each shareholder it is sent to the company's auditors (who have a week to decide whether in fact a meeting should be held) and is subject to the matters contained in section 381B of the Companies Act 1985 referred to below.

Written resolutions cannot be used to remove a director under section 303 or an auditor under section 386 of the Companies Act 1985.

Section 381B provides that a written resolution is not effective until seven days after a copy of it has been received by the auditor or the auditor certifies that it does not affect him as auditor. If it does "concern" the auditor in that capacity, the auditor may, within seven days, require that a general meeting is held.

In some cases, additional information must be supplied in accordance with Schedule 15A to the Companies Act 1985. For example, Schedule 15A(7) to the Companies Act 1985 requires each shareholder to be given a copy of the proposed service agreement involving a director, if it is a service agreement requiring approval under Companies Act 1985, s. 319 (see paragraph 12.15).

14. Basic Company Finance and Maintenance of Share Capital

A. Equity and Debt

1. Introduction, the Nature of Equity Securities and the Various Classifications of Ordinary Shares

14.1　It goes without saying that, in order to trade and/or provide a service, a private limited company must raise finance. Without money, a company cannot hope to purchase premises and stock, employ staff, and fund projects such as the acquisition of existing businesses in the area of trade with which it is concerned.

Initially, companies raise finance in one of two ways. First, the promoters of the business concerned may subscribe for shares in the company in return for an investment of cash or some other asset. In this way, the promoters become shareholders and owners of the company concerned. The shares with which the promoters are issued represent their units of ownership in the company and their title to those shares is evidenced by the share certificates that they hold. As the company trades and decides to expand its operations (thus requiring extra finance), more shares may be issued by it to existing or new shareholders. Investments of cash or other assets by shareholders in this way represent the company's share capital, which cannot generally be returned to shareholders by the company during its lifetime but rather must be "maintained" (*i.e.* represented in its assets) for the benefit of third-party creditors who trade with the company and provide credit to it and who are entitled to assume that the company does have assets to the nominal value of its issued share capital (see paragraphs 14.26–14.34 for a discussion on maintenance of share capital).

Secondly, a private limited company may borrow money from a bank or some other lending institution under the terms of a loan agreement or "debenture" in order to raise finance. Loans do not confer the status of owner or shareholder on the individual making the advance; that person or, as is usual, bank is a creditor of the company and the monies so advanced are subject to the terms of the loan agreement or debenture. Typically, this contract will provide for the monies to be repaid in full over a period of time or on or before a specified date or on the occurrence of a specified event such as failure by the company to meet an interest payment on time. In this way, creditors are entitled to a return of their money during the lifetime of the company unlike shareholders who, as already noted, generally cannot obtain a return of their capital from the company during its lifetime. It should be noted that it is not only banks and other lending institutions that advance monies to companies in this way. There may be very good legal, commercial and taxation reasons why someone who is a key promoter of the company and working full time in it to earn his living should invest all or some of his money and other assets in it not by way of share capital but by way of loan to the company. Such reasons will become apparent throughout this chapter. At this stage, it is sufficient to note that in many small, private limited companies, those who are the directors and shareholders may have also lent money to the company and therefore be creditors of it in accordance with a loan agreement or debenture.

As the company trades, it will hopefully make a profit. This money pro- **14.2** vides an additional source of finance to the company with which to fund its business generally and expand its operation. However, not all of the profit may be retained in the business of the company in this manner. It may be decided to pay some or all of the profits made to the owners of the company who invested in it by way of shares and thus provided it with its capital. Profits that are distributed to shareholders in this way are referred to as dividends and represent an "income" for them or a "return" on their capital investment. In addition to the receipt of such income profits, shareholders will hope that the value of their shares or capital asset will increase itself as the company trades successfully, expands and adds profits generated to its existing asset base. There may come a time in the future when a shareholder wishes to realise any such capital gain (*i.e.* the difference between the price paid for the shares and their current value). As has been noted already, it is generally not possible for a company to return this capital investment to a shareholder during its lifetime. Instead, the owner of the shares concerned will need to sell or transfer his shares to a third party in order to realise any capital gain. Alternatively, the owner may decide to make a lifetime gift of his shares or leave them on his death by will to a beneficiary. Any sale, gift or transmission of shares may be subject to rights of pre-emption contained in the company's articles of association (see generally Chapter 11) *and* any such transaction may give rise to a charge to tax (see generally Chapter 16). In any event, the new shareholder will step into the shoes of the old shareholder and become entitled to any future income generated by the shares and any future increase in the capital value of them.

Whether or not a company is successful and whether or not it makes a profit or loss, it will be required to pay interest on monies lent to it by its creditors and that are outstanding at any given time if this is an obligation imposed by the loan agreement or debenture. Needless to say, nearly all loan agreements will provide for the payment of interest on monies lent as well as for the eventual repayment of the original sum. In this way, the return or income earned by creditors on monies lent is in some sense guaranteed given that it is not dependant upon the company making profits as is the case for shareholders. The company is bound in accordance with its agreement to make the annual or monthly interest payments. Of course, capital that is lent to a company does not itself increase in value for the bank or the individual creditor concerned because it is not represented in the net worth of the company, which increases as profits are made and operations expand. In view of this, only the initial monies advanced, interest payments due to date and any other costs incurred are paid to the bank or individual creditor concerned when the monies are repaid in full in accordance with the terms of the loan agreement.

The nature of equity securities

14.3   The vast majority of shares issued by private limited companies are ordinary shares. Such shares are sometimes referred to as "equity" or "risk capital" because they represent ownership of and control over a company and carry the real risks that they will generate no income in the form of dividends if no profits are made *and* the capital value of them will never be returned to their owners if, when the life of the company is brought to an end, no assets remain because they have been used in full to meet the obligations of the company to its then existing creditors.

As well as any rights conferred by statute, the rights that attach to any type of shares may be specifically spelt out in the contract between the company issuing them and the new member or "subscriber" when he takes them up but more than likely these rights will be spelt out in the company's articles of association so that any subsequent member taking the shares will be bound by such rights in accordance with section 14 of the Companies Act 1985. The current version of table A articles of association sets out the rights that attach to the ordinary shares issued by any company adopting them for its articles. Whether the rights attaching to a company's ordinary shares derive from statute or its articles, the hallmarks of such shares are as follows:

(a) Ownership of ordinary shares confers control over the affairs of a company by giving voting rights that are usually directly proportionate to the size of the shareholding concerned. Hence, article 54 of table A provides that on a poll vote taken at a meeting of members, every member shall have one vote for every share of which he is a holder. Hence, a shareholder who owns a majority of the ordinary shares currently in issue (*i.e.* 50 per cent plus one share) can pass an ordinary resolution and a shareholder who owns 75 per cent of the ordinary shares currently in issue can pass a special resolution. Obviously, the greater the size of the shareholding, the greater the control over the company's affairs. This position is distorted somewhat if the articles of association provide enhanced voting rights to certain shareholders in certain circumstances (see generally Chapter 12: "*Bushell v. Faith*" clauses).

(b) Ordinary shareholders are entitled to a return on, or income from, their capital investment in the form of a dividend *provided that* such a dividend is declared by ordinary resolution of the company. Any dividend so declared *must not* exceed the amount recommended by the directors (see article 102 of table A). In addition, there are strict statutory controls on the payment of dividends in order to ensure that they are paid out of profits and do not constitute a return of share capital to a shareholder. Hence section 263(1) of the Companies Act 1985 provides that a company shall not make a distribution of its assets to its members except out of profits available for the purpose. Such profits are a company's accumulated, realised profits less its accumulated, realised losses. In view of these restrictions, there is no pre-determined amount that an ordinary shareholder will receive by way of dividend. The risk for such a shareholder here is that the company will never perform well and hence never generate profits available for distribution that the directors feel and the company sanctions can be utilised to make a dividend payment! Conversely, if a company performs extremely well, there is no predetermined limit on the amount that an ordinary shareholder can potentially receive once profits available for distribution are generated. The risk nature of ordinary share capital can sometimes work in the shareholder's favour!

(c) Ordinary shareholders are entitled to a return from the company of their capital invested when the company is wound up and its life is brought to an end. They are not entitled to a return of their capital during its lifetime. When a company is wound up, there is a strict order of entitlement to the money that is raised on the sale of its assets by a liquidator. The reader is referred in this regard to section B.4 of Chapter 15 (Corporate Insolvency: Liquidation). Basically, all creditors of the company must be paid in full before any money is distributed to shareholders. In the vast majority of cases, when a company is wound up it is insolvent or unable to pay its debts in full. This means that it is extremely rare for any money to be left to return to shareholders when a company is wound up. This highlights another real risk for the holder of ordinary share capital.

The various classifications of ordinary shares
A number of concepts and terms have been discussed elsewhere in relation to ordinary shares and share capital generally. For the sake of completeness in relation to the matters covered in this chapter, some of those concepts are discussed below:

(a) *Authorised and issued share capital.* A company's *authorised share* **14.4**
capital as stated in its memorandum of association is the maximum amount of share capital that it may issue at any given time. That proportion of the authorised share capital which has at any time been allotted by the company to shareholders, is referred to as the *issued share capital.* For example, a company may have an authorised share capital of £500,000 but only have issued £400,000 of it leaving it free to issue a further £100,000 without the need to increase its authorised share capital in accordance with section 121 of the Companies Act 1985 and its articles of association. The issued share capital of a company must always be the equivalent to or less than the authorised share capital; it can never exceed it!

(b) *Par or nominal value.* The *par or nominal value* of each share is stated **14.5**
in the memorandum of association and is simply a classification that measures the shareholder's unit of ownership. For example, a company's authorised share capital may be £100,000 divided into 100,000 ordinary shares of £1 each. A shareholder who holds 75,000 of such £1 ordinary shares holds a 75 per cent stake or interest in the company concerned and can pass a special resolution at a members' meeting. This par or nominal value of £1 says

nothing at all about the share's actual or *market value*. The market value of the £1 ordinary share depends upon a variety of factors such as the success and profitability of the company, its asset base and market conditions generally. Naturally, market value will fluctuate over a period of time. The market values of shares in some public limited companies are quoted daily on markets such as the London Stock Exchange. In the case of private limited companies, it will be necessary to obtain market valuations of their shares from the company auditors.

14.6   (c) *Discount*. A private limited company cannot issue shares at a *discount* to their nominal or par value (see Companies Act 1985, s. 100). Hence, when a £1 ordinary share is issued by a company, there is an obligation on the shareholder to provide £1 to the company either now or at some time in the future. In view of this, a company is unable to gift its shares to someone. However, a company is able to issue *partly paid-up shares*. Hence, if the par or nominal share value of a company's shares is £1 each, that company can issue a share for anything under £1 initially but there remains a liability on the shareholder who owns that share to pay the full amount up to £1 when called for by the company and in any event when that company is wound up (see Insolvency Act 1986, s. 74). For example, a £1 ordinary share is issued to X in return for 50p. That £1 ordinary share is said to be partly paid up. There remains a liability on X or anyone to whom he transfers the share to pay the remaining 50p to the company when called for and in any event if the company is wound up. The company cannot issue the £1 ordinary share to X for 50p without further obligation on X in respect of the outstanding 50p as this would be issuing shares at a discount to par or nominal value and section 100(2) of the Companies Act 1985 makes the allottee liable to pay up the discount plus interest in these circumstances.

14.7   (d) *Premium*. A private limited company is able to issue shares at a *premium* to nominal or par value. For example, a £1 ordinary share can be issued for £1.20p or £1.40p, etc. The difference between the par value and the price paid by the new shareholder for the share is referred to as the share premium. Section 130(1) of the Companies Act 1985 provides that this premium must be paid into a share premium account in order to ensure that, save in limited circumstances, it is treated as share capital and maintained for the benefit of the company's creditors. A company may wish to issue shares at a premium to par value because at the time of the proposed issue the market value of its shares is well in excess of the par value. For example, a £1 ordinary share may be worth £4.50 if the company is preforming well and market conditions are healthy. In this case, the company wishing to raise new finance may issue new shares for a price well in excess of the par or nominal value of £1. Of course, a company may be performing so badly that the market value of its shares is well below their par value. For example, a £1 ordinary share may only be worth 50p. In this case, the company concerned could not issue any new shares for anything less than £1 as to do so would amount to issuing shares at a discount to par value (see Companies Act 1985, s. 100, above). If such a company needed to raise new finance, it would have to subdivide its £1 ordinary share into shares of a smaller amount (*e.g.* one £1 ordinary share becoming two 50p ordinary shares) in accordance with section 121 of the Companies Act 1985 and its articles of association and issue new shares with the lower nominal value.

2. THE STATUTORY FRAMEWORK SURROUNDING THE ISSUE OF ORDINARY SHARES BY A PRIVATE LIMITED COMPANY

The power to issue shares is one of the general powers of a company carried out by its directors. Whenever new shares are issued by a private limited company, the position of its existing shareholders cannot help but be affected. The main concern for an existing shareholder is that if new shares, which carry with them an entitlement to vote, are issued to third-party outsiders then that existing shareholder will find his proportionate control over the affairs of the company diluted to some extent. It is clear that unless it is regulated in some way, this power provides directors with an opportunity to issue shares for quite improper purposes such as for the purpose of weakening the control of a particular shareholder over the affairs of the company rather than for the purpose of raising finance. Case law has established that as part of their fiduciary duties to act bona fide for the benefit of the company as a whole, directors must exercise this power for a proper purpose only; namely, to raise finance that is required by the company and not to strengthen or weaken the control of particular shareholders over the affairs of the company (see *Piercy v. Mills* [1920] 1 Ch. 77 and *Hogg v. Cramphorn* [1967] Ch. 254). Nowadays, in addition to common law considerations, the power to issue shares is heavily regulated by statute.

14.8

There are three important provisions of the Companies Act 1985 to take into account when directors exercise their powers to issue new shares in a private limited company. These provisions have been looked at elsewhere but are raised here for the sake of clarity as regards the matters discussed in this chapter.

Alteration of Share Capital (Companies Act 1985, s. 121)

It may be that at the time when the directors wish to issue new shares, all of the company's current authorised share capital is in issue. In this case, it will be necessary to increase the company's authorised share capital by at least the amount of new shares that it is proposed to be issued. Section 121 of the Companies Act 1985 provides that a company may increase its share capital by new shares of such amount as it thinks expedient provided that it is authorised to do so by its articles and provided that it is done by an ordinary resolution of the members in general meeting. For those companies that have adopted table A articles of association, article 32(a) provides the necessary authorisation. The effect of this section is that, where all of a company's share capital is in issue, only a simple majority of the members in general meeting can increase its share capital with a view to the issue of further shares and not the directors themselves. If the members do not pass the requisite ordinary resolution in these circumstances then the directors will be unable to make any further issue of shares.

14.9

Section 123 of the Companies Act 1985 provides that notice of the increased share capital in the prescribed form (form G123) together with a printed copy of the ordinary resolution authorising the increase must be forwarded to the registrar of companies within 15 days of the passing of the resolution. This is one of the very few examples of when a company must file an ordinary resolution with the registrar. Given that any increase in the authorised share capital will necessarily alter the capital clause of the memorandum of association, it is also necessary to file a printed copy of the altered memorandum with the registrar.

Authority to issue shares (Companies Act 1985, s. 80)

14.10   Before the directors of a company are able to exercise the power to issue shares, they must obtain an authority to do so either from an ordinary resolution of the members of the company or from the company's articles of association as provided for in the important section 80 of the Companies Act 1985. For those companies that have adopted table A articles of association, there is no such authority contained in them and therefore the directors must seek an ordinary resolution of the members to authorise any proposed share issue.

The authority given may relate to a particular share issue or it may be general but it must state the maximum amount of shares that may be issued under it and the date on which it will expire. In the case of an authority contained in the company's articles at the time of its original incorporation, the expiry date must be not more than five years from the date of the company's incorporation. In the case of an authority obtained by resolution passed by the company's members, the expiry date must be not more than five years from the date of the resolution. It should be noted that a private limited company is able to dispense with this time-period requirement and give the authority for an indefinite period if an elective resolution is used pursuant to section 80A of the Act.

Authorities of any kind (whether contained in a company's articles or given by ordinary or elective resolution) can be revoked or varied by an ordinary resolution of the members of the company concerned.

A director who contravenes section 80 is liable to fine but the validity of the share issue is not affected.

If an authority is obtained by an ordinary or elective resolution, it must be filed with the registrar of companies within 15 days after it is passed. Again, this is one of the few examples of when a company must file an ordinary resolution with the registrar.

Pre-emption rights on the issue of shares (Companies Act 1985, s. 89)

14.11   It was noted above that the major concern of existing shareholders whenever directors propose to issue new shares is the threat of dilution of their own stakes in the company and consequent reduction in control over its affairs. Section 89 of the Companies Act 1985 provides that any new shares, which it is proposed to be issued, must first be offered to existing shareholders on the same or more favourable terms in proportion that is as nearly as practicable equal to the proportion of existing shares held by them. Section 89 thereby creates "pre-emption" rights over new shares that are to be issued thus conferring on existing shareholders an opportunity to maintain their current proportion of the company's entire share capital and thus their proportionate influence or control by taking up their rights in respect of the shares to be issued. Only if rights of pre-emption are not taken up can the new shares be issued to a third party. These pre-emption rights only apply to the issue of shares in exchange wholly for cash. If the new shares are to be issued wholly or partly for non-cash consideration then the provisions of Section 89 do not apply and existing shareholders do not have rights of pre-emption.

The rights of pre-emption contained in section 89 can be excluded by a private limited company in one of two ways:

(a) Section 91 of the Companies Act 1985 provides that a private limited company can exclude the provisions in its memorandum or articles of association.

(b) Section 95 of the Act 1985 provides that where the directors of the company are generally authorised to issue shares for the purposes of section 80, they can be given power to issue the shares concerned as if section 89 of the Companies Act did not apply to that issue by way of special resolution of the members of the company.

For those companies which have adopted table A articles of association, there is no provision excluding section 89 pre-emption rights and therefore they may only be disapplied by such a company by way of special resolution of the members. A copy of any special resolution which disapplies pre-emption rights will have to be filed with the registrar of companies within 15 days of being passed. It should be noted that as well as excluding the pre-emption rights on share issues, it is possible for a private limited company to increase those rights by way of a provision in its articles of association (*e.g.* it may be prudent to extend pre-emption rights to cover *all* new share issues and not just those in exchange wholly for cash consideration).

If there is a contravention of section 89, the company and every officer who authorised or permitted the contravention are jointly and severally liable to compensate any person to whom an offer should have been made under that section for any loss, damage, costs or expenses that that person has sustained or incurred.

Once all of the statutory provisions have been complied with, directors will be able to issue the new shares to the proposed allottees. This power will usually be exercised in board meeting following the passing of any requisite members' resolutions in general meeting of the company or by the written resolution procedure. Section 88(2) of the Companies Act 1985 requires the company to deliver to the registrar of companies within one month after any share issue, a return of allotments (form G88(2)) which states the number and nominal amount of the shares, the names and addresses of the allottees, and the amount (if any) paid or due and payable on each share. If the shares are issued wholly or partly in exchange for non-cash consideration, a copy of the written contract of allotment must also be sent to the registrar or if that contract was not reduced to writing then particulars of it on the prescribed form should be forwarded in its place.

3. OTHER SECURITIES ISSUED BY PRIVATE LIMITED COMPANIES

There is nothing to stop a company from creating different classes of shares with different rights if it is able to do so in accordance with its articles of

14.12

association. Article 2 of table A provides that any share may be issued with such rights or restrictions as the company may by ordinary resolution determine. As mentioned previously, the rights and restrictions attaching to any class of shares may be detailed in the contract of allotment between the company and the new shareholder when the shares are issued or more likely in the company's articles of association. While table A articles of association envisage only one class of shares with the same rights attaching to all, there is nothing to prevent a company, which has adopted table A articles, from determining that new shares will be issued with different rights and/or altering its articles to specifically include the rights of a new class of shares.

Some classes of shares other than straight forward ordinary shares are fairly common in private limited companies:

Preference shares

14.13   Typically, a preference share will confer on the holder of it a right to an annual dividend of a fixed amount that must be paid before any dividend is paid to other shareholders. Preference shares are said to be "cumulative" in that if a dividend cannot be paid to the holders of them in any given year because profits are not available for distribution then that dividend payment is rolled over into the next year and so on until payment in full. In addition, it is usual to provide that when the company is eventually wound up, the holders of preference shares are entitled to a return of their capital from the company in priority to all other members. Of course, as with other members, preference shareholders receive no payment of capital on a winding up until all existing creditors are repaid in full. Usually, preference shares are not "participating" in the sense that once the holders of them have received their fixed dividends, they do not take a further share of any profits distributed to all other members and once their capital is returned to them on a winding up, they do not share in any surplus assets distributed to all other contributories. In addition, it is usually the case that preference shareholders are not entitled to vote except in respect of matters that affect them as a class of shareholders and then only in accordance with the rights and procedures conferred in the company's articles.

Redeemable shares

14.14   Generally, a company cannot repurchase its own shares because this would amount to a return of share capital to members during the company's lifetime and such capital must generally be maintained for the benefit of its creditors. (See section 143(1) of the Companies Act 1985). However, section 159(1) of the Companies Act 1985 provides that a company may, if authorised to do so by its articles, issue shares that are to be redeemed at the option of the company or the shareholder. For those companies that have adopted table A articles of association, article 3 provides the requisite authorisation.

In effect, redeemable shares represent a temporary shareholding in a company with membership coming to an end when the shares are "redeemed" (*i.e.* repurchased by the company) in accordance with the terms of redemption set out in the company's articles. Redeemable shares may only be issued at time when there are some issued shares that are not redeemable and the redeemable shares themselves may not be repurchased unless they are fully paid up. Shares that are redeemed are treated as cancelled and the amount of the company's issued share capital is reduced by the nominal value of the redeemed shares.

Generally, redeemable shares may only be redeemed out of distributable profits of the company or the proceeds of a fresh issue of shares made for the purposes of the redemption (see Companies Act 1985, s. 160). However, a private limited company is able to redeem shares out of capital provided a strict statutory procedure is followed. This procedure for payments out of capital applies generally whenever a private company is able to purchase its own shares whether such shares are issued as redeemable or not and is set out in some detail at paragraph 14.30 below.

4. THE NATURE AND CLASSIFICATION OF DEBT

In most cases, when money is lent to a company, the arrangement is subject to the terms of a written loan agreement. Loan agreements are sometimes referred to as "debentures", especially where the monies advanced represent some or all of an individual's long-term commitment or investment in the company (as is the case with a director/shareholder who, for whatever reason, decides to invest some of his money in the company by way of debt capital, *i.e.* a loan rather than in the form of share capital). **14.15**

The loan agreement will impose various obligations on the company borrowing the money. In particular:

(a) There will be an obligation on the company to pay interest at a certain rate on the outstanding balance of monies advanced at regular intervals; and

(b) There will be an obligation on the company to repay the capital monies advanced on or before a specified date or alternatively by way of instalments at regular intervals. In addition, there will be an obligation to repay the monies on the occurrence of certain defined events (*e.g.* failure to meet an interest payment on time) and in any event when repayment in full is demanded by the lender at any time during the currency of the loan.

In this way, a loan agreement confers some comfort on the lender in that he has contractual entitlements to annual interest or income from the monies advanced and to the return of those monies at any time. Of course, whether or not the lender is able to enforce these contractual rights effectively very much depends on the company's ability to pay. It is the possibility that at some stage the company will be unable to meet its contractual obligations that leads many lenders to insist that additional clauses are inserted into the loan agreement or debenture that provide them with "security" over the company's assets for the monies advanced. In effect, the company charges or mortgages its assets to the lender under the terms of the loan agreement and the lender is able to take action to sell those assets or "enforce his security" if the company fails to meet payments to the lender as required under the agreement. The various types of security taken by a lender over the assets of a company are discussed at paragraphs 14.16–14.20.

Classification of debt
Depending on the terms of the loan agreement, debt can be classified as follows: **14.16**

(a) *Unsecured debt*. This means that the lender of money or the provider of credit has no security over the assets of the company in respect of the debt. Hence, if the company concerned was to fail to repay the monies advanced and any interest was agreed would be paid, the lender merely has a claim or claims for breach of contract. The lender is at liberty to pursue the matter through the Courts and obtain judgment for the debt against the company but whether that judgment can be effectively enforced very much depends upon the company's ability to pay its unsecured creditors at that time see generally in this regard Chapter 15, section B: Liquidation. The lender cannot take action himself to sell the assets of the company and recoup payment. It is common for trade suppliers to provide reputable or well-known companies with unsecured credit when supplying goods and stock in trade. For example, the supply contract may provide for payment in full for the goods delivered to the company within three months of the invoice date. It should be appreciated that, though the debt owed to the trade supplier is unsecured, the terms of the supply contract may include a valid retention of title clause that reserves title in the goods supplied by the supplier until payment in full for them is obtained from the company.

14.17   (b) *Debt with quasi-security*. This means that the obligations of the company under the loan agreement are in some way guaranteed by a third party. It is extremely common for the directors of small, private limited companies to be required to guarantee the debts and obligations contained in loan agreements with banks and other lending institutions. Usually, the effect of such a guarantee is that the director concerned becomes personally liable to meet all of the obligations of the company in the event that the company breaches any of them under the terms of the principal loan agreement. Such guarantees reduce the effectiveness of the limited liability principle when the director giving the guarantee is also a shareholder of the company concerned.

14.18   (c) *Secured debt*. This means that in accordance with the terms of the loan agreement, the company charges or mortgages some or all of its assets to the lender of the monies. If the company breaches the loan agreement and, in particular, if it fails to pay or repay monies when required to do so, the lender is able to enforce his security by appointing a receiver or administrative receiver to take control of the charged assets, sell them and apply the proceeds primarily in discharging the company's outstanding debts to the lender.

There are numerous types of security that can be created in a loan agreement or debenture. In particular the following two types of security are very common:

14.19   *Fixed charges*. These are mortgages or charges over specific assets such as freehold land, leasehold property, plant and machinery. If an asset is subject to a fixed charge, it cannot be dealt with (*i.e.* sold) by the company without the consent of the lender.

14.20   *Floating charges*. Typically, these will be charges over all of the constantly changing assets and undertaking of the company concerned whatever they may be from time to time. The floating charge leaves the company free to deal in the assets that are subject to such security (*i.e.* it can sell them and replace them with new ones). However, the floating charge is said to "crystallise" and become a fixed charge over assets held by the company on the occurrence of certain events. The most important events that trigger crystallisation are set out in the loan agreement or debenture; for example, when the lender appoints a receiver or administrative receiver to enforce his security in accordance with the terms of the agreement because the company has failed to repay the monies advanced to the lender when due or demanded. Once the floating charge has crystallised the company is no longer free to deal in the assets that are subject to this security and they will be available to the lender's administrative receiver to sell for the benefit of his appointee and certain other creditors of the company.

Banks and other lending institutions will rarely be satisfied with mere contractual rights to the payment of interest and the repayment of capital monies advanced at any time. In practice, they may well insist on taking both fixed and floating charges over the assets of the company and personal guarantees from its directors. In view of this, debt advanced on these terms is often referred to as "secured capital." In addition to the security obtained via the terms of the loan agreement and ancillary guarantees, creditors with security over the company's assets also enjoy the added comfort of knowing that in the event that the company is wound up and its life brought to an end, they are entitled generally to be paid in full before anything is paid to the company's ordinary unsecured creditors who in turn are entitled to be paid in full before any capital is returned to shareholders. The reader is referred to Chapter 15, section B: Liquidation generally in this regard.

5. The Statutory Framework and Other Regulation Surrounding Borrowing by a Private Limited Company

It is common for a company to include express powers to borrow money   **14.21** and grant security over its assets in the objects clause of the memorandum of association. This puts beyond doubt any question that an act of borrowing and granting security over the company's assets in favour of a lender may be *ultra vires* the company. In fact, the lender has nothing to fear from the *ultra vires* principle because section 35(1) of the Companies Act 1985 now provides that the validity of an act done by a company shall not be called into question on the ground of lack of capacity by reason of anything in the company's memorandum. Nevertheless, in practice lenders are best advised to check the objects clause of the memorandum of association of the company to ensure that the proposed borrowings are *intra vires* the company.

The exercise of the power to borrow money and grant security is governed by the company's articles of association. For those companies that have adopted table A articles of association, the directors will exercise the power in accordance with their general right to exercise all the powers of the company under article 70. Some companies incorporate a special article that specifically declares that the directors are able to borrow money up to any amount and charge the assets of the company as security for such borrowings. Other companies incorporate a special article that actually restricts the directors in the exercise of their power to borrow to a certain specified sum and any borrowings in excess of that amount are required to be sanctioned by the members of the company in general meeting.

14.22   A prudent lender will carry out a number of investigations in relation to the company seeking the loan before entering into the agreement:

(a) As stated earlier, although this is not strictly necessary, a lender is best advised to check the company's constitutional documents to ensure that it has a power to borrow money and grant security over its assets and that the directors are able to exercise this power free from any limitation.

(b) an up-to-date search against the company should be obtained from the registrar of companies and the lender should check that those directors and/or secretary who are to commit the company to the loan agreement are validly appointed and continuing in office. Original directors appear on form G10 and any subsequent appointments and resignations appear on form G288. By virtue of section 36(4) of the Companies Act 1985, a document that is signed by a director and the secretary or by two directors and expressed to be executed by the company, has the same effect as if executed under the company's common seal.

(c) The search against the company will also reveal details of any prior charges in its charges register. If a prior charge has been discharged, a memorandum of satisfaction (form M403a) should appear in the register. If a prior charge is undischarged, the lender will need to assess the effect of any such charge on the value of the security that he is proposing to take. Where there are numerous charges over the same assets, there is a strict order of priority, the detail of which is beyond the scope of this book. In practice, problems may arise where there is a competing fixed and floating charge over the same assets. Generally, the fixed charge will prevail even if created after the floating charge *unless* the loan agreement or debenture which creates the floating charge prohibits the creation of later fixed charges ranking in priority to or equal with it *and* the subsequent fixed chargee has "notice" of this prohibition when he takes his charge (what constitutes notice is doubtful to say with certainty; it may amount to the prohibition being included in the particulars of the floating charge that are delivered to the registrar of companies at the time of its creation and thus appearing in the company's register of charges at Companies House). Copies of all charges revealed on the company search can be obtained from the company's registered office and a prudent lender may wish to investigate the terms of them. If any undischarged floating charges are revealed, the lender will require the directors to confirm that no events that trigger crystallisation have as yet occurred. In practice, a prior ranking charge over the company's assets may be unacceptable to a bank or other lending institution. The lender concerned may insist that the debt secured by the prior ranking charge is to be subordinated to the monies to be advanced by it or that such debt is converted into equity if this is at all feasible.

(d) The search against the company at Companies House will also reveal whether an insolvency procedure has been commenced against the company or whether any prior charge-holder has commenced action to enforce his security. The appointments of administrative receivers, administrators and liquidators must be notified to the registrar of companies who registers the relevant details against the company concerned. Of course, there may be a delay between the appointment of such an insolvency officer and the appearance of the notice on the register and therefore the complete up-to-date picture can never be guaranteed. A prudent lender may check with the court that no winding-up petitions have been lodged against the company concerned immediately prior to entering into the loan agreement.

(e) All lenders will need to check the financial position of the company, which is revealed on the search made against it. This will entail reviewing the last sets of accounts with a view to verifying the financial standing of the company and its ability to meet the proposed interest payments and capital repayments.

Once the loan agreement is entered into there are certain registration requirements to be complied with: **14.23**

(a) Section 395 of the Companies Act 1985 provides that charges to which that section applies are void against the liquidator or administrator and any creditor of the company, unless the prescribed particulars of the charge together with the instrument by which the charge is created are delivered to the registrar of companies for registration within 21 days of the date of the charge's creation. Section 396 of the Act sets out the charges to which section 395 applies and these include floating charges and fixed charges over land, book debts and goodwill.

(b) It is the duty of the company to forward the prescribed particulars (contained in form M395) and the actual charge instrument to the registrar within 21 days of execution of the charge but such registration may be effected by any person interested in it. Because of the effects of section 395 on the lender's security if registration is not effected properly, it is common for him to effect the registration.

(c) The registrar will register the details of the charge that are contained in the prescribed particulars (date of creation, amount secured by charge, short particulars of property charged, person entitled to the charge) and issue a certificate of registration. The original charge instrument is returned to the company.

(d) If the charge is not registered within the 21-day period the Court may, on the application of the company or a person interested, order that the time for registration shall be extended but this is on such terms and conditions as seem to the court just and expedient (see Companies Act 1985, s. 404). The court will only exercise its powers in this regard if it is satisfied that the omission to register the charge within the time limit was accidental or due to inadvertence or some other sufficient cause or is not prejudicial to creditors or shareholders or it is just and equitable to do so. In particular, the court will be keen to ensure that the rights acquired by innocent third party creditors are not disturbed and will impose conditions to ensure that this is the case.

(e) Section 395 of the Companies 1985 has a very dramatic effect on a lender's security if the charges are not registered with the registrar and the company goes into liquidation or administration. If this is the case, the lender cannot enforce his security against the company's assets and instead he ranks as an ordinary unsecured creditor to paid out after those with valid security over the company's assets have been paid in full. Until such time as the company goes into liquidation or administration, the lender can enforce his security against the company; section 395(2) of the Act guarantees the lender's contractual rights to repayment of the capital monies advanced, which become immediately repayable when the charge itself becomes void. If a charge does become void under section 395, the lender cannot enforce it against a third-party creditor of the company who may acquire rights over the charged assets.

(f) Once the debt which is secured by the charge is discharged a statutory declaration in the prescribed form (form M403a) should be submitted to the registrar who will enter a memorandum of satisfaction on the register.

(g) The company itself is required to keep a register of its charges at its registered office in accordance with section 407 of the Companies Act 1985 and this together with copies of the instruments creating the charges must be open to inspection of any creditor or member of the company without fee during business hours in accordance with section 408 of the Act.

(h) Finally, if a lender takes a charge over land owned by the company then this will have to be registered as appropriate at H.M. Land Registry for registered land or the Land Charges Department for unregistered land.

6. A BRIEF COMPARISON BETWEEN EQUITY AND DEBT

14.24   It was stated earlier that those who promote a company and work full time in it to earn a living may have a choice as to whether to invest their money in the company in the form of shares or in the form of a loan or both. The position of a shareholder and the position of a creditor or debenture holder are very different in numerous ways:

(a) Shareholders are members of the company and as owners of it they have the ability to control its affairs through the exercise of votes at meetings of members. The right to vote at meetings of members is usually conferred on shareholders by a company's articles of association. Article 54 of table A confers on each member of the company one vote for every one share held on a poll taken at a members' meeting. In contrast, creditors of the company or debenture holders are not members and do not ordinarily have any right to vote at meetings.

(b) Shareholders only receive a return on their investment in the form of a dividend if the company generates profits available for distribution through its business activities. In contrast, debenture holders will have a contractual entitlement to yearly or monthly interest on the monies advanced and outstanding at any given time. This interest must be paid by the company whether or not profits are generated from its business activities. The position in relation to income generated from equity and debt serves to highlight the risk nature of share capital as opposed to the relatively secure nature of loan capital. Of course, if the company performs well and generates profits then there is no pre-determined limit on the amount of dividends which can be distributed.

Dividends and interest payments made by a company are subject to different taxation treatments. In particular, as far as the company is concerned, a payment of debenture interest is treated ordinarily as a charge on income that is deductible from its profits before those profits are charged to corporation tax whereas a payment of a dividend is treated as neither a charge on income nor a business expense and so cannot be deducted from its profits before they are charged to corporation tax. In view of this, it is generally considered more tax effective for a company to distribute income by way of debenture interest rather than by way of dividends to shareholders. However, it must be appreciated that taxation savings can not be the only reason for structuring the capital of a company in any given way. It may be difficult to obtain loans from banks and other lending institutions if the promoters of the company have invested all of their money as loan capital with first ranking security over the company's assets!

(c) Share capital invested by members must be maintained for the benefit of the company's creditors throughout its lifetime. This means that ordinarily a company cannot repurchase its shares from members. Creditors are entitled to assume that the nominal value of the share capital of the company will remain represented in its asset base for its lifetime when they trade with it because this is the fund that will be used to repay some or all of their debts if the company is to be wound up. There are some statutory exceptions to this rule and these will be discussed in more detail in paragraphs 14.26–14.34. In contrast, a debenture holder will have a contractual entitlement to the return of monies advanced on the occurrence of specified events at any time during the lifetime of the company.

(d) In the event of a company being wound up and its life brought to an end, there is a strict order of entitlement to the company's assets. The reader is referred to "Chapter 15: section B: Corporate Insolvency: Liquidations" for more detail. Generally, creditors with security over a company's assets are repaid in full before ordinary, unsecured creditors who in turn are repaid in full before any capital is returned to shareholders. The position of equity and debt on a winding up serves to highlight again the risk nature of share capital as opposed to the secure nature of loan capital, particularly where the loan capital is supported by security over the assets of the company.

14.25   The distinction between equity and debt is sometimes blurred when a company issues securities with a variety of rights and entitlements. For example, preference shares usually confer on the holders a right to a fixed dividend or annual income that is not unlike the status of debenture interest save that a preference dividend cannot be paid if there are no profits available for distribution (in which case the dividend would be rolled over into the next year and so on). In addition, preference shares usually confer on the holder a right to have his capital repaid before any other members receive their capital when the company is wound up. Hence, the preference shareholder has priority over the ordinary shareholder on a winding up as does a debenture holder. However, it must be remembered that a preference shareholder is not in the same secure position of such a debenture holder on a winding up as *all* creditors (including unsecured trade creditors) must be paid in full before *any* capital of whatsoever nature (including preference share capital) is returned to shareholders in accordance with their rights under the company's articles of association. Finally, given their preferential status as to dividends and return of capital on a winding up, preference shares do not normally carry an entitlement to vote at members' meetings as is the case for debenture holders. Although the distinction is sometimes blurred, it remains a crucial one in many cases; preference shares are share capital and not debt.

B. Maintenance of Share Capital

1. INTRODUCTION: GENERAL PROHIBITION ON THE REDUCTION OF SHARE CAPITAL

14.26   It is a long established principle of company law that no part of a company's share capital can be returned by that company to its members during the company's lifetime unless it is authorised by statute. Share capital must be maintained (*i.e.* represented in the assets of the company) for the benefit of those who trade with the company throughout its lifetime. Those who trade with the company and provide it with credit are entitled to assume that the pool of assets represented by the nominal value of the share capital fund will remain in tact and be available for distribution to them to settle their debts in whole or in part when the company is wound up and its life brought to an end. In addition, shareholders in the company are entitled to assume that its capital will be used for the purposes defined in its objects clause and not for any unlawful or improper purpose. Consequently, a company may only part with money to its shareholders by making a payment of profit (*i.e.* dividend). We have already seen that there are strict statutory controls on the payment of dividends by a company in order to ensure that they are paid out of profits available for distribution and not capital.

The maintenance of share capital rule has been the subject of some fairly complex statutory exceptions. Section 135(1) of the Companies Act 1985 provides that a company can reduce its share capital in any way by special resolution of its members provided it is authorised to do so by its articles and the reduction is confirmed by the court. For those companies which have adopted table A articles of association, article 34 provides the requisite authorisation. The section is fairly wide ranging as it entitles a company to reduce its share capital "in anyway." However, the involvement of the court is an essential ingredient in a reduction of capital of this kind and it will be concerned to ensure that the interests of creditors are adequately protected in deciding whether or not to confirm the proposals. The court has power to confirm the reduction on "such terms as it thinks fit" (see Companies Act 1985, s. 137(1)). In practice, the use of this procedure is often reserved for fairly complicated rearrangements of share capital or the extinguishing of share capital no longer represented in the diminishing asset base of the company concerned.

2. PURCHASE BY A PRIVATE LIMITED COMPANY OF ITS OWN SHARES:
COMPANIES ACT 1985, ss. 159–181

One of the consequences of the maintenance of share capital rule is that generally a company cannot purchase its own shares from its existing shareholders (and it cannot agree to subscribe for new shares in itself). This rule, as established in *Trevor v. Whitworth* (1887) 12 App. Cas. 409, has been given statutory authority in section 143 of the Companies Act 1985. The rule itself is subject to statutory exceptions which result in a company being able to reduce its share capital without the necessity of implementing a court approved reduction in accordance with section 135 of the Act.   **14.27**

First, it has already been noted that a company can issue redeemable shares provided it is authorised to do so by its articles (see Companies Act 1985, s. 159). When these shares come to be redeemed, the company is in effect returning capital to shareholders during its lifetime. As previously stated, strict statutory controls exist in relation to the way in which a company is permitted to finance the redemption. Generally, a company can only use distributable profits or the proceeds of a fresh issue of shares to finance the redemption (see Companies Act 1985, s. 160). If the company's distributable profits are used to finance the redemption, then capital must be maintained and the amount by which the company's share capital is diminished on redemption must be transferred to the "capital redemption reserve." Here, it must be maintained in much the same way as share capital and treated as a liability to shareholders which is not to be reduced until the company is wound up (Companies Act 1985, s. 170). If the proceeds of a fresh issue of shares are used to finance the redemption, then the share capital which is diminished is effectively replaced by the newly contributed capital.

In addition, a private company can redeem its shares out of capital provided it is authorised to do so in its articles (article 35 of table A provides such authorisation) and a strict statutory procedure is followed. This procedure is the same as that to be followed when a company purchases its own shares of any type out of capital (whether they are issued as redeemable or not) and is set out in detail at paragraph 14.30 below. Shares that are redeemed are treated as cancelled and the amount of the company's issued share capital is reduced accordingly (Companies Act 1985, s. 160(4)).

14.28   Secondly, a company is able to purchase its own shares whether they are issued as redeemable or not provided it is authorised to do so by its articles (Companies Act 1985, s. 162). For those companies that have adopted table A articles of association, article 35 provides the necessary authorisation. One of the purposes of this wide-ranging exception to the general rule is to create what may be much-needed markets in the shares of private limited companies. For example, it may be in the best interests of the company as a whole for a dissident shareholder to leave the company and yet no market can be found for his shares either in the shape of existing shareholders or third parties. Additionally, it may be necessary for an existing shareholder to sell his shares to meet a pressing liability and yet again no market can be found for them. Given the threat to the maintenance of share capital and the consequential risks for those who trade with the company and provide it with credit, the purchase or "buy-back" of shares by a company is subject to a strict and fairly complex statutory procedure:

(a) The shares to be bought back must be fully paid-up (Companies Act 1985, s. 59(3)). After the buy-back is complete, those shares are cancelled and the issued share capital of the company is reduced accordingly (Companies Act 1985, s. 160(4)). The amount of the company's authorised share capital remains unaltered. Further, after the buy-back is complete, there must remain at least one member of the company holding a share(s) other than shares that are issued as redeemable (Companies Act 1985, s. 162(3)).

(b) Generally, the shares in question must be bought back out of distributable profits of the company or out of the proceeds of a fresh issue of shares (Companies Act 1985, s. 160). If the company's distributable profits are used to finance the buy-back, then capital must be maintained and the amount by which the company's share capital is diminished on buy-back must be transferred to the "capital redemption reserve." Here it must be maintained in much the same way as share capital and treated as a liability to shareholders not to be reduced until the company is wound up (Companies Act 1985, s. 170). If the proceeds of a fresh issue of shares are used to finance the buy-back, then the share capital which is diminished is effectively replaced by the newly contributed capital.

14.29   (c) Section 164(1) of the Companies Act 1985 provides that a buy-back of shares by a company "off-market" (*i.e.* not on a recognised stock exchange, as will be the case in relation to a private limited company) is only permissible if it is in pursuance of a contract that is approved in advance in accordance with that section of the Act. Section 164(2) of the Companies Act 1985 provides that the terms of the proposed contract must be authorised by a special resolution of the company before the contract is entered into. The shares that are to be bought back must not be voted; if they are, the resolution is not effective if it would not have been passed without those votes (Companies Act 1985, s. 164(5)).

The proposed contract or a written memorandum of its terms must be available for inspection by members of the company both at the company's registered office for not less than 15 days ending with the date of the meeting at which the resolution is passed and at the meeting itself (Companies Act 1985, s. 164(6)). This latter requirement will reduce the effectiveness of any efforts made by the members of the company to consent to the meeting that is held to pass the special resolution being so held on short notice. Of course, the resolution to approve the contract may be adopted by the company by way of written resolution pursuant to section 381A of the Act in which case a copy of the proposed contract would need to be circulated to each member before or at the time that the resolution is supplied to him.

Once the shares are bought back, there are certain administrative matters to be dealt with. Section 169 of the Companies Act 1985 requires the company to submit a return in the prescribed form (form G169) within 28 days of the shares bought back being delivered to it, which states the number and nominal value of those shares and the date on which they were delivered to the company. In addition, a copy of the special resolution approving the contract for the buy back will have to be delivered to the registrar. In accordance with section 169(4), the company must keep a copy of the contract for the purchase of the shares or a memorandum of its terms for 10 years from completion of the purchase of all the shares at its registered office.

(d) Section 171(1) of the Companies Act 1985 provides that a private limited company can make a payment for the purchase of its shares out of capital (*i.e.* "otherwise than out of its distributable profits or the proceeds of a fresh issue of shares") if it is authorised to do so by its articles. Article 35 of table A provides the requisite authorisation. However, if a private limited company is to use its capital in this way then certain procedures must be followed in addition to those mentioned immediately above. The procedures to be followed for payments out of capital also apply where a private limited company makes a payment out of capital for the redemption of any redeemable shares issued by it.   **14.30**

Section 173(2) of the Companies Act 1985 provides that the payment out of capital must itself be approved by a special resolution of the company. In addition, section 173(3) of the Act provides that the directors of the company must make a statutory declaration of solvency; namely, that having made full inquiry into the affairs and prospects of the company, they have formed the opinion that there will be no grounds on which the company could be found unable to pay its debts immediately following the date on which the payment out of capital is proposed to be made and that the company will be able to continue to carry on business as a going concern (and will accordingly be able to pay its debts as they fall due) throughout the year immediately following that date. Section 173(5) of the Act provides that this statutory declaration must have annexed to it a report by the company's auditors, which verifies the opinion expressed by the directors after having made enquiries into the company's state of affairs.

The special resolution approving the payment out of capital must be passed on or within the week immediately following the date on which the directors make the required statutory declaration and the payment out of capital must be made between five and seven weeks after the date of the resolution (Companies Act 1985, s. 174(1)). The shares to be bought back must not be voted on the special resolution (Companies Act 1985, s. 174(2)). The statutory declaration and auditors' report must be available for inspection at the meeting at which the resolution is passed (Companies Act 1985, s. 174(4)).

Within five weeks of the date on which the resolution was passed, any member who did not consent to or vote in favour of the resolution and any creditor of the company may apply to the court for cancellation of the resolution (Companies Act 1985, s. 176). The court can make an order on such terms and conditions as it thinks fit either confirming or cancelling the resolution (Companies Act 1985, s. 177).

Finally, there are certain additional administrative and publicity matters to be dealt with in relation to payments out of capital. Within the week immediately following the date of the resolution, the company must publish a notice in the *London Gazette* giving details of the payment out of capital and stating that any creditor of the company may apply to court for an order prohibiting the payment under section 176 of the Companies Act 1985 within five weeks of the date of the resolution (section 175 of the Companies Act). An additional notice should be published in a national newspaper or sent to each of the company's creditors. Together with a copy of the special resolution, the company must deliver a copy of the directors' statutory declaration and auditors' report to the registrar of companies (Companies Act 1985, s. 175(5)) and keep a copy of the same at its registered office for five weeks after the date of the resolution (Companies Act 1985, s. 175(6)).

3. FINANCIAL ASSISTANCE BY A PRIVATE LIMITED COMPANY FOR THE ACQUISITION OF ITS OWN SHARES: COMPANIES ACT 1985, SS. 151–158

14.31 As well as the general prohibition on a company's ability to purchase its own shares, it is also generally unlawful for a company to assist financially anyone to purchase its shares or shares in its holding company. This general prohibition, which again is subject to statutory exceptions, originates from the maintenance of share capital rule. If a company assists anyone to purchase its shares then, as will be seen from the examples of financial assistance given below, the capital assets of that company may well be at risk.

Section 151(1) of the Companies Act 1985 makes it unlawful for a company or any of its subsidiaries to give "financial assistance" directly or indirectly for the purpose of an acquisition of its shares by any person before or at the same time as the acquisition takes place. In addition, section 151(2) of the Act makes it unlawful for a company or any of its subsidiaries to give "financial assistance" directly or indirectly for the purpose of reducing or discharging a liability incurred by any person who has already acquired shares in the company. If the company breaches section 151 it is liable to a fine and every officer in default is liable to imprisonment or a fine or both (Companies Act 1985, s. 151(3)). These criminal sanctions are not the only ramifications for breach of the section; any contract entered into for the acquisition of the company's shares that contains the provision of illegal financial assistance is generally void for illegality (property transferred is irrecoverable and guarantees/security unenforceable) although severance of the illegal part may be possible in certain circumstances leaving the remainder enforceable. In addition, directors procuring the company to enter into illegal transactions are clearly in breach of their fiduciary duties.

Section 152 of the Companies Act 1985 provides that financial assistance includes, *inter alia*, such things as financial assistance given by way of gift, guarantee, security, release and loan. Examples are helpful:

(a) *Gift:* ABC Ltd makes a gift of £100 to P who acquires 100 £1 **14.32** ordinary shares at par in ABC Ltd with the money. Clearly, ABC Ltd has assisted P to buy the shares and its assets have been reduced accordingly; it appears that P has contributed £100 worth of share capital which in fact, ABC Ltd has paid for itself!

(b) *Guarantee:* P wishes to acquire shares in ABC Ltd using the proceeds of a loan to be taken out with his bank. ABC Ltd agrees to guarantee P's indebtedness to his bank and P uses the monies advanced to acquire the shares in ABC Ltd. Clearly, if P defaults on his loan repayments to his bank, ABC Ltd will be required to repay the loan in accordance with the terms of the guarantee. Again, the assets of ABC Ltd are at risk if the guarantee is enforced; the company would have to pay for P's contributed share capital.

(c) *Security:* Assume that the facts are as in the guarantee example given above but instead of actually guaranteeing P's indebtedness to his bank, ABC Ltd allows its assets to be charged to the bank as security for P's loan. If P defaults on his loan payments in this case, the bank will be entitled to sell ABC Ltd's assets to repay the loan. Again, the assets of ABC Ltd are at risk.

(d) *Release:* P acquires shares in ABC Ltd using the proceeds of a loan taken out with his bank. Once P has subscribed for the shares, ABC Ltd discharges the loan on P's behalf thus releasing him from his debt. The end result is that ABC Ltd's assets have been used to fund P's share capital contribution. Like the examples of financial assistance given by way of guarantee or security detailed above, this is an example of indirect assistance given to a third party.

(e) *Loan:* P wishes to acquire shares in ABC Ltd. Either ABC Ltd or one of its subsidiary companies funds the purchase price by making a loan to P. Clearly, if P were to default on his loan repayments then it is only ABC Ltd's assets (or those of its subsidiary) that have been used to fund P's share capital contribution. Further, if P was to acquire his shares using his own cash, it would be unlawful for ABC Ltd to lend P money after he has subscribed for the shares if it were given for the purposes of restoring P's financial position and thus funding the acquisition of the shares. This last example is one of financial assistance occurring after the acquisition of shares has taken place pursuant to section 151(2) of the Companies Act 1985.

Section 152 of the Companies Act 1985 also provides that financial assistance includes "any other financial assistance" given by a company whose net assets are materially reduced by it or that has no net assets. The result of this helpful definition(!) is that financial assistance has no precise or technical meaning. The definition has the potential to be widely construed and it is essential to analyse the facts of each transaction to decide if the sections have been offended. In the case of a private limited company which has doubts about any transaction, it may be wise to use the relaxation procedure provided for in sections 155–158 of the Companies Act 1985, which permits private companies to give financial assistance provided certain conditions are met and steps are followed (see paragraph 14.34 below).

14.33   There are two important statutory exceptions to the general prohibition on the giving of financial assistance. The first exception applies to both public and private companies and is contained in section 153 of the Companies Act 1985. This section provides that a company is not prohibited from giving financial assistance if its principal purpose in giving that assistance is not to give it for the purpose of any such acquisition or the giving of the assistance for the purpose of the acquisition is but an incidental part of some larger purpose of the company. In either case, the assistance must be given in good faith in the interests of the company. This principal and larger purpose exception has been the subject of judicial interpretation (see *Brady v. Brady* [1989] A.C. 755, H.L.) with the result the ambit of the exception is unclear. Again, in the case of a private limited company which has doubts about any transaction, it may be wise to use the relaxation procedure set out below (see paragraph 14.34).

14.34   The second exception to the general prohibition on the giving of financial assistance applies to private companies only. By virtue of section 155(1) of the Companies Act 1985, a private company is able to give financial assistance of any kind subject to certain conditions and provided a strict procedure is followed:

(a) A private company may only give financial assistance in accordance with this exception if its net assets are not reduced by it or if they are so reduced, the assistance is given out of distributable profits. The net assets of a private company giving financial assistance by way of loan will not be reduced (the reduction in cash is matched by the debt owed to it by the borrower) but net assets will be reduced (and so the assistance provided must come out distributable profits) if the company makes a gift of the monies.

(b) The directors of the company proposing to give the financial assistance must make a statutory declaration of solvency in the prescribed form (form G155(6)(a)), which contains details of the financial assistance to be given and their opinion that there will be no ground on which the company could be found unable to pay its debts immediately after the date on which the assistance is given and that the company will be able to pay its debts as they full due in the year following that date (Companies Act 1985, ss. 155(6), 156(1)(2)). The statutory declaration must have annexed to it a report of the company's auditors that verifies the declaration of the directors after enquiry into the state of the affairs of the company.

(c) On the date that the directors make their declaration or within a week immediately following that date, the company must approve the giving of the financial assistance by way of special resolution (Companies Act 1985, ss. 155(4), 157(1)). The statutory declaration and auditors' report must be available at the meeting held to pass the resolution (Companies Act 1985, s. 157(4)(a)). If the company adopts the special resolution using the written resolution procedure then the documents must be circulated to each member either before or at the time that the written resolution is circulated to them.

(d) The statutory declaration and the auditors' report must be filed with the registrar of companies together with a copy of the special resolution (Companies Act 1985, s. 156(5)).

(e) Within 28 days of the date of the special resolution, an application may be made to court for cancellation of it by the holders of not less than 10 per cent in nominal value of the company's issued share capital but the application cannot be made by a person who consented to or voted in favour of the resolution (Companies Act 1985, s. 157(2)). The court may make an order cancelling or confirming the resolution on such terms and conditions as it thinks fit. Where it is possible that an application could be made, there are strict time limits as to when the financial assistance can be given by the company which are set out in section 158 of the Act. The assistance must not be given before a period of four weeks beginning with the date on which the special resolution is passed and must not be given after a period of eight weeks beginning with the date of the directors' statutory declaration. Where an application for cancellation of the resolution is made under section 157, the assistance cannot be given until the final determination of the application unless the court decides otherwise (Companies Act 1985, s. 158(3)).

15. Corporate Insolvency

A. Introduction and the Nature of Corporate Insolvency

1. INTRODUCTION

15.1 This chapter will consider what can happen to a company that finds itself in financial difficulties:

(a) The worst-case scenario is that the company concerned is found to be insolvent (or "unable to pay its debts") and is consequently "liquidated" or "wound up"; this involves bringing a company's existence as a legal entity to an end and, eventually, removing its name from the register of companies. It is stressed that this is a final step in the history of the company concerned and that other, so-called "insolvency procedures" can be invoked in relation to a company in financial difficulties; which procedure is invoked and who actually invokes it depends upon the circumstances of each case (see paragraphs 15.5–15.28).

(b) In some circumstances, a company that is the subject of a particular insolvency procedure may be liable to have certain transactions entered into by it prior to commencement of the procedure concerned set aside. The aim of the relevant legislation in this case is to prevent an unlawful dissipation of the troubled company's assets that would otherwise swell any cash fund available to its creditors once such a procedure is invoked (see paragraphs 15.29–15.34).

(c) The directors and others involved in the management of a company in financial difficulties may find themselves subject to all sorts of liabilities and penalties in the event that the company concerned becomes insolvent and is liquidated. The aim here is to increase the responsibility of those who control the affairs of the troubled company for its debts and liabilities and, if necessary, to regulate and control their future business activities. In this respect, the relevant legislation operates to restrict the application of the limited liability rule for those directors and managers who are also shareholders of an insolvent company (see paragraphs 15.35–15.40).

2. THE NATURE OF CORPORATE INSOLVENCY

15.2 The main statute dealing with the law relating to corporate insolvency is the Insolvency Act 1986. It is supplemented by the Insolvency Rules 1986 (S.I. 1986 No. 1925) and, in relation to certain issues, by the Company Directors' Disqualification Act 1986.

A company is considered to be insolvent if it is "unable to pay its debts" because in these circumstances the company *could* be "wound up" (or liquidated) by the court in accordance with section 122(1)(f) of the Insolvency Act 1986.

Basically, by virtue of section 123 of the Act, a company is deemed unable to pay its debts if one of two circumstances exist. These circumstances are as follows:

(a) First, a company is unable to pay its debts if a creditor who is owed in excess of £750 by the company concerned has, by leaving it at its registered office, served on that company a written demand in the form prescribed by the Insolvency Rules 1986 (see rule 4.5 Insolvency Rules 1986) requiring the company to pay the sum due and the company has not paid or otherwise dealt with it to the reasonable satisfaction of the creditor for three weeks thereafter (see section 123(1)(a) of the Insolvency Act 1986).

Alternatively in this regard, execution or other process issued on a judgment or court order in favour of a creditor of the company concerned is returned unsatisfied in whole or in part following a visit from the court officer (see section 123(1)(*b*) of the Insolvency Act 1986).

This is often referred to as the "cash flow" test of insolvency; in principle, if the company concerned cannot find the funds necessary to discharge the debt owed in the demand or the amount detailed in the judgment or order then it is insolvent and faces the threat of being wound up regardless of the company's overall value or net worth.

(b) Secondly, a company is unable to pay its debts if it could be proved to the satisfaction of the court that the value of the company's assets is less than the amount of its liabilities, taking into account its contingent and prospective liabilities.

This is often referred to as the "balance sheet" test of insolvency; in principle, if the liabilities of the company concerned exceed its assets then it is insolvent and faces the threat of being wound up regardless of the extent of its cash reserves. However, if petitioned, the court always has a discretion to refuse to make an order winding up the company: see section 125(1) of the Insolvency Act 1986.

Many companies carry on business even though they would satisfy one or both of the tests referred to above and are in effect insolvent. The mere fact that a company has not got sufficient cash reserves to meet a statutory demand or the requirements of a court order if one of them were to be served on it and/or that its total liabilities exceed its assets does not mean that an insolvency procedure will be *imposed* on it or that necessarily some other drastic event will occur in relation to it and/or its property.

For an insolvency procedure to be invoked, someone (usually a creditor or director or shareholder) must take appropriate action against the company concerned and these procedures are looked at in some detail in section B below. What is important to note here is that if a company is insolvent on the above mentioned tests, then it is exposed to the *risk* of someone taking appropriate action with the result that an insolvency procedure is invoked in

15.3

relation to it; for example, as has already been indicated, if the company is unable to pay its debts then it risks being wound up (*i.e.* its existence brought to an end) by the court.

15.4   In addition, many other types of risks arise for the company and its directors:

> (a) Transactions entered into by the company are at risk of being set aside in certain circumstances (see paragraphs 15.29–15.34);
> (b) Directors and others may become personally liable to contribute to the assets of the company and face further penalty (see paragraphs 15.35–15.40);
> (c) The company's contracts with third parties may be affected by any procedure that is invoked by creditors, shareholders or directors. Some contracts will contain a term that provides for their automatic termination on, for example, the presentation of any petition to wind up the company. The business activity and, therefore, the very heart of the company concerned is at risk if it is in financial difficulty and such contractual terms are applicable.

B. The Insolvency Procedures

15.5   In this section, the following insolvency procedures will be looked at:

> (a) Administrative receivership
> (b) Voluntary arrangements
> (c) Administration
> (d) Liquidation

One or more of these procedures may be invoked by a variety of people when a company is in financial difficulty.

1. ADMINISTRATIVE RECEIVERSHIP

15.6   Receivers are persons who are appointed by creditors of the company to realise (*i.e.* sell) their appointees' security which is held by them over the company's assets. Security of a variety of forms is usually taken by sophisticated lenders such as banks and financial institutions when they lend money to companies. Typically, the loan agreement or debenture will contain terms creating the security over the company's assets and allowing the creditor to appoint a receiver to realise the security in the event that certain terms in the loan agreement are not complied with by the company (for example, a term requiring the company to repay the loan in full when requested by the creditor).

From this it can be seen that the power to appoint a receiver to act is usually derived from the contractual terms agreed to between lender and borrower; the Court is rarely involved in this type of procedure. It follows that strictly there is no need for a company to be insolvent within the meaning set out in paragraph 15.2–15.3 above before a bank or other secured creditor invokes this procedure; the key question is: can the lender enforce his security in accordance with the terms of the debenture or loan agreement? However, it should be appreciated that the procedure is invariably only invoked in relation to companies that find themselves in financial difficulties and therefore fail to comply with their repayment obligations pursuant to the terms of the loan agreement; if repayments under the loan facility concerned are made on time, the secured creditor will not enforce its security!

It is important to distinguish between ''a receiver'' and ''an administrative receiver.'' ''A receiver'' is appointed by a secured creditor to take control of and realise specifically charged or mortgaged property (for example, freehold property or leasehold land and buildings specifically identified as being the subject of a *fixed charge* in the loan agreement).

''An administrative receiver'' is defined in section 29(2) of the Insolvency **15.7** Act 1986 to mean:

(a) a receiver or manager of the whole (or substantially the whole) of a company's property appointed by or on behalf of the holders of any debentures of the company secured by a charge which, as created, was *a floating charge*, or by such a charge and one or more other securities; or

(b) a person who would be such a receiver or manager but for the appointment of some other person as the receiver of part of the company's property.

An administrative receiver *must* be a qualified insolvency practitioner.

In practice, a loan agreement entered into between a sophisticated lender such as the bank and the company will contain a multitude of charges, one of which invariably will be a floating charge over the whole or substantially the whole of the company's property. Others charges may include fixed charges over land held by the company but these do not prevent the secured creditor from appointing an administrative receiver. Inevitably, the secured creditor will appoint one and the same person or persons to be both receivers of the specifically charged or mortgaged property such as land and administrative receivers over the remaining total of the company's property.

Because the administrative receiver is appointed in respect of the whole **15.8** of the company's property and has sole authority to deal with it, he replaces the directors in the management of the company for most purposes. Therefore, the appointment of such a receiver has an instant and dramatic effect for the company's officers as well as the creditors of the company and the members. His main duty is to realise the assets that are the subject of his appointee's security and account to him for the proceeds. He may attempt to perform this duty by selling the whole of the business of the company as a going concern or he may sell off the assets that are the subject of the charge individually; his chosen course of action will depend upon numerous factors but, like his appointee, he is under a duty to take reasonable care to obtain the true market value of the property.

The following points should be noted in relations to his powers, obligations and ability to deal with the company's property:

(a) The administrative receiver will have all the powers that were conferred on him by the terms agreed to between the lender and the company in the loan agreement. These will be wide ranging in themselves but in addition he will have all the powers conferred by section 42(1) and Schedule 1 to the Insolvency Act 1986. Examples of such powers include the power to sell the property of the company, the power to raise or borrow money and grant security for it over the property of the company and the power to carry on the business of the company. The powers contained in the Insolvency 1986 can be excluded in the loan agreement itself but this will rarely be the case.

(b) Pursuant to section 43(1) of the Insolvency Act 1986, an administrative receiver may apply to court for permission to dispose of company property that is subject to a charge that is ranked prior to that under which he is appointed. The court may authorise the administrative receiver to dispose of the charged property as if it were not subject to such security if it is satisfied that the disposal (with or without other assets) would be likely to promote a more advantageous realisation of the company's assets than would otherwise be effected. The net proceeds of the disposal and the difference (if any) between such proceeds and the market value must be paid to the prior chargeholder.

15.9   This section is of benefit to an administrative receiver when, once appointed, he attempts to sell the whole of the business of the company as a going concern (such a sale *generally* yields more cash proceeds than the sale of individual assets held by the company). The sale of the going concern may well be jeopardised if the administrative receiver cannot include in it property that is in fact charged to some other secured creditor (*e.g.* stock which is the subject of a floating charge created and registered before his appointee's floating charge). The court order made under section 43(1) Insolvency Act 1986 will allow him to complete the sale of the business as a going concern and include in that sale the property that is subject to the prior charge thus maximising the cash proceeds available generally to him with which to realise his appointee's security. Naturally enough, the administrative receiver must account to the secured creditor with priority for monies realised from the property that is subject to the prior charge (and any shortfall in market value); thus the position of that creditor is protected throughout.

(c) Many trade suppliers will supply goods to companies under their standard terms and conditions that will invariably contain a so-called retention of title clause or "Romalpa" clause (named after the leading case in this area: *Aluminium Industrie Vaasen BV v. Romalpa Aluminium* [1976] 2 All E.R. 552). This clause provides that title to the goods supplied does not pass to the company concerned until payment in full has been received by the supplier. Basically, the effect of the clause is that until full payment is received, the goods concerned belong to the supplier and not the company; they do not form part of the company's property and the trader is, prima facie, entitled to reclaim them from any administrative receiver who is appointed. It must be stressed that, given their basic effect, retention of title clauses have been widely used in a variety of circumstances; however, their very validity and effect will depend on the wording of the clause and the circumstances of each case.

(d) In carrying out his main task of realising the security and accounting for the proceeds to his appointee, the administrative receiver must take note of the entitlement of other creditors: **15.10**

    (i) Those creditors with the benefit of fixed charges (*i.e.* charges or mortgages over specifically identified property) rank in priority to everyone (including "preferential creditors": see below) in relation to the specifically charged property (*i.e.* proceeds realised from such property belong in total to the relevant chargeholder). As mentioned earlier, it is common for lenders to take both fixed and floating charges in the loan agreement and appoint the same persons to be receivers and administrative receivers over the relevant property respectively.

    (ii) The administrative receiver's expenses are payable first out of proceeds realised by him from the property over which he is appointed (it would be difficult to find anyone to do the job otherwise!).

    (iii) As we shall see (paragraph 15.26), when a company is wound up or liquidated, certain "preferential" creditors are entitled to be paid in priority to those creditors with the benefit of a floating charge where the assets available to general, unsecured creditors are insufficient to meet the preferential debts concerned. Such preferential debts include certain amounts owed by the company concerned to the Inland Revenue and its employees. It follows that, when a company is not being wound up but an administrative receiver is appointed in relation to it in order to realise the floating chargeholder's security, section 40(2) of the Insolvency Act 1986 provides that the administrative receiver must pay preferential debts out of the assets coming into his hands in priority to his appointee. In keeping with the position under a winding up mentioned above, section 40(3) of the Act 1986 entitles the administrative receiver to recoup the payments made by him to preferential creditors out of assets of the company that are available for general unsecured creditors, provided such assets exist once the administrative receiver has completed his task!

    (iv) Finally, the administrative receiver may account to his appointee for the net proceeds realised from the property that was the subject of the floating charge.

The legal position of an administrative receiver is provided for in section 44 of the Insolvency Act 1986. This section makes him an agent of the company, unless and until the company goes into liquidation. Generally this means that his acts (*e.g.* entering into contracts) will bind the company. He is not an agent of his appointee who generally incurs no liability for acts carried out by the administrative receiver on behalf of the company. **15.11**

Section 44 of the Insolvency Act 1986 also provides that the administrative receiver is personally liable on any new contract that he himself enters into in the carrying out of his functions unless the contract otherwise provides. Needless to say, administrative receivers will usually attempt to contract out of such personal liability. In any event, section 44 provides that the administrative receiver is entitled to an indemnity out of the assets of the company in respect of his personal liability and in practice an additional indemnity is always taken from his appointee (*i.e.* the secured creditor).

The administrative receiver's position in relation to the company's *existing* contracts of employment merits a special mention. Section 44 makes an administrative receiver personally liable for any existing contracts of employment that he "adopts" (*i.e.* he will be liable for such things as salaries and occupational pension scheme contributions after such adoption incurred while he is in office). He cannot contract out of such liability. Following recent case law (see *Re Paramount Airways Ltd (No. 3)* [1993] B.C.C. 662), Parliament has enacted the Insolvency Act 1994 that provides that the administrative receiver is not to be taken to have adopted a contract of employment by reason of anything done or omitted to be done within 14 days after his appointment (section 44(2) of the Insolvency Act 1986 as amended by the Insolvency Act 1994). The aim of the new legislation is to give administrative receivers a limited period in which to ascertain if the business of the company can be sold as a going concern with all or some of the existing employees. If at the end of the limited period a sale as a going concern is not possible and he is forced to dismiss the workforce for redundancy reasons then the administrative receiver will not incur personal liability in respect of the existing contracts.

The administrative receiver who continues to employ and pay persons after the 14-day period has expired will have adopted those contracts and be personally liable in respect of them in accordance with section 44 of the Insolvency Act 1986. Finally, the above is the position of *existing* employment contracts adopted by administrative receivers in the course of the receivership; if he enters into *new* contracts of employment himself then, like any other new contract under section 44, he will be personally liable on them but with the ability to contract out of liability.

Under section 47 of the Insolvency Act 1986, an administrative receiver can require various persons (usually directors of the company) to make out and submit a statement in the prescribed form that addresses the affairs of the company (*e.g.* details of company assets, debts and liabilities, names and addresses of creditors, etc.). Under section 48 of the Act, within three months of being appointed (or such longer period as the court may allow), the administrative receiver must send a report to the registrar of companies and the company's creditors that details such things as the events leading up to his appointment, the disposal by him of any property held by the company, the amounts owing to his appointee and preferential creditors and the amount (if any) likely to be available for payment to other, general creditors. The legislation provides for the subsequent holding of a meeting of the unsecured creditors of the company. In practice, once the administrative receiver has completed his task and realised his appointee's security, there may be very few assets remaining (if any!) and the company is likely to be wound up or liquidated (see paragraphs 15.21–15.28). If a liquidator has been appointed to wind up the company or is subsequently appointed during the receivership, the administrative receiver should deliver his report to the liquidator and not the company's creditors.

2. VOLUNTARY ARRANGEMENTS

Sections 1–7 of the Insolvency Act 1986 make provision for the proposal, approval and implementation of an arrangement between a company and its creditors in respect of that company's debts. Although any proposed arrangement must be reported to the Court, it does not require the Court's approval. The aim of the legislation is to promote voluntary agreements between a company in financial difficulties and its creditors as to a composition in satisfaction of the company's debts; the intention being that such an agreement provides an advantageous distribution to all creditors and (hopefully!) the long-term survival of the company concerned (paragraphs 15.21–15.28). For example, creditors may agree to take 50p for every £1 owed to them by the company in difficulty in total satisfaction of their debts with the result that they are actually paid more than what would have been achieved for them by a liquidator on a winding-up and the company is able to continue trading once freed from its current debt burden.

15.12

It is the directors of the company who may make such proposals to the members and creditors of the company. The proposals must provide that some person ("the nominee") will act in the supervision and implementation of the voluntary arrangement. That person must be a qualified insolvency practitioner. The nominee must submit a report to Court stating whether, in his opinion, meetings of the company and its creditors should be summoned to consider the proposal. Directors are under a duty to submit the terms of the proposal and details of the assets and liabilities of the company to the nominee in order to assist him in preparing this report. If the nominee reports that meetings should be held, he is then required to summon them.

In addition to directors, such voluntary arrangements may be proposed by an administrator when an administration order is in force (see paragraphs 15.14–15.20) or by a liquidator when a company is being wound up (see paragraphs 15.21–15.28). In this case, the arrangement is usually supervised by the administrator or liquidator (*i.e.* he is the nominee for these purposes) and he can summon meetings of the creditors and members as he thinks fit without reference to the court.

In practice, it is very difficult for directors to implement a voluntary arrangement outside of administration. This is because, while proposals are being drawn up, there is nothing to stop any creditor "spoiling the show" and taking his own steps to obtain payment of his debt. For example, a creditor may petition the court for the winding up of the company or take other steps to repossess goods supplied to the company. As we shall see, if the company is in administration there is, in effect, created a "moratorium" that prevents actions being commenced or continued against the company (see paragraph 15.16). The creditor is, in effect, unable to take action to obtain payment of his debt. This gives the company the "breathing space" needed to prepare proposals and submit them to creditors and members for approval. Therefore, it is wise for directors to petition the court for an administration order if they wish to implement a voluntary arrangement. The approval of such an arrangement is one of the specific grounds on which the court may be petitioned for such an order (see paragraph 15.14: Administration). However, the granting of an administration order can be blocked by those entitled to appoint administrative receivers (*i.e.* those who hold floating charges over the company's assets) and so their agreement must be sought by the directors before the court is petitioned.

15.13   The members' and creditors' meetings that are summoned by the nominee or administrator or liquidator must decide whether or not to approve the proposed voluntary arrangements with or without modifications. The meetings cannot approve a proposal that affects the rights of a secured creditor to enforce his security unless that creditor agrees nor can they approve a proposal that affects the priority of preferential debts (as to the meaning of preferential debts, see paragraph 15.26). Members approve the arrangement by a simple majority vote in favour in accordance with the voting rights attached to their shares. The voluntary arrangement is imposed on all creditors who in accordance with the Insolvency Rules 1986 had notice of and who were entitled to vote at the creditors' meeting if a three-quarters majority (in value) of the company's unsecured creditors vote in favour. The results of the meetings must be reported to court and any approved arrangement can be challenged within 28 days by a member, creditor, the nominee or liquidator or administrator on the grounds of unfair prejudice or material irregularity. If it is challenged, the court may revoke or suspend the approvals given by the meetings and make directions for revised proposals to put before further meetings.

The approved arrangement is implemented by the nominee who is from this point referred to as the supervisor.

3. ADMINISTRATION

15.14   Administration is a procedure initiated by court order and is designed as an alternative to the winding up or liquidation procedure (see paragraphs 15.21–15.28). Whereas, generally, on a winding up the assets of the company in financial difficulties are sold and the proceeds distributed amongst creditors with the end result that the company is dissolved and removed from the register, an administration order provides the company with a breathing space during which time proposals can be implemented that will hopefully result in the survival of all or some part of the business of the company or a more advantageous sale of the company's assets than would be achieved by a liquidator in a winding up. For example, an administrator may take control of and manage an insolvent company until certain contracts are completed or assets sold which have the effect of returning it to a solvent state. Alternatively, an administrator may sell all or part of the business of a company as a going concern thus producing more cash proceeds for creditors than would have been produced by a liquidator selling off the company's assets individually in a winding up.

On the petition of the company or its directors or any creditor, the court can make an administration order under section 8 of the Insolvency Act 1986 directing that, during the period for which the order is in force, the affairs, business and property of the company shall be managed by a person ("the administrator") appointed for the purpose by the court. The administrator so appointed must be a qualified insolvency practitioner. The court can only make such an order if the company is or is likely to become unable to pay its debts (*i.e.* it is insolvent or likely to become insolvent in accordance with section 123 of the Insolvency Act 1986; see paragraphs 15.2–15.3) *and* the making of the order is likely to achieve one or more of the purposes mentioned in section 8(3) of the Act; namely:

(a) the survival of the company, and the whole or any part of its undertaking as a going concern;
(b) the approval of a voluntary arrangement: (see paragraphs 15.12–15.13) or the sanctioning of a compromise or arrangement between the company and its members or creditors under section 425 of the Companies Act 1985;
(c) a more advantageous realisation of the company's assets than would be effected on a winding up.

It is important to note the relationship between administration and the other insolvency procedures. **15.15**

(a) In relation to administrative receivership, section 9(2) of the Insolvency Act 1986 provides that where a petition for an administration order is presented to court, notice of it shall be given forthwith to any person who has appointed, or is or may be entitled to appoint, an administrative receiver of the company (*i.e* the holder of a floating charge). Section 9(3) of the Act provides that, except in limited circumstances, the Court shall dismiss the petition for an administration order where it is satisfied that an administrative receiver is in office.

These provisions mean that those who have the benefit of floating charges can effectively block the making of an administration order by appointing their own administrative receiver in accordance with the terms of the loan agreement once they receive notice of the petition under section 9(2) of the Insolvency Act 1986 but before that petition is heard; where such action is taken, the petition must be dismissed upon being heard in accordance with section 9(3) of the Act. It is for these reasons that administrative receiverships are much more common than administrations in the United Kingdom. Although, as we shall see, the administration procedure has certain advantages, the holder of a floating charge faced with a choice of appointing his own administrative receiver or agreeing with the directors and/or company and/or other creditors to petition the court for an administration order may well feel that, for purely selfish reasons, it is more expedient to elect for the former where the primary duty of the person appointed is to realise the security of his appointee. The result is that in practice the support of those holding floating charges is necessary before a petition for administration can be successful; section 9(3) provides that floating chargeholders can consent to the making of the administration order if they have already appointed an administrative receiver and section 11 provides that on the making of such an order, any current administrative receiver shall vacate office and none can be appointed while the order remains in force.

(b) In relation to voluntary arrangements, it has already been noted that the approval of such an arrangement is one of the very proposes for which an administration order will be made. As we shall see, the administration order confers major advantages (*i.e.* the creation of a moratorium) that make the implementation of such an arrangement much more likely to succeed under this procedure than outside of it in practice.

(c) In relation to winding up or liquidation, given that administration is meant to be an alternative to this procedure, no resolution of the company may be passed and no order of the court may be made for the winding up of the company in the period during which a petition for administration is pending (*i.e.* the petition has been presented but has not yet been heard) and in the period during which an administration order is actually in force. While the administration order is pending, a petition for the winding up or liquidation of the company may be presented to court but it will only be considered if the administration order is not made. If the administration order is made, section 11 of the Insolvency Act 1986 provides that the winding up petition must be dismissed. Equally, no administration order can be made if a company has gone into liquidation. The result is that these two procedures, like administration and administrative receivership, are mutually exclusive; they cannot be on-going at the same time.

15.16   The appointment of an administrator has major consequences for the company, its directors and its creditors:

(a) Section 14(1) of the Insolvency Act 1986 provides that an administrator may do all such things as may be necessary for the management of the affairs, business and property of the company. He also has the powers specified in Schedule 1 to the Act, which include the power to sell the assets of the company. The powers are so wide ranging that, in effect, the administrator takes over control of the company from the directors who must not interfere with the exercise by the administrator of his powers (see Insolvency Act 1986, s. 14(4)).

(b) Section 11(3) of the Insolvency Act 1986 provides for a moratorium preventing creditors from enforcing their rights against the company while an administration order is in force. This provision is at the very crux of an administration. The aim is to provide the company with the breathing space required so that the administrator can implement his proposals and, hopefully, achieve the aim of the order without fear of any one particular creditor taking steps against the company that could wreck the plan. Hence, on the making of an administration order:

  (i) as we have already seen, any outstanding petition for the winding up of the company is dismissed and no resolution may be passed or order made for the winding up of the company;

 (ii) again, as we have already seen, any current administrative receiver of the company vacates office and no new administrative receiver may be appointed;

(iii) no other steps may be taken to enforce security over the company's property or to repossess goods in the company's possession under any hire-purchase agreement except with the consent of the administrator or the leave of the court; and

(iv) no other proceedings and no execution or other legal process may be commenced or continued and no distress may be levied against the company or its property except with the consent of the administrator or the leave of the court.

In order to preserve the assets of the company while a petition for an administration order is pending (*i.e.* it has been presented but not heard), section 10 of the Insolvency Act 1986 provides for similar provisions in relation to the enforcement of creditors' rights at this stage as those contained in section 11. It would be pointless going to Court to try to obtain an administration order if one particular creditor were able to wreck the plan by taking steps to enforce his rights against the company once he discovered what was being applied for by others. Hence, during the period beginning with the presentation of a petition and ending with the making of such an order or the dismissal of the petition: **15.17**

  (i) as we have already seen, no resolution may be passed or order made for the winding up of the company;

 (ii) no steps may be taken to enforce any security over the company's property or to repossess goods in the company's possession under any hire-purchase agreement, except with the leave of the court; and

(iii) no other proceedings and no execution or other legal process may be commenced or continued, and no distress may be levied, against the company or the property except with the leave of the court.

The important exception in this particular period is that a floating-charge holder may appoint an administrative receiver (Insolvency Act 1986, s. 10(2)(b)). As we have already seen, such a charge holder must be given notice of the petition when it is presented to Court and no administration order will be made where an administrative receiver has been appointed by him in the interim unless he consents to the making of the order whereupon his administrative receiver must vacate office. This reiterates the point that usually a petition for an administration order will not be successful unless those who hold floating charges over the assets of the company consent to it by not appointing an administrative receiver as they are entitled to do or by agreeing to the vacation of office of one already so appointed.

In addition in this period, a petition for the winding up or liquidation of the company may be *presented* to court but, as we have already seen, the petition must be dismissed and no winding up order made if the administration order is granted. The winding-up petition will only be considered if the petition for administration is dismissed.

15.18   Armed with his wide-ranging powers, the aim of the administrator is to achieve the purpose of the order; namely, the survival of the whole or some part of the business of the company or the approval of some voluntary arrangement or an advantageous sale of the company's assets. He is deemed to act as the agent of the company in exercising his powers (s. 14(5) of the Insolvency Act 1986) but, unlike an administrative receiver (see paragraph 15.11), he has no personal liability on contracts entered into or adopted by him during the administration. Obviously, the administrator may well find that some or all of the company's assets, which are to be affected by his proposals, are subject to some form of security granted before the order was made. Section 15 of the Insolvency Act 1986 provides as follows:

(a) An administrator may dispose of property that is the subject of a floating charge as if it were not subject to it. In this case, the holder of the charge has the same priority in respect of the property representing the property disposed of as he would have had in respect of the property that was subject to his security. Hence, this allows the administrator to sell property freely while preserving the floating chargeholder's priority position in respect of the company's assets generally.

(b) On application of the administrator, the court may authorise the administrator to dispose of property subject to any other security (*e.g.* a fixed charge) or goods in the possession of the company under a hire-purchase agreement, conditional sale agreement, chattel-leasing arrangement or retention of title agreement as if it were not subject to the security or terms of the relevant agreement. Here, the court must be satisfied that the disposal would be likely to promote one or more of the purposes specified in the administration order. In these cases, the proceeds of sale (and any deficiency between that and market value) must be used to discharge amounts secured by the security or payable under the relevant agreements.

In carrying out his function of attempting to achieve the aim of the administration order, the administrator is under a duty to ensure that (a) a statement of affairs relating to the company is submitted to him (see Insolvency Act 1986, s.22) and (b) a statement of his proposals for achieving the purpose of the order is sent to all creditors of whom he is aware (see Insolvency Act 1986, s.23):

15.19   (a) *Statement of affairs.* The administrator can require any or all of many people to submit this statement to him (see section 22(3) of the Insolvency

Act 1986) but it will usually be prepared by the directors of the company and/or some of its employees. When such persons are required to submit a statement, they must normally do so within 21 days of being requested to do so. The statement itself contains such details as the company's assets, debts and other liabilities and the names and addresses of its creditors and any security held over the assets.

(b) *Statement of proposals*. Within three months of the administration order **15.20** being made (or such longer time as the court may allow) the administrator must send to the registrar of companies and all creditors of whom he is aware a statement of his proposals for achieving the purpose or purposes specified in the order and he must lay a copy of this statement before a meeting of the company's creditors, which must be summoned on not less than 14 days' notice. The creditors' meeting decides whether to approve the administrator's proposals. If the meeting modifies the proposals, the administrator must consent to each such modification before they can be effective. The result of the meeting is reported to Court. If the meeting does not approve the proposals the court may discharge the administration order or, *inter alia*, make any order that it thinks fit. If the proposals are approved then they are implemented by the administrator. Any substantial revision to approved proposals must be put before a creditors' meeting and approved by it.

Finally, an administrator must apply to Court for the discharge of an administration order if it appears to him that the purpose of the order either has been achieved or is incapable of achievement. The administrator will vacate office if the administration order is discharged.

4. LIQUIDATION

Liquidation or winding up involves bringing the existence of a company to **15.21** an end. The aim of such a procedure is to ensure that the company's assets are collected in, "liquidated" (or sold) and distributed to creditors and original contributories (*i.e.* shareholders) in a strict order of entitlement. Ultimately, the company in liquidation will be "dissolved"; *i.e.* its name will be removed from the register of companies and it will cease to be a separate legal entity.

There are two types of winding-up procedure that can be invoked in respect of a company; these are referred to as voluntary liquidations and compulsory liquidations. There are in fact two types of voluntary liquidations in themselves; namely, a members' voluntary liquidation and a creditors' voluntary liquidation. Both types of voluntary liquidation are commenced by members of the company concerned passing resolutions at general meetings without any involvement of the court. As we shall see, a members' voluntary winding up can only be used in relation to a solvent company (and so it is somewhat confusing to find it addressed in a chapter concerning corporate insolvency procedures!); if the company concerned is unable to pay its debts then any voluntary liquidation will be a creditors' voluntary liquidation. A compulsory liquidation is commenced by a petition to the court that the company be wound up by reason of one of the grounds contained in section 122 of the Insolvency Act 1986; by far the most common ground used by petitioners is that the company is unable to pay its debts (see paragraphs 15.2–15.4).

Members' voluntary winding-up

Directors and/or members of many solvent companies may conclude that, for a variety of reasons, it is prudent or desirable to cease trading but that they require some time to settle the existing obligations of the company; in this case, a members' voluntary liquidation may be an appropriate procedure to invoke. Generally, a members' voluntary liquidation is commenced when the members of the company resolve by special resolution that it be wound up voluntarily (Insolvency Act 1986, s. 84(1)(b)). In addition, at some time in the five weeks immediately preceding the date of the passing of that resolution or on that date but before it is so passed, the directors (or a majority of them if there are more than two) *must* make a statutory declaration at a board meeting to the effect that they have made a full inquiry into the company's affairs and that, having done so, they have formed the opinion that the company will be able to pay its debts in full, together with interest at the official rate within a specified period not exceeding 12 months from the commencement of the winding up. The declaration must contain a statement of the company's assets and liabilities. A notice of the resolution must be placed in the *London Gazette* within 14 days of it being passed. In addition, a copy of the resolution and a copy of the declaration must be delivered to the registrar of companies within 15 days of the resolution being passed. The winding up is deemed to commence when the resolution is passed. A director who makes the declaration without reasonable grounds for his opinion is liable to imprisonment or a fine, or both. Where the resolution is passed by members but no declaration is made by the directors, the liquidation is taken to be a creditors' voluntary winding up (Insolvency Act 1986, s. 90; see below).

A company using this procedure is meant to be solvent and so the legislation provides that it is the members in general meeting who appoint the liquidator for the purpose of winding up the company's affairs and distributing its assets. The liquidator must be a qualified insolvency practitioner. On his appointment, the powers of the directors cease, except in so far as the company in general meeting or the liquidator permits them to continue.

Creditors' voluntary winding-up

15.22   Directors and/or members of a company may conclude that the company is insolvent and yet no action has been taken by a secured creditor (*e.g.* a floating charge holder has not appointed an administrative receiver), no unsecured creditor (*e.g.* a trade supplier) has petitioned the court for the winding up of the company and there are no viable grounds on which to petition the court for an administration order or implement some voluntary arrangement with all creditors. Given the increasing personal liabilities that directors face where they continue trading and the company concerned goes into insolvent liquidation (see paragraphs 15.35–15.40), it may be prudent to invoke a creditors' voluntary winding up. Generally, this procedure is commenced by the members of the company concerned passing an extraordinary resolution to the effect that it cannot by reason of its liabilities continue its business, and that it is advisable to wind up (Insolvency Act 1986, s. 84(1)(c)). The winding up is deemed to commence when the resolution is passed. The resolution must be filed with the registrar of companies within 15 days of its being passed. The members may nominate a person to be a liquidator at the meeting held to pass the extraordinary meeting. However, given that the company is insolvent when this procedure is invoked, section 98 of the Insolvency Act 1986 requires the company to hold a creditors' meeting within 14 days of the meeting of the members at which the extraordinary resolution was passed. At this meeting, the directors must lay a statement of affairs before the creditors detailing, *inter alia*, the company's assets, debts and liabilities and the names and addresses of the company's creditors and details of any security held by creditors. The creditors themselves are then given the opportunity to nominate a different liquidator. The creditors may confirm the choice of the members as liquidator or replace him with their own choice. If they do not nominate a different liquidator, the members' choice remains in office. In order to protect the creditors' position in relation to the assets of the insolvent company, section 166 of the Act provides that a liquidator appointed at the members' meeting passing the extraordinary resolution shall not exercise his powers except for limited purposes (*e.g.* to take control of the company's property) prior to the holding of the creditors' meeting. Any liquidator appointed must be a qualified insolvency partitioner. On his appointment, all the powers of the directors cease unless the liquidator or creditors permit them to continue.

In a creditors' voluntary winding up, the creditors are given the right to appoint a liquidation committee to assist the liquidator in his task of winding up the company and distributing its assets. The committee is given wide powers (*e.g.* to sanction the liquidator's proposals to make any compromise or arrangement with creditors).

Compulsory winding-up

In the case of the compulsory winding up, a petition to court may be presented by a variety of persons; namely, the company itself, the directors, a contributory or contributories (*i.e.* shareholders) or any creditor or creditors (see Insolvency Act 1986, s. 124). Petitions are usually presented by unsecured creditors who are owed money by the company concerned. The grounds on which a winding up order may be granted are set out in section 122 of the Act and in practice the most common ground made out is that contained in section 122(1)(f); namely, the company is unable to pay its debts. A detailed discussion of what is meant by "inability to pay debts" (see Insolvency Act 1986, s. 123) is set out in paragraphs 15.2–15.3 of this chapter and the reader is advised to re-read them at this stage. If the order is granted, the winding up is deemed to commence at the time of presentation of the petition for winding up (Insolvency Act 1986, s. 129(2)). A copy of the order must be forwarded to the registrar of companies.

15.23

As soon as the winding up order is made, the official receiver becomes the liquidator of the company and continues in office until another person becomes liquidator (see Insolvency Act 1986, s. 136(2)). Under section 136(4) of the Act, the official receiver *may* call separate meetings of creditors and contributories for the purpose of choosing a person to be a liquidator of the company in his place. He must decide whether or not to do this within 12 weeks of the order being granted and if he decides not to, he must give notice of his decision to the Court, the creditors and the contributories before the end of the 12-week period. He must call such meetings if requested to do so by one-quarter (in value) of the company's creditors. Where the meetings are held, both creditors and contributories may nominate persons to be the liquidator and if they nominate different people, the creditors' choice prevails (see Insolvency Act 1986, s. 139). Any liquidator appointed must be a qualified insolvency practitioner.

Where meetings of the creditors and contributories are held to appoint a liquidator, these meetings may establish a liquidation committee to assist the newly appointed liquidator in his task of winding up the company and distributing its assets. The committee is given wide powers (*e.g.* to sanction the liquidator's proposals to carry on the business of the company or compromise any creditor's claim).

15.24   Section 143(1) of the Insolvency Act 1986 specifically provides that the functions of the liquidator are to get in, realise and distribute the assets of the company to its creditors and, if there is a surplus, to the persons entitled to it. In order to ensure that the assets of the company available to the liquidator for such purposes are not jeopardised, the compulsory winding up procedure has certain dramatic effects:

  (a) once a winding-up petition is presented, the company, a creditor or a contributory may apply to court for a stay in any action or proceeding pending against the company (Insolvency Act 1986, s. 126);

  (b) once the winding up is commenced (*i.e.* the time of the presentation of the petition if an order is made), any disposition of the company's property is void unless the court otherwise orders (Insolvency Act 1986, s. 127);

  (c) once the winding-up order has been made, no action or proceeding may be proceeded with or commenced against the company or its property except by leave of the court (Insolvency Act 1986, s. 130(2) of the Insolvency Act).

Powers of liquidators

The powers which all liquidators have are set out in sections 165 and 167 of the Insolvency Act 1986 and are contained in Schedule 4 to the 1986 Act. In the case of a members' voluntary winding up, the liquidator will require the sanction of an extraordinary resolution of the company if he is to exercise the powers contained in Part I of Schedule 4. Similarly, in the case of a creditors' voluntary winding up, he will require the sanction of the court or the liquidation committee/creditors for the exercise of such powers. Finally, in the case of a compulsory winding up he well require the sanction of the court or the liquidation committee. Examples of powers contained in Part I of Schedule 4 include the power to pay any class of creditors in full and the power to make any compromise or arrangement with creditors.

In the case of a compulsory liquidation only, the liquidator will require the sanction of the court or the liquidation committee to exercise the powers contained in Part II of Schedule 4; namely, the power to bring or defend legal proceedings in the name and on behalf of the company and the power to carry on the business of the company for the purpose of a beneficial winding up. No sanction is required in relation to these powers for a liquidator of any voluntary liquidation.

Finally, in the regard, the powers contained in Part III of Schedule 4 are exercisable by all liquidators without any sanction whatsoever. Examples of the powers contained in Part III include the power to sell any of the company's property and the power to raise money on the security of the assets of the company.

In addition to these powers, it should be noted that a liquidator is able to disown or "disclaim" property of the company that is "onerous"; namely, unprofitable contracts and property which is unsaleable or not readily saleable (see Insolvency Act 1986, s. 178).

Distribution of assets by liquidators

In distributing the assets of a company in liquidation to its creditors (and, if **15.25** there is any surplus, to those entitled to it), the liquidator must adhere to a strict order of entitlement. Creditors are classified in groups and these groups are ranked according to their entitlement to the company's assets. This ranking system is subject to the *pari passu* rule; namely, *all* creditors in any one group are paid *in full* before *any* creditor in the next ranking group is paid *anything* and when there are insufficient funds to pay *all* creditors in *any one* group, the creditors in that group must each receive the same proportion of their claims (*e.g.* 10p per £1 of claim for each creditor; the amount paid out being dependant upon the value of the remaining assets).

The order of entitlement is somewhat complicated but can be summarised **15.26** as follows:

(a) any person with the benefit of a fixed charge over any of the company's assets is entitled to realise that security and discharge amounts owed by the company to him in priority to all other creditors and/or claimants. If the secured creditor does enforce his security then clearly the assets that are the subject of the fixed charge are not then available to any liquidator of the company for distribution to ordinary creditors;

(b) (ignoring the rights of fixed-charge holders detailed above) the first category of debts to be paid in full are the expenses of the liquidation; including the liquidator's renumeration (see Insolvency Act 1986, ss. 115, 175(2)(a));

(c) secondly, section 175(1) of the Insolvency Act 1986 provides that the company's preferential debts shall be paid in priority to all other debts. If there is insufficient assets to pay all preferential debts in full then all creditors in this group will receive the same proportion of their claims in accordance with the *pari passu* principle. Preferential debts include:

    (i) Debts due to the Inland Revenue (*i.e.* sums due for deductions of income tax from salaries paid during the previous 12 months under the PAYE system).

    (ii) Debts due to customs and excise (*i.e.* VAT referable to the previous six months).

    (iii) Social security contributions due and referable to the previous 12 months/certain contributions due to occupational pension schemes.

(iv) Wages owed to employees in respect of the previous four months up to a current maximum of £800 per employee/certain accrued holiday renumeration.

The full list of preferential debts is contained in Schedule 6 to the Insolvency Act 1986.

(d) thirdly, any person with the benefit of a floating charge over the company's undertaking who is entitled to realise that security and discharge amounts owed by the company to him ranks in priority to all general, unsecured creditors of the company for repayment of his debt to the extent of his security.

Why does a *secured* creditor with the benefit of a floating charge rank below the costs of the liquidation and the preferential debts for payment in a winding up?

(i) with regard to the costs of the liquidation, it is a settled principle that these are paid in full in priority to all other claims; including preferential debts (see section 115 of the Insolvency Act 1986 for voluntary liquidations and section 175(2)(a) of the Act for both compulsory and voluntary liquidations);

(ii) with regard to the preferential debts themselves, we have already seen that if the holder of a floating charge had enforced his security when the company was not being wound up, his administrative receiver would have had to pay the preferential debts out of assets coming into his hands in priority to the appointee subject to his power to recoup such payments out of any assets available for payment to general creditors (Insolvency Act 1986, s. 40(2) and (3): see paragraph 15.10). In the case of a winding up, section 175(2)(b) of the Act similarly provides that preferential debts have priority over the claims of those with the benefit of floating charges in so far as the assets available to general creditors are insufficient to meet them.

(e) fourthly, general, unsecured creditors are entitled to be paid in full. Again, if there is insufficient assets to pay all general creditors in full then all creditors in this group will receive the same proportion of their claims in accordance with the *pari passu* principle.

15.27   Some unsecured trade creditors may have supplied goods to the company on terms that included a retention of title clause (see paragraph 15.9). As in the case of a company in administrative receivership, provided the clause is valid and effective then title in the goods will not have passed to the company in liquidation if payment for them was not received in full by the trade creditor concerned and he is entitled to reclaim the goods from the liquidator. This point illustrates why such clauses are commonly found in commercial contracts; they provide a safeguard for those creditors without security over the company's assets and disrupt the strict order of entitlement applicable on a liquidation.

(f) fifthly, once all debts are paid in full, then interest is payable on them in respect of the period during which they have been outstanding since the company went into liquidation. Interest payable ranks equally, whether or not the debts on which it is payable rank equally (see Insolvency Act 1986, s. 189).

(g) next, certain general, unsecured creditors whose debts have been "postponed" (*i.e.* paid only after all other general creditors are paid in full and all interest on those debts is paid in full in accordance with section 189 of the Insolvency Act 1986) are entitled to payment. An example of such a postponed debt would be any debt owed to a person found liable to contribute to the assets of the company by the court for wrongful trading, if the court so directs; (see section 215(4) of the Insolvency Act 1986 and generally paragraphs 15.36–15.37 below).

(h) finally, any surplus is returned to members in accordance with their rights under the company's articles of association: The articles may provide for different classes of members to be treated differently on a winding up; in particular, any preference shareholders may be entitled to a return of their capital investment before ordinary shareholders.

Once a liquidation is complete, the company concerned will be "dissolved"; namely, its name will be removed from the register of companies and it will cease to exist as a legal entity. In the case of a compulsory liquidation, a final meeting of creditors is summoned to receive the liquidator's report of the winding up. The liquidator must give notice to the registrar of companies that the meeting has been held and of the decisions (if any) of the meeting. The registrar must register this notice and the company is dissolved automatically at the end of three months. In the case of a voluntary liquidation, the liquidator must make up an account of the winding up as soon as the affairs of the company are fully wound up. After the appropriate meetings of members and creditors have been held, the liquidator must file the account with the registrar of companies. The registrar must register the account and the company is dissolved automatically at the end of three months. **15.28**

C. The Avoidance of Transactions Entered into by a Company Prior to Liquidation or Administration

1. INTRODUCTION

Directors and others who are managing the affairs of a company in financial difficulty may be tempted to take action that causes the assets of the company to be placed beyond the reach of any liquidator or administrator who is eventually appointed if and when the company goes into liquidation or an administration order is made in respect of it. Needless to say, any such action will reduce the general fund available to liquidators and administrators. As a result, the Insolvency Act 1986 contains several provisions that are designed to reverse the effects of any such action so far as is possible in all the circumstances. The main provisions under the Act are as follows: **15.29**

section 238 Transactions at an undervalue
section 239 Preferences
section 245 Avoidance of certain floating charges
section 423 Transactions defrauding creditors.

2. TRANSACTIONS AT AN UNDERVALUE (INSOLVENCY ACT 1986, S. 238)

15.30   Section 238 of the Insolvency Act 1986 seeks to reverse the effects of a gift given or an undervalue transaction entered into by a company that then goes into liquidation or has an administration order made in relation to it. Where the company concerned has entered into such a transaction at a "relevant time" (see below for an explanation of what is meant by this) then the liquidator or administrator may apply to court for an order under this section. The court can make such order as it thinks fit for restoring the position to what it would have been if the company had not entered into that transaction. Some guidance on the type of orders to be awarded is provided in section 241(1) of the Insolvency Act 1986 *and* the position of bona fide third parties is protected by section 241(2) of the Act.

What is meant by a transaction at an undervalue? Basically, section 238(4) of the Insolvency Act 1986 provides that a company enters into a transaction with a person at an undervalue if:

(a) the company makes a gift to that person or
(b) the company enters into a transaction with that person and the value of consideration received by the company is significantly less than the value of the consideration provided by the company.

Clearly, the section is aimed at preventing the company concerned from simply giving away or selling cheaply assets that would otherwise be available to the liquidator or administrator.

Under section 238(5) of the Insolvency Act 1986, the Court will not make an order if it is satisfied that the company entered the transaction in good faith and for the purpose of carrying on its business and that at the time there were reasonable grounds for believing that the transaction would benefit the company.

It is often the case that a company faced with a severe shortage of cash reserves will be forced to sell assets at a discount to market value in order to ensure the immediate payment of pressing debts. If the company concerned does not enter into the undervalue transaction and realise some cash for payment of such debts, then any creditor may well force a liquidation, thus effectively bringing the business of the company to an end. When the company enters into the undervalue transaction, there must be reasonable grounds for believing that the transaction will benefit the company (for example, reasonable grounds for believing that the cash realised from it for payment of the pressing debts concerned will alleviate the financial problems of the company and allow it to carry on its business).

For the court to make an order under section 238 of the Insolvency Act 1986, the transaction concerned must be entered into at the "relevant time". Section 240 of the Act provides that in the case of a transaction at an undervalue the relevant time is in the period of two years ending with the "onset of insolvency."

In the case of an administration, the onset of insolvency is the date of the presentation of the petition for an administration order and in the case of a liquidation it is the date of the commencement of the winding up.

The company must be unable to pay its debts at the time of the transaction or it must become unable to pay its debts as a result of the transaction (*i.e.* the company must be insolvent at the time of the transaction or become insolvent as a result of it). Insolvency is presumed if the transaction is with a person connected with the company unless the contrary is shown.

3. PREFERENCES (INSOLVENCY ACT 1986, s. 239)

Section 239 of the Insolvency Act 1986 seeks to reverse the effects of a company "preferring" one of its creditors or a surety or a guarantor to the detriment of others prior to it going into liquidation or administration. Where the company concerned has given a preference at the relevant time (see below for an explanation of what is meant by this) then the liquidator or administrator may apply to Court for an order under this section. The court can make such order as it thinks fit for restoring the position to what it would have been if the company had not given that preference. Some guidance on the type of orders to be awarded is provided in section 241(1) of the Insolvency Act 1986 *and* the position of bona fide third parties is protected by section 241(2) of the Act.

15.31

What is meant by a preference? Basically, section 239(4) of the Insolvency Act 1986 provides that a company gives a preference to a person if:

(a) that person is one of the company's creditors or a surety or guarantor for its debts or liabilities; and
(b) the company does anything or suffers anything to be done that has the effect of putting that person into a better position than he would have been in on a liquidation if that thing had not been done.

This section is aimed at preventing the company paying off one of its favoured creditors in full while others of the same status remain unpaid. In a liquidation, assets would be distributed to creditors in a strict order of entitlement (see paragraphs 15.25–15.27) and where there were insufficient assets to pay creditors in any given class then they would each receive an equal proportion of their respective debts. Clearly, this principle is disregarded if one creditor is given preferential treatment.

Under section 239(5) of the Insolvency Act 1986, the Court will not make an order unless the company was influenced by a desire to put the person concerned into the better position mentioned above. Under section 239(6) of the Act 1986, this desire is presumed in the case of preferences given to persons connected with the company concerned unless the contrary is shown.

It is often the case that a company in financial difficulty is faced with a choice of paying off one particular creditor or being forced into liquidation by him. In this case, payment of the debt concerned in full may not amount to a preference by the company concerned because, rather than being influenced by a desire to put that creditor in the better position, the company is responding to real commercial pressure.

For the court to make an order under section 239, the preference must be given at the "relevant time". Section 240 provides that, in the case of a preference, the relevant time is in the period of two years ending with the "onset of insolvency" (see above paragraph 15.30) for what is meant by this) where the preference is given to a person who is connected with the company. Where the preference is given to someone who is not so connected, the relevant time is in the period of six months ending with the onset of insolvency.

The company must be unable to pay its debts at the time of the preference or it must become unable to pay its debts as a result of the preference. Insolvency is not presumed in the case of a preference.

4. AVOIDANCE OF CERTAIN FLOATING CHARGES (INSOLVENCY ACT 1986, s. 245)

15.32
(a) Section 245 of the Insolvency Act 1986 provides that, where a company has gone into liquidation or administration, a floating charge on the company's undertaking or property created at the "relevant time" (see below for an explanation of what is meant by this) is invalid *except* to the extent of consideration paid or supplied to the company at the same time as, or after, the creation of the charge *and* consideration consisting of a discharge or reduction of any debt of the company at the same as, or after, the creation of the charge *and* interest payable (*if any*) on such consideration.

This section aims to prevent specifically a company uplifting the status of an ordinary unsecured creditor to that of a secured creditor. Hence, a floating charge created for the benefit of an ordinary creditor who is already owed a sum of money by the company without the provision of fresh consideration by such a creditor is clearly invalid if created within the relevant time provided the company goes into liquidation or administration. Where the creditor provides further consideration (for example, in the form of further cash advances or the provision of new goods or services on credit) at the time of, or after, the creation of the charge then that charge will be valid only to the extent of the value of the new consideration and interest payable thereon (if any). The rational here is that the interests of existing ordinary creditors cannot be prejudiced by a new floating charge that is supported by fresh valuable consideration of which the company did not have the benefit prior to the new arrangements.

(b) A floating charge is only invalid if created at the "relevant time." Section 245(3) of the Insolvency Act 1986 provides that the relevant time is in the period of two years ending with the "onset of insolvency" (defined as above, see paragraph 15.30) if the charge is created in favour of a person who is connected with the company. Where the charge is created in favour of someone not so connected, the relevant time is in the period of 12 months ending with the onset of insolvency.

In the case of a charge created in favour of a person who is connected with the company, there is no requirement that the company is unable to pay its debts at the time of the transaction or becomes unable to do so as a result of the transaction. In the case of unconnected persons, the reverse is true and the company must be insolvent at the time of creation of the charge or become insolvent as a result of it before it is invalid.

5. Meaning of "Connected" with the Company

For the purposes of sections 238, 239 and 245 of the Insolvency Act 1986 **15.33** a person is connected with a company if:

(a) he is a director or shadow director or an associate of such a director or shadow director, or
(b) he is an associate of the company.

(See Insolvency Act 1986, ss. 249, 435.)

6. Transactions Defrauding Creditors (Insolvency Act 1986, s. 423)

Finally, in addition to the above provisions, it should always be remembered **15.34** that any transaction entered at an undervalue may amount to a transaction defrauding creditors pursuant to section 423 of the Insolvency Act 1986. This is so if the Court is satisfied that the transaction was entered into for the purpose of putting assets beyond the reach of a person who is making, or may at some time make, a claim against the company or that otherwise prejudices the interests of such a person.

This section is far more wide ranging that the ones mentioned previously and does not only apply to companies in liquidation or administration. There are no "relevant time" limits and so transactions defrauding creditors can be set aside at any time. The real difficulty for those seeking a court order under this section is the requirement that it must be established that the transaction was entered into with the specific intention or purpose of putting assets beyond their reach or otherwise prejudicing their interests. Needless to say, this intention or purpose is difficult to prove; the section is reserved for truly fraudulent activity and is not invoked as often as the other sections.

D. The Personal Liabilities of Directors (and Others) in the Event of a Company's Insolvent Liquidation

1. Introduction

The Insolvency Act 1986 and related legislation provide for a variety of **15.35** liabilities that may be imposed on directors and others who control or manage the affairs of a company that eventually goes into insolvent liquidation. This section will provide a very brief overview of the most important areas of liability which are as follows:

> section 214: Wrongful trading
> section 213: Fraudulent trading
> section 212: Summary remedy against delinquent directors ("misfeasance")
> sections 6 and 10 of the Company Directors Disqualification Act 1986: Disqualification as directors

Invariably, the aim of the legislation is either to force directors and others who have controlled or managed the affairs of an insolvent company to contribute to the assets available to the liquidator where there has been wrongdoing or to somehow punish those participating in such wrongdoing. Given the threat of such personal liability, this body of legislation is of increasing concern to company directors and the like. In particular, for those directors who are also shareholders in a company, the legislation that forces them to contribute to the assets of the insolvent company represents a major limitation on the effectiveness of the limited liability principle.

2. WRONGFUL TRADING: INSOLVENCY ACT 1986, s. 214

15.36   By far the most pressing form of liability for directors of insolvent companies is that of wrongful trading set out in section 214 of the Insolvency Act 1986.

Section 214(1) of the Act provides that, on the application of the liquidator during the course of a winding up, the Court may declare that a person is to be liable to make such contribution to the company's assets as the court thinks proper.

Section 214(2) provides that the court will only make such order in relation to that person if:

(a) the company has gone into insolvent liquidation;
(b) at some time *before* the commencement of the winding up of the company, that person knew or ought to have concluded that there was no reasonable prospect that the company would avoid going into insolvent liquidation; and
(c) that person was a director of the company at that time.

Section 214(3) provides for a defence for the director concerned. The court will not make a declaration if it is satisfied that the director concerned took *every* step with a view to minimising the potential loss to the company's creditors as he *ought* to have taken.

Section 214 provides that the director concerned must be regarded as a person having both the general knowledge, skills and experience that may reasonably be expected of a person carrying out the same functions as are carried out by that director in relation to the company *and* the general knowledge, skill and experience that that director has.

Where does all of this leave a director of a company in financial difficulty? Basically, before any liability for wrongful trading can arise, the company concerned must go into insolvent liquidation. Once this has occurred, it is for the liquidator alone to decide whether or not to seek an order under section 214 for a contribution to the assets from a person who is or has been a director of the company. The liquidator will decide whether or not to seek the order by reference to the acts of the director concerned prior to the insolvent liquidation; namely, at any time prior to liquidation, did the company continue to trade when that director knew or ought to have concluded that there was no reasonable prospect of avoiding the insolvent liquidation?

The ingredients of wrongful trading mean that directors of companies in financial difficulty but not yet insolvent must always consider whether or not insolvent liquidation in a real prospect and cannot reasonably be avoided. If it is such a prospect and the company continues to trade then the directors concerned are exposed to the risk of liability for wrongful trading. For example, directors who continue to accept goods or services on credit once they know that insolvent liquidation is a real prospect are likely to be held liable to contribute to the assets of the company.

Directors will escape liability if, knowing or having ought to have concluded that there was no reasonable prospect that the company would avoid going into liquidation, they take *every* step to minimise loss to creditors as they ought to have taken. What amounts to every such step depends on the facts of each case but may include: **15.37**

    (a) petitioning the court for an administration order if one of the grounds for the granting of such an order exists;

    (b) petitioning the court for a winding-up order;

    (c) seeking the implementation of a creditors' voluntary winding up;

    (d) inviting the holder of a floating charge to appoint an administrative receiver;

    (e) seeking advice and assistance from a qualified insolvency practitioner as to the overall strategy to be employed.

In assessing a director's liability for wrongful trading, he will be regarded as possessing the knowledge and skill that one might reasonably expect such a person in his position to have as well as his actual knowledge and skill. This means that those directors with substandard skills will always be judged in accordance with reasonable standards while those with superior skills to those that one can reasonably expect will be judged in accordance with those superior standards. The result is that those directors with wide-ranging knowledge and expertise are more vulnerable to a charge of wrongful trading than others.

In conclusion here, it cannot be stressed enough that directors of companies in financial difficulties must always be aware of the risks of wrongful trading. Many company directors may have viable financial strategies that enable them to conclude reasonably that insolvent liquidation can be avoided. Clearly, such strategies should be discussed and implemented at fully attended and fully minuted board meetings. It is advisable to have such strategies reviewed and approved by the company's auditors and major creditors. Further, at every appropriate opportunity, the directors' conclusions that insolvent liquidation can be avoided should be minuted. If at any stage doubt is thrown on such conclusions the directors should seek the assistance of a qualified insolvency practitioner and take every step to protect creditors (see above in this paragraph for examples of such steps).

3. FRAUDULENT TRADING (INSOLVENCY ACT 1986, S. 213)

15.38   Where the business of a company has been carried on by any persons with intent to defraud creditors of the company or creditors of any other person or for any fraudulent purpose then section 213 of the Insolvency Act 1986 provides that, during the course of a winding up, a liquidator may seek an order of the court that such persons are liable to make such contributions to the company's assets as the court thinks proper.

Any person (and not just a director) who carries on the business of the company in a fraudulent manner is liable to make a contribution to the assets of the company. Such activity is also a criminal offence under section 458 of the Companies Act 1985 whether or not the company is in the course of being wound up. A person convicted of such a crime is liable to imprisonment or a fine, or both.

In the case of civil liability to contribute to the assets of the company under section 213 of the Insolvency Act 1986, the company must go into liquidation before such liability can accrue and it is the liquidator alone who may seek the relevant order. In deciding whether or not to seek such an order, the liquidator will make reference to the acts of any persons who were knowingly parties to the carrying on of the business of the company at any time prior to the winding up.

Because fraud is such a serious matter, it is essential to establish deliberate and actual dishonesty. For example, directors who continue to accept goods and services on credit knowing that the debts that are run up will *never* be paid by the company are clearly acting dishonestly and may be subject to a charge of fraudulent trading.

It is because of the onerous requirement of establishing such dishonest intent that section 213 of the Insolvency Act 1986 is not invoked as often of section 214 of the Act. In the case of wrongful trading, the intention of the director concerned is of no importance; the question is: ought he have concluded that there was no reasonable prospect that the company would avoid going into insolvent liquidation?

4. SUMMARY REMEDY AGAINST DELINQUENT DIRECTORS ("MISFEASANCE"): (INSOLVENCY ACT 1986, S. 212)

15.39   Section 212 of the Insolvency Act 1986 applies during the course of a winding up to a "person" who has misapplied or retained, or become accountable for any money or other property of the company, or been guilty of any misfeasance or breach of any fiduciary or other duty in relation to the company.

Such a "person" must be or have been an officer of the company (*e.g.* a director) or have acted as liquidator, administrator or administrative receiver of the company or be or have been concerned or taken part in the promotion, formation or management of the company.

Section 212(3) of the Act provides that on the application of the liquidator or any creditor or contributory (*i.e.* shareholder), the Court may examine the conduct of such a person and compel him to repay, restore or account for money or property or contribute a sum to the company's assets as compensation for the misfeasance or breach of duty as the court thinks just.

This section simply provides efficient summary proceedings for the recovery of money or property by the liquidator or others from those (primarily, directors) who have committed the wrongs detailed in the section.

5. DISQUALIFICATION AS A DIRECTOR: (SS. 6 AND 10 OF THE COMPANY DIRECTORS' DISQUALIFICATION ACT 1986)

Finally, this piece of legislation has severe ramifications for directors of insolvent companies that may result in the loss of their personal livelihoods. **15.40**

Section 10 of the Company Directors' Disqualification Act 1986 provides that if a Court makes an order under section 213 of the Insolvency Act 1986 (fraudulent trading) or section 214 of that Act (wrongful trading) then the court *may*, if it thinks fit, also make a disqualification order against the person to whom the declaration relates. This means that the director concerned is disqualified from acting as a director of a company in the future. The maximum period of disqualification here is 15 years.

Section 6 of the Company Directors' Disqualification Act 1986 provides that the Court *shall* make a disqualification order against a person if it is satisfied that he is or has been a director of a company that has at any time become insolvent (whether while he was a director or subsequently), and that his conduct as a director of that company makes him unfit to be concerned in the management of a company. Here, the minimum period of disqualification is two years and the maximum period is 15 years. It is for an appropriate office-holder (*i.e.* liquidator, administrator or administrative receiver) to report to the Secretary of State that the conditions set out in section 6 are satisfied in respect of a person who is or has been a director of the company concerned. The Secretary of State may then make the appropriate application to Court for the disqualification order if it appears to him to be expedient in the public interest. Matters to be taken into account by the Court in determining whether or not a person is unfit to be involved in the management of a company are set out in Schedule 1 to the Act.

16. Company Taxation

A. Introduction

16.1   This chapter deals with the taxation of companies and employees.

Companies pay corporation tax under the Income and Corporation Taxes Act 1988 by reference to Schedule D which deals with the profits from a trade or profession.

Employees pay income tax under the Income and Corporation Taxes Act 1988 and the income received in that capacity is allocated to Schedule E.

As with taxation issues concerning sole traders and partners, the legal adviser's task is becoming increasingly specialised. Unless a solicitor is a tax expert, it will be prudent to liaise with the firm's tax section or otherwise seek assistance.

As far as the solicitor advising a company it is important that:

(a) potential tax problems are recognised;
(b) tax planning suggestions are made and investigated; and
(c) that advice is given in the light of the wider commercial circumstances pertaining to the company.

As with partnerships and sole traders, companies pay taxation on their income profits. The income profits are classified in accordance with the income Schedules.

The ingredient elements of taxation are as follows:

(a) it is a compulsory levy;
(b) imposed by a government or local authority;
(c) for raising revenue for public purposes.

1. CLASSIFICATION OF TAXES IN THE UNITED KINGDOM

Direct taxes

16.2   (a) Income tax
(b) Capital gains tax
(c) Inheritance tax
(d) Corporation tax
(e) Stamp duty
(f) Petroleum revenue tax
(g) Council tax

Indirect taxes
(a) Value added tax
(b) Car tax
(c) Customs and Excise duty

2. DISTINCTION BETWEEN DIRECT AND INDIRECT TAXES

    (a) *Direct* taxes are borne by the taxpayer and not passed on to any other person.   **16.3**

    (b) *Indirect* taxes are passed on so that the burden of the tax is borne by another, person, *e.g.* VAT is paid by the retailer and then passed on to the customer.

B. The Income Schedules

Income tax for the companies is levied according to the source of the income   **16.4** profits. Income is categorised according to the five schedules set out in the Income and Corporation Taxes Act 1988.

    Each type of income will fall within a schedule, *i.e.* a *trading* company having no other source of income will use Schedule D, Case I to complete its profits.

Schedule	Source	Basis of assessment
A	Rents and other receipts from land in the U.K.	Rents receivable less outgoings of the current year of assessment
C	Public Revenue	Income of the current year of assessment
D		
Case I	Profits of a trade in the U.K.	
Case II	Profits of a profession or vocation in the U.K.	
Case III	Interest, annuities and other payments	Schedule D operated on a preceding year basis. It is being brought into line with the other schedules so as to operate on a current year basis from 1997–98 see sections 60–69 of the Income and Corporation Taxes Act 1988. It is currently operating with regard to transitional rules.
Case IV	Securities out of the U.K. not charged under Schedule C	

Schedule	Source	Basis of assessment
Case V	Possessions out of the U.K. not charged under Schedule C (but excluding foreign employment)	
Case VI	Annual profits or gains not falling under Cases I–V and not charged by virtue of any other Schedule; and certain income directed to be so charged.	
E Cases I, II III	Offices, employments and and pensions (both "home" and foreign). Also, chargeable benefits under the social security legislation.	Income in the year of receipt.
F	Dividends and certain other Income of the current year of assessment. distribution by companies	

C. Background Concepts

16.5   As with the taxation of individuals, there are several concepts that have a bearing on the company's taxation liability. These concepts have already been discussed in Chapter 6 but are also discussed here for the sake of convenience.

Among such concepts are the following:

(a) *Expenses*. These are the costs of running the business that can be *deducted* from the income profits and thereby reduce the taxable income profits of the company. There are detailed rules in the legislation as to what type of expenses are deductible and the conditions which have to be satisfied

(b) *Capital allowances*. This refers to the depreciation of capital assets that, whilst of a capital nature, *reduce* the income profits and therefore the liability to corporation tax.

(c) *Capital gains tax*. This is charged on the increase in value over and above the pending inflation rates for certain assets owned by the company and subsequently disposed. Capital gains are *added* to the income profits made by a company. Capital gains *reliefs* act either to delay or reduce the capital gains tax liability.

(d) *Qualifying distributions.* These are payments made by the company that allow the company to *pre-pay* parts of its mainstream tax liability. The portion of tax liability pre-paid is known as advance corporation tax (ACT).

(e) *Losses.* These can be *set-off* against other income. That other income may be in relation to:
   (i) another schedule; or
   (ii) another tax year, *i.e.* before or after the loss is incurred.

(f) *Charges on income.* These are amounts that the company is under legal obligation to pay to a third party as set out in section 8(8) of the Taxes Management Act 1970. As such, they are deducted before the income profits are added up. The main charge on income incurred by a company will be an interest payment paid to a third party for a loan.

D. The Taxation of Companies

Just as individuals pay income tax on their assessable income profits, companies pay corporation tax on their income profits, subject to authorised deductions pursuant to the Income and Corporation Taxes Act 1988, s. 12.

16.6

Corporation tax is also known as Mainstream Corporation Tax (MCT).

There are two periods to be borne in mind when looking at the assessment to corporation tax of companies, namely:

(a) the accounting period; and
(b) the financial year, which is also known as the corporate tax year.

1. THE ACCOUNTING PERIOD

The Accounting Period is a period of one year, chosen by the company. It is a period for which the company's annual accounts are prepared (also known as the annual accounts reference). A common accounting period will be January 1–December 31, *i.e.* an ordinary calendar year.

2. THE FINANCIAL YEAR

The financial year is a period of 12 months which provides the reference period for all British companies for the calculation of their mainstream corporation tax (MCT) liability (the *payment* of MCT is dealt with separately).

The financial year for companies is April 1 of a year to March 31 of the following year.

As a result of the accounting period and financial years overlapping, many companies will pay MCT based on two financial years and possibly different rates of MCT.

Example: Overlapping Accounting Period and Financial Year. Assume that Ninja Ltd Accounting Period was January 1, 1991–December 31, 1991.

    (a) The accounting period was spread over two financial years, *i.e.* April 1, 1990—March 31, 1991 (the 1990 FY) and April 1, 1991—March 31, 1992 (the 1991 FY).

    (b) The MCT rate in 1990 was 34 per cent.

    (c) The MCT rate in 1991 was 33 per cent.

    (d) Therefore, in Ninja Ltd's case, by reference to its accounting period:

        (i) the period January 1, 1991—March 31, 1991 will be treated to MCT at 34 per cent; and

        (ii) the period April 1, 1991—December 31, 1991 will be treated to MCT at 33 per cent.

3. CORPORATION TAX RATES

16.7   The standard rate of taxation for companies (Mainstream Corporation Tax or MCT) is 33 per cent of the income profits. The standard rate may change from financial year to year. The MCT rate has come down from 50 per cent in 1983 and has been 33 per cent for a few years.

4. THE SMALL COMPANIES RATE

16.8   Section 13 of the Income and Corporation Taxes Act 1988 provides relief for "small companies" in respect of the amount of corporation tax they are required to pay.

    If a company's income profits do not exceed £300,000, the applicable rate is 25 per cent of income profits, *i.e.* a company with profits of £100,000 pays £25,000 MCT.

    For those companies making income profits in a relevant year in excess of £300,000 but not exceeding £1,500,000 the applicable corporation tax rate is set by reference to a tapering formula (in section 13(2) of the Income and Corporation Taxes Act 1988).

E. Losses Made by a Company

16.9   So far we have dealt with the situation where the company makes a profit. What happens, however, if the company makes a loss, *i.e.* its costs and expenses in a financial year outweigh its revenue, capital gains and other schedule income?

    A company can put its loss to good use as far as MCT is concerned. Essentially, what is involved in the use of the loss is that it is set off against other income profits of the company, thereby reducing MCT payable in profit making areas of the company's business or profit-making years.

    The applicable principle is that if the company makes a trading loss, it is the company, as a separate legal entity (and not the members) who are entitled to claim the tax relief.

1. TAX RELIEF FOR LOSSES

16.10   Both trading losses and unrelieved charges on income will be available to the company for tax relief purposes. To be used for income tax relief purposes such amounts must be set against profits from the same trade (known as the "same trade rule"). To be carried forward, charges on income must be wholly and exclusively used for the company's trade.

They may be set off against profits for:

    (a) the same accounting period
    (b) future accounting periods ("carried forward"); or
    (c) previous accounting periods ("carried back").

2. Same Accounting Period Losses (Income and Corporation Taxes Act 1988, s. 393)

Trading losses or charges on income can be set off against income profit, of the same accounting period in which they were incurred. **16.11**

The same trade rule applies.

3. Losses Carried Forward (Income and Corporation Taxes Act 1988, s. 393)

Alternatively to setting off losses against income from the same accounting period in which they are incurred (or if the trading loss or unrelieved charges on income are not used up), the trading loss/unrelieved charges on income may be carried forward against the trading profits of future years (but not against the capital gains of future years). The Revenue must be notified within six years of the end of the accounting period in which loss occurred. **16.12**

4. Losses Carried Back (Income and Corporation Taxes Act 1988, s. 393A)

Trading losses can be set off against profits of the previous three accounting periods. **16.13**

The loss must be set off against the income profits of the later years before the earlier years, *i.e.* a loss incurred in 1994, will first be set off against income from 1993, then 1992, etc.

The same trade rule applies. See paragraph 16.12.

F. Business Reliefs

As was discussed in Chapter 6, the notion of a relief in relation to tax is either that it: **16.14**

    (a) reduces a taxpayer's liability to pay tax because of the taxpayer's personal circumstances, such as retirement relief; or
    (b) delays the payment of tax by virtue of reinvestment in replacement assets (such as rollover relief) or by way of an election (request) by the taxpayer (such as holdover relief on the gift of business assets).

Allowances refer to exemptions from the payment of tax due to an individual's circumstances.

The reliefs and allowances looked at are at follows:

INCOME TAX RELIEFS AND ALLOWANCES

Personal allowance—the first £3,765 of income is exempt from income tax
Married couple's allowance—£1,790
Others such as the blindness allowance; age related allowance

CAPITAL GAINS TAX RELIEFS AND ALLOWANCES

16.15   Annual allowance—the first £6,300 of capital gain is exempt
Replacement of business assets
Hold-over relief (instalments option)
Incorporation relief
Entrepreneurial relief

INHERITANCE TAX RELIEFS AND ALLOWANCES

Annual allowance—£3,000 annually
Threshold value of estate—£200,000 as from April 6, 1996
Business property relief (instalments option)

REPLACEMENT OF BUSINESS ASSETS RELIEF (TAXATION OF CHARGEABLE GAINS ACT 1992, ss. 152–158)

16.16   As we discussed in Chapter 6, rollover relief can be claimed by an individual who owns assets which are used by the business. In that case, it is the individual who must purchase the replacement asset and claim the relief.

Rollover relief operates on the same principles in relation to companies. It can be claimed by either:

(a) the company as a separate entity; or

(b) by an individual who owns an asset which is used by his personal company (which is defined in relation to an individual as one in which he exercises at leat 5 per cent of the voting rights);

(c) by an employee who owns an asset which is used or in the case of land-buildings, is occupied for the purpose of the employment.

Replacement of business assets relief postpones the payment of CGT. The relief works by rolling the capital gain made on the sale of an asset into the purchase price of the replacement asset thereby reducing the deemed acquisition price of the replacement asset. Capital gains tax will be paid when the replacement asset is sold and not replaced. The rationale for the relief is to encourage the investment by business in business assets.

As mentioned above, rollover relief can be claimed by individuals where they own one of the nominated business assets which is used by the business. The relief is then available to the individual rather than the business, *i.e.* the individual must purchase the replacement asset in order to claim the relief.

16.17   The conditions that have to be met in order to claim rollover relief are as follows:

Those who can claim rollover relief: either the company or an individual who owns the asset which is used by the business;

Type of asset: see Taxation of Chargeable Gains Act 1992, s. 155. The list includes buildings, fixed plant and machinery, land and goodwill. The old asset and the replacement asset need not be of the same type, *e.g.* a gain on the sale of plant can be rolled into the purchase of land;

Timing of purchase of replacement asset: the replacement asset must be purchased within three years of the sale of the old asset or can be purchased no more than one year before the sale of the old asset, *i.e.* the old and replacement asset can both be owned at the same time for up to one year.

Use of assets in successive trades: the replacement asset need not be used in the same trade as the old asset but can be used by another trade (in which the taxpayer is involved) which is being operated at the same time as or in succession to the trade in which the old asset was used. In the case of a successive trade it must commence trading within three years of the former trade ceasing.

Example: Roll-over relief. ABC Ltd sells land and makes a capital gain of £100,000. One year later it purchases replacement land for £500,000. ABC Ltd can roll the £100,000 gain into the purchase price of the second piece of land, reducing the land price to £400,000, *i.e.* actual price of £500,000 less gain rolled into it of £100,000—so, in effect, ABC Ltd is *delaying* the repayment of CGT on the sale of the first piece of land until such time as ABC Ltd sells the replacement land and does not purchase a replacement asset.

16.18

RETIREMENT RELIEF (TAXATION OF CHARGEABLE GAINS ACT 1992, ss. 163 AND 164)

As discussed in Chapter 6, retirement is available to individuals including directors, employees, sole traders and partners. It acts to reduce a taxpayer's capital gains liability on retirement from a business. The rationale for the relief is to encourage the turnover of business assets and the continuity of businesses.

16.19

Those who can claim
Individuals who retire from the business at the age of 50 or more or earlier through ill health, in which case they would need medical proof in order to satisfy the Revenue.

Type of asset
Retirement relief is only given in respect of the capital gains made on the "material disposal" of "chargeable business assets". For other assets, *e.g.* private rather than business investments, the taxpayer will have to pay CGT. Chargeable business assets are generally those which qualify for capital allowances and include:

(a) land
(b) goodwill
(c) plant and machinery.

A "material disposal" includes the disposal of:

(a) a sole tradership business;
(b) a partner's interest in a partnership business;
(c) a shareholder who retires from a "personal company", *i.e.* a company in which he holds at least 5 per cent of the voting rights. In the case of a shareholder he must also prove in relation to the personal company that he was:

   (i) a full-time working officer or employee;
   (ii) who devoted substantial time to the company; and
   (iii) was involved in a managerial or technical capacity.

Retirement relief will apply to what is referred in section 164 as "associated disposals". These arise for instance in the case of companies where an asset which is owned by an individual in his own name is used by his "personal company". In order to get retirement relief he must (in addition to disposing of his shares in the company) sell that asset as part of his complete withdrawal from the company.

Amount of retirement relief

16.20   In order to qualify for the retirement relief the taxpayer must have owned the interest for at least one year before claiming the relief.

Thereafter, the retirement relief claimable increases by 10 per cent per year on a straight line basis. Thus whilst ownership of an asset for two years gives 20 per cent relief, ownership for eight years gives 80 per cent relief.

The maximum amount of retirement relief claimable is available on disposals or associated disposals involving capital gains in excess of £1,000,000. The relief applicable in such situations is £625,000 calculated as follows:

(a) £250,000, *i.e.* 100 per cent of £250,000; plus
(b) £375,000, *i.e.* 50 per cent of the £750,000 balance up to £1,000,000.

With full retirement relief therefore, a capital gain of £1 million can be reduced by £625,000 to a taxable gain of £375,000.

Such relief is claimed by written application to the Revenue (together with supporting medical evidence of ill health if the claimant is less than 50 years of age).

HOLD-OVER RELIEF

16.21   Hold-over relief acts to delay the payment of capital gains tax. It is governed by the Taxation of Chargeable Gains Act 1992. It covers:

(a) transfers between spouses (s. 58); and
(b) the gift or undervalue sales (*i.e.* where less than market vaue is paid) of business assets (s. 165). In this situation the donee and donor can make a joint election to hold over the capital gain. When the donee *sells* the asset in question he will be liable to pay:

   (i) his own capital gains tax for the period of his ownership; plus

   (ii) the capital gains tax for the period relating to the donor's period of ownership.

The conditions which have to be met to claim hold-over relief under section 165 of the Taxation of Chargeable Gains Act 1992 are as follows:

Type of asset
An asset which is used for the purpose of a trade, profession or vocation (see s. 165(2)).

Conditions
A joint election to hold over the capital gain is made by the donor and donee to the Revenue in respect of a gift or undervalue sale of a business asset.

ENTREPRENEURIAL RELIEF
Dealt with in paragraph J below

INCORPORATION RELIEF (SEE CHAPTER 6)

Incorporation relief may be claimed when a sole tradership or partnership business becomes a private limited company and the owners of the business (*i.e.* the sole trader or the partners as the case may be) thereby make a capital gain. The capital gain can be rolled into the return from the new company. **16.22**

   Example: Incorporation relief. Bob sells his sole tradership to ABC Ltd for a capital gain of £20,000. He receives shares worth £50,000 in ABC Ltd.
   The incorporation relief will apply as follows: the £20,000 gain will be rolled into the actual acquisition price of the shares which is £50,000 giving the shares a deemed acquisition price of £30,000. When Bob sells the shares in ABC Ltd, subject to other reliefs, he will pay CGT based on the share's deemed acquisition price of £30,000.

G. The Taxation of Payments Made by the Company

1. THE PAYMENT OF DIVIDENDS

The company will make or be obliged to make certain payments in any one accounting period. These will broadly be of two kinds: **16.23**

   (a) distributions: chief amongst these is the payment of dividends to shareholders; and

   (b) charges on income: chief amongst these is the payment of interest.

The "classical" system for the payment of dividends that was in operation between 1966 and 1973 had two central features:

   (a) company distributions (including dividends) were not allowed as deductions by a company in calculating its income profits. Instead, distributions were payable out of net profits and were subject to income tax in the hands of he shareholder. Dividends were in effect subject to double taxation—both the company and shareholder paid tax on them; and

(b) the close company was created with its own taxation rules and the treatment.

The dividend imputation system that has been in operation from 1973, introduced the concept of Advance Corporation Tax or ACT. ACT is generally payable on "distributions" made by the company.

ACT serves the following purposes:

(a) it is a pre-payment of part of the company's MCT liability; and

(b) it is a payment of the amount basic rate income tax (as a general principle and subject to any transitional provisions) for the shareholder in respect of the particular distribution and result in a tax credit such that a basic rate taxpayer need pay no more tax on it.

A dividend is not a deductible expense for the company in arriving at its income profits. Distributions may either be "qualifying" or "non-qualifying." A dividend is a qualifying distribution. The two main features of a qualifying distribution are:

(a) the payment of ACT by the company to the Revenue, *i.e.* as we have noted, it represents a partial pre-payment of the company's mainstream corporation tax bill;

(b) a tax credit for the shareholder, *i.e.* the shareholder is given a tax credit for the ACT paid in respect of the dividend he receives so that he will receives his dividend payment together with a national credit equivalent to basic rate income tax.

Example: ACT and tax credits for the recipient

16.24   The ACT rate for the current tax year is $\dfrac{I}{100 - I}$

where I equals the basic rate income tax for 1996–97 of 20 per cent.

$$i.e. \text{ It is currently } \frac{20}{100 - 20} = 1/4$$

The ACT rate is 1/4 of the amount of the dividend itself. So if a dividend of £80 is proposed to be paid by a company to a shareholder, the company will pay ACT, *i.e.* £20 to the Revenue.

ACT is 1/4 of the dividend itself or 1/5 of the "grossed-up" amount of such dividend. The grossed up amount simply refers to the dividend *and* the ACT, *i.e.* which in the case would be £100 in total.

The shareholder in this example receives the dividend of £80 and a tax credit of 20 per cent. This means that the shareholder will only have to pay more tax in respect of the dividend if he is a 24 per cent or 40 per cent taxpayer.

ACT avoids the "double taxation" of both:

(a) the company; and
(b) the shareholder.

It allows a company when it pays dividends to shareholders to pay in advance part of its MCT liability. The shareholder is given a tax credit and receives "franked" dividends, *i.e* dividends on which the company has already paid tax.

Example: ACT payment by the company to the revenue. A company Betannix Ltd wishes to pay dividends totalling £100,000 to its shareholders. How much ACT will Betannix pay?

(a) It will pay a sum equivalent to 1/4 of the £100,000 dividend.
(b) Betannix pays £25,000 ACT to the revenue.
(c) Each shareholder in Betannix receives a 20 per cent tax credit.
(d) the ACT of £25,000 is 20 per cent or 1/5 of the "grossed-up" amount of the dividend which is £125,000.

ACT paid on dividends can be deducted from the MCT bill on income profits for the relevant accounting period. In this way, a company can plan its tax arrangements by reference to cash reserves at a given time.

For the shareholders, dividends are assessed to income tax under Schedule F on the gross sum received, *i.e.* the dividend actually paid, together with the ACT paid on it.

The individual receives a tax credit equal to the basic rate of income so that only if the shareholder is subject to the higher rate will there be a further income tax charge.

2. DEBENTURE INTEREST, *I.E.* INTEREST PAID BY THE COMPANY ON A LOAN

"Charges on income", as already noted, are amounts that fall to be deducted on computing total income. They are defined but consist of certain transfer that the taxpayer is obliged to make. **16.25**

The theory is that such income ceases to be the payer's and becomes that of the payee so that the payer should not be taxed on it.

Charges on income are, therefore, deducted from income profits *before* personal reliefs are taken into account.

Some interest payment will be paid in gross and the recipient will be assessed to income tax under Schedule D, Case III.

For interest payable under a debenture, the company deducts the basic rate income tax at source which, for 1994–95 is 25 per cent, and notifies the Revenue that the payment has been made.

The bank (or payee) will be assessed for income tax on the amount it receives and will get a credit equivalent to the basic rate of tax income:

Example: Interest payments

(a) A company, Chelsea Ltd, has a mortgage debenture interest payment of £1,000 to pay to the lender Bank.

    (b) Chelsea Ltd pays £250 to the Revenue.

    (c) The bank receives £750.

    (d) The bank will get a tax credit for the 25 per cent deducted and paid to the Revenue.

3. Loans to Participators in Close Companies (Income and Corporation Taxes Act 1988, ss. 419–422)

16.26   Special taxation rules apply to "close" companies.

A close company is one in which there is an overlap between ownership (the shareholders) and management (the directors). Close companies are defined by section 414 of the Income and Corporation Taxes Act 1988 to include companies:

    (a) with five or fewer participators; or

    (b) any number of participators who are also directors.

A "participator" means in general terms a shareholder of a company.

The "associate" of a participator includes immediate family, a partner in a partnership, a trustee or fellow beneficiary. Both terms are defined in section 417 of the Act.

When a close company makes a loan to a participator, whilst such payment is not a qualifying distribution (see section G above), it is treated in much the same way. The company making the loan to a participator is required to pay an amount to the Revenue equivalent to the rate of ACT then in force pursuant to section 419 of the Income and Corporation Taxes Act 1988.

The sum received by the Revenue whilst it is equivalent in amount to ACT is not classified as ACT and the borrower is not entitled to any tax credit.

The payment is best described as a "forced loan" so that, if the participator repays the sum lent to him the Revenue will repay to the company the sum that it received.

If the loan is released or written off by the company however, the sum paid to and held by the Revenue is forfeited *and* the participator will be assessed to income tax at the higher rate on the "grossed-up" amount of the loan pursuant to section 421 of the Income and Corporation Taxes Act 1988. Section 421 provides that the amount of the loan written off by the close company is treated as income in the hands of the recipient after deduction of "income tax at the lower rate from a corresponding gross amount".

16.27   *Example: Loans to participators in close companies.* ABC Ltd lends Bob, a shareholder, the sum of £100,000. A few months later it releases the debt.

Such a situation will be subject to the following taxation treatment:

ABC Ltd will pay £25,000 (a sum equivalent to ACT) to the Revenue in accordance with section 419(1).

When the debt is released by the company, the Revenue will retain the £25,000 which it has been holding. It will treat the amount of the loan released or written off as income in Bob's hands, and subject to the rules in section 421.

Bob will be subject to pay tax on the amount of the loan grossed up by the ACT equivalent of £25,000 making a total of £125,000.

The total tax payable by Bob will be 40 per cent, *i.e.* £50,000.

He will get a tax credit of 20 per cent, *i.e.* for the £25,000 (1/5 of £125,000) already held by the Revenue and will have to pay a further 20 per cent or £25,000 to satisfy the tax liability in respect of the loan.

H. Schedule E

Schedule E, Cases I, II and III concerns income from "offices, employment and pensions". This covers the directors, the company secretary and other employees of a company. It also covers employees employed by partnerships or sole traders.   **16.28**

Approximately 75 per cent of income tax collected falls under Schedule E. Schedule E includes PAYE taxpayers.

1. EMOLUMENTS

In broad terms, Schedule E taxes in the hands of the employee: **16.29**

    (a) "taxable emoluments" dealt with in sections 131 to 152 of the Income and Corporation Taxes Act 1988; *less*

    (b) "deductible expenses" dealt with primarily ins sections 153 to 168 (which concerns employees earning more than £8,500 per year and directors), and miscellaneous other provisions such as section 198 (necessary expenses) and section 577 (business entertaining expenses) of the Income and Corporation Taxes Act 1988.

"Emoluments" is a very broad term defined in section 131 of the Income and Corporation Taxes Act 1988 which includes:

    (a) salaries, fees, wages, profits (*i.e.* cash benefits) paid to an employee; and

    (b) the provisions of certain non-cash benefits also known as "benefits in kind" or "fringe benefits", *e.g.* clothing allowance, medical insurance, etc.

Emoluments are taxed under Schedule E of the income Schedules.

2. THE TAX TREATMENT OF EMOLUMENTS PAID TO "LOWER PAID" AND "HIGHER PAID" EMPLOYEES

The income tax legislation distinguishes between: **16.30**

    (a) lower paid employees; and

    (b) employees earning £8,500 or more per annum and (most) directors.

Some emoluments will not be treated as emoluments and hence, not taxed, *e.g.* free coal for mine workers, removal and relocation expenses.

Some emoluments will be taxed regardless of the category of employee, Examples include:

    (a) "cheque vouchers"—provided to employees to purchase goods or services; and

(b) "living accommodation"—section 145 of the Income and Corporation Taxes Act 1988, provides that such accommodation is taxed on the market value of the accommodation, less any sum actually paid by the employee for its use.

No charge to tax arises under section 145 of the Income and Corporation Taxes Act 1988 however, for "representative occupation", which is that occupation that is:

(a) necessary for the proper performance of an employee's duties, *e.g.* a caretaker;
(b) customary for the better performance of an employee's duties, *e.g.* a police house next to the police station; or
(c) necessary because of a special threat to an employee's security.

Emoluments will be taxed, whether they are supplied only for the director's benefit, such as medical insurance, or for the director's family as well as the director, such as the provision of a car or accommodation.

Directors and higher paid employees (*i.e.* those who earn more than £8,500/non-directors? —

(a) a benefits in kind is taxable in the hands of the employee if it is convertible in to money;
(b) if the benefit is convertible into money, tax is levied on the value of the benefit to the employee, *i.e.* on the secondhand value of the benefit.

Example: Secondhand value of a perquisite. In the case *Wilkins v. Rogerson* [1961] 1 All E.R. 358 an employee had been given a clothing allowance of £15. He purchased a suit for £14.50.

It was *held* that the clothing allowance received by the employee was a benefit in kind convertible into a money value of £5. The taxpayer was liable to pay tax on the sum of £5, which was in effect the second-hand value of the suit.

3. EXPENSES AND DEDUCTIBLE EXPENSES PAID UNDER SCHEDULE E

16.31   As we saw in Chapter 6, a business entity—whether a sole trader, a partnership or a company—is likely to derive its income under Schedule D Case I (for trades) and Case II (for professions), so that the rules as to deductibility of expenses are found primarily in the Income and Corporation Taxes Act 1988, s. 74 (refer to Chapter 6).

A director or employee on the other hand is taxed under Schedule E and the principle provision as to deducbility of expenses under Schedule E is the Income and Corporation Taxes Act 1988, s. 198.

Generally speaking the rules for deductibility of expenses are more generous under Schedule D.

Section 198 differentiates between:

(a) travelling expenses; and
(b) other expenses.

Travelling expenses

In order to be deductible from income profits, section 198 of the Income **16.32**
and Corporation Taxes Act 1988 provides that travelling expenses must be
"necessarily" incurred "in the performance" of the employee's duties, *i.e.*
travelling to and from work is incurred before and after the duties and the
costs are not deductible but the expense of travelling between places of work
is deductible.

Expenses other than travelling expenses

For expenses, other than travelling expenses, section 198 specifies that
they will only be deductible income profits if they are incurred "wholly,
exclusively and necessarily" in the performance of the employees duties.
This is therefore a stricter test than that which applies to the deductibility of
expenses under Cases I and II in Schedule D. It has three requirements as
follows:

(a) it has to be an expense incurred in actually performing the duties,
i.e. it does not refer to preparing for duties or to be better equipped
to carry them, *e.g.* no deduction is allowed for a fee paid to an
employment agency in seeking work;
(b) The expense must be "necessarily incurred".
(i) it is not an objective test.
(ii) It is irrelevant whether the employer requires the expenditure, to be made by the employee, *e.g.* a bank manager has
required to join a London club. It was held that it was not
necessary to make him better at his job and therefore was
not a deductible expense (*Brown v. Bullock* [1961] 1 All
E.R. 206); and
(iii) The nature of the employer's duties must require the
expenditure by the taxpayer; and
(c) The expense must be "wholly and exclusively" incurred in the performance of the employee's duties (*i.e.* this is the same requirement
as that for Schedule D, Cases I and II specified in section 74 of the
Income and Corporation Taxes Act 1988).

Example: The taxation treatment of a director's emoluments package. **16.33**
Below we will examine an emoluments package paid to a director from both
the company's point of view and the recipient's point of view.
Facts: Sandy Smith has been offered a position as marketing director of
Samson's Tyres Ltd, a Bristol-based company which manufactures and sells
a new type of tubeless tyre. He is offered the following emoluments package:

1. *Fees*—£40,000 per annum.
2. *Motor vehicle*—use of a Ford Mondeo for work purposes only. It is a
"pooled car"—available to several employees and normally garaged at the
premises.
3. *Accommodation*—provision of a flat to him at half its monthly market
rental of £2,000 which is situated within half a mile of work, *i.e.* he pays
rent of £1,000 per calendar month.
4. *Expense account*—up to £500 per month, to include client entertainment.

5. *Private health insurance*—to include comprehensive medical and hospital treatment.

6. *Loan arrangement*—£20,000 at an interest rate of 3 per cent below commercial rates.

7. *Shares in Samson's Tyres Ltd*—1,000 of them offered to him at their par value of £2, *i.e.* he is to purchase them so that they will be fully paid. At the expiration of 12 months he may be entitled to share options, depending on his performance.

8. *A mobile telephone*

Required

Advise the company and Smith of their tax position in respect to each part of the emoluments package.

General advice

Samson's Tyres Ltd, as a trading company, is likely to derive its income under Schedule D Case I, so that the rules as to deductibility of its expenses should be found primarily in Income and Corporation Taxes Act 1988, s. 74 which provides that expenses wholly and exclusively laid out for the purpose of the trade are prima facie deductible.

As a director Smith is taxed under Schedule E and the principal provision as to deductibility of expenses is Income and Corporation Taxes Act 1988, s. 198. He is a "higher paid" employee (see section H above).

Specific advice re the emoluments package

1. Fees

16.34 For Smith the fees are a taxable emolument under Schedule E; his marginal tax rate will be 40 per cent.

For the company the fees paid to Smith are a deductible expense under Schedule E; it will deduct Pay As You Earn tax from Smith as well as National Insurance contributions (see section L below).

2. Motor vehicle

For Smith, he will not be charged to tax for the use of the car or petrol if he did not use the vehicle for his personal use. This is the case with a pooled care, as here.

If the car had been a non-pool car the following matters would need to be taken into account:

  (a) if the car is available for private use he is taxed on the cash equivalent of the car as provided in the Income and Corporation Taxes Act 1988, s. 157 and Schedule 6 which is 35 per cent of the list price, *i.e.* the manufacturer's published price for the vehicle as new. This is referred to as the "price of the car as regards a year",

  (b) if the car which is provided is over 15 years of age and worth more than £15,000 (referred to in section 168F as a classic car) the price of the car as regards a year will be the market value if it is more than the list price;

    (c) the cap on the market value of the vehicle in any case is deemed by section 168G to be £80,000, *i.e.* the maximum amount of emolument that an employee can be taxed on in relation to a vehicle is 35 per cent of £80,000, *i.e.* £28,000;

    (d) pursuant to Schedule 6 the price of the car as regards a year will be reduced as follows:

        (i) by 1/3 if the employee does at least 2,500 business miles (*i.e.* miles required by the nature of his employement) per year; or

        (ii) by 2/3 if the employee does at least 18,000 business miles

    (e) for the company sections 34 and 41 of the Capital Allowances Act 1990 allow it claim a writing down allowance in respect of the vehicle of 25 per cent of a deemed market price of £12,000 for vehicles unless the market price is less. This is due to the fact that vehicles are usually used for private use as well. In effect then, the company can only claim a write down of £3,000 per year.

3. Accommodation

For Smith, he will be treated as receiving a taxable emolument for the difference between what he actually pays and the market price, unless he can show that it is representative occupation (see section 2 above);   **16.35**

    For the company the provision of the subsidised portion of the accommodation could be a deductible expense if it could show it was provided wholly and exclusively for the purpose of the trade pursuant to the Income and Corporation Taxes Act 1988, s. 74.

4. Expense account

For Smith as a director-higher paid employee the expense account will be treated as an emolument under the Income and Corporation Taxes Act 1988, s. 153.

    For the company the provision of the expense account could be a deductible expense if it could show it was provided wholly and exclusively for the purpose of the trade pursuant to the Income and Corporation Taxes Act 1988, s. 74. However for those parts of the expense account provided for "business entertaining", it will not be deductible pursuant to the Income and Corporation Taxes Act 1988, s. 577.

5. Private health insurance

For Smith it is a taxable emolument, taxed on its "cash equivalent" basis.

    For the company the provision of private health insurance could be a deductible expense if it could show it was provided wholly and exclusively for the purpose of the trade pursuant to the Income and Corporation Taxes Act 1988, s. 74.

6. Loan arrangement

For Smith this is classified as a beneficial loan arrangement, which is taxed under the Income and Corporation Taxes Act 1988, s. 160 on its cash equivalent which is the difference in interest between what Smith pays and the commercial or "official rate" rate. If the loan is written off he is treated as receiving an emolument equivalent to the loan amount.

For the company the provision of a loan could be a deductible expense if it could show it was provided wholly and exclusively for the purpose of the trade pursuant to the Income and Corporation Taxes Act 1988, s. 74 and was not otherwise prohibited.

7. Shares

16.36 For Smith as he has paid for the shares in full, he has not received a taxable emolument unless it can be shown that £2 is below the market value for the shares. In that case the Income and Corporation Taxes Act 1988, s. 162 provides that the employee is treated as having the benefit of an interest-free loan which will be treated as released when he sells the shares.

For the company, provided the shares have been paid in full there should be no tax consequences, until payment of dividends.

Share options

The rules concerning share options are complex and under review.

The main provisions are the Income and Corporation Taxes Act 1988, ss. 19, 135 and 162.

In general terms, the employee will be taxed on the gain in value of the shares when the option is exercised.

8. Mobile telephone

For Smith he is treated as receiving a benefit of £200 per year under the Income and Corporation Taxes Act 1988, s. 159A, unless he can show he did not use it for private use or actually reimbursed the company in respect of such use.

For the company the provision of the phone could be a deductible expense if it could show it was provided wholly and exclusively for the purpose of the trade pursuant to the Income and Corporation Taxes Act 1988, s. 74.

4. THE TAXATION OF SPECIFIC OTHER EMOLUMENTS

16.37 Not all payments made by an employer to an employee will be emoluments taxable under Schedule E. To be chargeable to tax, an emolument must:

(a) be a reward for services; or
(b) arise from the employment.

Three types of payments made by the company to an employee cause problems in that they do not fit easily into the above requirements:

(a) gifts. In general terms a gift is distinguishable from a reward for services. A gift will be received tax free; if not a gift it will be an emolument. A gift is likely if the payment is:
(i) a one off payment;
(ii) paid to only person, rather than a group;
(iii) paid by a person other than the employer; and
(iv) is not a contractual entitlement.

(b) contractual benefits unconnected with the employment, *e.g.* a sign-ing-on fee paid to an amateur rugby player who turns professional. It has been held that such a payment is not an emolument but is designed to compensate a player for the permanent loss of his ama-teur status (note that such a ruling may no longer be valid in light of the professionalisation of rugby union); and

(c) payments made on or after the termination of the employment. For example "gratuitous payments" made to directors under section 312 of the Companies Act 1985.

Certain lump sum payments are taxed in full under Schedule E as a reward for services past, present and future, *e.g.* any payment made under a contrac-tual obligation will be taxed in full even though it is paid because of the termination of the employment. For example a director's service agreement that provides for him to be paid £10,000 if it should be prematurely terminated.

Restrictive covenant payments received by an employee are taxed as emoluments under the Income and Corporation Taxes Act 1988, s. 313 and are deductible expenses for the employer, For example, if Sue is paid £10,000 by Computers Ltd in consideration of her not joining a competing within 20–40 miles of Computers Ltd office for the period of one year.

5. The Taxation of Termination Payments

Specific tax rules apply to those payments made to an employee on or after the termination of the employment. Essentially the rules allow the first £30,000 of any such payment to escape tax liability, so that the employee is only paying tax on any balance over and above the first £30,000. These payments are dealt with by sections 148 and 188 of the Income and Corpora-tion Taxes Act 1988.

16.38

Sections 148 and 188 of the Act apply to the following specific types of payments made by a company to an employee:

(a) "golden handshakes"—a payment to which there is no contractual right;

(b) compensation and damages paid for wrongful dismissal; and

(c) redundancy payments.

The first £30,000 of any payment falling within sections 148 and 188 of the Act is exempt from tax. Only the balance over and above the first £30,000 is subject to tax at the taxpayer's marginal rate.

Example: Compensation for loss of office (Income and Corporation Taxes Act 1988, s. 148). Diana receives a lump sum, on termination of her employ-ment, of £50,000. The first £30,000 will be free from tax and only £20,000 (the balance) will be subject to tax at her marginal rate, which we will assume is 40 per cent, *i.e.* she will have tax to pay of £8,000 (40 per cent of £20,000), in respect of the compensation payment received for loss of office.

I. Retirement Provisions for Employees and Officers

16.39   If taxes and death are two certainties, retirement is close behind as a near certainty.

Pensions involve making financial provision for retirement and/or old-age. There are three broad types of pension available:

(a) the State scheme funded through National Insurance contributions, which is comprised of two parts, the first being compulsory and the second part able to be opted out of in favour of an occupational pension scheme (see (b) below) or a private pension (see (c) below);

(b) an Occupational Pension Scheme provided by the employer for the benefit of its employees; or

(c) a Personal Pension used by self-employed individuals or employees who wish to top up their other pension arrangements.

2. STATE RETIREMENT PENSIONS

16.40   The State Retirement pension is a government administered scheme funded by national insurance contributions made by employees (their contributions are referred to as Class One). It provides a flat rate pension (the old-age pension). The first part cannot be contracted out of by employers.

It has an inflexible retirement age:

(a) 65 years for men; and
(b) 60 years for women.

Employees need to have made national insurance contributions for 90 per cent of their working lives in order to get the full amount of benefit. This translates as 44 years for men and 39 years for women. The full pension entitlement is low, being approximately £60 for a single person and £94 for a married couple.

A self-employed person such as a partner (who pays Class 2 National Insurance and can satisfy the contributions criteria) is also entitled to a part one flat-rate state pension.

The second part of the State pension is the State Earnings Related Pension. These are provided to an employee unless the employer has its own scheme or the employee has a personal pension arrangement.

National Insurance contributions
16.41   For the employer, National Insurance contributions paid on *behalf* of an employee are able to be deducted by the employer in arriving at income profits, *i.e.* they are an allowable expense of the business.

For employees, contributions to national insurance are not deductible expenses.

A self-employed person or a partner can in limited circumstances deduct one half of the national insurance contributions made as a charge on income.

3. OCCUPATIONAL PENSION SCHEME (INCOME AND CORPORATION TAXES ACT 1988, ss. 590–612)

As already noted, employees have a choice of: **16.42**

    (a) the State scheme; or

    (b) a private occupational pension scheme provided by the company.

As mentioned in section 1 above the State scheme is funded by national insurance contributions and is in two-parts, or tiers. The second part of the State scheme is an earnings-related pension (a "SERP", *i.e.* State Earnings Related Pension) which:

    (a) is an *additional* pension related to individual employees' earnings; and

    (b) which employers and employees may "contract out" by providing an appropriate occupational scheme.

An occupational scheme, if taken up, involves *diminished* payments of national insurance and payments instead being made to the private scheme.

The terms of the private scheme must be approved by:

    (a) the Occupational Pensions Board; and

    (b) the Inland Revenue Superannuation Fund Office.

Most private schemes involve contributions by *both* the employer and the employee—known as contributory schemes.

With a non-contributory scheme all contributions are made by the employer (and none is made by the employee. The contributions made by the employer are not taxed as emoluments in the hands of the employee (*i.e.* the employee receives a tax-free fringe benefit). The contributions by the employer are deductible in arriving at the employer's taxable income profits without limit (however, pension schemes must keep the surplus of assets over liabilities within a prescribed limit).

The employee or director can contribute 15 per cent of his gross emoluments to an occupational pension scheme and can obtain tax relief for those contributions. The fund itself is tax-free, *i.e.* no tax is paid on it by company/employee as it accumulates. An employee can, in general, take 25 per cent (subject to variations) of the lump sum tax free on retirement.

The main advantages and disadvantages of an occupational pension scheme for the employer and employee are as follows:

For the employer
Advantages: tax deductibility of its contribution without limit
Disadvantages: assets in the fund must be maintained at prescribed levels.

For the employee
Advantages:

    (a) the employer is also contributing to the fund, so that it grows more quickly;

    (b) tax deductibility of contributions up to 15 per cent of income;

(c) the employee can take up to 25 per cent tax fee as a lump sum on retirement.

Disadvantages:

(a) is the money properly and prudently invested?
(b) is it transferable to a new employer?

4. PERSONAL PENSIONS

16.43 Such pensions may involve an employee opting out of, or taking on a pension in addition to the second part of the State scheme or the occupational pension scheme ("SERP") provided by the company.

Prior to July 1, 1988, the self-employed and employees in non-pensionable employment, made provision for their retirement by entering into *retirement annuity contracts* approved by the Inland Revenue under section 619 of the Income and Corporation Taxes Act 1988.

From July 1, 1988, it has not been possible to take out new retirement annuity contracts as they have been superseded by *personal pensions*.

Personal pension schemes are available in the following circumstances:

(a) for the self-employed;
(b) for the employee in non-pensionable employment;
(c) for the employee who wishes to "top-up" his occupational pension;
(d) for an employee who has contracted out of his occupational pension scheme

Such schemes may often be high risk and the final project is not set by reference to an individual's earnings but, ultimately, by the purchase of an annuity (the pension) from a life insurance company.

Tax relief in respect of pension contributions made by an individual under Schedule E depends on the contributor's age:

Age	Maximum contribution
Under 36	17.5 per cent
36–45	20 per cent
46–50	25 per cent
51–55	30 per cent
56–60	35 per cent
61 or more	40 per cent

16.44 *Example: Tax deductibility of pension contributions.* Ed is 62 and earns £40,000 per year. He can make contributions to a personal pension scheme of up to £16,000 per year, *i.e.* 40 per cent of his income in light of his age and he is able to claim those contributions so as to reduce his taxable income to £24,000.

The tax relief is limited by reference to a maximum income of £75,000 per annum, *i.e.* if Ed had been earning £80,000 per annum he could have claimed tax relief on pension contributions of up to £30,000, *i.e.* 40 per cent multiplied by £75,000.

Generally, 25 per cent of the *lump sum* may be taken tax-free.

The main problems perceived with the State scheme are as follows:

(a) low entitlements even if claimed to its full value;
(b) there is no tax relief for the National Insurance Contributions made by the employee;
(c) the retirement age is inflexible;
(d) the first part provides, even on its maximum basis, a small pension;
(e) the second part—the SERPs—has rules which cap the payout to an employee;
(f) none of the state scheme pension can be taken as a tax free lump sum, but must instead be taken on a payment by payment basis;
(g) hence, a lack of flexibility and commerciality has seen a boom in the private pensions market.

J. Taxation Issues Concerning Shares

1. GENERAL PRINCIPLES

A shareholder will not be subject to any tax consequences in respect to the purchase of shares at their market value. If they are provided at less than their fully paid price or below market price, the taxpayer may be treated in the same way as if he had received a beneficial loan from the company (see section H). **16.45**

The shareholder will receive a tax credit in respect of income tax (satisfying the basic rate) if and when he receives a dividend in respect of his shares.

The sale of shares by a shareholder will attract CGT in line with the general principles (see Chapter 6). The price of the shares will be reflected in the increase in value of the assets owned by the company, *e.g.* land, premises, goodwill, retailed profits, *i.e.* the "asset backing."

The sale of shares may be:

(a) at arm's length, *i.e.* at market value where full consideration is paid; or
(b) to a "connected person" and if so, it will be reviewed by the Revenue as being at *market value* or if is not the Revenue will *impose* the market price. "connected persons" include:
  (i) the spouse of the shareholder;
  (ii) companies under common control;
  (iii) a partner or fellow partner; and
  (iv) a trustee is connected with the settlor of a trustee (but not with a beneficiary); or
(c) by the shareholder to the company, *i.e.* involving a redemption or buy-back of shares.

2. ENTREPENEURIAL RELIEF (TAXATION OF CAPITAL GAINS ACT 1992, s. 164A TO N)

16.46 Entrepeneurial relief is a new form of capital gains relief. It works like roll-over relief to *delay* the payment of CGT liability.

In order to qualify for entrepeneurial relief the following conditions must be satisfied:

- (a) the claimant makes a chargeable capital gain;
- (b) in respect of the disposal of chargeable assets; and
- (c) following the disposal, there must be a reinvestment of the proceeds of sale in a "qualifying investment" within the qualifying period.

The following points clarify the above conditions:

- (a) a "qualifying investment" *includes* the purchase of ordinary shares in an unquoted company carrying on a "qualifying trade";
- (b) a "qualifying trade" *excludes*, amongst others, the following activities:
  - (i) dealing in land, commodities; shares
  - (ii) financial activities
  - (iii) insurance
  - (iv) property development.

i.e. a qualifying trade is a wholesale/retail/manufacturing type business rather than a finance/speculative type business:

- (a) the claimant need not work in the company, *i.e.* the investment may be a "pure" investment;
- (b) the qualifying investment must be purchased within one year before or three years after the disposal of the asset;
- (c) the gain on the sale is rolled into the purchase price of the qualifying investment thereby reducing the acquisition price of the qualifying investment;
- (d) when the qualifying investment is sole and not replaced, the deferred capital gain will be subject to the payment of tax; and
- (e) the annual capital gains tax of £6,300 can be deducted from the capital gain rolled forward.

3. STAMP DUTY ON THE TRANSFER OF SHARES

16.47 The stamp duty payable on the transfer of shares (stock transfer form) is 0.5 per cent of the consideration paid or the market value payable by the transferee (purchaser) stamp duty is paid before the purchaser's name is entered in the register of members at the company's registered office.

4. SALE OF SHARES BY THE SHAREHOLDER TO THE COMPANY

16.48 A buy-back or redemption of shares involves the company purchasing shares from the shareholder usually for cash. The shareholder return, and the return the share certificate to the company.

Ordinarily, the payment by the company will be taxed in the shareholder's hands as a qualifying distribution.

As such it attracts the payment of ACT and, a tax credit at the basic rate of income tax for the shareholder.

If the payment made by the company is not to be treated as a distribution, prior clearance is required from the Inland Revenue. Certain information will have to be forwarded to the Revenue in relation to the proposed transaction, including:

(a) details of the vendor;
(b) details of the purchaser; and
(c) the reasons for the sale.

If the payment to the shareholder is not treated as a distribution, the shareholder's liability will be to CGT on the chargeable capital gain made on the sale of the shares.

When the distribution rules apply, it is only the excess of the purchase proceeds over the amount originally paid to the company for the shares that is treated as a distribution in the hands of the taxpayer/former shareholder. The payments made by a company to its shareholder, whether distributions or not, will not be expenses for the company which are deductible from income profits.

With a buy-back, or redemption of shares, the company as purchaser, pays stamp duty at the rate of 0.5 per cent of the purchase price, or the market price (whichever is the greater) paid to the shareholder.

5. LOANS TO PURCHASE SHARES IN A CLOSE COMPANY

An individual can deduct from his taxable income profits the interest payable on a loan if the purpose of the loan is to buy shares in a close company. He has to satisfy the following criteria: **16.49**

(a) the company in question is a trading company; and
(b) he is involved in the management of the company *or* he controls more than 5 per cent of the ordinary share capital.

K. Inheritance Tax

1. BACKGROUND

IHT is governed by the Inheritance Tax Act 1984. A charge to IHT may arise where the taxpayer: **16.50**

(a) makes a gift of an asset, *i.e.* receives no consideration from the donee of the gift; or
(b) makes an under value transaction to the effect that less than the market price is received from the donee.

Such transactions have the affect of diminishing the taxpayer's taxable pool of assets available at the date of death of the taxpayer.

Under the Inheritance Act 1984 what began as a general tax on gifts and under value transactions has been limited, in the main, to gifts on or within seven years of the death of the transferor. **16.51**

A gift of shares:

    (a) for IHT purposes is a "potentially exempt transfer" (PET); and

    (b) for CGT purposes is a disposal giving rise to a chargeable gain.

For a charge to IHT to arise, whether immediately or in the future, there must be a chargeable transfer that may be:

    (a) a potentially exempt transfer (a "PET") in which case IHT will only be charged if the donor dies within seven years of the transfer, otherwise it is exempt; or

    (b) is chargeable immediately because it does not fall within the definition of a PET. A supplementary charge may arise if the donor dies within seven years.

If the taxpayer dies more than three years after the date of the "chargeable transfer", tapering relief applies as follows:

—between 3 and 4 years—80 per cent of the IHT liability is payable
—between 4 and 5 years—60 per cent of the IHT liability is payable
—between 5 and 6 years—40 per cent of the IHT liability is payable
—between 6 and 7 years—20 per cent of the IHT liability is payable

Sections 1 and 2 of the Inheritance Act 1984 defined "a chargeable transfer." It has three elements:

    (a) a transfer of value, *i.e.* any disposal that reduces the value of the donor's estate and includes certain deemed transfers;

    (b) made by an individual; and

    (c) which is not exempt.

Examples: Chargeable transfers—IHT

    (a) Tom is owed £4,000 by Enid. Tom releases the debt.

    (b) Edward gives his house worth £51,000 to Barry, his son.

    (c) Andrew sells his car worth £4,000 to Caroline, his daughter, for £400.

For transactions where there is no "gratuitous intent" they are not chargeable to IHT. The onus to prove no gratuitous intent on the taxpayer. If Adam buys a set of encyclopedias in Chad's name, the onus is on Adam to show the Revenue that no gratuitous intent is being conferred on Chad.

2. INHERITANCE TAX IN THE COMPANY CONTEXT

16.52   As inheritance tax affects individuals, it may, in a company context, affect:

    (a) shareholders; and

    (b) directors (who are shareholders).

Shares form part of someone's estate just as say the family home does. The issue for inheritance tax planning purposes is how to deal with the taxpayer's estate so as to minimise inheritance tax and thereby avoid imposing financial difficulties on beneficiaries.

The IHT general exemptions and allowances are as follows:

(a) an annual exemption of £3,000 which allows a taxpayer to make gifts up to that amount annually without paying IHT;
(b) incidental gifts of up to £250 per person per annum;
(c) IHT is charged at 40 per cent on estates worth in excess of £200,000 at the date of death of the taxpayer.

In examining a transaction for its IHT consequences the legislation distinguishes between:

(a) market value transfers, *i.e.* where the arm's length price is paid. In this situation there is no reduction in the value of the taxpayer's estate and there should be no IHT consequences; and
(b) gifts or undervalue sales during the taxpayer's lifetime, *i.e.* where less than market price is received, where there is a loss to the estate. Such a transaction will usually be a PET and taxable if the transferor dies less than seven years after making the gift;
(c) gifts on the taxpayer's death which diminishes the estate. These will usually attract IHT liability unless the taxpayer's estate can claim a relief, which in the business context includes business property relief.

3. BUSINESS PROPERTY RELIEF (INHERITANCE TAX ACT 1984, SS. 103–114)

There are exemptions from IHT liability for certain lifetime and death gifts, for example: **16.53**

(a) inter-spousal transactions (Inheritance Tax Act, s. 18)
(b) agricultural property relief;
(c) heritage property;
(d) gifts to political parties;
(e) gifts to charities; and
(f) *business property relief* (BPR).

The purpose of BPR is to prevent a business, *e.g.* sole trader or partnership, having to be sold in order to pay the IHT bill. It *reduces* the loss to the donor's estate. BPR is given automatically. Any IHT liability payable after allowing BPR may often be made by interest-free instalments.

BPR is claimed in relation to relevant business property. Two provisos need to be met:

(a) the relevant business property for replacement property is owned at the time of death of the donor or donee;
(b) the property is classified as "relevant business property" at the time of both the transfer of property and the death two years later.

Definitions of relevant business property include:

(a) a business, *e.g.* a sole trader or sole practitioner—100 per cent relief is available;
(b) on interest in a business, *e.g.* a partner's share—100 per cent relief is available;

   (c) shares or securities that gave the transferor control of the company (total control does not have to be transferred, the key point is that at the time of transfer the transferor should have such control)—50 per cent relief;

   (d) shares in an unquoted company that give the transferor more than 25 per cent of the votes (a substantial minority shareholding)—100 per cent relief is available;

   (e) other unquoted shareholdings—50 per cent relief is available;

   (f) any land or building, plant or machinery that immediately before the the transfer was used by a partnership in which the transferor was a partner, or by a company of which he had control—50 per cent relief is available.

Relevant business property needs to be owned for two years prior to the gift being made.

Pursuant to section 227–228 of the Inhertance Tax Act 1984, the IHT liability may often be payable over 10 years by 10 interest-free instalments.

17.   A Common Commercial Transaction: Sale and Purchase of a Private Limited Company

A. Introduction

This chapter outlines what is involved for solicitors in acting on behalf of commercial clients on the sale or purchase of a private limited company; it is designed to provide the reader with an insight into a fairly common example of what "company" or "commercial" lawyers do in practice. The subject area is complicated and the chapter can only serve as an introduction to such a transaction and the role of the lawyer in the preparation, negotiation and formal completion of relevant documentation. Numerous commercial and taxation issues influence the negotiations and the structure of the documentation in such transactions and many of these issues are beyond the scope of this chapter.

17.1

Paragraphs 17.4–17.6 will outline the various steps and procedures involved in the sale and purchase of a private limited company. At this point it is helpful to explain what is involved in such a transaction overall:

17.2

(a) The sale of a private limited company involves the sale or transfer of the entire "issued" share capital of it by existing shareholders or members (known as "vendor(s)") to a third party or parties (known, obviously enough, as "purchaser(s)")

(b) The company whose issued shares are to be sold is often known as the "target company." Vendors and purchasers of the issued shares are often individuals but more commonly they are companies themselves in which case the target company will be the "subsidiary" company of the "parent" vendor company and, after the sale is completed, of the "parent" purchaser company.

(c) The target company's issued shares are legally transferred from vendor to purchaser by means of a stock transfer form (see chapter 11) but, typically the *agreement* between vendor and purchaser to sell or transfer the shares is documented in a *legal contract* that is usually drafted, negotiated and concluded on behalf of the parties by solicitors. This contract is known as a *share sale and purchase agreement*.

(d) Historically, there has never been any regulation, statutory or otherwise, of the sale of companies. In effect, the principle of *caveat emptor* applies to such transactions and a purchaser of the target company's issued shares will take the target company and all its contractual/financial obligations as they are unless specific provision is made in the agreement to sell the issued shares that in some way modifies this rule (see paragraph 17.16): One consequence of this is that there is no standard or prerequisite form for a share sale and purchase agreement and ancillary documentation to take in order to properly represent the sale of a company. In effect, such documentation is tailor-made by solicitors to meet the needs and wishes of the vendor and purchaser concerned. In addition, there is no standard or prerequisite time limits or procedures that must be adhered to in putting the transaction into effect. Nevertheless, lawyers have adopted fairly standard practices and procedures in the drafting, negotiation and completion of documentation representing the sale of a company and these are discussed in detail at section C of this chapter.

17.3   Once the issued shares of the target company are sold to the purchaser then there are certain legal consequences or effects:

(a) In accordance with the general principles of company law, on the sale of its entire issued share capital, the target company remains a legal entity entirely separate from its shareholder members. However, ownership of the issued shares and therefore control over the target company's activities has changed hands. Hence, the purchaser, as the current shareholder member after the sale is complete, has the power, *inter alia*, to:

    (i) appoint directors;

    (ii) alter the company's constitution;

    (iii) change the company's name;

    (iv) commit the company to new contractual obligations;

    (v) charge the assets of the company as security in relation for a loan and otherwise raise finance;

either in its capacity as shareholder member or through the company's agents; namely the directors appointed by it.

(b) As the target company has not ceased to exist following the transfer of its issued shares then, prima facie, any contractual and financial obligations entered into by it prior to the sale of the shares will survive and continue to take effect (although some contracts which the target company has entered into prior to the sale of its issued shares may contain a term that provides that they cease automatically when the shares are transferred to a third party and/or control of the company's affairs passes to a third party). As a result, purchasers will need to ascertain the nature of the target company's obligations from the vendor of the issued shares at the time of the sale in the share sale and purchase agreement. Given that the principle of *caveat emptor* applies to the sale of companies, purchasers will seek to elicit certain representations concerning the obligations of the target company from the vendor in the agreement with a view to having legal redress against the vendor if the representations made by it concerning such information prove to be false. Such representations and their practical effect serve to modify the caveat emptor rule (see paragraph 17.16). In addition, the purchaser of the target company's issued shares will need the information divulged in the agreement in order to plan effectively the future contractual and financial obligations of the target company once the transaction is completed.

B. Outline of the Sale and Purchase of a Private Limited Company

It was mentioned in section A of this chapter that there are no standard form documents or procedures to follow or adhere to when selling the target company but that nevertheless lawyers have adopted certain precedents when drafting, negotiating and completing the documentation that represents the transaction. A typical scenario for the sale and purchase of a private limited company is set out below and a detailed explanation of the documentation and procedures referred to follow in paragraphs 17.7–17.37.

17.4

A typical company sale and purchase transaction may proceed roughly as follows:

(a) The vendor and purchaser of the target company's issued shares will instruct separate solicitors giving a brief resume of the transaction or "deal" agreed by them and its main terms. The information disclosed to the solicitors may include the names and addresses of the other party and its solicitors, the details of the target company and its business, the price agreed for the shares and how it is to be satisfied and any particular or unusual terms agreed between the parties.

The most important terms of the "deal" as "agreed" by the vendor and purchaser may have been set out by them in so-called "heads of agreement". Most of the terms contained in the heads of agreement are expressed to be "subject to contract" or, in effect, non-legally binding on the parties. The solicitors acting for the vendor and purchaser will need to check this document carefully as it represents the commercial intentions of the parties and will be helpful in drafting the legally binding share sale and purchase agreement and ancillary documentation in due course.

Solicitors can gain detailed financial and administrative information concerning the target company (and indeed the vendor and purchaser if either also happens to be a company limited by shares) by carrying out a company search against the relevant details held on the public register of companies by the companies registrar at Companies House. The information disclosed by such a search may not always be up to date as there will be a delay between the lodging of the information and its appearance against the relevant company details.

(b) The purchaser's solicitors may prepare some *preliminary enquiries* (or requests for information) regarding the target company and submit them to the vendor's solicitors for formal replies.

(c) The vendor's solicitors may require the prospective purchaser to sign a *letter of confidentially* before releasing any information relating to the vendor or the target company. Thereafter, the vendor's solicitors *may* reply to the preliminary enquiries but in practice this may take some time and very often not all of the questions are answered!

(d) In order to ascertain more detailed information about the financial state of the target company and to assess its true market value, purchasers may engage accountants (usually, their own auditors if they are corporate entities themselves) to investigate and report on the target company. In addition, the purchaser's solicitors may be engaged to carry out a detailed investigation of the target company's contractual obligations. This whole process is known as due diligence. Naturally the vendor will have to agree to such a process being carried out as it will require detailed disclosure of all relevant financial and legal information. In these circumstances, the confidentiality undertaking of the purchaser is of crucial importance to the vendor.

(e) The purchaser's solicitors will produce the first draft of the *share sale and purchase agreement* together with a first draft of any separate *tax deed of indemnity* for comment and amendment by the vendor's solicitors. Until formal signing of the agreement at the completion meeting these documents should be marked "subject to contract" in order to prevent any inference that a legally binding agreement has been reached before the parties desire this to be the case.

(f) The vendor's solicitors will produce amended versions or "markups" of the share sale and purchase agreement and any separate tax deed of indemnity to take account of the vendor's requirements and understanding of the transaction. The vendor's solicitors will also produce a first draft of a *disclosure letter*.

17.5

(g) The purchaser's solicitors will produce an amended or marked up version of the disclosure letter to take account of the purchaser's requirements and understanding of the transaction.

(h) There may then follow fairly protracted negotiations between the solicitors and their respective clients in relation to all of the above documents and ancillary materials. The extent and nature of the negotiations depend on the facts of each particular transaction and numerous amendments to the original documentation may be made.

(i) Once all of the documentation is agreed between vendor and purchaser, the agreement and ancillary legal documents will be signed by both parties and the shares will be transferred to the purchaser on stock transfer forms in return for the agreed purchase price or other consideration at the completion meeting (this is sometimes referred to as a "signing" or "closing" meeting).

At the completion meeting it will be necessary for the target company to hold a meeting of directors to approve the transfer of the shares to the purchaser and record the removal of any existing directors retiring at completion of the transaction (*i.e.* the vendor's appointees) and the appointment of the new directors (*i.e.* the purchaser's appointees) as well as to deal with any ancillary matters arising out of the transaction. To this end, *completion board minutes* will be drafted by the purchaser's solicitors detailing the business to be transacted.

There may be a gap between the formal signing of the contract and the execution of the stock transfer forms if certain conditions have to be met before the vendor can transfer the shares to the purchaser as provided for in the share sale and purchase agreement (see paragraphs 17.38–17.41).

(j) Post-completion of the transaction, a variety of documents may have to be filed with the Registrar of Companies at Companies House including, *inter alia*, Form G288: Notification of change of particulars of directors and secretary and the target company's statutory books will have to be amended by the purchaser's solicitors (these books include the register of directors, the register of members and the register of directors' interests in shares and debentures).

(k) Finally, it may be that the share sale and purchase agreement together with ancillary documentation places each party under "post-completion obligations." For example, these may include, in the case of the vendor, a negative covenant requiring that party not to compete in business with the target company for a certain period of time and within a certain geographical area. In the case of the purchaser, the agreement may require that party to pay additional consideration for the company's shares as it is "earned" by, for example, the annual profits of the target company reaching a specified level in the period immediately following completion of the transaction.

The above-mentioned documents and procedures, which are explained in detail in the *next section* of this chapter, form the crux of any company sale transaction but they are by no means the only requirements of any such transaction. In practice numerous ancillary contracts and legal documents will be drafted, negotiated and completed in addition to those that have been mentioned in this section. The nature and extent of what is required will depend upon the facts of each case. For example, at completion of the transaction, the purchaser may require that the target company enters into new service agreements with any directors who are to remain in post after the purchaser takes control of its affairs. In this case, new service contracts would have to be drafted, negotiated and completed accordingly.

17.6

C. The Main Documentation Representing the Sale and Purchase of a Private Limited Company

1. PRELIMINARY ENQUIRIES RELATING TO THE TARGET COMPANY

The preliminary enquiries drafted by the purchaser's solicitors and sent to the vendor's solicitors are simply a list of questions concerning the target company together with a request to supply various documents and information. It is one of the first steps taken by a purchaser in ascertaining the nature

17.7

of the target company's general situation and financial/contractual obligations at the time of the share transfers. The answers furnished allow the purchaser's solicitors to tailor the first draft of the share sale and purchase agreement to the particular facts of the transaction in hand. In addition, the information will also assist the vendor's solicitors in the drafting of the disclosure letter.

Typically, the preliminary enquiries will ask for details of any subsidiary companies held by the target company, copies of the up-to-date memorandum and articles of association of the target company, information concerning the target company's pension scheme, its personnel, its inland revenue/taxation dealings, its trading agreements and other material contracts and commitments as well as details of all property held by it. It may take some time for the vendor's solicitors to gather all the relevant information and produce a comprehensive reply. Quite often, some questions remain unanswered at completion of the transaction!

2. LETTER OF CONFIDENTIALITY

17.8 Before divulging to the purchaser information regarding the vendor and the target company which may be of great benefit to competitors in the particular area of business concerned, the vendor's solicitors may insist that a prospective purchaser signs an undertaking in letter form whereby that party agrees to hold information divulged by the vendor in strict confidence and not to disclose or use such information other than for the purpose of appraisal of the target company and the negotiations for the purchase of it.

This undertaking as to confidentiality is of great importance to a vendor if the transaction is not carried through to a successful completion. Typically, the undertaking will provide that if negotiations are not proceeded with then the purchaser must return all documents entrusted to it and destroy all copies. Further, the undertaking usually continues indefinitely unless the transaction is completed and the shares are transferred to the purchaser whereupon it lapses save in so far as the information divulged related to the vendor and that party's remaining business interests.

3. THE SHARE SALE AND PURCHASE AGREEMENT

Agreement to sell shares

17.9 In this legal agreement or contract the vendor agrees to sell and the purchaser agrees to buy the target company's issued share capital. The shares themselves will be transferred to the purchaser by means of a stock transfer form that will normally be executed at the completion meeting (unless the contract is a conditional one: see below, section D of this chapter). This section explains some of the more important clauses that will be contained in this agreement.

Sale and purchase clause/consideration clause

In this clause, the vendor undertakes to sell the target company's shares to the purchaser in return for the consideration agreed between the parties. The consideration for the shares may be satisfied by the purchaser in a number of ways:

17.10   (a) *cash* payable by the purchaser at the completion meeting; typically by way of a telegraphic transfer from the purchaser's solicitors client account to the vendor's solicitors client account or by presentation of a banker's draft. A purchaser company may raise cash for the purchase of the shares in a variety of ways. It may use profit reserves or new monies raised from existing shareholders who are asked to subscribe in cash for additional shares in the company. Alternatively, a purchaser may make use of bank borrowings to finance the purchase of the shares. However the transaction is financed, it is essential that the target company and/or its subsidiary company (if any) do not provide financial assistance to the purchaser for the acquisition of the target company's shares unless permitted in accordance with sections 151–153 of the Companies Act 1985 (see Chapter 14). For example, if a purchaser was to borrow money and use this to acquire the target company's shares and the target company (or its subsidiary company, if any) subsequently made a loan to the purchaser and this was used to discharge the initial loan raised by the purchaser then, prima facie, this would amount to unlawful financial assistance on the part of the company;

(b) if the purchaser is itself a company limited by shares, it may issue **17.11** *shares* credited as fully paid up to the vendor that represent the current market value or selling price of the target company so that in effect the vendor becomes a shareholder member of the purchaser company (*i.e.* the vendor receives shares instead of cash and may retain them as an investment or sell them at a later date. This is only an attractive alternative to cash for a vendor if there is a ready market for the purchaser's shares such as those of a public company quoted on the London Stock Exchange);

(c) the purchaser may issue *loan stock* to the vendor in return for the shares in the target company.

In addition, this clause may provide that, whatever the nature of the consideration, it is to be *deferred* (*i.e.* paid at some date after completion of the share transfers) pending, for example, the future profit results or performance of the target company. Alternatively, this clause may provide that there is to be a *retention* of part only of the consideration to cover, for example, the eventuality of projected profits not being met by the target company or, alternatively, any claim of the purchaser against the vendor as the result of a warranty proving false (see paragraphs 17.16–17.30). In each case the clause will be coupled with *an adjustment to purchase price provision* so that the purchase price will be reduced and the deferred or retained consideration not paid by the purchaser if actual profits of the target company do not meet agreed projections after completion of the transaction or, alternatively, the purchaser establishes a valid warranty claim for a specified amount against the vendor. Occasionally, if actual profits of the target company exceed agreed projections after completion of the transaction the purchase price may be actually increased.

Waiver of pre-emption rights clause
It may be that the target company's articles of association or a separate agree-   **17.12**
ment of its shareholders provides for pre-emption rights on the sale or transfer

the shares (see Chapter 11). This clause will provide that the vendor agrees to waive any such rights to have any of the shares offered to it or any other person for purchase prior to the transfer of the shares to the purchaser.

Completion clause

17.13   Usually this clause will fix a date for the completion meeting when the contract is signed and dated and the stock transfer forms are executed thus completing the transfer of the shares in the target company.

If conditions have to be fulfilled before the shares can be transferred (see paragraphs 17.38–17.41), this clause will provide that the stock transfer forms are not to be executed and the transaction not completed until the last condition is fulfilled.

Restrictions clause

17.14   It is common in the agreement for the vendor to enter into certain negative covenants concerning the business of the target company. Examples are as follows:

(a)   The vendor will not divulge any confidential information concerning the business of the target company at any time after completion of the share transfers.

(b)   For a reasonable period of time and within a reasonable geographical limit the vendor will not carry on the business of the target company nor employ in a business competing with the target company any person who was an employee of the target company within a reasonable period prior to signing the agreement.

To be valid such restrictions or "non-compete" clauses must be in the public interest, reasonable as between the parties in duration and geographical area and only protect the legitimate business interests of the purchaser. Purchasers will require the inclusion of such restrictions in the agreement because the consideration to be paid may well include a substantial premium for the goodwill of the business of the target company that could itself be severely damaged by competition from the vendor who may possess expert knowledge and considerable reputation in the business of the target company. Share sale and purchase agreements that contain such negative covenants may require registration with the Office of Fair Trading pursuant to the Restrictive Trade Practices Act 1976.

Costs clause

17.15   Where two commercial clients are negotiating for the sale of a company at arm's length, it is usual (although by no means always the case) for this clause to provide for both parties to bear their own costs in connection with the transactions as a whole.

The warranties clause/warranties schedule

17.16   Often regarded as the most important aspect of any company sale and purchase transaction, the warranties are a set of statements made in the agreement by the vendor of the target company shares that disclose certain important factual information about the current financial, trading and general state of the target company to an intending purchaser. This section will cover:

(a) the function of warranties;
(b) examples of warranties;
(c) remedies available to purchasers against vendors if a warranty proves false;
(d) the negotiation of warranties.

(a) *Function of warranties.* Warranties elicit disclosure of information **17.17** about the target company that would not otherwise be available to a purchaser. As stated earlier (see paragraph 17.2) the principle of *caveat emptor* applies generally to company sale and purchase transactions and a purchaser will acquire the target company and all its trading/financial commitments as they are at the time of the share transfers. This represents a considerable risk for intending purchasers and, therefore, the information elicited by the warranties will hopefully give them an insight into the overall position of the target company; helping them to make informed judgments about the future financial structuring and new contractual obligations that the target company will be committed to after completion of the share transfers.

The warranties clause in the agreement will typically provide that the representations made by the vendor and contained in the warranties schedule annexed to the agreement induced the purchaser to agree to purchase the shares in the target company and that the vendor acknowledges that the purchaser is relying upon them in purchasing the shares and can thus treat them as major terms of the agreement. Additionally, therefore, warranties enable the purchaser to have legal redress against the vendor where it transpires after the sale of the target shares that, for example, a particular asset or liability of the target company is not as represented to the purchaser in the warranty schedule or, for example, the overall position of the target company is not as represented and thus it is not worth the amount paid for it. The warranties are said to *allocate risk or responsibility* for the pre-completion state of the target company as between vendor and purchaser. In this way, the warranties modify the application of the principle of *caveat emptor* to company sale and purchase transactions. The purchaser does not simply take the target company and its trading/financial commitments as they are at the time of the share transfers; the purchaser takes them as they are represented to be in the warranty schedule by the vendor so that if such representations prove to be false then the purchaser has recourse to the vendor in an action for breach of a contractual term or, possibly, for misrepresentation. These remedies are discussed later in this section of the chapter.

During the negotiations relating to the share sale and purchase agreement and in particular the precise wording of warranties, a vendor may often refuse to make a particular representation on the basis that he/she or it lacks the personal knowledge required to support such a statement. This line of argument ignores the risk allocation function of warranties. It is not an entirely unreasonable demand for a purchaser to insist that the vendor makes the representation concerned regardless of whether or not the vendor is satisfied as to the complete accuracy of the statement. In this scenario, purchasers may well argue that the accuracy or otherwise of the statement is not of primary importance and that what really matters is that the vendor bears the loss for the pre-completion state of the target company if and when the statement proves to be inaccurate. It must not be forgotten that warranties are subject usually to the vendor being able to disclose certain matters of which the vendor is aware and that affect the accuracy of the warranties concerned to the purchaser in the disclosure letter thus escaping risk or liability in relation to the matter disclosed. The disclosure letter is discussed in paragraphs 17.31 to 17.32.

Finally, in relation to the risk allocation function of warranties, purchasers must appreciate that warranties are only worth something if the vendor making them is worth suing for damages if and when they prove inaccurate. Once the target company is sold to the purchaser, the vendor may be left with very few assets or business interests. If this is the case, purchasers may well insist on a retention of part of the consideration price (see paragraph 17.11) until, for example, the time period for bringing claims for breach of warranty has expired (this period is usually stated in the warranties clause in the share sale and purchase agreement).

(b) *Examples of warranties*. The most important warranties seek to establish the financial and trading position of the target company immediately prior to the transfer of the shares to the purchaser.

17.18   *Accounts*. Usually, the vendor will be required to represent that the accounts of the target company made up to the last accounting date comply with all relevant statutes and show a true and fair view of the assets and liabilities and of the state of affairs of the company at the last accounting date. Usually, this warranty is of crucial importance to purchasers as the commercial decision to buy the target company at the purchase price will usually be borne out of a detailed analysis of the target company's financial records.

17.19   *Changes since the last accounting date*. It may have been a considerable period of time between the target company's last accounting date and the date set for completion of the share transfers. Consequently, vendors may be asked to represent that no material changes have occurred in the assets and liabilities shown in the accounts or in the financial/trading position of the company and that the business of the company has been carried on in the ordinary course. In addition to such protection, purchasers may insist that, if available, monthly management accounts dating from the last accounting date to completion are produced and their accuracy is warranted by the vendor.

17.20   *Business*. The vendor may be asked to represent that the target company has obtained all licences, permissions and consents necessary for the carrying on of its business and that such things are in full force and effect.

17.21   *Employment*. The purchaser will require the vendor to represent that accurate details of all significant employees' contracts have been furnished to it and that the target company has complied with all relevant employment legislation in respect of all employees.

Assets. Vendors may have to represent that the target company has good **17.22** and marketable title to all its assets and that they are sufficient for the proper and efficient conduct of the business of the target company.

Agreements and commitments. Vendors may be required to state that the **17.23** target company is not a party to any onerous or long-term contracts or any contract not entered into in the normal course of business. Purchasers may require that vendors state that accurate details of all significant company contracts have been furnished to them.

Litigation. A statement may be made to the effect that otherwise than a **17.24** plaintiff in the collection of debts, the target company is not engaged in any litigation or other legal proceedings and no such proceedings are threatened or pending.

In addition to the above, specific representations may be made in relation to the target company's pension scheme, insurance cover, real and leasehold property and the target company's tax affairs (*e.g.* details of any disputes with the Inland Revenue and confirmation of orderly submission of tax returns). The list is not exhaustive and in practice warranties can take up tens of pages of the share sale and purchase agreement.

(c) *Remedies available to purchasers against vendors if a warranty proves* **17.25** *false.* The *main* potential actions available to purchasers are set out below although it must be appreciated that this list is not exhaustive; it is possible, for example, that a purchaser may have a claim in tort for negligent misstatement; see *Hedley Byrne and Co. Ltd v. Heller and Partners Ltd* [1964] A.C. 465.

An action for damages following a breach of contractual term. The war- **17.26** ranties constitute terms of the share sale and purchase agreement. When a warranty transpires to be false there has been a breach of contract committed by the vendor for which the purchaser may seek damages. The contractual measure for damages aims so far as money can do it to put the purchaser in the position in which he would have been in if the contract had been properly performed. The damages aim to compensate the purchaser for loss of bargain. In essence this means that contractual damages for breach of a warranty equal the difference between the market value of the target shares as they are and their value as they would have been if the warranty had been true (*i.e.* their value if the contract had been properly performed). The major difficulty for a purchaser following this course of action is that the breach of warranty may not necessarily lead to any diminution in the market value of the target company shares or at least it may be difficult to prove loss of such market value.

An action for damages following misrepresentation pursuant to section *2(1) of the Misrepresentation Act 1967.* As stated earlier, the warranties **17.27** clause in the contract will usually provide that the vendor acknowledges that the warranties contained in the warranty schedule annexed to the agreement induced the purchaser to agree to purchase the target company shares. Hence, a claim may be made by a purchaser on the basis that the untrue warranty constitutes a mistatement of fact that, as well as being a contractual term of the agreement, actually induced the contract before signing and therefore amounts to a misrepresentation. This claim will typically be for negligent misrepresentation pursuant to section 2(1) of the Misrepresentation Act 1967. In this case, damages are assessed on the tortious basis; namely to put the purchaser in the position he would have been in if the tort had not been committed. In essence this means that damages in tort for breach of warranty equal the difference between the market value of the target company shares as they are and the actual price paid for them.

The difference between contractual damages and damages in tort is important.

Example: Purchaser and vendor agree the sale of target shares for £800,000. The target company's accounts do not disclose an outstanding liability for £80,000. The accounts also do not disclose a completely unrelated asset of the target company worth £80,000 to it. In the contract, the vendor gave the purchaser a warranty to the effect that the accounts showed a true and fair view of all the assets and liabilities of the company as at the last accounting date. This warranty is clearly false as the accounts did not disclose the outstanding liability and, prima facie, the purchaser has an action for breach of contract and/or misrepresentation. Under a claim for breach of contract, provided the purchaser can show that the undisclosed liability reduced the market value of the target company's shares correspondingly (this is by no means an easy task; see paragraph 17.26), then the purchaser is entitled to recover £80,000; this being the difference between the market value of the target shares as they are (£800,000) and their value if the warranty had been true (£880,000). The essential function of contractual damages is to compensate for loss of bargain hence the existence of an unrelated asset that covers the deficit is of no relevance in this case because if the warranty had been true and accurate then the purchaser would have had the benefit of the unrelated asset as part of his bargain (*i.e.* he would have made a good bargain). Under a claim in tort on the same facts, the purchaser would be unable to recover anything since the existence of the unrelated asset means there is no difference in the market value of the shares as they are and the actual price paid for them. In essence, there is no damage or loss in tort because the distinctly unrelated liability and asset cancel each other out; the target company is worth the price paid.

17.28   *A claim pursuant to a contractual term providing for damages to be assessed on an indemnity basis.* Occasionally, purchasers will insist that a term is included in the share sale and purchase agreement itself whereby both parties agree that a purchaser is entitled to recover damages against a vendor for a breach of a warranty on an indemnity basis. That is, the vendor must by way of damages pay in full the amount necessary to put the target company into the position that would have existed if the warranty in question had been true. Hence, if an asset is worth less than is represented the vendor must compensate the purchaser for the shortfall in full (or, at the purchaser's option, must pay an amount equal to the diminution thereby caused in the value of the target company's shares). Similarly, the vendor must pay in full the value of any undisclosed liability (or the loss in value caused to the shares). Such a contractual indemnity confers major benefits on a purchaser in that damages are easily quantifiable, they are not limited by rules of law relating to the measure of damages or the causation/remoteness of loss and finally the purchaser relying on such a clause is not subject to the normal duty to mitigate his loss. Such a clause is a contentious one and insistence of its inclusion in the contract is often taken as evidence of an over-aggressive attitude on the part of the purchaser. The parties are, of course, free to include such a provision in the contract provided it is not a penalty but rather a genuine pre-estimate of actual loss that will be suffered by an innocent purchaser. The issue of its inclusion will invariably be settled by reference to the respective bargaining strengths of the vendor and purchaser at the negotiating table. It may be possible to compromise by identifying any particularly important warranties for which recovery should be on an indemnity basis.

Repudiation of the share sale and purchase agreement following the breach of a contractual term. Ordinarily, a breach of warranty will entitle the purchaser to claim damages only for breach of contract; he will not be entitled to treat the contract as at an end or repudiated.

Rescission of the share sale and purchase agreement following a misrepresentation. Finally, in relation to remedies available to a purchaser for a **17.29** breach of warranty, it is highly unlikely that a purchaser will be able to rescind his contract after the target shares have been transferred to him following subsequent discovery by him of a misrepresentation since, except for a very short period of time after completion of the transaction, he could not return the target company to the vendor in the state it was in prior to completion. The target company will undoubtedly be subject to new contractual and financial obligations (note however, the situation in respect of conditional contracts at paragraphs 17.38–17.41: where there is a gap between the signing of the agreement and completion of the share transfers, rescission should be possible and purchasers often assist on a specific contractual right of rescission during that time if a breach of warranty is discovered before completion).

(d) The negotiation of warranties. Usually, the solicitors advising the **17.30** vendor and purchaser will negotiate the terms of the share sale and purchase agreement and in particular the form that the warranties are to take. This may well prove the crux of the transaction. Indeed, lengthy negotiations on warranties between solicitors are often the reason for a transaction failing to proceed to completion. Warranties are not cast in stone. If an impasse is reached solicitors should attempt to generate solutions and not just identify problems:

(a) A purchaser may prefer to re-negotiate the consideration price for the target shares downwards rather than insist on warranties in a particular form.

(b) It is possible to state exceptions to a particular warranty if a particular issue is of concern to the vendor and the purchaser agrees to such an exception (see paragraphs 17.31 to 17.32).

(c) It is also possible to limit the extent of warranties by the use in the contract of concepts of *materiality* (for example, the vendor warrants that the target company has no *material* hire purchase agreements) and *reasonableness* (*e.g.* the vendor warrants that as far as it is *reasonable* to do so, the company has complied with its statutory obligations imposed by X).

(d) Certain warranties can be limited by reference to the knowledge of the vendor (*e.g.* so far as the vendor is aware, there are no breaches committed by the target company of any intellectual property rights held by third parties).

(e) Warranties which duplicate others in the agreement should always be deleted.

4. THE DISCLOSURE LETTER

17.31   The disclosure letter sent by the vendor to the purchaser of the shares in the target company is a list of qualifications to the warranties. The share sale and purchase agreement will provide that the warranties given by the vendor are subject to the disclosures contained in the disclosure letter. Hence, whilst the purchaser may insist that the vendor gives certain warranties in relation to the situation of the target company, the vendor is given the opportunity in the disclosure letter to make any relevant qualification to a particular warranty or warranties and so avoid liability to the purchaser in respect of the qualification that is detailed. Such disclosures must be truthful as purchasers will require that vendors warrant in the share sale and purchase agreement that the facts in the disclosure letter are true and accurate in all respects.

Like warranties, disclosures are frequently a source of negotiation between the parties as they also affect the allocation of "risk" between vendor and purchaser. During negotiations, the disclosures drafted by the vendor's solicitors will give the purchaser some idea of any major problems affecting the current financial and trading position of the target company. If the purchaser is concerned about anything revealed, it has a variety of options open to it, including; re-negotiating the purchase price downwards if the problem disclosure is to remain as drafted by the vendor's solicitors on execution of the agreement *or* accepting the disclosure as drafted by the vendor's solicitors but insisting on an indemnity for any loss incurred by the purchaser as a result of a problem at a later date *or* insisting that the problem disclosure is deleted from the disclosure letter so that the vendor is bound by the warranties without such a qualification *or* withdrawing from the negotiations because the problem is too much to contemplate!

Disclosure letters are usually divided into two distinct sections:

17.32   (a) First, there will be a list of *general* disclosures where there is deemed to be disclosed to a purchaser a series of documents/matters that relate to all warranties given by the vendor in the agreement generally. Such general disclosures usually relate to matters of public record or information in the public domain that a purchaser should satisfy itself about. For example, there is often deemed disclosed to a purchaser all matters registered against the target company at Companies Registration Office and all matters registered against the target company's property at H.M. Land Registry. In addition, all matters revealed by inspection of the statutory books of the company or contained in the accounting records of the company will be deemed disclosed. Such general disclosures are justified in that it is reasonable to expect that the intending purchaser should have no legal redress against a vendor in relation to matters affecting the target company that are of public record and that can be assessed adequately by the purchaser prior to completion of the transaction. However, purchasers should be wary of accepting general disclosures drafted by the vendor's solicitors that stray beyond this area. For example, vendors may attempt to disclose (and therefore have no liability in relation to) the purchaser's knowledge of economic, financial and trading conditions and prospects covering the area of business in which the target company operates. This is vague and imprecise. The purchaser is left not knowing exactly what has been disclosed.

(b) Secondly, there will be a list of specific disclosures whereby certain specific documents and matters are disclosed against the warranties given by the vendor in the share sale and purchase agreement itself to which the disclosures are most likely to relate (but without removing their applicability to all warranties). These specific disclosures will depend on the particular circumstances of the target company concerned:

Example: A warranty may provide that the target company has complied with its obligations in respect of all relevant employment legislation. In fact, one ex-employee has a valid claim for unfair dismissal against the target company that it is hoped can be settled out of court. Clearly, the purchaser would not accept the deletion of the warranty as it is left with no legal redress for any or all lack of compliance with the relevant legislation on the part of the target company. In this case, the vendor would disclose as much detail as possible about the one outstanding claim in the disclosure letter and therefore have no liability under the warranty in respect of it.

Any documents or correspondence to be disclosed should be detailed precisely in the disclosure letter and legible copies of them should be appended to it.

The disclosures contained in a disclosure letter are not the only way a vendor may seek to limit its liability to a purchaser in relation to warranties. It is common for vendors' solicitors to draft certain limitations into the share sale and purchase agreement as follows:

Trivial claims

In order to avoid petty claims, a clause is often inserted requiring that no claims under the warranties are brought unless, in aggregate, they exceed a **17.33** specific *de minimus* level. Once this level is reached the clause may provide that either only the excess is recovered by a purchaser or alternatively the total of all claims to date.

Maximum liability

17.34   Usually, vendors will seek to limit their maximum liability under the warranties to the amount of consideration paid by the purchaser to the vendor for the target company.

Time periods

17.35   It is not uncommon for the purchaser to agree to a time limit in the agreement in respect of which any claims under the warranties must be brought; this is often a maximum of two or three years from the completion date on the general commercial understanding that two or three audits of the target company carried out after completion of the transaction should be enough for the purchaser to identify any major warranty claims. This may vary depending on the particular business activities of the target company. Such a clause reduces the limitation periods otherwise applicable to claims for breach of contract or claims in tort.

5. Tax Indemnities

17.36   A tax deed of indemnity is often entered into by "covenantors" (namely the vendors of the shares in the target company) whereby they agree to indemnify the purchaser of the shares in the target company and hold it harmless against liability for any target company tax charge that is essentially unpaid and due on or before the completion date subject to specific exceptions such as, for example, unpaid taxation for which provision has been made in the target company's accounts.

    Historically, the indemnities contained in the tax deed of indemnity were made by the vendors in favour of both the purchaser and the target company itself (hence the need for a separate document over and above the share sale and purchase agreement; the target company is not a party to the agreement by which its shares are sold from vendor to purchaser!). Following the case of *Zim Properties Ltd v. Proctor* [1985] S.T.C. 90, it is thought likely that the total amount of any indemnity payment received by the target company would be a capital receipt and hence liable to a charge to CGT in full (*i.e.* tax would have to be paid by it on the payment made by the vendors to satisfy a tax bill!). For this reason, tax indemnities are no longer made in favour of the target company but rather in favour of the purchaser alone. Indemnity payments made by vendors to purchasers are not subject to the "Zim" principle but instead the amount of any such payment simply operates to reduce the consideration received by the vendor in calculating his charge to CGT on the disposal of the shares in the target company to the purchaser and consequently to reduce the purchaser's acquisition base cost in calculating its future charge to CGT in the event of disposal of the target shares at a later date by it. This latter principle applies equally to payments made by vendors to purchasers pursuant to a valid claim for breach of warranty.

    The tax indemnities serve a separate function to that of any warranties given by the vendor in the share sale and purchase agreement concerning the tax affairs of the company (see paragraph 17.24). The main function of such warranties is to elicit information about the target company's tax status and its dealings with the Inland Revenue for the planning of its future financial structure and for subsequent dealings with the Inland Revenue. If such warranties prove to be false, purchasers must normally pursue a claim for breach of contract or misrepresentation against the vendor for the loss suffered. It does not normally mean that the vendor must indemnify the purchaser for the full amount of any loss suffered by the purchaser as a result of such warranties proving to be false (although this position may be modified in the agreement itself if it is provided that damages can be claimed on an indemnity basis: see paragraph 17.28). The tax indemnities ensure that any unpaid tax not disclosed and provided for prior to completion of the transaction is the responsibility of the vendor, *i.e.* the vendor must pay the total value of any such amounts that are billed to the target company after the completion date. It is not normal for purchasers to allow vendors to disclose material against indemnities as it does in relation to the warranties as this would simply negate or reduce the liability to pay in full for the outstanding amounts.

6. COMPLETION BOARD MINUTES

At the completion meeting where the share sale and purchase agreement is signed and the share transfers are executed, a board (and, possibly, general) meeting of the target company will be necessary and this will be recorded in minutes which are normally drafted by the purchaser's solicitors to ensure all requirements of the new owners of the target company are met. The board minutes will normally record the following business: **17.37**

(a) the signing of the share sale and purchase agreement between the vendor and the purchaser as well as the signing of any separate tax deed of indemnity between the parties;

(b) the stock transfer forms will be produced to the meeting transferring the shares in the target company from the vendor to the purchaser. These stock transfer forms will be approved and the purchaser will be registered as the holder of shares in the target company. Share certificates will be sealed and issued accordingly;

(c) the bank mandate in favour of the target company's existing bankers will be revoked and replaced with a mandate in favour of the purchaser's chosen bankers;

(d) the registered office of the target company will be changed in accordance with the purchaser's requirements;

(e) the accounting reference period of the target company may be changed to coincide with the purchaser's group of companies;

(f) if required by the purchaser, the resignation of the current directors will be accepted as from close of meeting and the purchaser's nominees will be similarly appointed; and

(g) if required by the purchaser, the resignation of the target company's auditors will be accepted and the new auditors of the target company will be appointed. The outgoing auditors are required to state that there are no circumstances connected with their resignation that should be brought to the attention of shareholders or creditors (see section 394(1) of the Companies Act 1985).

Following the meeting, certain documents will have to be filed at Companies House and these include:

(a) form G287—change in situation of registered office
(b) form G225(1)—change of accounting reference date
(c) form G288—change of directors/secretaries particulars
(d) copy of auditor's resignation letter.

Following the meeting, the target company's statutory books will have to be amended by the purchaser's solicitors; these include the register of directors/secretary, the register of members and the register of directors' interests in shares and debentures.

D. Conditional Contracts for the Sale and Purchase of a Private Limited Company

1. INTRODUCTION

17.38 An agreement for the sale and purchase of shares of a private limited company may well provide that certain conditions have to be met before those shares can be transferred. Hence, the contract is said to be a conditional one and there will be a gap between the signing of it and completion of the share transfers by execution of stock transfer forms. Typically, the agreement will provide that the transfers shall not take place until the final condition is met or fulfilled. If conditions remain unfulfilled at the expiration of a certain period of time the contract may well provide that the agreement shall terminate and that the obligations of the parties under it will lapse.

2. EXAMPLES OF CONDITIONS

17.39 It is often the case that consents, clearances, approvals or permissions are required before the shares in the target company can be transferred. For example:

(a) An acquisition of shares in a private limited company may require the consent of the Commission of the European Community (E.C.) if, for example (a) it constitutes an agreement prohibited by Article 85(1) of the Treaty of Rome in that the restrictive or negative covenants entered into by vendor shareholders restrict competition between members states or (b) it constitutes an abuse of a dominant position by the purchaser as prohibited by Article 86 of the Treaty of Rome whereby the purchaser company, already holding a dominant position within the relevant business area in the E.C., strengthens its position by acquiring control of the target company.
(b) If the vendor and/or the purchaser are public limited companies

listed on the London Stock Exchange, then the Stock Exchange requirements in respect of the sale and purchase contained in its Listing Rules (or "Yellow Book") will need to be complied with.

(c) The acquisition may require the consent of a body that regulates the business activity of the target company/vendor/purchaser (for example, the consent of the target company's self-regulating organisation when it is involved in the provision of financial services).

(d) The consideration being paid by the purchaser for the shares in the target company may involve the issue of new shares in its share capital to the vendors and this may require the purchaser to obtain its shareholders' consent to increase its authorised share capital and to authorise its directors to allot the relevant shares (see sections 121 and 80 of the Companies Act 1985).

This list is not exhaustive. The particular conditions that apply to any share sale and purchase agreement depend on the facts of each case.

3. REMEDIES: THE RIGHT OF RESCISSION IN CONDITIONAL CONTRACTS

17.40 It was mentioned in paragraph 17.28 of this chapter that it is highly unlikely that a purchaser would be able to rescind his share sale and purchase agreement once the share transfers are executed since, except for only a short period following completion, the purchaser will be unable to return the target company to the vendor in the state it was in prior to completion given that new contractual/financial obligations will be in place. However, in the case of conditional contracts, purchasers will often argue for the inclusion in the share sale and purchase agreement of a specific right to rescind the contract where a material breach of a warranty or warranties is discovered *after* signing the agreement but *before* the shares are transferred to the purchaser; namely in the period during which the conditions are being satisfied since in this period legal title to the shares is still held by the vendor and rescission would simply involve the purchaser not going ahead with its obligation to take the shares in exchange for the agreed price. This is safer than relying on any potential right of rescission for misrepresentation under the Misrepresentation Act 1967; in that case the Court may have a discretion to award damages instead of rescission and in any event the purchaser would have to show that the untrue warranty that constitutes a contractual term also was a misstatement of fact that induced the agreement prior to the signing of it.

E. The Financial Services Act 1986 and Share Sale and Purchase Agreements

17.41 It has been stated already that the sale and purchase of private limited companies has been remarkably free of regulation by statute or otherwise and that the overriding principles to be applied to such transactions have been those of freedom of contract and *caveat emptor*. This is hardly surprising when the subject matter involved is in essence a commercial agreement negotiated by the parties freely at arm's length. However, even such agreements have not failed to escape entirely the regulatory regime introduced by the Financial Services Act 1986 and this section outlines the main relevant provisions.

There are four major provisions of the Act that may be relevant in a share sale and purchase transaction:

1. SECTION 47(1) OF THE FINANCIAL SERVICES ACT 1986

17.42   *Inter alia*, this section confers criminal liability on any person making a misleading or false or deceptive statement, promise or forecast that he knows to be misleading, false or deceptive for the purpose of inducing another person to enter into an investment agreement. In addition, a person who recklessly makes such a statement, promise or forecast is also guilty of the offence. It is also an offence under this section to dishonestly conceal material facts for the same purpose.

Investment agreements include share sale and purchase agreements and therefore it goes without saying that vendors and their advisers should only make truthful statements based on actual facts and should not intentionally conceal any material facts in respect of the target company in the share sale and purchase agreement and ancillary documentation.

2. SECTION 47(2) OF THE FINANCIAL SERVICES ACT 1986

This section confers criminal liability on any person who does any act or engages in any course of conduct which creates a false or misleading impression as to the:

(a) the market in;
(b) the price of; or
(c) the value of,

investments if he does so for the purpose of creating that impression and inducing another to acquire or refrain from acquiring investments. A course of conduct could include intentional omissions from the Share Sale and Purchase Agrement and ancillary documents by the vendor which induce the purchaser to invest.

3. SECTION 56(1) OF THE FINANCIAL SERVICES ACT 1986

17.43   This section prohibits persons entering into investment agreements such as share sale and purchase agreements with third parties in the course of or as a result of unsolicited visits and/or telephone calls by such persons to such third parties. An investment agreement entered into in breach of section 56(1) is generally unenforceable against the party on whom the call was made. That party is entitled to the recovery of money/property paid or transferred by him under the agreement together with compensation for any loss sustained by him: see section 56(2)(b) of the Financial Services Act 1986. The court has power under section 56(4) of the Financial Services Act 1986 to permit the agreement to be enforced under certain circumstances. Vendors should generally steer clear of such "cold calling" tactics in a bid to "drum up" a purchaser for the target company!

4. Section 57(1) of the Financial Services Act 1986

This section provides that no person other than an authorised person shall issue or cause to be issued an investment advertisement in the United Kingdom unless its contents have been approved by an authorised person. Breach of this section constitutes a criminal offence and any investment agreement entered into as a result of the breach is rendered unenforceable (although the court has a discretion to permit enforcement in certain circumstances). **17.44**

An investment advertisement is defined in section 57(2) of the Act to include any advertisement inviting persons to enter into an investment agreement.

As stated earlier, investment agreements include share sale and purchase agreements and therefore "every form of advertising" inviting persons to enter into such an agreement will be an investment advertisement.

This section is of more relevance where the vendor is auctioning the target company off to the highest bidder and so sends:

(a) an offer document;
(b) a draft agreement; or
(c) information memorandum,

about the target company to several possible purchasers, hence "advertising" it for sale.

There are a large number of exceptions to the general rule which are contained in section 58 of the Financial Services Act 1986 and in various orders of the Secretary of State made under section 58. It is often the case that one such exception can often be relied on in any given situation.

18.   Specialist Topics

18.1   The following section of this guide deals with topics that are of either a specialist nature or fall outside a central consideration of the three business entities already discussed. Given the increasingly sophisticated and complex nature of legal practice it may well be that a high degree of specialisation operates within particular law firms. It will not usually be the case anymore that a lawyer can service a commercial client by being proficient across several areas of law. Delegation and assistance may be required. Solicitors within firms are taking an increasingly co-operative approach as regards clients. The client may well receive advice from many departments working across a range of issues, in respect of a single transaction or matter, which is headed by a particular partner. A crucial part of the lawyer's role whatever his role in a transaction, will be a correctly identify and classify a potential legal problem or area of advice. Just as crucially, a lawyer should realise when the advice of a specialist in a particular field may be required to assist with a matter. It may involve an issue of taxation or European Community law that a solicitor, who deals with private limited companies, has not encountered before. Rather than "going it alone" the solicitor would be prudent to consult the firm specialist on these matters.

Among those areas of law that have already been mentioned in passing in this guide and that are increasingly handled by specialists within a firm, are the following:

(a) taxation advice and planning;
(b) company acquisitions and mergers;
(c) flotations of public companies;
(d) company finance;
(e) employment law;
(f) pensions law;
(g) intellectual property; and
(h) local government advice.

In the following chapters we will deal briefly with the following specialised and complex areas of law including:

(a) European Community law;
(b) competition law (both in the United Kingdom and Europe);
(c) international business advice (whether involving a European or other party);
(d) joint venture agreements;
(e) agency and trusts;
(f) marketing and distribution agreements.

It would be impossible in this guide to provide other than a brief outline of some of the relevant issues relevant to the solicitor advising a commercial client in these areas of the law.

19. International Business Transactions

By the term "international business transaction" reference is made to a trans-action involving two or more parties operating between two or more countries. **19.1**

Such transactions present difficulties to the legal adviser.and to the parties because there will be two different systems of law competing for supremacy. This raises the issue, for example, of how disputes will be solved.

Example: International transactions: choice of law. Investco Ltd, a U.K. company wishes to set up a joint venture arrangement with Bonanza Mining, an Australian company, in Malaysia. There are immediately three choices of law—United Kingdom, Australian, Malaysian. Which will govern?

This guide will concentrate on international transactions involving E.C. members, but is should not be forgotten that such transactions may involve a party or party from anywhere in the world. If an international business transaction is contemplated the legal adviser in the United Kingdom may well have to liaise with lawyers from the other participants' country. Some of those matters that will require particular attention and advice include: **19.2**

(a) *Choice of law clauses.* Whose law will apply and why? What are advantages and disadvantages in addition to those of knowledge of the local system, inconvenience etc.

(b) *Submission to jurisdiction.* Will the parties submit to have matters heard in the Courts of the country nominated under the choice of laws clause.

(c) *Arbitration.* Instead of seeking to solve disputes in the Courts the par-ties may wish to solve them by means of arbitration. In international transac-tions, this has proved common in the areas of the building and engineering industry and in respect of shipping contracts.

(d) *Exclusion of liability.* Certain international contracts involving a British-based party may seek to exclude liability for certain types of acts or damage. Such exclusions might, if both parties were in the United Kingdom or the United Kingdom was the place of business of or both of them, be in breach of domestic U.K. legislation such as the Unfair Contract Terms Act 1977. Such an issue will need to be resolved in light of the choice of laws outcome.

(e) *Taxation*. Do the countries from which the business entities originate have a double tax treaty or some other mutual form of tax arrangement as exists for example between the United Kingdom and Australia. In which country is it preferable that tax is paid?

(f) *Foreign investment controls*. What are the rules governing investment in countries? It may be that permission or a licence is required.

(g) *Insurance*. What matters will require insurance? Where should the policies be effected? Will this affect the choice of law clauses?

20. The European Community and European Community Law

A. Background

Whilst only a few years ago a legal adviser assisting a business client could **20.1**
assume that a point of E.C. law would not arise on a matter, the presumption
is increasingly being reversed *i.e.* that a point of E.C. law may well have a
bearing on the particular matter being dealt with. E.C. law is particularly
pervasive in civil law and business matters. E.C. law points will arise in the
following commercial circumstances:

(a) with business entities involved in trade with an inter-state element,
for example, where two or more Member States are involved;

(b) with employees and employment practices, for example, on a point
involving the free movement of workers; and

(c) the rights of employees, for example, the retirement age for men
and woman in the United Kingdom is now 65 for both men and
women following a ruling from the European Court of Justice. The
notion of "pure domestic" law is becoming increasingly difficult
to define because even if there is not a physical or geographic inter-
state element, E.C. law may still apply as in such cases; and

(d) "public procurement" or "tendering" whereby governments—
national, local and the like and other public bodies, seek work to
be undertaken and goods and services provided by private concerns.

The rationale for the establishment of a European community—legal, eco- **20.2**
nomic and political—attributed to the Second World War. In 1951, the first
"community initiative" was the Treaty Establishing the European Coal and
Steel Community (ECSC). The European Economic Community Treaty
("E.C. Treaty" or "Treaty of Rome") was signed in Rome in 1957 and
came into force on January 1, 1958, as did Euratom (the European Atomic
Energy Community). The preamble to the Treaty of Rome contains the desire
of the Member States to "lay the foundations of an ever closer union among
the peoples of Europe". The community's stated aims were to promote
within the community:

(a) a harmonious development of economic activities;

(b) a continuous and balanced expansion;

(c) an increase in stability;

(d) an accelerated raising of the standard of living; and

(e) closer relations between the Member States.

The two principal means by which these aims are to be achieved are:

(a) establishing a common market; and
(b) "progressively approximating" the economic policies of the Member States.

The United Kingdom did not become a member of the so-called "three communities", EEC, Euratom and ECSC until January 1, 1973, although having since 1960 been a "would be" member.

Article 5 of the E.C. Treaty provides that Member States are required to "take all appropriate measures, whether general or particular, to ensure fulfilment of the obligations arising out of this Treaty or resulting from action taken by the institutions of the community," and shall also "abstain from any measure which could jeopardise the attainment of the objectives of this Treaty". As early as 1974, a mere year after Britains full membership of the Community, Lord Denning characterised the E.C. Treaty when it concerned matters with a European element as "like an incoming tide. It flows into the estuaries and up the rivers. It cannot be held back. Parliament has decreed that the Treaty is hence forward to be part of our law. It is equal in force to any statute." *H.P. Bulmer Ltd. v. J. Bollinger SA* [1974] Ch. 401 at page 418.

In *Bollinger*, Lord Denning identified two continuing themes for U.K. domestic law:

(a) the ever encroaching domain of E.C. law; and
(b) the fact that E.C. law has supremacy over the national law of a Member State. That is, if there is a conflict between a provision of national law and community law, community law will prevail.

B. The Sources of European Community Law

20.3   The sources of E.C. law are as follows:

(a) *Primary legislation.* This includes the Treaty of Rome and Protocols, as amended by various treaties the latest of which is the 1992 Treaty on European Union ("TEU") better known as the Maastricht Treaty. Treaties, in general terms, are the organising documents setting up the broad framework of the Community.
(b) *Secondary legislation.* This is in the form of regulations, directives and decisions. Regulations are binding and have *direct* application as law in the Member States. Regulations are provided for in Article 189 of the Treaty of Rome as are directives. A directive is binding as to the *result* to be achieved but leaves the *implementation* (referred to in Article 189 as the "forms and methods") up to each of the Member States. Decisions are binding in respect of those whom they address. Recommendations and opinions do *not* have the force of law and are only "persuasive" as regards the Member States.
(c) *International agreements.* These are agreements that are entered into

by certain institutions of the Community, such as the General Agreement on Trades and Tariffs ("GATT").

(d) *Judicial decisions*. These are judgments of the European Court of Justice and the Court of First Instance. These also comprise general principles and opinion on the basis that they deal with E.C. law.

C. The Institutions of the European Community

The four principal institutions of the E.C. are:

1. THE COUNCIL OF MINISTERS

The Council consists of one delegate from the governments of each of the Member States. The delegates are ministers within the national governments and are required to have the power to *bind* the Member State to whatever is agreed, in both a political and legal sense. The Presidency of the Council is held for six monthly periods in turn by Member States, in accordance with a specified order of rotation.

20.4

The Council's brief is two-fold:

(a) to ensure co-ordination of the general economic policies of the Member States; and

(b) the power "to make decisions." This includes adopting and approving the Community's budget.

The Commission's role as co-ordinator of economic policy is becoming more important as advance towards Economic and Monetary Union ("EMU") is made.

The method of voting is by reference to the size of the population of particular Member States. For example Germany, the United Kingdom, France and Italy each get 10 votes whereas Ireland and Denmark get three. For a measure to be passed, 54 votes out of a possible 76 must be obtained. These voting details are in the process of being amended to take into account the joining of Austria, Finland and Sweden.

2. THE EUROPEAN COMMISSION

The primary role of the Commission (which is located in Brussels) is to:

20.5

(a) initiate matters that are decided by the Council of Ministers; and

(b) to put into effect the decisions taken by the Council of Ministers.

The Commission does not represent Member States but rather the community as a whole. There are 20 E.C. Commissioners. The Commission is divided into 23 departments known as Directorates, each responsible for a different area of policy. For example Directorate-General IV deals with competition policy.

The members of the Commission are required:

(a) to be independent of the Member States or other body once they are appointed (even though they are appointed by the Member States); and

(b) to act in the Community's best interests.

The Commission develops formulates, manages and implements policy decisions taken by the Council of Ministers. Decisions are made within the Commission on a simple majority basis.

3. THE EUROPEAN PARLIAMENT

20.6   The European Parliament was originally called the Assembly. It is presently comprised of 567 members (known as ''MEPs''—Members of the European Parliament). The United Kingdom together with France and Italy is entitled to provide 87 members. The number of MEPs is based roughly on the populations of Member States. The Parliament is organised across political party lines rather than Member State lines.

The MEPs are directly elected for a five-year term, but the voting systems in the Member States are not uniform. The parliament is informally organised on party rather than national lines. It conducts its work in several cities:

(a) Strasbourg where plenary sessions are held one week per month:

(b) Brussels where committee and plenary sessions are held; and

(c) Luxembourg where the organising Executive is based.

The powers of the European Parliament have gradually increased since the first elections were held in 1976.

Its role is consultative. In general terms:

(a) the Commission proposes legislation;

(b) the Council provides preliminary approval; and

(c) the Parliament is given time to comment. Its comments must be considered even though they are not binding.

The 1992 Treaty on European Union has provided, in limited areas at least, that the Parliament is given ''co-decision'' status working alongside the Council.

4. THE EUROPEAN COURT OF JUSTICE

20.7   The European Court of Justice (''ECJ'') is based in Luxembourg. The ECJ is becoming more and more influential in respect of U.K. domestic law. This is due to two matters:

(a) the supremacy of E.C. law over domestic U.K. law on a point of where the two differ; and

(b) the ability of any court or decision making body in the U.K. or any other Member State to refer a matter to the ECJ for a preliminary ruling under Article 177 of the Treaty of Rome. The definition of a decision-making body is very broad. It includes a court or tribunal. It applies to any body using law or facts that makes a decision or finding that is binding on the parties. It does *not* cover a body providing merely an opinion, *i.e.* something that is *not* binding on the parties.

Decisions emanating from the ECJ are treated with caution by practitioners. This is due to the nature of the Court's composition and decision-making process. The full court is comprised of 13 judges, one from each Member State. The court produces one written judgment that will inevitably be a "lowest common denominator" compromise.

Irrespective of the language in which the arguments were conducted before the court, the judgment will be in French. The judgment will then need to be translated. Inevitably, there may be some dispute over the correct nuances of the translation. This has led at times to protracted litigation trying to clarify the original decision.

Written submissions by the parties form the basis of the litigation process. The parties usually get 15 minutes each to further clarify their arguments.

The judges are assisted by six Advocates-General who are assigned to cases and whose task it is to assist the judges. They prepare opinions based on the case papers. Such opinions are not binding on the Court.

The Court's jurisdiction includes:

(a) references to it by a national court under Article 177 of the Treaty of Rome;
(b) reference when the Commission brings action against a Member State under Article 169 of the Treaty of Rome; and
(c) reference when one Member State brings action against another Member State under Article 170.

The Court is not bound by precedent.

D. European Community Law for Business Clients

Use of the term "E.C. law" immediately draws a distinction between "Community law" on the one hand and the domestic or national law of the member states on the other. E.C. law is a separate and distinct body of law that is expanding in scope and importance all the time. The interface between community law and national law will be a key practical concern for the legal adviser when dealing with a business client because, as already noted, E.C. law will apply if there is an inconsistency between the two. The matters of E.C. law that may be relevant to a business client are the discussed below.   **20.8**

1. FREE MOVEMENT OF GOODS

Article 30 of the Treaty of Rome principally provides for this freedom which is designed to create a single market. There is extensive case law interpreting the extent of Article 30 which is beyond the scope of this text.   **20.9**

2. FREE MOVEMENT OF WORKERS

Article 48 of the Treaty of Rome provides for the free movement of workers within the European Community.   **20.10**

3. FREEDOM OF ESTABLISHMENT AND PROVISION OF SERVICES

20.11 The right of establishment refers to the right for an E.C. national to permanently establish a business in another Member State (see Article 52). Article 52 provides that the business must comply with the host Member's domestic laws in relation to establishing and operating the business in question, so that there is a level playing field for citizens of the host state.

The freedom to provide services refers to a business providing services beyond its home country to other Member States—see Article 59. As is the case with the right of establishment, the person claiming the right cannot be put in a better position than nationals of the Member State in which the right is sought to be exercised. Special rules may apply as concerns professionals which are beyond the scope of this guide.

4. COMPETITION POLICY

20.12 Article 3 of the Treaty of Rome which lists the E.C.'s activities, includes the institution of a system to ensure that "competition in the common market is not distorted." The underlying philosophy is that unfettered competition within the Community is seen as essential to a "market" economy and also as a stimulant of economic activity. The Community's competition law aims to ensure that the market is not structured so as to advantage any country, individual or entity, *i.e.* that there is a level playing field or true market in which goods and services can compete for market share.

A second theme of competition law already touched on—for example as far as customs duty is concerned, is that the E.C. market should be *common*. This means that as between members there must be common policies and application of those policies concerning goods, persons, services and capital (Treaty of Rome, Article 3a). These are referred to as "the Four Freedoms."

The primary source of E.C. law on competition law is provided by Articles 85–94 of the Treaty of Rome. In terms of E.C. law this guide will focus on competition law. It should be stressed that the discussion will serve only as an introduction to some of the legal issues of which the legal adviser should be aware and that advice will invariably and increasingly be provided by a practitioner specialising in E.C. law.

Competition law is investigated further in Chapter 21.

21. Competition Law

A. Introduction

The term "competition law" refers broadly to practices, arrangements and the like, that hamper the workings of the free market in respect of goods and services. Economic theory and the concept of the market, free markets, goods and services provide that competition law is both very broad in its theoretical scope and rapidly evolving in the light of developments concerning the political and economic integration of Europe.

The term "competition law" is not a term of art with a tightly defined and agreed definition. The expression may not be used in some countries. For example, in Australia the preferred terms are "trade practices" and "restrictive trade practices." In the United States the term "anti-trust" may be used.

Competition law may involve an examination of:

(a) *Domestic competition law*, *i.e.* those statutes and principles applying to parties operating wholly within the United Kingdom; or

(b) *International competition law*, *i.e.* international agreements and the like designed to regulate competition issues between parties from two or more different countries or operating across more than two countries. Such international competition may, depending on the parties and the scope of the market, involve a consideration of E.C. competition law. Alternatively it may involve consideration of the law of the particular country. For example a joint venture agreement between a U.K. and a U.S. company may hinge on U.S. anti-trust law. The application of U.S. law will depend on the "choice of laws" clause in the joint venture documentation.

As mentioned above, economic principles will inform competition law. Competition law examines matters which create unfair distortions of the marketplace such as for example the charging of excessive prices. Included in those economic principles are the following matters:

(i) *market power and its concentration.* The competition authorities will examine a situation where there is a high degree of market power vesting in an organisation or organisations. There are several theoretical models ranging from:

    (a) a monopoly (*i.e.* where one organisation has 100 per cent of the market); to

    (b) "dispersed" markets where there is a great deal of competition between competing organisations.

Between these there are:

    (c) duopolies, *i.e.* two organisations one of whom will typically set prices, etc., and the other who will follow; and

    (d) oligopoly, *i.e.* in which a market is dominated by a small number of either suppliers or buyers.

    (ii) *entry barriers and their importance.* What is meant essentially by an "entry barrier" is something that makes a new firm's entry onto the market more difficult than it would otherwise be. In a given situation entry barriers might include the following areas:

    (a) government laws and regulations;
    (b) intellectual property
    (c) start-up capital requirements; or
    (d) existing brand loyalties

In E.C. competition law terms, entry barriers are given significance in the way that Articles 85 and 86 of the Treaty of Rome (see section C below) are interpreted, *i.e.* the Commission takes the view that:

    (a) entry barriers are a significant matter hindering competition (compare this to the so-called Chicago school of economics which regards entry barriers in a global economy as relatively unimportant); and so
    (b) Articles 85 and 86 will be read widely in respect of an anti-competitive practice.

    (iii) *Inter- and intra-brand competition.*

    (a) Inter-brand competition is competition between rival brands of the one product, *e.g.* with softdrinks Coke, Pepsi, Virgin and others are in inter-brand competition;
    (b) Intra-brand competition is competition between different sellers of the same brand of product, *e.g.* between the retailers of Virgin Cola.

Determining the levels of inter- and intra-brand competition will be an important facet affecting the competition authority's stance. For example, generally speaking intra-brand competition will be strong in a monopoly, duopoly or oligopoly, whilst inter-brand competition will be weak in such situations.

    In looking at inter- and intra-brand competition, regard will be had to vertical and horizontal agreements:

    (a) "horizontal" agreements involve competitors at the same level of trade, *e.g.* between manufacturers;
    (b) "vertical agreements" involve competitors at different levels of trade, *e.g.* between a manufacturer and a wholesaler.

For the purposes of this guide, we will focus on E.C. competition law. Before doing so, it is necessary to briefly review domestic competition law.

B. U.K. Competition Law

The first crucial point is that if there is a conflict on a point of competition law between:　21.2

(a) U.K. domestic competition law; and
(b) E.C. competition law,

the situation will be governed by the latter.

U.K. competition law may be either statutory or common law. The key statutes are:

(a) the Fair Trading Act 1973
(b) the Restrictive Trade Practices Act 1976
(c) the Resale Prices Act 1976
(d) the Competition Act 1980

1. COMMON LAW PRINCIPLES

Certain principles at common law may also be relevant. For example, the　21.3
test of reasonableness imposed by the courts is still applied in respect of
restrictive covenants in service agreements that seek to restrict an employee's
employment opportunities once he leaves the employment.

Such restraint of trade clauses will be void, as against public policy, unless
they seek to protect a legitimate business interest, such as trade contacts or
confidentiality.

The restraint of trade clause must be reasonable in three separate respects:

(a) the *market* in which the parties are operating and the type of work
done by the employee in relation to that market;
(b) the *time* period covered commencing from the employee's departure
from the business. The longer the period of restraint, the more likely
that it will be held unreasonable; and
(c) the geographical *distance* covered by the clause. This is usually
expressed in terms of a radius implying a notional circle with the
business as being at the centre of that circle.

The reasonableness or otherwise of the restraint of trade clause will depend
on all the facts and circumstances of a case including:

(a) the type of business;
(b) the seniority of the employee and the responsibilities and duties
undertaken;
(c) the length of service of the employee;
(d) the special know-how or trade secrets to which the employee has
access;
(e) the number of similar businesses within the proposed restricted area;
(f) the personal circumstances of the employee, and
(g) any other facts or matters relevant to the situation.

2. U.K. Competition Law Statutes

21.4   A brief review of the U.K. statutes dealing with competition law is given below.

Fair Trading Act 1973/Restrictive Trade Practices Act 1976
The Restrictive Trade Practices Act 1976 is concerned more with the form and content of potentially restrictive practices than the broader affects of those practices.

The Act focuses on:

(a) the form of individual drafted agreements; and
(b) particular clauses within the agreements that may restrict competition.

The Restrictive Trade Practices Act requires the registration of any agreement:

(a) between two or more persons who carry on business in the United Kingdom; and
(b) under which two or more parties to the agreement accept trade practices restrictions in respect of those matters specified in section 6(1) of the Restrictive Trade Practices Act. It is essential that the restrictions are *agreed* rather than *imposed* by one party on the other.

Examples: relevant restrictions requiring registration:

(a) specifying the quantity of goods to be purchased;
(b) specifying the territory in which the goods are to be sold; and
(c) specifying the class of customers who can be supplied with goods.

Examples: agreements requiring registration:

(a) An agreement between suppliers where it is stipulated that one will supply retail outlets and the other wholesale outlets.
(b) An agreement between suppliers whereby they specify an upper limit on the quantity or volume of goods to be sold in a year.

If the Act does apply to a particular agreement:

(a) the parties to the agreement are required to file particulars of the agreement with the Director-General of Fair Trading; and
(b) those particulars are then held on a public register;
(c) the agreement *may* be referred to the Restrictive Practices Court, in order to further examine the restrictions placed upon the agreement by the Director-General;
(d) if particulars are not furnished to the Director-General of Fair Trading, any competition restrictions in the agreement are void.

Resale Prices Act 1976
The Resale Prices Act prevents resale price maintenance except in limited situations. "Resale price maintenance" involves the manufacturer or supplier specifying, in relation to the goods that they supply or manufacture, a min-

imum price at which those goods are to be resold (so as to keep prices artificially high).

The prohibition on resale price maintenance extends to indirect methods. For example, the supplier cannot recommend a price for a particular product to be resold and then boycott any retailer who sells the goods at less than the recommended price.

The Net Book Agreement (which was abandoned in October 1995) was one of the few exceptions under the Act.

Another exception to the prohibition is where the retailer is loss leading on a particular brand or product. Resale price maintenance is justified in that instance on the basis that not to allow it would adversely affect the supplier's reputation and ability to sell to other retailers.

Competition Act 1980

The Competition Act covers "anti-competitive practices", *i.e.* practices which are likely to have the effect of restricting, distorting or preventing competition, other than those practices which arise as a result of an agreement which is registrable under the Restrictive Trade Practices Act, *i.e.* the Competition Act and the Restrictive Trade Practices Act are mutually exclusive. Examples of anti-competitive practices are:

(a) predatory pricing; *i.e.* pricing aimed at reducing competition in the market; and

(b) full line forcing, *i.e.* forcing a retailer, etc., to accept a whole line of products rather than allowing the ability to pick and choose to suit their needs.

Suspected anti-competitive practices may be investigated by the Monopolies and Mergers Commission and, where necessary, the Secretary of State for Trade and Industry may make an appropriate order where it is found that a particular monopoly operates against the public interest.

Compare the situation under Article 86 of the Treaty of Rome where heavy fines may be imposed by the Commission.

C. European Community Competition Law

Competition law issues involving E.C. Member States will generally arise in the context of business law or litigation.

21.5

Example: Competition law litigation. Tobacco Ltd imports tobacco stem from Germany. The Customs and Excise authorities classify the product as "waste" rather than "leaf" and impose a correspondingly higher rate of duty. Under Article 177 of the Treaty of Rome, such a decision can be challenged in the European Court of Justice.

As for *business law*, European competition issues may arise in the following areas:

(a) agency,

(b) distribution agreements,
(c) purchase and supply,
(d) franchising,
(e) brand licensing, and
(f) patents and trademarks.

The Commission is empowered to regulate competition law under Council Regulation 17/62.

The threshold test for the application of European Competition law is the "inter-state" element, *i.e.* that two or more members of the Community are involved in a transaction. Competition issues may thereafter be relevant, depending on the circumstances. E.C. competition law is enforced by the European Commission. The Commission is divided into several departments known as Directorates-General ("DGs"). DG IV deals with competition policy.

The main sources of European Community Competition law are Articles 85 and 86 of the Treaty of Rome.

The broad aims of E.C. competition law are as follows:

(a) to ensure, as far as possible that companies and other trading entities take decisions independently and do not collude with one another;
(b) to ensure, free trade in markets, subject to regulation;
(c) to protect consumers and customers; and
(d) to stop or prevent abuses of market power.

1. ARTICLE 85 OF THE TREATY OF ROME

21.6 In broad terms, Article 85 outlaws any "agreement" (broadly defined) dealing with trade between two or Member States that either deliberately or unintentionally distorts the workings of the market in so far as competition is concerned. The term "agreement" is given wide scope. It includes written and non-written agreements as well as formal and informal arrangements, including "gentlemen's agreements". Article 85 also refers to:

(a) "undertakings"—this is widely construed to cover all commercial activity; and
(b) "concerted practices"—basically this refers to cartels where competitors collude with each other to partition the market for their benefit.

Article 85 provides as follows:

(a) The following shall be prohibited as incompatible with the Common Market: all agreements between undertakings, decisions by associations of undertakings and concerted practices that may affect trade between Member States and that have as their object or effect the prevention, restriction or distortion of competition within the Common Market, and in particular those which:
　　(i) directly or indirectly fix purchase or selling prices or any other trading conditions;

    (ii) limit or control production, markets, technical development, or investment;

    (iii) share markets or sources of supply;

    (iv) apply dissimilar conditions to equivalent transactions with other trading parties, thereby placing them at a competitive disadvantage;

    (v) make the conclusion of contracts subject to acceptance by the other parties of supplementary obligations that, by their nature or according to commercial usage, have no connection with the subject of such contracts.

(b) Any agreements or decisions prohibited pursuant to this article shall be automatically void.

(c) The provisions of paragraph 1 may, however, be declared inapplicable in the case of:

    (i) any agreement or category of agreements between undertakings;

    (ii) any decision or category of decisions by associations of undertakings;

    (iii) any concerted practice or category of concerted practices;

which contributes to improving the production or distribution of goods or to promoting technical or economic progress, while allowing consumers a fair share of the resulting benefit, and which does not:

    (i) impose on the undertakings concerned restrictions that are not indispensable to the attainment of those objectives;

    (ii) afford such undertakings the possibility of eliminating competition in respect of a substantial part of the products in question.

2. ARTICLE 85 IN OPERATION

For the legal adviser, the practical application of Article 85 is as follows: **21.7**

    (a) does the agreement under consideration breach Article 85(1)? If it does, the agreement, in that respect, will be void under the terms of Article 85(2) unless:

    (b) the agreement may be exempted from the application of Article 85(2) by falling within the terms of Article 85(3).

Under Article 85(3) there is a general "benefit" test comprising the following elements:

    (a) "improving the production or distribution of goods";

    (b) "promoting technical or economic progress"; and

    (c) "allowing consumers a fair share of the resulting benefit."

If there is a benefit that can be expressed within this broad framework, the next point is to establish that the *benefit* outweighs any *detriment* to competition within the market.

The Commission (DG IV) may grant exemptions to agreements and the like under Article 85(3) either:

(a) by reference to the terms of the *particular* agreement; or
(b) by reference to the class of or category of agreement. This is known as *block exemption*.

Block exemptions may be either by reference to the type of service the agreement provides (for example, distribution, purchasing, licensing) or they may be by reference to the type of goods the subject of the agreement (for example motor vehicles).

Block exemptions

21.8   The Commission by Regulation (*i.e.* that has direct effect in Member States) has provided general exemption from the operation of Article 85(1) for certain categories of agreements.

The following block exemptions apply to Member States by regulation:

> Regulation 1983/83 on Exclusive Distribution Agreements
> Regulation 1984/83 on Exclusive Purchasing Agreements
> Regulation 2349/84 on Patent Licensing Agreements
> Regulation 1475/95 on Motor Vehicle Distribution Agreements
> Regulation 417/85 on Specialisation Agreements
> Regulation 418/85 on Research and Development Agreements
> Regulation 4087/88 on Franchising Agreements
> Regulation 556/89 on Know-how Agreements.

Block exemptions contain the following sections:

(a) a "white list" of clauses, *i.e.* those clauses whether in the nature of restrictions or otherwise, that are permitted in the document;
(b) a "black list" of clauses, *i.e.* those clauses whether in the nature of restrictions or otherwise, that are *not* permitted in the document. If any one of the "black list" clauses were included, the agreement would not fall within the block exemption;
(c) a "grey list" of clauses, *.e.* those clauses that whilst they would not usually come within the terms of Article 85(1) (and therefore be void under Article 85(2)), are for the sake of certainty, provided to be expressly permitted. In other words, the inclusion of "grey clauses" will not result in the agreement falling outside the scope of the block exemption;
(d) "recitals," these are statements of policy issued by the Commission. As with statements of practice issued by the Inland Revenue, they do not have the force of law. They are aids to the interpretation and application of the block exemption.

Dealing with the Commission in respect of Block Exemptions

21.9   If an agreement is within the ambit of the block exemption, it will not be caught by Article 85(1) and will not therefore require an exemption or clearance from the Commission in relation to its contents. The whole of the agreement in question must fall, as a matter of construction; within the terms of the particular block exemption that is being claimed. An agreement can not "straddle" two or more block exemptions. It must be wholly within the terms of one block exemption.

The following points in relation to dealings with the Commission can be made:

(a) if an agreement falls within the scope of the block exemption claimed, no delaying as such is required;

(b) if the agreement contains a "block list" clause it will fall outside the scope of the block exemption;

(c) if the agreement contains white and grey list clauses and other clauses (other than black list clauses) it should be notified to the Commission depending on the type of agreement, for example, with franchising and research and development agreements, are notified to the Commission in such circumstances. If the Commission makes no comment within six months, the agreement is deemed to be exempt from any problem under Article 85(1).

Commission Notices

As with the recitals contained in the block exemptions, notices issued by the Commission are meant as an aid to the interpretation of Article 85(1) and in particular whether certain provisions in various categories of agreement fall inside or outside its terms.   **21.10**

Among Commission notices that have been issued are the following:

(a) 1962—Announcement on exclusive agency contracts;

(b) 1968—Co-operation Agreements;

(c) 1986—Agreements of Minor Importance.

This notice deals with those sorts of agreements that, because of:

(a) the aggregate turnover; and

(b) the market share

of the parties to the share, will not exceed the financial specifications contained in the notice.

3. ARTICLE 86 OF THE TREATY OF ROME

Article 86 on the other hand deals with a single business or trading entity within a relevant market that is appreciably free from the normal market forces of competition. The general underlying principle behind article 86 is that a business entity in a special position of strength owes reciprocally "special responsibilities" to the market within which it operates.   **21.11**

Article 86 provides as follows:

"Any abuse by one or more undertakings of a dominant position within the Common Market or in a substantial part of it shall be prohibited as incompatible with the Common Market in so far as it may affect trade between Member States. Such abuse may, in particular, consist in:

(a) directly or indirectly imposing unfair purchase or selling prices or other unfair trading conditions;

(b) limiting production, markets or technical development to the prejudice of consumers;

(c) applying dissimilar conditions to equivalent transactions with other
trading parties, thereby placing them at a competitive disadvantage;

(d) making the conclusion of contracts subject to acceptances by the
other parties of supplementary obligations which, by their nature or
according to commercial usage, have no connection with the subject
of such contracts.''

4. EXCLUSIVE DISTRIBUTION AGREEMENTS

21.12   *Introduction*

Exclusive distribution agreements are those agreements where ''only two
undertakings are party and whereby one party agrees with the other to supply
certain goods for resale within the whole or a defined area of the Common
Market only to that other.'' Exclusive Distribution Agreements are subject
to the 1983 Block Exemption (see paragraph C above). The basis of the block
exemption provides that Article 85(1) of the Treaty of Rome does not apply
because such types of agreements are not considered to be anti-competitive,
i.e. Exclusive Distribution Agreements falling within the terms of the 1983
Block Exemption will not be void under Article 85(2) of the Treaty of Rome.

Overview of a standard exclusive distribution agreement

An Exclusive Distribution Agreement will generally provide as follows:

(a) there will be two parties, the appointing party and the distributor.
The distributor will be appointed on an exclusive basis for the duration of the agreement as distributor of the contract goods which will
themselves be sufficiently specified and defined, usually by way of
a schedule;

(b) the appointor will supply, at a nominated price, contract goods to
the distributor;

(c) the distributor may be required to hold certain stock levels of the
contract goods; to take steps to market the contract goods, etc.; and

(d) miscellaneous clauses such as those dealing with the appointing
party's trademark in respect of the goods; confidentiality; termination and notice provisions and execution clauses.

Possible steps involved in dealing with the commission

In advising a client in relation to a distribution agreement the following lines
of inquiry will be relevant:

(a) does Article 85(1) apply? Prima facie if Article 85(1) does apply,
the agreement will be void under Article 85(2).
Checklist for Article 85(1)
   (i) Does the agreement involve two or more Member States?
   (ii) Does it restrict, prevent or distort competition and or trade
   between states?
   (iii) The Commission will look at the *actual* effect on trade and
   competition as well as *potential* effects.

(b) Even if Article 85(1) does apply, does the agreement fall within the terms of the 1983 block exemption? If it falls *wholly* within the terms of the block exemption, it will be exempt from the effect of Article 85(2).

Alternatively, even if Article 85(1) does apply, the agreement may fall within the 1986 Commission notice dealing with ''Agreements not to contravene Article 85(1) because they do not have an 'appreciable effect' on trade or competition within the Common Market.'' This will depend on:

    (i) the size of the company;

    (ii) the market share the subject of the agreement.

Again the minor agreements notice is not legally binding on the Commission. It is, however, indicative of Commission policy.

(c) Assuming there is, prima facie, a problem under the terms of Article 85(1), does the Commission need to be notified? This will involve seeking either:

    (i) a specific exemption under the terms of Article 85(3) to the effect that the terms of Article 85(1) do not apply. Specific exemptions are rarely sought; or

    (ii) more commonly, a comfort letter. A letter of comfort is not legally binding on the Commission or any other party. The letter of comfort can be obtained quite quickly. The basis of the comfort letter is that the Commission does not intend to take action on the agreement; this, however, does not prevent a third party from taking action.

The comfort letter provides as follows:

(a) that the Directorate-General IV (''DG IV'' responsible for competition policy) of the Commission has completed a preliminary investigation of the agreement which has not revealed the grounds for further investigation; and

(b) that if the underlying factual or legal situation were to change, the Commission could reconsider the case and its stance.

(c) the legal adviser will want to advise the client in writing in respect of whether the agreement is in breach of Article 85(1). This will of course be a legal judgment. The ultimate commercial decisions will be for the client. However, if the client does not heed the legal advice, the client may be subject to large fines. The fine can be as much as 10 per cent of group turnover, based on the most recent year's accounts.

5. PRACTICAL MATTERS CONCERNING THE DRAFTING OF DISTRIBUTION AGREEMENTS

(a) *Exclusive appointment of the distributor*

The appointment of the distributor provided in the agreement must be *exclusive*, *i.e.* it is the one person or organisation that is being appointed rather   **21.13** than two or more parties. The agreement must not provide for a second party to be able to carry out the functions of the distributor.

Source of law
Article 1 of the 1983 Regulation provides that Article 85(3) of the Treaty of Rome does not apply to agreements to which "only two undertakings are party and whereby one party agrees with the other to supply certain goods for resale within the whole or a defined area of the common market only to that other".

Drafting solutions
In summary an exclusive distribution agreement will, in order to comply with these requirements, have the following features:

(a) there is one supplier and one distributor who are generally the only parties to the agreement (but see below);
(b) the distributor is given exclusive rights to distribute the contract goods within the agreed territory.

The appointment of a successor to the distributor may be allowable so long as the successor has no right to sell contract goods until *after* the termination of the current distributor's appointment. If the distribution agreement provides for such an arrangement it should not contravene the Regulation.

(b) *Minimum resale price*

21.14   The party appointing the distributor can *recommend* the price at which the distributor sells the goods onto third parties in the contract territory but cannot create a legally binding obligation on the distributor to sell them at a particular price.

Source of law
Article 2(2) of the 1983 Regulation provides as follows:

"No restriction on competition shall be imposed on the exclusive distributor other than:

(a) the obligation not to manufacture or distribute goods which compete with the contract goods;
(b) the obligation to obtain the contract goods for resale only from the other party;
(c) the obligation to refrain from, outside the contract territory and in relation to the contract goods, from seeking customers, from establishing any branch, and from maintaining any distribution depot."

Prima facie then, any other restriction on the distributor unless specifically allowed elsewhere for example in Article 2(3) of the 1983 Regulation, will not be allowed. Such restrictions will include attempting to fix the price at which the distributor sells the goods to third parties.

The matter is further clarified by the following E.C. laws:

(a) Recital 8 of the 1983 Regulation which specifically refers to the exclusive distributor's right to "determine his prices and conditions of sale."

(b) Paragraph 17 of the 1983 Commission Notice provides that "an agreement will exceed the bounds of (the 1983 Regulation) if the parties relinquish the possibility of independently determining their prices or conditions of business."

Drafting solutions

The exclusive distribution agreement will generally contain reference to two sets of prices;

(a) the price at which the supplier is supplying the contract goods to the distributor. This will be specified, *e.g.* at the supplier's published prices less a 2 per cent discount;

(b) the recommended price at which the distributor will on-sell the contract goods to third parties within the contract territory. This price can only be a recommended one.

(c) *Selective distribution network*

The appointing party cannot *generally* require the distributor or retailers and others with whom the distributor will deal, to possess technical skills or qualifications in order to sell or otherwise deal with the contract goods.

21.15

Source of law

Provisions in the distribution agreement which seek to impede the distributor's free choice of customers are prima facie not permissible as being in contravention of:

(a) Recital 8 of the 1983 Regulations which provides that clauses which seek to "limit the exclusive distributor's choice of customers . . . cannot be exempted under (the 1983 Regulation); and

(b) Paragraph 17 of the 1983 Commission Notice which states in part "among other clauses which in general are not permissible under the (1983 Regulations) are those which impede the reseller in his free choice of customers."

However, paragraph 20 of the 1983 Commission Notice relaxes these restrictions in respect of certain goods. Paragraph 20 provides that

"the reseller may be forbidden to supply the contract goods to unsuitable dealers. Such clauses are unobjectionable if admission to the criteria is based on objective criteria of a qualitative nature relating to the professional qualifications of the owner of the business or his staff or the suitability of his business premises, if the criteria are actually applied in a non-discriminatory manner."

Whether paragraph 20 can be relied on will depend on the nature of the contract goods in a particular case. It has been applied in the main to luxury goods such as electronic equipment and perfumes.

Drafting solutions
Whether paragraph 20 can be relied on will depend on the type of contract goods. The criteria applied must be objective and non-discriminatory in their application.

(d) *Export ban*

21.16   The agreement cannot attempt to ban on the distributor from supplying the goods the subject of the agreement to a third party whose place of business is outside the territory specified in the distribution agreement.

Relevant law
A central aim of the 1983 Regulation is that exclusive distribution agreements should not be deployed to isolate and/or protect the national markets of Member States. This is spelt out in recitals 11 and 12 of the 1983 Regulation and paragraphs 17, 28 an 31 to 33 of the 1983 Commission Notice.

The compromise position is set out in Article 2(2) of the 1983 Regulation which provides as follows:

> "No restriction on competition shall be imposed on the exclusive distributor other than:
>
> (a) the obligation not to manufacture or distribute goods which compete with the contract goods;
> (b) the obligation to obtain the contract goods for resale only from the other party;
> (c) the obligation to refrain from, outside the contract terrritory and in relation to the contract goods, from seeking customers, from establishing any branch, and from maintaining any distribution depot."

Drafting solutions
The compromise in Article 2(2) enables the parties to provide that the distributor can sell goods outside the contract area in response to unsolicited orders (*i.e.* passive sales) but cannot make active sales where the distributor would initiate the sale.

(e) *Servicing of contract goods ban*

21.17   The distributor cannot be banned from providing servicing facilities in respect of contract goods which were purchased outside the contract territory.

Relevant law
To allow such a clause is to limit the distributor's free choice of customers under recital 8 of the 1983 Regulation.

It also contravenes Article 3(d) of the 1983 Regulation in that it makes it "difficult for intermediaries or users to obtain the contract goods from other dealers inside the (E.C.)."

Drafting solutions
Do not include in the agreement such miscellaneous criteria which can be construed as a difficulty in the path of the distributor in carrying out its functions.

(f) *Non-competition*

The appointing party cannot try and restrict the distributor from undertaking its commercial activities once the distribution agreement comes to an end.

Relevant law

The restrictions able to be imposed on the distributor as set out in Article 2(2) of the 1983 Regulations (see paragraph 21.14 above) can only apply during the duration of the agreement and not beyond it.

This time-limit is also specifically referred to in recital 8 of the 1983 Regulations and paragraph 18 of the 1983 Commission Notice.

Drafting solutions

Make sure that the distributor is restricted by reference to the duration of the agreement and not beyond it.

22. Joint Ventures

A. Introduction

22.1   The term "joint venture" is not a legal term of art. The term first arose in commercial rather than legal context. The term "joint venture" may have different meanings between countries. For instance, in the United States and Australia the term usually refers to:

  (a) a single venture or undertaking;
  (b) between two or more participants (natural or artificial legal persons);
  (c) a common rather than joint ownership of assets;
  (d) typically involving joint (shared) control of the project; and
  (e) the sharing of an end product and the profits and losses arising.

In the United Kingdom, the term "joint venture" has not been given a less narrow and specialised meaning. It has been used in the United Kingdom in several contexts including:

  (a) a loose management arrangement between two or more natural or legal entities;
  (b) a partnership on a formal basis; or
  (c) a company interposed between two or more participants.

As a minimum common requirement of joint ventures it could be said that they involve some element of an intention on the part of the participants parties to co-operate with each other in respect of a commercial enterprise.

Joint ventures have not been recognised as a separate and distinct legal entity as, for example, have companies. Instead, joint ventures have been defined and described using the other available forms of business entity, namely partnership and company, together with reference to the principles of contract law.

For the legal adviser, joint ventures will therefore demand a legal knowledge and commercial understanding across a range of possible topics including:

  (a) partnerships,
  (b) companies,
  (c) contract,
  (d) the co-operative enterprise itself—its form and how the joint venturers will deal with one another and get along in spite of possibly quite different "cultures", ideas and aims in so far as the joint enterprise is concerned.

22.2   Each joint venture is a particularly tailor-made endeavour. As such, no two joint ventures will be the same. Therefore the legal adviser will need very full instructions before he can provide commercially sound advice to the particular joint venturers. For example, he will require details on the following points:

    (a) Is it a one-off venture or an ongoing enterprise?
    (b) How will the joint venturers raise finance?
    (c) How will the joint venturers bear liabilities?
    (d) How will the joint venturers share profits or the "end product" of the operation?
    (e) How will disputes be settled?
    (f) What happens if one joint venturer wants to leave the operation?
    (g) By what law is the joint venture governed if, for example, the joint venture participants are from different countries?
    (h) How will the joint venture be terminated?

All these issues and others should be clearly set out in the joint venture document, which should provide a comprehensive working framework for the participants. Drafting the joint venture document is both a very specific and demanding task for the legal adviser.

B. Types of Joint Ventures

Given the relatively broad meaning given to joint ventures in the United Kingdom, three types of joint venture can be identified.   **22.3**

1. THE "JOINT VENTURE COMPANY"

This is otherwise known as an incorporated joint venture. This involves the two or more joint venture participants setting up a company vehicle in which they will each own shares and control the activities. The immediate advantages of this type of joint venture will be the ability of the company to raise finance by way of fixed and floating charge over its assets (depending on its asset base) and the ability of the participants to limit their liability as shareholders in the joint venture company. It may be in practice, of course, that a lender to the joint venture company requires personal guarantees to be given by directors in respect of borrowings made by the joint venture company.

2. THE "JOINT VENTURE PARTNERSHIP"

This is an unincorporated joint venture. Such an arrangement will be treated as if it were a partnership and will be governed by the terms of the Partnership Act 1890 unless the joint venturers agree to vary its terms either orally, by a written agreement or both.

In order to meet the threshold test for a "partnership", a joint venture partnership must satisfy the criteria specified in section 1 of the Partnership Act 1890, that is:

    (a) a relation that subsists between two or more persons;
    (b) carrying on a business in common;
    (c) with a view to making a profit.

If these elements are not satisfied, but nevertheless a joint venture arrangement is held to exist, it will be of the third type set out below.

3. An Unincorporated Association

This is not a joint venture partnership but is nevertheless a joint venture. Such joint ventures will be governed by principles of contract law and the particular principles that have been developed by the courts in relation to "associations". It is very important therefore with such a joint venture arrangement, that the joint venture agreement is particularly detailed in setting out the rights and liabilities of the parties.

C. The Advantages and Disadvantages of Joint Ventures

22.4   The benefits or problems associated with joint venture structures will depend on all the circumstances in the particular commercial context. Such analysis can only take place knowing:

(a) the requirements of the parties;
(b) the nature of the venture;
(c) whether or not there is an international element;
(d) the number and type of participants, etc.

In broad terms the advantages could be identified as follows:

(a) *Shared objectives.* There may be several participants each with different skills resources and general objectives, but for the purpose of the particular joint venture project(s) they share some of the same fundamental aims commercial or otherwise.

(b) *Pooling of resources.* The combined resources of the participants should make borrowing easier because of the increased assets available as security. The credibility of an operation should be enhanced by the coming together of the available resources—people, expertise, reputations, assets, know how and the like.

(c) *Cohesion between the participants.* As the joint venturers usually have a joint right of control and management, there should not be domination by the "big" over the "small" as is often the case with respect of majority shareholders over minority shareholders in respect of companies. Such cohesion and dispute resolution will largely depend on the quality of the joint venture documentation.

(d) *Sharing profits and losses.* Again this will depend on the documentation and the wishes of the parties—will liability be several in respect of joint venture liabilities, losses, etc? Will a participant be able to deal with an "end product" of the joint venture and sell it on and retain the profits?

D. The Use of Joint Venture Arrangements

As with trying to define joint ventures, it is not possible to say when a joint   **22.5**
venture venture arrangement will be appropriate. They have been used in
several areas of commercial activity and have been very common in the
United States, Australia, Japan and Germany. They have also been very popular as regards international transactions.

Joint ventures have been applied to the following areas:

  (a) natural resources, *e.g.* mining, oil and gas;
  (b) engineering construction, *e.g.* bridges, airports;
  (c) production—manufacturing;
  (d) buying—selling;
  (e) the provision of services; and
  (f) research and development purposes.

This list is by no means complete and the use and application of joint venture
techniques is increasing rather than diminishing.

23.   Agents and Distributors

A. Introduction

23.1   The purpose of this chapter is two-fold. First, to examine and compare the general principles concerning agents and distributors and, second, to apply those principles in a practical context to the various business entities.

B. Defining Agency

23.2   The law relating to agency is not a discrete and easily defined area. By agency we mean a legal relationship based on the following elements:

  (a) there is an agent either in name or in law;
  (b) there is a principal on whose behalf the agent acts;
  (c) the agent owes certain duties and responsibilities to the principal;
  (d) the principal may be obliged to pay the agent for the duties undertaken depending on the type of agency;
  (e) the principal will generally be liable to third parties for acts carried out by the agent acting within the scope of the agency arrangement.

C. Types of Agent

1. AGENTS IN LAW

23.3   The following categories of people whilst not actually referred to as agents are, in law, agents:

  (a) company directors and the board of directors to the company as principal;
  (b) the company secretary to the company as principal;
  (c) partners of a firm to the firm and each and every partner as principal;
  (d) employees under contracts of service to the employer as principal;
  (e) certain "professionals" such as solicitors and accountants when acting for clients.

2. AGENTS IN NAME AND LAW

23.4   Under this category, there are various types of "commercial agents" whose task it may be to:

  (a) deal with customers;
  (b) seek new customers; or

(c) enter contracts for and on behalf of a principal.

The following types of commercial agent can be identified.

General and special agents
As a general rule, a special agent acts in respect of a particular transaction whereas a general agent may act in relation to a type of transaction or business for a principal.

The labels "special" and "general" are no longer frequently used and neither are they terms of art. It would therefore be necessary to examine the documents and instructions giving rise to the agency.

Brokers and factors
Brokers negotiate the sale and purchase of goods on the principal's behalf and do not have possession of those goods. Factors on the other hand sell goods on the principal's behalf and for that purpose, have possession of the goods.

Marketing agents
Marketing agents are not authorised to enter into contracts binding on the principal. The agent's task is to find suitable potential customers, to carry out preliminary negotiations with those customers and then to put them in touch with the principal who will be the contracting party. The principal retains a high degree of control with such arrangements.

Sales agents
Sales agents are authorised to enter into contracts on behalf of the principal. The principal will be contractually bound by such contracts. Sales agents therefore have more powers than marketing agents.

Del credere agents
Such agencies are unusual because of the degree of risk potentially falling on the agent. The contract is entered into between the principal and the third party, with the agent guaranteeing the performance (*i.e.* payment) of the contract by the third party. Because of the risks inherent in such an arrangement, the agent will usually be provided with a correspondingly higher rate of commission by the principal.

3. MARKETING ARRANGEMENTS OTHER THAN AGENCY

A business may use several techniques for the purpose of getting its goods to the ultimate consumers. These may or may not amount in law to agency relationships. Several other commercial arrangements may be used instead. These are in the nature of "vertical" agreements in that they involve parties at different levels in the chain of manufacture and distribution, whereas joint venture arrangements (see Chapter 22) will usually be "horizontal", *i.e.* involving parties at the same level.

It is necessary to examine the particular facts and documentation in any one case to determine the precise nature of the relationship. In *general* terms the following arrangements listed below may be used.

23.5

Franchising

23.6   The franchisor authorises the franchisee to sell a product or service to the public. In return for being able to sell the product, the franchisee accepts that the business will be conducted in the manner specified by the franchisor. On payment of a fee by the franchisee to the franchisor, the franchisee gets the benefit of the logo, the goodwill, the trade name, etc., already built up by the franchisor. It is a separate business although it appears as if it is part of a uniform organisation.

The franchisee deals in the capacity as *seller*, *i.e.* as a principal to the public.

Licensing

23.7   A business (the licensor) grants another entity (the licensee) a licence to manufacture or sell its products in accordance with the intellectual property rights owned by the licensor.

Subsidiaries

Subsidiairies—businesses having common ownership or elements of common ownership—may be agents of the parent organisations or may contract as sellers direct with the public.

Distribution agreements

These are discussed in paragraph 23.11

D. Agency Relationships in the Context of the Business Entities

23.8   Agency relationships may affect each of the business entities.

For example:

    (a) *A sole trader* may appoint an agent to sell goods on behalf of the business. The sole trader will be the principal in this situation and will be bound by the acts of the agent that are within the scope of the agency relationship.

    (b) Each of the *partners* is a partnership business acts in the capacity of an agent when dealing with third parties. Agency principles are included in various sections of the Partnership Act 1890. For example, section of the Act deals with the question of the scope of the agent partner's authority in a transaction with a third party.

    (c) A director of a *company* in dealings with third parties is an agent for the principal company.

23.9   In all of these relationships, if in law they are construed as principal–agent relationships, the following points will generally apply:

    (a) The principal will be liable to the third party for the acts of the agent carried out within the scope of the agency.

    (b) The agent owes certain duties to the principal including those of trust, confidence and honesty.

(c) The third party can sue the principal in respect of the act done by the agent. For example, if a director executes a contract on behalf of Investco Ltd. to purchase land from Hardsell PLC, Hardsell PLC will pursue the principal Investco Ltd.

This principle may be subject to exceptions.

In terms of identifying and analysing principal–agent relationships therefore we need to bear in mind:

(a) Who is the agent in the relationship?
(b) For whom does the agent act, *i.e.* who is the principal?
(c) What is the *source* of the agents' authority? For example, is it oral, in writing or partly oral-partly written?
(d) What is the *scope* of the agent's authority?

It may be that the agent habitually acts beyond the scope of his authority. Will these acts bind the principal?:

(a) When is the *principal liable* for the agent's acts?
    The answer is that the principal is liable when the agent acts within the scope of his agency authority, which is as we have seen difficult to ascertain.
(b) When is the agent himself *personally liable* for his own acts? The agent will be liable for "frolics of his own" beyond the scope of the agency authority.
(c) Is a *particular* act or event within the scope of the agency?

It is quickly apparent that there are many aspects to an agent–principal relationship that give rise to potential difficulty.

E. Types of Agency Agreements

The type of agency agreement will depend on the powers vested by the principal. These may be simply to seek contracts so that the principal as supplier can supply goods to customers. Such an agent would usually be referred to as a *marketing agent*. Alternatively, the agent may actually be given contractual powers so as to deal, on the principal's behalf with the clients. Such an agent would usually be referred to as *sales agent*.   **23.10**

Sales agents may be classified as described below.

Exclusive agency
The principal cannot appoint another agent in respect of the goods.

Sole agency
The principal cannot appoint another agent, but can solicit goods himself.

Non-exclusive agency
The principal can not only appoint several agents but can also seek customers directly.

F. Commercial Agents Regulations 1993

Agency agreements are as from January 1, 1994 regulated by the Commercial Agents (Council Directive) Regulations 1993 (S.I. 1993 No. 3053). For a detailed discussion of these Regulations, it is necessary to consult a specialist Agency text.

In broad terms the Commercial Agents Regulations can be summarised as follows:

(a) they implement an E.C. directive the aim of which is to harmonise the relevant domestic legislation of Member States in so far as "commercial agents" are concerned so that they will be bound by the same rules and able to claim the same rights wherever they operate within the E.C. A commercial agent is defined as "a self-employed intermediary who has continuing authority to negotiate the sale or purchase of goods on behalf of (the principal) or to negotiate and conclude the sale and purchase of goods on behalf of and in the name of the principal";

(b) they are mandatory, *i.e.* they cannot be contracted out of;

(c) they are based on the German model of law applying to commercial agents and alters U.K. domestic law in so far as they confer more extensive protection on the agent. For example, under the Regulations:

    (i) compensation may be payable to the agent when the agency ceases or alternatively, the agent may have a right to an indemnity. These rights can extend to the situation where the agent dies; and

    (ii) there are detailed provisions regarding the period of notice to be given to the agent on termination of the agency.

    (iii) the duties owed by the agent to the principal are broadly similar to those set out by the common law, *i.e.* the duty to act in good faith and honestly; the duty of disclosure, etc.

    (iv) in the United Kingdom at least, agency relationships, as far as the principal is concerned, may no longer as commercially attractive as when they were governed by U.K. domestic agency law. For the agent concerned, no doubt the opposite is the case.

G. Distribution and Distribution Agreements

23.11 Whereas agents do not generally have liability independent of the principal for whom they act, distribution differ in several respects. In general terms, distributors will:

(a) contract in their own capacity. As such, they will ordinary assume liability for any obligations undertaken or agreements entered into;

(b) deal with the third party on an "as equals basis," both sides fully bearing contractual liabilities and obligations;

(c) not need to refer back to a "principal" or other person "behind the scene" before making a contractual commitment;

(d) in so far as the wording of the documentation between the third party and the distributor is concerned, unlike the agent, not be signing "for and on behalf of the principal" but will be signing in his independent and complete contractual capacity;

(e) in respect of any litigation proceedings arising out of the documentation issue or defend such proceedings, as the case may be, without recourse to a principal or another party acting in a similar capacity.

24.   Trusts

A. Introduction

24.1   In general terms, a trust is a relationship established by a settlor or founder and arising between a trustee and a beneficiary.

The settlor will usually "settle" a sum (the trust sum or fund) on the trustee, obliging the trustee to deal with the trust fund and any accretions, additions, interest, etc, in accordance with written or oral instructions. The general and overriding duty of the trustee is to safeguard the trust sum for the benefit of the beneficiary.

There is a distinction drawn between the apparent or legal ownership of the trust sum and the beneficial ownership of the trust sum. The trustee has the legal ownership and the beneficiary, the beneficial ownership. This means that the trustee cannot treat the trust sum as his own but must have constant regard to the interests of the beneficiary to whom the trust sum will eventually pass in accordance with the governing documents.

In order for a trust to be valid, three certainties must exist.

(a) *Certainty of words.* Technical expressions are not required. It is a question of the intention of the parties.

(b) *Certainty of subject.* This can be ambiguous. It may mean that the property of the trust must be certain or that the interest of the beneficiaries must be certain.

(c) *Certainty of objects.* This involves ascertaining the aim of the trust.

B. Trusts in Relation to the Business Entities

24.2   For present purposes we can distinguish between two broad ways in which trusts are created, namely:

(a) by the parties intentionally by way of some form of declaration; or
(b) imposed by operation of law by the courts. This second group is known as "constructive trusts." They arise as the result of the conduct of the trustee and their existence is independent from the *intention* of the parties to actually establish a trust. They are imposed *ex post facto* in that the counts will review a situation and impose a trust relationship retrospectively on the parties.

Both types of trusts may arise in relationship to the business entities but we shall focus briefly on the constructive trust.

C. Constructive Trusts

In relation to the business entities, constructive trusts have been imposed **24.3** most commonly in relation to:

(a) *Director and company, i.e.* the director is deemed by the court to be a trustee in relation to the company as beneficiary.

(b) *Partner and co-partner, i.e.* one partner is deemed by the court to be a trustee in relation to the rest of the partners.

Constructive trusts have also been applied in a commercial context to people already in a relationship of trustee–beneficiary or agent–principal.

The rationale for the imposition of a constructive trust are, in general terms, two-fold:

(a) the result of fraudulent, unconscionable or inequitable conduct by the would be trustee; or

(b) the result of a breach of fiduciary duty by the would be trustee.

Appendix 1   Sole Traders

1.1 Terms, Definitions and Legislation

Legislation to Consider

Business Names Act 1985
Income and Corporation Taxes Act 1988
Insolvency Act 1986
Value Added Tax Act 1985
Taxation of Chargeable Capital Gains Act 1992

Definitions to Consider with Sole Traders

Business names	a name adopted by a business that complies with the Business Names Act 1985.
Management	control and administration of the business as distinct to ownership of the business.
Third party	a generic term referring to a party existing and operating outside the business.
Unlimited liability	where the owner of the business is solely responsible to pay the debts incurred by the business.
VAT registration	registering under the Value Added Tax Act (1985) which is necessary depending on the turnover of the business.

For other terms and definitions, see Appendix 2.1.

1.2 Sole Trader Self-Test Questions and Answers (see Chapters 2 and 5)

Sole Trader Self-test Questions

1. What are the restrictions on the choice of name for a business operated by a sole trader?

2. How is a sole trader taxed on income profits?

3. What is meant by the phrase ''a separate legal entity'' when used in relation to a company?

4.   What are the advantages of operating as a sole trader?

5.   What are the disadvantages of operating as a sole trader?

6.   What is the personal bankruptcy threshold debt?

7.   What alternatives are there to formal bankruptcy for a sole trader?

8.   Explain the concept of Capital Gains Tax for an asset owned by a sole trader.

9.   Could a sole trader adopt the name "Royal Enterprises"? Give reasons.

10.   What formalities are there in setting up business as à sole trader?

11.   Is a sole trader required to have his name on the business letterhead?

12.   Is a sole trader entitled to retirement relief and, if so, what are the conditions applicable?

13.   Can a sole trader be sued in his own name?

14.   Is a sole trader bound by the terms of the Unfair Contract Terms Act 1977?

15.   If declared bankrupt, can someone continue to run a business?

ANSWERS TO SOLE TRADER SELF-TEST QUESTIONS

1.   The restrictions are contained in the regulations issued by the Secretary of State under the Business Names Act 1985. Business names that contain a word in the regulations list require the approval of a particular body, the Secretary of State, or both, before use. The main restrictions are words associated with the Crown, government—national and local—and offensive or illegal words.

2.   A sole trader is subject to pay income tax under the Income and Corporation Taxes Act, 1988 for all personal income, which includes income from the sole trading business. The relevant schedules are Schedule D, Case I (for a trade) and Case II (for a profession or vocation). For businesses formed before April 6, 1994, they will be taxed on a preceding year basis pursuant to Schedule D until 1997–98. For businesses commending on or after April 6, 1994, Schedule D will operate on a current year basis.

3.   That the company is separate and distinct from the members who are the owners of it. This means that the company can assume liabilities; it can sue and be sued in its own name, etc.

4. Flexibility and speed of decision-making. The sole trader does not have to consult others before deciding on a decision affecting the sole trading business. Another is the "privacy" offered to the sole trader, *i.e.* no public registration of documents is required.

5. Personal, unlimited liability, *i.e.* the debts of the business, are borne solely by the owner of the business.

6. £750 for an unsecured debt owed to one or more creditors (Insolvency Act, s. 267(4)).

7. An IVA made by the sole trader in conjunction with his creditors (Insolvency Act, 1986, ss. 252–263) and the assistance of a nominee supervisor of the debtor whereby the creditors can meet and approve a scheme. It then binds each creditor who had notice of the meeting. Alternatively, the Deeds of Arrangement Act 1914 may be used, but is rarely done so, because arrangements entered into under it, only bind those creditors who *actually agree* to the arrangement.

8. CGT is a tax imposed on "chargeable assets" (as defined by the Taxation of Capital Gains Act 1992), that takes into account an asset's increase in value over and above the inflation index, subject to expenses incurred in purchasing and selling the asset.

9. A problem under section 2(1)(a) of the Business Names Act 1985, *i.e.* the word "Royal" provides the impression of connection with "Her Majesty's Government". The word "royal" is also on the list requiring the Secretary of State's approval (see s. 2(1)(b)).

10. There are no registration requirements, unless a business name is adopted. Also VAT registration depending on turnover

11. Yes, by section 4 of the Business Names Act 1985. If a business name is adopted, it must be complied with.

12. Retirement relief is a reduction of CGT due to a sole trader's personal situation. The conditions are:

    (a) retirement from the business;
    (b) age—55 or earlier, due to ill health;
    (c) ownership of the business for at least one year (maximum retirement relief is available after ownership of 10 years);
    (d) the amount of relief is 100 per cent up to £250,000 and 50 per cent for amounts between £250,000 and £1,000,000.

13. Yes, or in his or her own name trading as (business name).

14. Yes. The Unfair Contract Terms Act 1977 refers to a person "dealing as a consumer" with another which includes someone acting in the

"course of business," which includes all three of the business entities, *i.e.* sole trader, partnership, company (Unfair Contracts Terms Act 1977, ss. 12 abd 14).

15.   A bankrupt's assets vest in the trustee in bankruptcy on the making of the bankruptcy order by the court. The bankrupt cannot be a director or act in the management of a company once the bankruptcy order has been made. There is no bar on acting as a sole trader but practically this will be very difficult because of the vesting of property in the trustee and the many offenses under the Insolvency Act 1986, *e.g.* section 360—obtaining credit, etc.

Appendix 2   Partnerships

2.1 Terms, Definitions and Legislation

Legislation to Consider

Limited Partnership Act 1907
Business Names Act 1985
Partnership Act 1890

Definitions to Consider with Partnerships

Active partners	are active in the day-to-day management and business of the partnership.
Articles of partnership	see "Partnership deed".
Capital	(capital contribution) the permanent investment whether in assets, money or in kind made by a partner into the partnership.
Capital partner	a partner entitled to share in the profits of the partnership in accordance with the terms of the partnership agreement. A capital partner will usually receive income in addition to a share of profits.
Firm	in law, a business organisation, usually a partnership.
Income partner	a partner entitled only to receive an income from the partnership and not to share in the profits (see Capital partner).
Joint liability	where liabilities rather than being shared between two or more people are theoretically able to be imposed on one of those people alone. For example A, B, C and D in partnership have joint liability, for a debt of £100,000 and B, C and D are bankrupt, A will be liable for the whole £100,000 debt.
Joint and several liability	a combination of joint liability and several liability. For example if A, B, C and D have joint and several liability in respect of a debt of £100,000, A may be held liable by the creditor for either £25,000 (several liability) or the whole £100,000 (joint liability).
Limited partnership	a partnership governed by the Limited Partnership Act 1907 whereby the partners will have limited liability rather than unlimited liability

312

as is the usual case. Note, however, that at least one of the partners in a limited partnership must bear unlimited liability. Section 717 of the Companies Act 1985 and section 4 of the Limited Partnership Act 1907 limits the number of partners in a limited partnership to no more than 20.

Partnership   defined by section 1 of the Partnership Act 1890 as a relationship between two or more persons carrying on a business in common with the intention of making a profit.

Partnership deed or agreement   the document governing the relationship between partners that complements and/or replaces the Partnership Act 1890.

Professional partnership   not a term of art but a partnership comprised of professionally qualified groups being one of the following:

> (a) solicitors;
> (b) accountants/auditors;
> (c) members of a recognised stock exchange;
> (d) others as prescribed by regulation.

Several liability   where liabilities are shared between two or more people. For example, if A, B, C and D are in partnership and have equal several liability and a debt of £100,000, they will each be responsible for £25,000 only.

Sleeping partners   are partners who have contributed "capital", *i.e.* "permanent investment" in the partnership but they are not active in the management of the business.

Trading partnerships   as distinct from professional partnerships; they are comprised of members other than those listed in section 716 of the Companies Act 85. Limited in size to no more than 20 partners:

> (a) management, or
> (b) decision-making.

2.2.1 Example Partnership Agreement

THIS PARTNERSHIP AGREEMENT dated [   ] IS MADE BETWEEN

1. Name and Address of Partner A.

2. Name and Address of Partner B.

RECITALS

Whereas:

(i) Partner A is a [Trade or Occupation] with [Particular interest], *e.g.* Bob is a Computer Programmer with computer design experience.

(ii) Partner B is a [Trade or Occupation] with [Particular Interest], *e.g.* Wendy is an Investor with capital wishing to invest in a business venture.

(iii) A and B wish to set up a partnership business together on the terms and conditions set out in this Agreement.

OPERATIVE PART DEFINITIONS

1.1 The following terms shall have the following meanings under this Agreement:

"Accounting Period" means the period of [ ].

"Advances" means all loans, extended credit and other financial arrangements or moneys other than capital contributions extended by a Partner or Partners to the Partnership Business.

"Competing Business" means an Outside Business carrying on the same or substantially similar business to that of the Partnership Business.

"Commencement Date" means the [date].

"Defined Event" means in relation to any Partner

(a) bankruptcy;

(b) death;

(c) expulsion in accordance with the terms of this Partnership Agreement;

(d) the making of an order under the Mental Health Act 1983; or

(e) retirement.

"Dispute" means any dispute, difference, disagreement of whatsoever nature arising out of or in relation to this Partnership Agreement or the Partnership Business.

"Further Capital" means all contributions of capital made to the Partnership Business other than the Initial Capital.

"Initial Capital" means the capital investment contributed to the Partnership Business on or about the Commencement Date.

"Nominated Agent" means a person acting in the following capacities:

(a) the Personal Representative in the event of the death of a Partner;

(b) the Trustee in Bankruptcy in the event of the bankruptcy of a Partner;

(c) the Receiver under the Mental Health Act 1983 in the event of the provisions of that Act or its replacement being applied to a Partner.

(d) the Partner himself in the event of his retirement or expulsion from the Partnership.

"Outside Business" means any business, partnership, employment, occupation, trade, whether of a remunerative or profitable nature or not other than the Partnership Business set out in this Agreement.

"Partnership Accountant" means [ ] appointed by the Partners.

"Partnership Bank" means [branch/bank] appointed by the Partners.

"Partnership Business" means the business of [ ] and refers to the net value of the Partnership Business taking into account all assets of the Partnership (including the goodwill, if any) less all liabilities of the Partnership Business, including Third Party Debt, Advances and Profits.

"Partnership Debt" means any debts, liabilities or losses of whatsoever nature payable by the Partnership.

"Partnership Documents" means all documents, written materials, memoranda of whatsoever nature relating to or incidental to the Partnership Business.

"Partnership Premises" means [address].

"Precedent Partner" means the partner nominated and appointed by the other Partners (and consented to by the nominee) to deal with Accounting Records, the Partnership Taxation Return and such other matters as may be agreed by the Partners from time to time.

"Profits" means all amounts of a profit nature made by the Partnership Business and includes profits drawn by Partners and Undrawn Profits.

"Tax Act" means the Income and Corporation Taxes Act of 1988 and regulations and includes any reference to its replacement, amendment or modification.

"Third Party Debts" means any liabilities and debts of whatsoever nature of the Partnership Business owed to third parties.

"Undrawn Profits" means profits left in the Partnership Business by a Partner without prejudice to that Partner's entitlement to draw those profits at a later date.

1.2 A reference to either gender shall be taken to include reference to both genders.

1.3 A reference to the singular shall, where appropriate, be a reference to the plural and vice versa.

COMMENCEMENT AND NAME

2. The parties to this Agreement ("the Partners") will from the commencement date carry on the Partnership Business in partnership, on the terms of this Agreement under the business name of [ ].

DURATION

3. Each Partner shall remain a member of the Partnership until he ceases to be a member by reason of a Defined Event and if after he ceases to

be a partner, there are at least two continuing Partners, the Partnership shall not determine as regards the continuing Partners.

PLACE OF BUSINESS

4. The Partnership Business shall be carried on at the Partnership Premises.

CAPITAL

Initial capital

5.1 The Initial Capital of the Partnership shall consist of the sum of [£] of which each Partner shall pay [   ] into the Partnership bank account as agreed by them.

5.2 The Initial Capital shall belong to the Partners equally.

Further capital

6.1 All matters relating to the contributions of Further Capital shall be decided by the Partners by way of a majority vote at a Partner's meetings held from time to time.

6.2 Further Capital shall belong to the Partners in accordance with the contributions made by them.

Undrawn profits

7.1 Undrawn Profits shall not be added either to Initial Capital or to Further Capital.

BANK AND ACCOUNTANT

8.1 The Partners shall as soon as is practicable after the Commencement Date:

(a) open the partnership account at the Partnership Bank; and
(b) appoint the Partnership Accountant.

8.2 Any money or security for money belonging to the Partnership shall be paid into the Partnership Bank. Signatures on cheques on a Partnership account shall comply with the mandate from time to time lodged with the Partnership Bank.

DRAWINGS OF PROFITS

9.1 Each Partner shall be entitled to receive the Partnership Bank account on account of his share of profits such monthly sums as may be agreed by the Partners from time to time.

9.2 If, at the request of any Partner, the Partnership Accountant certifies that any Partner has drawn sums that exceed the level of drawings reasonably prudent in the circumstances, such excess shall be repayable by the Partner concerned within fourteen days of receiving written notification.

9.3 Each Partner shall be entitled to draw out of the Partnership Bank account any undrawn balance of his share of any profits shown in any profit and loss account of the Partnership, at any time after the account in question has been signed by the Partners, *provided* that no Partner may withdraw such part of his undrawn balance as the Partnership Accountant shall certify as appropriate to be retained to meet the estimated income tax and National Insurance liability of the Partnership.

9.4 Subject to the proviso in clause 9.3, a former Partner whose partnership share is purchased under clause 20 of this Agreement shall be entitled to receive any balance of his share of Undrawn Profits at the date when the purchase takes effect.

PROFITS AND LOSSES

10. The Partners shall share profits and losses of the Partnership business equally.

ACCOUNTING RECORDS

11. The Precedent Partner shall ensure that proper accounting records as the Partnership Accountant shall reasonably recommend are prepared and kept up to date.

ANNUAL ACCOUNTS

12.1 The Partnership Accountant shall be instructed to prepare accounts in respect of each Accounting Period of the Partnership.

12.2 The Partners shall agree and sign the accounts in accordance with clause 13.

TIME DEVOTED TO BUSINESS

13.1 Each Partner shall devote at least 40 hours per working week of his time and attention to the Partnership Business and shall diligently and faithfully work for the benefit of the Partnership.

13.2 Each partner may take [ ] weeks holiday in each Accounting Period at such times as the Partners may agree from time to time in accordance with clause 15.1.

13.3 Without prejudice to clause [Expulsion] a Partner shall not be in breach of clause 13.1 above where his absence is caused by ill health or injury duly certified (if the other Partners so require) by a medical practitioner.

ROLE OF PARTNERS

14. [The content of this clause will obviously be subject to instructions from the clients.
    Example
        Partner "A" shall be the managing partner responsible for:
        — day-to-day administrative matters;
        — all matters relating to employees (other than Partners); and
        — such other matters as are specifically designated by the other partners.
        Partner "B" shall be responsible for:
        — recording and maintaining the Partnership's financial records.
        Partner "C" shall be responsible for:
        — marketing and sales regarding the Partnership Business.]

DECISION-MAKING

15.1 Those decisions specifically referred to in clause 15.2 shall require the unanimous agreement of the partners and other decisions relating to the Partnership Business or the terms of this Agreement shall require the unanimous agreement of the Partners except that:
    (a) a majority of the Partners may take decisions on . . . [a list would be inserted].
        [*Example*
        The taking of holidays, new stationery designs, etc. There is no set rule as to what can be covered and it is up to each partnership business to decide these matters.]
    (b) any Partner may take decisions on . . . [a list would be inserted].
        [*Example*
        This might be conferences to be attended in the U.K., but as above, it depends on the Partnership Business].

15.2 Decisions requiring the unanimous agreement of the Partners shall include, but not be limited to the following matters:
(a) appointment of the Partnership Accountant;
(b) signing the Partnership Accounts;
(c) changing the nature of the Partnership Business; and
(d) admitting a new partner.

15.3 Regular Partnership meetings shall take place every [ ].

PAYMENT OF PRIVATE DEBTS

16. Each Partner shall punctually pay his personal debts and discharge his personal obligations and shall indemnify the other Partners and their representatives and successors against any liability in respect of his personal debts and obligations.

NEGATIVE COVENANTS

17. No Partner shall except with the consent in writing of all of the other Partners:
(a) carry on or be concerned with or interested directly or indirectly in any Outside Business;
(b) release or discharge any third party from any Partnership Debt without receiving the full amount;
(c) assign, mortgage, charge or otherwise encumber his interest in the Partnership;
(d) except in the usual and regular course of the Partnership Business, draw accept or sign any cheque or other bill of exchange or promissory note, or contract any debt on account of the Partnership, or use any of the Partnership's money or property, or in any manner pledge the credit of the Partnership;
(e) engage or dismiss any employee of the Partnership;
(f) lend any money belonging to or give any credit or guarantee on behalf of the Partnership (other than credit given in the usual course of business).

RETIREMENT OF A PARTNER

18.1 Any Partner may retire from the Partnership on giving (after one year from the date of this Agreement) not less than three months' notice in writing to the other Partners.

18.2 At the expiration of such notice the Partnership shall determine as regards the Partner giving notice.

EXPULSION OF A PARTNER

19.   If any Partner:
    (a) allows his share in the Partnership to be charged in respect of a debt unconnected with the Partnership; or
    (b) becomes a patient within the meaning of the Mental Health Act 1983; or
    (c) commits any serious breach or commits persistent breaches of this Agreement; or
    (d) fails to pay any money owing by his to the Partnership within twenty-one days of a request in writing by the other Partners; or
    (e) is guilty of any conduct likely to have a serious adverse effect upon the Partnership business; or
    (f) absents himself from the Partnership business (or is otherwise unfit to conduct his equal share of the work of the Partnership) for more than [ ] days in any period of twelve months by reason of ill health or injury the other Partners may by notice in writing expel such partner and the Partnership shall immediately cease as regards such Partner. Expulsion shall be without prejudice to the remedies of the other Partners for any breach of this Agreement.

OPTION TO PURCHASE A PARTNER'S SHARE

20.1   If any Partner ceases to be a Partner of the Partnership for any reason whatsoever, the remaining Partners may purchase the share of the former Partner in the Partnership Business upon them giving a notice in writing to the Partner to that effect within [ ] months of the cessation to his personal representative, trustee in bankruptcy, or receiver under the Mental Health Act 1983 or to the outgoing Partner himself (as the case may require), and the purchase of the share shall be deemed take effect in accordance with this clause.

20.2   If the remaining Partners do not wish to exercise the option to purchase the Partnership interest within the period specified in clause 20.1 the Partnership Business shall be dissolved.
    [*Note*: The partners could provide for other solutions. Clause 20.1 is a pre-emption provision in favour of the present partners. It gives them control over the affairs of the business.
    Alternatively, a third party could purchase the interest of the outgoing partner. The partners would want the right to vets such a sale if it was to a purchaser of whom they did not approve.]

20.3   The purchase price of the share of the outgoing Partner shall be a proportion of the value of the Partnership Business at the date on which the purchase takes effect in accordance with the profit-sharing ratio:
    The value of the Partnership Business shall be the value of the Part-

nership assets (which include the Partnership's goodwill) after deducting:

(a) third party debts, Partners (and the former Partner);

(b) advances;

(c) profits.

20.4 If the Partners are unable to agree between themselves the value to be attributed to the former Partner's share of the Business, it shall be referred forthwith to the Partnership Accountant for determination. If the Partners can not agree with the Partnership Accountant's decision as to the value of the share, such matters shall then be deemed to be a Dispute to be settled in accordance with clause 25.

PAYING FOR THE SHARE

21.1 The purchase price so ascertained shall be paid by the purchasing Partners ("the Purchasers") to the former Partner or his personal representative, trustee in bankruptcy or receiver under the Mental Health Act 1983 as appropriate ("the Vendor") by four equal instalments at the expiration of six, twelve, eighteen and twenty-four months respectively from the day on which the purchase takes effect, with interest on the instalments for the time being remaining unpaid. For each day in respect of which interest is due, interest shall be calculated as the daily equivalent of two per cent per annum above the base rate prevailing at the Partnership bank prevailing on that day.

21.2 The Purchasers shall indemnify the Vendor against the debts and liabilities taken into account in ascertaining the purchase price of the Vendor's share in the Partnership.

21.3 Any costs reasonably incurred in implementing the provisions of this clause (other than costs incurred in respect of any legal or arbitration proceedings, which may be the subject of an order for costs) shall be borne equally by the Partners (including the former partner).

21.4 The Vendor shall, at the request of the Purchasers, do and execute all acts, deeds and things necessary or proper, for vesting the share so purchased in the Purchasers and for enabling the Purchasers to get in the outstanding assets of the Partnership.

APPOINTMENT OF ATTORNEYS

22. Each Partner irrevocably appoints every other Partner and the persons deriving title under the last surviving or continuing Partner to be his attorney in the event of the Partnership being dissolved (as regards him), only for the purposes of getting in any assets and completing

payment of any debts of the Partnership and of giving notice to any customers or suppliers of the change in the Partnership and for those purposes, the attorney may make any relevant deed or instrument.

RESTRICTIVE COVENANTS

23.1   No Partner shall within [ ] years of leaving the Partnership Business carry on or be concerned or interested either directly or indirectly in a Competing Business within a radius of [ ] miles from the Partnership Premises.

23.2   No Partner shall within two years of leaving the Partnership solicit orders for or on behalf of a Competing Business from any customer with whom (within the period of two years before that partner left the Partnership) the Partnership Business had dealt.

DOCUMENTS

24.1   Upon any of the Partners leaving the Partnership the property in and possession of the Partnership Documents shall remain with the continuing Partners.

24.2   A departing Partner shall return all Partnership Documents to the Partnership Business within 14 days of the departure date.

In the case of a Defined Event, the Nominated Agent shall be required by the Partners to comply with clause 24.1.

ARBITRATION OF DISPUTES

25.   If at any time (including after determination of the Partnership Business) any Dispute arises, such Dispute shall be referred to a sole arbitrator appointed by the Partners (or their Nominated Agents as the case may be). In default of agreement as to the appointee, an arbitrator shall be appointed by [*the Partners should nominate a third party to appoint an arbitrator*].

Any decision made by the Arbitrator in relation to dispute shall be final and binding upon the Partners.

SCHEDULES

e.g. the listing of Partnership Property.

_____

Signed and Delivered as his deed   )
by A in the presence of   )

Signed and Delivered as his deed　　　)
by B in the presence of　　　　　　　)

2.2.2 Index of a Typical Partnership Agreement (by Clauses)

The following points refer to the example partnership agreement in Appendix 2.2.1.

1. *Definitions*

2. *Commencement*
   The date of the partnership business.

3. *Duration*
   Will the duration of the partnership be fixed? Will it dissolve automatically?

4. *Place of business*
   Where will the business be operated from? Will the premises be lease-hold or freehold? Will it form part of the partnership property?

5/6. *Capital*
   Capital, as opposed to income, is comprised of partnership assets including:

   (a) the premises,
   (b) the goodwill (an intangible asset),
   (c) equipment,
   (d) stock-in trade,
   (e) cash contributions initially and later on.

7. *Profits and losses*
   The profit and losses (including capital)—how are they to be shared?

8. *Bank and accountant*
   Formalising the choice of partnership account and the accountant? Who will be signatories to the account?

9/10. *Profit and drawings*
   Arrangements for drawings from the partnership account on a monthly or other basis.

   Note: Such further details in the partnership agreement should be in writing to avoid problems, uncertainty and disputes.
   Profit drawings should be made subject to the following ongoing liabilities of the partnership:

(a) income tax,
(b) National Insurance contributions.

11. *Accounting records*

(a) Who prepares them?
(b) Who oversees their preparation?
(c) Who audits them?

12. *Annual accounts*
I.e. the accounting records for an accounting period or tax year prepared annually by the partnership accountant and signed by the partners.

13. *Time devoted to the partnership*
The usual formula is that each partner devotes his:

(a) "whole time and attention"; and
(b) "diligently and faithfully works for the benefit" of the partnership; and
(c) holidays as agreed.

14. *Role of partners*
Defining the different roles, for example, management, sales, advertising, accounts, marketing.

15. *Decision-making*
Options:

(a) unanimous agreement of all the partners, *e.g.* admission of a new partner;
(b) majority decisions;
(c) single partner decisions, *e.g.* day-to-day administration.

Partnership meetings—how often are they held?

16. *Payment of a partner's private debts*
Usually the partnership agreement will include provisions to the effect that:

(a) each partner is to punctually pay all their personal debts and obligations; and
(b) each partner is to indemnify the other partners and their successors and assigns in respect of such debts and obligations.

17. *Negative covenants*
These typically involve the situations where a partner is prohibited, except for example with the *consent in writing* of the other partners, from:

(a) being involved in a competing occupation or business;
(b) giving a release or discharging a partnership debt for less than the

full amount, *i.e.* if someone owes the partnership £100 and is given a release by paying £50, this would breach this provision;

(c) assigning or mortgaging their interest in the partnership business;

(d) using partnership property or money outside the *usual and regular course of the business*;

(e) engaging or dismissing any employee of the partnership unilaterally (but see clause 14—this may be delegated to a managing partner); and

(f) lending money or giving credit to someone from the partnership other than in the *usual course of business*.

18. *Retirement of a partner*
The length and form of notice, *e.g.* three months' written notice—at the end of three months, does the partnership determine or is the retiring partner's interest purchased by the other partners?

19. *Expulsion of a partner*
Specify the grounds and procedure involved. The expulsion power must be specific. The procedure must follow the specific power and be exercised bona fide. Is it to be based on a one-off incident or several, repeated incidents?

Depending on the type of business, the occurrence of one or more of the following events might justify the expulsion of a partner:

(a) *e.g.* the *charging* of partnership assets by a partner for the purpose of personal debts, *i.e.* partner A borrows £7,000 from bank B and as security "charges" or "mortgages" his share of the partnership assets to bank B;

(b) one of the partners becomes a mental patient;

(c) a partner in debt to the partnership for 21 days after receiving a written request from the other partners;

(d) a partner guilty of conduct "likely to have serious adverse effect on the Partnership";

(e) a partner absent from the partnership business for more than 56 days "due to ill health or injury."

Effect of the expulsion:

(a) Does it result in the dissolution of the partnership business?

(b) Is expulsion without prejudice to other remedies?

20/21. *Option to purchase outgoing partner's share of the partnership assets*

(a) Do the existing partners get a "pre-emption" or right of first refusal ahead of others to purchase the interest?

(b) How is it triggered, *e.g.* by notice?

(c) What is the form of notice, *e.g.* written?

(d) When must the option be exercised?

(e) Does it arise as a result of a person ceasing to be a partner through:
  (i) retirement,

        (ii) death,

       (iii) bankruptcy,

      (iv) mental illness,

       (v) expulsion.

(f) If the "purchase option" is not taken, will the partnership be *dissolved*?

(g) What is the purchase price of the outgoing partner's share and how is it determined?

(h) Is it based on the value of the partnership business at the date the purchase takes *effect* or some other basis?

(i) does the value of the Partnership Business equal the value of partnership assets (including goodwill) *less*:

    (i) the debts and liabilities of the partnership;

   (ii) advances by the partners, *i.e.* in excess of capital contribution requirements;

  (iii) a partner's undrawn balance of profits;

(j) Will failure to agree a valuation of the outgoing partner's share be resolved by arbitration or another method?

(k) Payment of the purchase price for outgoing partner's share—how will it be arranged? *e.g.* four equal instalments over two years with interest at a daily rate.

(l) Do the remaining partners indemnify the vendor (*i.e.* the outgoing partner) against debts and liabilities of the partnership that have been taken into account in determining the value of the partnership and liabilities of the partnership assets.

(m) Costs of the purchase of the outgoing partner's share—are they borne equally by *all* the partners?

(n) Is the co-operation of the vendor (outgoing partner) regarding the sale of his share of the business to be included as a term in the partnership agreement.

22. *Appointment of attorneys*

(a) Each partner appoints every other partner in the event of the *dissolution* of the partnership business.

(b) the attorney may be appointed for limited purposes:

    (i) to get in the partnership assets;

   (ii) to pay debts;

  (iii) to give notice to customers, suppliers.

23. *Restrictive covenants regarding a departing partner*

What time duration from the departure date and distance from the business is to be protected? There will usually be a prohibition on using the name of the business, and dealing with or soliciting clients of the business.

24. *Documents clause*

Is the outgoing partner required to leave all/any documents relating to the business with the ongoing partners?

25. *Arbitration*

   The disputes settlement procedure—how is the arbitrator appointed? Is it by:

   (a) the partners; or
   (b) a third party (*i.e.* someone with specialist knowledge).

   Arbitration is a popular alternative to court solutions—it is quick, inexpensive, expert, final and informal.

26. *Other clauses*

   Personal pension scheme—detail the type and method of payments, etc.

27. *Schedules*—for example, providing a list of partnership property;

28. *Execution clauses*—each partner signs the agreement as a *deed*; the witness to include his:
   (i) full name;
   (ii) address;
   (iii) occupation;

   VAT Registration:
   (i) required if the "taxable supplies" exceed the VAT limit in previous 12 months or are likely to in the next 30 days.
   (ii) the VAT registration threshold is presently £46,000.

2.3 Partnership Self-Test Questions and Answers

PARTNERSHIP SELF-TEST QUESTIONS

These questions should be attempted after looking at the Partnership Act 1890.

1. Once a partner retires from a partnership he is free from debts of the partnership. True or false? Explain your answer.

2. What are the essential elements of a partnership?

3. The power to expel a partner is always inferred by virtue of a partnership existing. True or false? Explain your answer.

4. All partnerships require partnership agreements. True or false? Explain.

5. A partnership without a specified fixed term cannot simply be ended at any moment by one of the partners. True or false? Explain.

6. On dissolution of a partnership, a partner's personal assets are immediately exposed to the payment of the partnership's liabilities. True or false? Explain.

7. On dissolution of a partnership, which of (a) the advance or (b) a capital contribution is repaid first? Explain.

8. Bob and Sue are in partnership. They ask their friend Chris to lend the firm £5,000 to enable it to meet its financial obligations.

   Bob and Sue offer Chris 20 per cent of the partnership's profits for the next three years in lieu of interest on the loan.

   Advise Chris on the possible problems with such a scheme. How could these problems be overcome?

9. Damon and Alain are in partnership trading as "Formula One Garage." Damon has many other business interests and takes no active part in the management of FOG.

   The partnership agreement for FOG provides that "neither partner shall without the consent of the other engage in the business of buying or selling motor vehicles, either in the name of FOG or in his own name." Without Damon's knowledge, Alain has been dealing, i.e. buying and selling used cars at FOG premises and has incurred considerable amounts payable to a third party "Nigel's Indy Experience."

   Advise Damon on his liability to meet the payments to "Nigel's Indy Experience."

10. Damon from question 9 has decided to leave the partnership. What steps would you advise him to take to protect himself?

Answers to Partnership Self-test Questions

1. False. See section 17(2) of the Partnership Act 1890. However, has the outgoing partner been indemnified by the other partners? or has agreement been reached as per section 17(3)? Consider also the novation of important contracts.

2. See the definition under section 1 of the Partnership Act 1890.

3. False. See section 25 of the Partnership Act 1890.

4. False, but:
   (a) certainty is promoted.
   (b) avoid terms of the Partnership Act 1890.

5. False. See section 26 of the Partnership Act 1890.

6. False. See section 39 of the Partnership Act 1890—the partnership property is exposed first.

7. (i) The advance. See section 44(b) of the Partnership Act 1890.

8. See section 2(3) of the Partnership Act 1890. In particular, consider section 2(3)(a) and (d):

(a) prima facie—a partner—receipt of profits;
(b) depends on the intention of the parties;
(c) the danger then is that C is exposed to the same liabilities as the partners.

To overcome:

(a) prevent C from profit sharing, *i.e.* wording of agreement;
(b) prevent C from having any control over the business.

9. Revolves around section 5 of the Partnership Act 1890 and the issue of apparent authority. The buying and selling of cars is part of Alain's ostensible authority probably. Also, (a) part of the business and (b) the usual way of carrying it on. The prohibition on Alain's authority is ineffective unless the prohibition is actually known to the third party (see Partnership Act 1890, s.5).

Conclusion: it is the partnership's liability—joint liability of the partners for a contractual debt.

10. (a) See section 17(3) of the Partnership Act 1890;
(b) take his name of the letterhead—see section 14(1) of the Act—holding out;
(c) also see section 36 of the Act.

Appendix 3　Companies

3.1 Terms, Definitions and Legislation

LEGISLATION TO CONSIDER

Companies Act 1985 (which includes the amending act of 1989)
Company Directors Disqualification Act 1986

DEFINITIONS TO CONSIDER WITH COMPANIES

Allotment	the unconditional right for a would-be share-holder to have his name inserted in company's register of members.
Alternate director	a director who stands in for the usual director, whilst they are away or unable to act.
Annual general meeting (AGM)	a meeting of shareholders of the company generally held each calendar year: the first is required to be held within 18 months of incorporation.
Annual return	a financial return made by the company to the registrar of companies each year.
Articles of association	a company's internal regulations of a contractual nature between the company and each shareholder, and between each shareholder *inter se* (see table A.)
Auditor	a person who audits and confirms the accuracy of the accounts of a company.
Board of directors	collectively the managers of a company.
Bonus share	a share issued by the company to a member usually in proportion to his existing holding.
Call	a written demand made on a member by the company (through the directors) to pay up the amount remaining or part of the amount remaining unpaid on his shares.
Certificate of incorporation	a document issued by the registrar of companies to confirm the date of formation of the company.
Company limited by guarantee	a company, the liability of whose members is limited by reference to a guarantee amount.
Company limited by shares	a company, the liability of whose members is limited by reference to shares.

330

Debenture	a document acknowledging the indebteness of A to B.
Director	an officer of the company, along with the secretary principally concerned with the management of the company.
Dividend	a distribution paid of a company's profits so the shareholder in proportion to his shares and in accordance with the rights attaching to his shares.
Elective resolution	resolutions made by private companies to relax procedural requirements under the Companies Act 1985 (see s. 379A).
Executive director	a director who is working full-time for the company or under an obligation to devote a substantial amount of his time to the management of the company.
Extraordinary general meeting (EGM)	a meeting of shareholders of the company other than the AGM held whenever:

(a) required by the Companies Act 1985, *e.g.* to dismiss a director (section 303); or
(b) if the directors feel appropriate.

Extraordinary resolution	a resolution passed by a majority of not less than three-fourths of the shareholders voting in person or by proxy at a general meeting.
General meeting	a meeting of the members of the company.
Listed securities	those securities listed on a recognised stock exchange.
Managing director	a director appointed to oversee the day-to-day administration of the company (see article 84 table A).
Meetings	a company usually conducts its business through meeting procedure, unless it adopts written resolution procedure.
	refer either to a director's meeting or a shareholder's meeting which may be AGMs, EGMs.
Memorandum of association	contains key information about the company, *e.g.* type, the number of shares available to issue; business aims (objectives).
Member/shareholder	interchangeable terms, *i.e.* someone who holds at least one share in a company in own name or as a "bare trustee" or "nominee" on behalf of someone else. The owner nominee's name will be in the register of members kept by the company secretary at the company's registered office.
Nominal capital	the amount up to which the company can issue shares. The nominal capital must be increased

if more shares are to be issued than have been created in the memorandum of association.

Nominee shareholder   a shareholder who holds his shares as nominee for another person.

Non-executive director   usually a director who is not under an obligation to devote the whole or substantially the whole of his time to the company affairs.

Officer   a broad term including a director, manager or secretary.

Ordinary resolution   a resolution passed by a simple majority of members present at a general meeting.

Ordinary shares   a share entitling its holder to receive a dividend after dividends have been paid on preference shares.

Par value   the authorised or nominal value of a share.

Poll   a method of voting enabling each member to vote for or against a resolution according to the number of shares he holds.

Pre-emption   a right of first refusal given to shareholders to purchase the shares of any member wishing to sell his shares. The term is also used to refer to the right of certain shareholders to subscribe for further shares on a new issue.

Preference shares   a share giving its holder preferential rights in respect of dividends, and/or return of share capital on a solvent winding up. Such shares usually have limited voting rights.

Pre-incorporation contract   a contract entered into before a company has been incorporated.

Private company   a company that is not a public company (Companies Act 1985, s. 1(3))

Promoter, subscriber, founder   a person who takes steps to form a company or set it in motion. The term can also extend to some one involved in its subsequent flotation.

Prospectus   an invitation to the public to subscribe for shares or debentures of the company.

Proxy   a person appointed by a shareholder to vote for him at a meeting.

Quorum   the minimum number of persons necessary to constitute a valid shareholders' meeting.

Redeemable shares   shares of a company that can be redeemed by the company.

Register of members   a register kept by the company of membership of the company.

Registered office   the office where the company is required to keep certain documents and records as required by the Companies Act 1985. Also, the place where court documents will be served on the company.

Registrar	the registrar of companies—the person with whom a company must file its public records, *e.g.* appointment, resignation or directors; appointment of an auditor.
Regulations	the articles of association.
Resolution	a formal decision by a majority of the members of the company of the board of directors.
Rights issue	a right given to an existing shareholder to subscribe for further shares in the company.
Shadow director	a shadow director (Companies Act, s. 741) is a person who is not formally appointed a director but in accordance with whose directions or instructions the directors of a company are accustomed to act. However, a person is not a shadow director merely because the directors act on advice given by him in a professional capacity.
Share	a shadow director (Companies Act, s. 741) is a person who is not formally appointed a director but Unit of ownership in a company—different rights attach to different classes of shares. Rights are set out in the contract of allotment, *i.e.* the contract between the company and the member, when the member is issued and allotted the shares, *e.g.* preferential shares usually denote that a shareholder has a preferred right over other shareholders to receive a dividend from the company and/or payment on winding up (dividends are paid at the discretion of directors and approved by members when the company makes a profit).
Special resolution	a resolution passed by a majority of not less than three-fourths of members voting at a general meeting of the company of which not less than 21 days' notice has been given (Companies Act 1985, s. 378(2)).
Stock exchange	an exchange that provides markets for the buying and selling of securities in public companies.
Subscriber of memorandum	see promoter, subscribes, founder—a person who signs the memorandum of association and is required to take at least one share in the company.
Table A	a model set of articles of association.
A trading company	not defined in the Companies Act 1985. An active as opposed to a "dormant" company (see Companies Act 1985, s. 250). "Dormant" is defined in this context as no significant

	accounting transaction occurring for a period of time.
Transfer (of shares)	*i.e.* transfer of the legal and beneficial ownership in the shares by sale or gift.
Transmission (of shares)	a vesting by operation of law of a shareholder's shares in another person on death.
Ultra vires	a company acting in excess of its object or powers as set out in its memorandum or articles.
Written resolutions	a resolution in written form signed by each shareholder replaces the need to hold meetings of shareholders (see Companies Act 1985, s. 381A). Written resolutions can be used for all company matters except the removal of a director or an auditor. Will often be used by small, private companies.

3.2 Table A, Articles of Association (Companies Act 1985)

Table A is reproduced in full below. Table A is simply a model set of articles which private limited companies can adopt, amend or not use, depending on the requirements of the promoters, etc., (see Companies Act 1985, s. 8).

INDEX TO TABLE A

Table A covers five basic areas:

REGULATIONS FOR MANAGEMENT OF A COMPANY LIMITED BY SHARES

INTERPRETATION

1. **In these regulations —**
"**the Act**" means the Companies Act 1985, including any statutory modification or re-enactment thereof for the time being in force.
"**the articles**" means the articles of the company.
"**clear days**" in relation to the period of a notice means that period excluding the day when the notice is given or deemed to be given and the day for which it is given or on which it is to take effect.
"**executed**" includes any mode of execution.
"**office**" means the registered office of the company.
"**the holder**" in relation to shares means the member whose name is entered in the register of members as the holder of the shares.
"**the seal**" means the common seal of the company.
"**secretary**" means the secretary of the company or any other person appointed to perform the duties of the secretary of the company, including a joint, assistant or deputy secretary.
"**the United Kingdom**" means Great Britain and Northern Ireland.
    Unless the context otherwise requires, words or expressions contained in these regulations bear the same meaning as in the Act but excluding any statutory modification thereof not in force when these regulations become binding on the company.

SHARE CAPITAL

2. Subject to the provisions of the Act and without prejudice to any rights attached to any existing shares, any share may be issued with such rights or restrictions as the company may by ordinary resolution determine.

3. Subject to the provisions of the Act, shares may be issued that are to be redeemed or are to be liable to be redeemed at the option of the company or the holder on such terms and in such manner as may be provided by the articles.

4. The company may exercise the powers of paying commissions conferred by the Act. Subject to the provisions of the Act, any such commission may be satisfied by the payment of cash or by the allotment of fully or partly paid shares or partly in one way and partly in the other.

5. Except as required by law, no person shall be recognised by the company as holding any share upon any trust and (except as otherwise provided by the articles or by law) the company shall not be bound by or recognise any interest in any share except an absolute right to the entirety thereof in the holder.

SHARE CERTIFICATES

6. Every member, upon becoming the holder of any shares, shall be entitled without payment to one certificate for all the shares of each class held by him (and, upon transferring a part of his holding of shares of any class, to a certificate for the balance of such holding) or several certificates each for one or more of his shares upon payment for every certificate after the first of such reasonable sum as the directors may determine. Every certificate shall be sealed with the seal and shall specify the number, class and distinguishing numbers (if any) of the shares to which it relates and the amount or respective amounts paid up thereon. The company shall not be bound to issue more than one certificate for shares held jointly by several persons and delivery of a certificate to one joint holder shall be a sufficient delivery to all of them.

7. If a share certificate is defaced, worn-out, lost or destroyed, it may be renewed on such terms (if any) as to evidence and indemnity and payment of the expenses reasonably incurred by the company in investigating evidence as the directors may determine but otherwise free of charge, and (in the case of defacement or wearing-out) on delivery up of the old certificate.

LIEN

8. The company shall have a first and paramount lien on every share (not being a fully paid share) for all monies (whether presently payable or not) payable at a fixed time or called in respect of that share. The directors may at any time declare any share to be wholly or in part exempt from the provisions of this regulation. The company's lien on a share shall extend to any amount payable in respect of it.

9. The company may sell in such manner as the directors determine any shares on which the company has a lien if a sum in respect of which the lien exists is presently payable and is not paid within 14 clear days after notice has been given to the holder of the share or to the person entitled to it in consequence of the death or bankruptcy of the holder, demanding payment and stating that if the notice is not complied with the shares may be sold.

10. To give effect to a sale the directors may authorise some person to execute an instrument of transfer of the shares sold to, or in accordance with the directions of, the purchaser. The title of the transferee to the shares shall not be affected by any irregularity in or invalidity of the proceedings in reference to the sale.

11. The net proceeds of the sale, after payment of the costs, shall be applied in payment of so much of the sum for which the lien exists as is presently payable, and any residue shall (upon surrender to the company for cancellation of the certificate for the shares sold and subject to a like lien for any monies not presently payable as existed upon the shares before the sale) be paid to the person entitled to the shares at the date of the sale.

CALLS ON SHARES AND FORFEITURE

12. Subject to the terms of allotment, the directors may make calls upon the members in respect of any monies unpaid on their shares (whether in respect of nominal value or premium) and each member shall (subject to receiving at least 14 clear days' notice specifying when and where payment is to be made) pay to the company as required by the notice the amount called on his shares. A call may be required to be paid by instalments. A call may, before receipt by the company of any sum due thereunder, be revoked in whole or part and payment of a call may be postponed in whole or part. A person upon whom a call is made shall remain liable for calls made upon him notwithstanding the subsequent transfer of the shares in respect whereof the call was made.

13. A call shall be deemed to have been made at the time when the resolution of the directors authorising the call was passed.

14. The joint holders of a share shall be jointly and severally liable to pay all calls in respect thereof.

15. If a call remains unpaid after it has become due and payable the person from whom it is due and payable shall pay interest on the amount unpaid from the day it became due and payable until it is paid at the rate fixed by the terms of allotment of the share or in the notice of the call or, if no rate is fixed, at the appropriate rate (as defined by the Act) but the directors may waive payment of the interest wholly or in part.

16. An amount payable in respect of a share on allotment or at any fixed date, whether in respect of nominal value or premium or as an instalment of a call, shall be deemed to be a call and if it is not paid the provisions of the articles shall apply as if that amount had become due and payable by virtue of a call.

17. Subject to the terms of the allotment, the directors may make arrangements on the issue of shares for a difference between the holders in the amounts and times of payment of calls on their shares.

18. If a call remains unpaid after it has become due and payable the directors may give to the person from whom it is due not less than 14 clear days' notice requiring payment of the amount unpaid together with any interest which may have accrued. The notice shall name the place where payment is to be made and shall state that if the notice is not complied with the shares in respect of which the call was made will be liable to be forfeited.

19. If the notice is not complied with any share in respect of which it was given may, before the payment required by the notice has been made, be forfeited by a resolution of the directors and the forfeiture shall include all dividends or other monies payable in respect of the forfeited shares and not paid before the forfeiture.

20. Subject to the provisions of the Act, a forfeited share may be sold, re-allotted or otherwise disposed of on such terms and in such manner as the directors determine either to the person who was before the forfeiture the holder or to any other person and at any time before sale, re-allotment or other disposition, the forfeiture may be cancelled on such terms as the directors think fit. Where for the purposes of its disposal a forfeited share is to be transferred to any person the directors may authorise some person to execute an instrument of transfer of the share to that person.

21. A person, any of whose shares have been forfeited, shall cease to be a member in respect of them and shall surrender to the company for cancellation the certificate for the shares forfeited but shall remain liable to the company for all monies which at the date of forfeiture were presently payable by him to the company in respect of those shares with interest at the rate at which interest was payable on those monies before the forfeiture or, if no interest was so payable, at the appropriate rate (as defined in the Act) from the date of forfeiture until payment but the directors may waive payment wholly or in part or enforce payment without any allowance for the value of the shares at the time of forfeiture or for any consideration received on their disposal.

22. A statutory declaration by a director or the secretary that a share has been forfeited on a specified date shall be conclusive evidence of the facts stated in it as against all persons claiming to be entitled to the share and the declaration shall (subject to the execution of an instrument of transfer if necessary) constitute a good title to the share and the person to whom the share is disposed of shall not be bound to see to the application of the consideration, if any, nor shall his title to the share be affected by any irregularity in or invalidity of the proceedings in reference to the forfeiture or disposal of the share.

TRANSFER OF SHARES

23. The instrument of transfer of a share may be in any usual form or in any other form which the directors may approve and shall be executed by or on

behalf of the transferor and, unless the share is fully paid, by or on behalf of the transferee.

24. The directors may refuse to register the transfer of a share which is not fully paid to a person of whom they do not approve and they may refuse to register the transfer of a share on which the company has a lien. They may also refuse to register a transfer unless:

(a) it is lodged at the office or at such other place as the directors may appoint and is accompanied by the certificate for the shares to which it relates and such other evidence as the directors may reasonably require to show the right of the transferor to make the transfer;

(b) it is in respect of only one class of shares; and

(c) it is in favour of not more than four transfers.

25. If the directors refuse to register a transfer of a share, they shall within two months after the date on which the transfer was lodged with the company send to the transferee notice of the refusal.

26. The registration of transfers of shares or of transfers of any class of shares may be suspended at such times and for such periods (not exceeding 30 days in any year) as the directors may determine.

27. No fee shall be charged for the registration of any instrument of transfer or other document relating to or affecting the title to any share.

28. The company shall be entitled to retain any instrument of transfer which is registered, but any instrument of transfer which the directors refuse to register shall be returned to the person lodging it when notice of the refusal is given.

TRANSMISSION OF SHARES

29. If a member dies the survivor or survivors, where he was a joint holder, and his personal representatives, where he was a sole holder or the only survivor of joint holders, shall be the only person recognised by the company as having any title to his interest; but nothing herein contained shall release the estate of a deceased member from any liability in respect of any share which had been jointly held by him.

30. A person becoming entitled to a share in consequence of the death or bankruptcy of a member may, upon such evidence being produced as the directors may properly require, elect either to become the holder of the share or to have some person nominated by him registered as the transferee. If he elects to become the holder he shall give notice to the company to that effect. If he elected to have another person registered he shall execute an instrument of transfer of the share to that person. All the articles relating to the transfer of shares shall apply to the notice of instrument of transfer as if it were an instrument of transfer executed by the member and the death or bankruptcy of the member had not occurred.

31. A person becoming entitled to a share in consequence of the death or bankruptcy of a member shall have the rights to which he would be entitled if he were the holder of the share, except that he shall not, before being registered as the holder of the share, be entitled in respect of it to attend or

vote at any meeting of the company or at any separate meeting of the holders of any class of shares in the company.

ALTERATION OF SHARE CAPITAL

32. The company may by ordinary resolution:
    (a) increase its share capital by new shares of such amount as the resolution prescribes;
    (b) consolidate and divide all or any of its share capital into shares of larger amount than its existing shares;
    (c) subject to the provisions of the Act, sub-divide its shares, or any of them, into shares of smaller amount and the resolution may determine that, as between the shares resulting from the sub-division, any of them may have any preference or advantage as compared with the others; and
    (d) cancel shares which, at the date of the passing of the resolution, have not been taken or agreed to be taken by any person and diminish the amount of its share capital by the amount of the shares so cancelled.

33. Whenever as a result of consolidation of shares any members would become entitled to fractions of a share, the directors may, on behalf of those members, sell the shares representing the fractions for the best price reasonably obtainable to any person (including, subject to the provisions of the Act, the company) and distribute the net proceeds of sale in due proportion among those members, and the directors may authorise some person to execute an instrument of transfer of the shares to, or in accordance with the directions of, the purchaser. The transferee shall not be bound to see to the application of the purchase money, nor shall his title to the shares be affected by any irregularity in or invalidity of the proceedings in reference to the sale.

34. Subject to the provisions of the Act, the company may, by special resolution, reduce its share capital, any capital redemption reserve and any share premium account in any way.

PURCHASE OF OWN SHARES

35. Subject to the provisions of the Act, the company may purchase its own shares (including any redeemable shares) and, if it is a private company, make a payment in respect of the redemption or purchase of its own shares otherwise than out of distributable profits of the company or the proceeds of a fresh issue of shares.

GENERAL MEETING

36. All general meetings other than annual general meetings shall be called extraordinary general meetings.

37. The directors may call general meetings and, on the requisition of members pursuant to the provisions of the Act, shall forthwith proceed to convene an extraordinary general meeting for a date not later than eight weeks after receipt of the requisition. If there are not within the United Kingdom sufficient directors to call a general meeting, any director or any member of the company may call a general meeting.

NOTICE OF GENERAL MEETINGS

38. An annual general meeting and an extraordinary general meeting called for the passing of a special resolution or a resolution appointing a person as a director shall be called by at least 21 clear days' notice. All other extraordinary general meetings shall be called by at least 14 clear days' notice but a general meeting may be called by a shorter notice if it is so agreed:

    (a) in the case of an annual general meeting, by all the members entitled to attend and vote thereat; and

    (b) in the case of any other meeting by a majority in number of the members having a right to attend and vote being a majority together holding not less than 95 per cent in nominal value of the shares giving that right.

The notice shall specify the time and place of the meeting and the general nature of the business to be transacted and, in the case of an annual general meeting, shall specify the meeting as such.

Subject to the provisions of the articles and to any restrictions imposed on any shares, the notice shall be given to all the members, to all persons entitled to a share in consequence of the death or bankruptcy of a member and to the directors and auditors.

39. The accidental omission to give notice of a meeting to, or the non-receipt of notice of a meeting by, any person entitled to receive notice shall not invalidate the proceedings at the meeting.

PROCEEDINGS AT GENERAL MEETINGS

40. No business shall be transacted at any meeting unless a quorum is present. Two persons entitled to vote upon the business to be transacted, each being a member or a proxy for a member or a duly authorised representative of a corporation, shall be a quorum.

41. If such a quorum is not present within half an hour from the time appointed for the meeting, or if during a meeting such a quorum ceases to be present, the meeting shall stand adjourned to the same day in the next week at the same time and place or to such time and place as the directors may determine.

42. The chairman, if any, of the board of directors or in his absence some other director nominated by the directors shall preside as chairman of the meeting, but if neither the chairman nor such other director (if any) be present

within 15 minutes after the time appointed for holding the meeting and willing to act, the directors present shall elect one of their number to be chairman and, if there is only one director present and willing to act, he shall be chairman.

43. If no director is willing to act as chairman, or if no director is present within 15 minutes after the time appointed for holding the meeting, the members present and entitled to vote shall choose one of their number to be chairman.

44. A director shall, notwithstanding that he is not a member, be entitled to attend and speak at any general meeting and at any separate meeting of the holders of any class of shares in the company.

45. The chairman may, with the consent of a meeting at which a quorum is present (and shall if so directed by the meeting), adjourn the meeting from time to time and from place to place, but no business shall be transacted at an adjourned meeting other than business which might properly have been transacted at the meeting had the adjournment not taken place. When a meeting is adjourned for 14 days or more, at least seven clear days' notice shall be given specifying the time and place of the adjourned meeting and the general nature of the business to be transacted. Otherwise it shall not be necessary to give any such notice.

46. A resolution put to the vote of a meeting shall be decided on a show of hands unless before, or on the declaration of the result of, the show of hands a poll is duly demanded. Subject to the provisions of the Act, a poll may be demanded:

   (a) by the chairman; or
   (b) by at least two members having the right to vote at the meeting; or
   (c) by a member or members representing not less than one-tenth of the total voting rights of all the members having the right to vote at the meeting; or
   (d) by a member or members holding shares conferring a right to vote at the meeting being shares on which an aggregate sum has been paid up equal to not less than one-tenth of the total sum paid up on all the shares conferring that right;

and a demand by a person as proxy for a member shall be the same as a demand by the member.

47. Unless a poll is duly demanded a declaration by the chairman that a resolution has been carried or carried unanimously, or by a particular majority, or lost, or not carried by a particular majority and an entry to that effect in the minutes of the meeting shall be conclusive evidence of the fact without proof of the number or proportion of the votes recorded in favour of or against the resolution.

48. The demand for a poll may, before the poll is taken, be withdrawn but only with the consent of the chairman and a demand so withdrawn shall not be taken to have invalidated the result of a show of hands declared before the demand was made.

49. A poll shall be taken as the chairman directs and he may appoint scrutineers (who need not be members) and fix a time and place for declaring the

result of the poll. The result of the poll shall be deemed to be the resolution of the meeting at which the poll was demanded.

50. In the case of an equality of votes, whether on a show of hands or on a poll, the chairman shall be entitled to a casting vote in addition to any other vote he may have.

51. A poll demanded on the election of a chairman or on a question of adjournment shall be taken forthwith. A poll demanded on any other question shall be taken either forthwith or at such time and place as the chairman directs not being more than 30 days after the poll is demanded. The demand for a poll shall not prevent the continuance of a meeting for the transaction of any business other than the question on which the poll was demanded. If a poll is demanded before the declaration of the result of a show of hands and the demand is duly withdrawn, the meeting shall continue as if the demand had not been made.

52. No notice need be given of a poll not taken forthwith if the time and place at which it is to be taken are announced at the meeting at which it is demanded. In any other case at least seven clear days' notice shall be given specifying the time and place at which the poll is to be taken.

53. A resolution in writing executed by or on behalf of each member who would have been entitled to vote upon it if it had been proposed at a general meeting at which he was present shall be as effectual as if it had been passed at a general meeting duly convened and held and may consist of several instruments in the like form each executed by or on behalf of one or more members.

VOTES OF MEMBERS

54. Subject to any rights or restrictions attached to any shares, on a show of hands every member who (being an individual) is present in person or (being a corporation) is present by a duly authorised representative, not being himself a member entitled to vote, shall have one vote and on a poll every member shall have one vote for every share of which he is the holder.

55. In the case of joint holders the vote of the senior member who tenders a vote, whether in person or by proxy, shall be accepted to the exclusion of the votes of the other joint holders; and seniority shall be determined by the order in which the names of the holders stand in the register of members.

56. A member in respect of whom an order has been made by any court having jurisdiction (whether in the United Kingdom or elsewhere) in matters concerning mental disorder may vote, whether on a show of hands or on a poll, by his receiver, *curator bonis* or other person authorised in that behalf appointed by that court, and any such receiver, *curator bonis* or other person may, on a poll, vote by proxy. Evidence to the satisfaction of the directors of the authority of the person claiming to exercise the right to vote shall be deposited at the office, or at such other place as is specified in accordance with the articles for the deposit of instruments of proxy, not less than 48 hours before the time appointed for holding the meeting or adjourned meeting

at which the right to vote is to be exercised and in default the right to vote shall not be exercisable.

57. No member shall vote at any general meeting or at any separate meeting of the holders or any class of shares in the company, either in person or by proxy, in respect of any shares held by him unless all monies presently payable by him in respect of that share have been paid.

58. No objection shall be raised to the qualification of any voter except at the meeting or adjourned meeting at which the vote objected to is tendered, and every vote not disallowed at the meeting shall be valid. Any objection made in due time shall be referred to the chairman whose decision shall be final and conclusive.

59. On a poll votes may be given either personally or by proxy. A member may appoint more than one proxy to attend on the same occasion.

60. An instrument appointing a proxy shall be in writing, executed by or on behalf of the appointor and shall be in the following form (or in a form as near thereto as circumstances allow or in any other form which is usual or which the directors may approve):

PLC/Limited

I/We,   of   being a member/members of the above-named company, hereby appoint   of   or failing him,   of
as my/our proxy to vote in my/our name[s] and on my/our behalf at the annual/extraordinary general meeting of the company to be held on
19   , and at any adjournment thereof.
Signed on   19

61. Where it is desired to afford members an opportunity of instructing the proxy how he shall act the instrument appointing a proxy shall be in the following form (or in a form as near thereto as circumstances allow or in any other form which is usual or which the directors may approve):

PLC/Limited

I/We,   of   being   a   member/members   of   the
above-named   company,   hereby   appoint   of
or failing him   of   ,as my/our proxy to vote
in my/our name[s]
and on my/our behalf at the annual/extraordinary general meeting of the company, to be held on   19   , and at any adjournment thereof.
This form is to be used in respect of the resolutions mentioned below as follows:

Resolution No. 1 *for *against
Resolution No. 2 *for *against

*Strike out whichever is not desired.

Unless otherwise instructed, the proxy may vote as he thinks fit or abstain from voting.
Signed this   day of   19

62. The instrument appointing a proxy and any authority under which it is executed or a copy of such authority certified notarially or in some other way approved by the directors may:

(a) be deposited at the office or at such other place within the United Kingdom as is specified in the notice convening the meeting or in any instrument of proxy sent out by the company in relation to the meeting not less than 48 hours before the time for holding the meeting or adjourned meeting at which the person named in the instrument proposes to vote; or

(b) in the case of a poll taken more than 48 hours after it is demanded, be deposited as aforesaid after the poll has been demanded and not less than 24 hours before the time appointed for the taking of the poll; or

(c) where the poll is not taken forthwith but is taken not more than 48 hours after it was demanded, be delivered at the meeting at which the poll was demanded to the chairman or to the secretary or to any director; and an instrument of proxy which is ·not deposited or delivered in a manner so permitted shall be invalid.

63. A vote given or poll demanded by proxy or by the duly authorised representative of a corporation shall be valid notwithstanding the previous determination of the authority of the person voting or demanding a poll unless notice of the determination was received by the company at the office or at such other place at which the instrument of proxy was duly deposited before the commencement of the meeting or adjourned meeting at which the vote is given or the poll demanded or (in the case of a poll taken otherwise than on the same day as the meeting or adjourned meeting) the time appointed for taking the poll.

NUMBER OF DIRECTORS

64. Unless otherwise determined by ordinary resolution, the number of directors (other than alternate directors) shall not be subject to any maximum but shall be not less than two.

ALTERNATE DIRECTORS

65. Any director (other than an alternate director) may appoint any other director, or any other person approved by resolution of the directors and willing to act, to be an alternate director and may remove from office an alternate director so appointed by him.

66. An alternate director shall be entitled to receive notice of all meetings of directors and of all meetings of committees of directors of which his appointor is a member, to attend and vote at any such meeting at which the director appointing him is not personally present, and generally to perform all the functions of his appointor as a director in his absence but shall not be entitled to receive any remuneration from the company for his services as an alternate director. But it shall not be necessary to give notice of such a meeting to an alternate director who is absent from the United Kingdom.

67. An alternate director shall cease to be an alternate director if his appointor

ceases to be a director; but, if a director retires by rotation or otherwise but is reappointed or deemed to have been reappointed at the meeting at which he retires, any appointment of an alternate director made by him which was in force immediately prior to his retirement shall continue after his reappointment.

68. Any appointment or removal of an alternate director shall be by notice to the company signed by the director making or revoking the appointment or in any other manner approved by the directors.

69. Save as otherwise provided in the articles, an alternate director shall be deemed for all purposes to be a director, and shall alone be responsible for his own acts and defaults and he shall not be deemed to be the agent of the director appointing him.

POWERS OF DIRECTORS

70. Subject to the provisions of the Act, the memorandum and the articles and to any directions given by special resolution, the business of the company shall be managed by the directors who may exercise all the powers of the company. No alteration of the memorandum or articles and no such direction shall invalidate any prior act of the directors which would have been valid if that alteration had not been made or that direction had not been given. The powers given by this regulation shall not be limited by any special power given to the directors by the articles and a meeting of directors at which a quorum is present may exercise all powers exercisable by the director.

71. The directors may, by power of attorney or otherwise, appoint any person to be the agent of the company for such purposes and on such conditions as they determine, including authority for the agent to delegate all or any of his powers.

DELEGATION OF DIRECTORS' POWERS

72. The directors may delegate any of their powers to any committee consisting of one or more directors. They may also delegate to any managing director or any director holding any other executive office such of their powers as they consider desirable to be exercised by him. Any such delegation may be made subject to any conditions the directors may impose, and either collaterally with or to the exclusion of their own powers and may be revoked or altered. Subject to such conditions, the proceedings of a committee with two or more members shall be governed by the articles regulating the proceedings of directors so far as they are capable of applying.

APPOINTMENT AND RETIREMENT OF DIRECTORS

73. At the first annual general meeting all the directors shall retire from office, and at every subsequent annual general meeting one-third of the dir-

ectors who are subject to retirement by rotation or, if their number is not three or a multiple of three, the number nearest to one-third shall retire from office; but, if there is only one director who is subject to retirement by rotation, he shall retire.

74. Subject to the provisions of the Act, the directors to retire by rotation shall be those who have been longest in office since their last appointment or reappointment, but as between persons who became or were last reappointed directors on the same day those to retire shall (unless they otherwise agree among themselves) be determined by lot.

75. If the company, at the meeting at which a director retires by rotation, does not fill the vacancy the retiring director shall, if willing to act, be deemed to have been reappointed unless at the meeting it is resolved not to fill the vacancy or unless a resolution for the reappointment of the director is put to the meeting and lost.

76. No person other than a director retiring by rotation shall be appointed or reappointed a director at any general meeting unless:

(a) he is recommended by the directors; or
(b) not less than 14 nor more than 35 clear days before the date appointed for the meeting, notice executed by a member qualified to vote at the meeting has been given to the company of the intention to propose that person for appointment or reappointment stating the particulars which would, if he were so appointed or reappointed, be required to be included in the company's register of directors together with notice executed by that person of his willingness to be appointed or reappointed.

77. Not less than seven nor more than twenty-eight clear days before the date appointed for holding a general meeting notice shall be given to all who are entitled to receive notice of the meeting of any person (other than a director retiring by rotation at the meeting) who is recommended by the directors for appointment or reappointment as a director at the meeting or in respect of whom notice has been duly given to the company of the intention to propose him at the meeting for appointment or reappointment as a director. The notice shall give the particulars of that person which would, if he were so appointed or reappointed, be required to be included in the company's register of directors.

78. Subject as aforesaid, the company may by ordinary resolution appoint a person who is willing to act to be a director either to fill a vacancy or as an additional director and may also determine the rotation in which any additional directors are to retire.

79. The directors may appoint a person who is willing to act to be a director, either to fill a vacancy or as an additional director, provided that the appointment does not cause the number of directors to exceed any number fixed by or in accordance with the articles as the maximum number of directors. A director so appointed shall hold office only until the next following annual general meeting and shall not be taken into account in determining the directors who are to retire by rotation at the meeting. If not reappointed at such annual general meeting, he shall vacate office at the conclusion thereof.

80. Subject as aforesaid, a director who retires at an annual general meeting

may, if willing to act, be reappointed. If he is not reappointed, he shall retain office until the meeting appoints someone in his place, or if it does not do so, until the end of the meeting.

DISQUALIFICATION AND REMOVAL OF DIRECTORS

81. The office of a director shall be vacated if:

(a) he ceases to be a director by virtue of any provision of the Act or he becomes prohibited by law from being a director; or

(b) he becomes bankrupt or makes any arrangement or composition with his creditors generally; or

(c) he is, or may be, suffering from a mental disorder and either:

(i) he is admitted to hospital in pursuance of an application for treatment under the Mental Health Act 1983, or, in Scotland, an application for admission under the Mental Health (Scotland) Act, 1960; or

(ii) an order is made by a court having jurisdiction (whether in the United Kingdom or elsewhere) in matters concerning mental disorder for his detention or for the appointment of a receiver, *curator bonis* or other person to exercise powers with respect to his property or affairs; or

(d) he resigns his office by notice to the company; or

(e) he shall for more than six consecutive months have been absent without permission of the directors from meetings of directors held during that period and the directors resolve that his office be vacated.

REMUNERATION OF DIRECTORS

82. The directors shall be entitled to such remuneration as the company may by ordinary resolution determine and, unless the resolution provides otherwise, the remuneration shall be deemed to accrue from day to day.

DIRECTORS' EXPENSES

83. The directors may be paid all travelling, hotel, and other expenses properly incurred by them in connection with their attendance at meetings of directors or committees of directors or general meetings or separate meetings of the holders of any class of shares or of debentures of the company or otherwise in connection with the discharge of their duties.

DIRECTORS' APPOINTMENTS AND INTERESTS

84. Subject to the provisions of the Act, the directors may appoint one or more of their number to the office of managing director or to any other executive office under the company and may enter into an agreement or arrangement with any director for his employment by the company or for the provision by him of any services outside the scope of the ordinary duties of a director. Any such appointment, agreement or arrangement may be made upon such terms as the directors determine and they may remunerate any such director for his services as they think fit. Any appointment of a director to an executive office shall terminate if he ceases to be a director but without prejudice to any claim to damages for breach of the contract of service between the director and the company. A managing director and a director holding any other executive office shall not be subject to retirement by rotation.

85. Subject to the provision of the Act, and provided that he has disclosed to the directors the nature and extent of any material interest of his, a director notwithstanding his office:

   (a) may be a party to, or otherwise interested in, any transaction or arrangement with the company or in which the company is otherwise interested;

   (b) may be a director or other office of, or employed by, or a party to any transaction or arrangement with, or otherwise interested in, any body corporate promoted by the company or in which the company is otherwise interested; and

   (c) shall not, by reason of his office, be accountable to the company for any benefit which he derives from any such office or employment or from any such transaction or arrangement or from any interest in any such body corporate and no such transaction or arrangement shall be liable to be avoided on the ground or any such interest or benefit.

86. For the purpose of regulation 85:

   (a) a general notice given to the directors that a director is to be regarded as having an interest of the nature and extent specified in the notice in any transaction or arrangement in which a specified person or class of persons is interested shall be deemed to be a disclosure that the director has an interest in any such transaction of the nature and extent so specified; and

   (b) an interest of which a director has no knowledge and of which it is unreasonable to expect him to have knowledge shall not be treated as an interest of his.

DIRECTORS' GRATUITIES AND PENSIONS

87. The directors may provide benefits, whether by the payment of gratuities or pensions or by insurance or otherwise, for any director who has held but

no longer holds any executive office or employment with the company or with any body corporate which is or has been a subsidiary of the company or a predecessor in business of the company or of any such subsidiary, and for any member of his family (including a spouse and a former spouse) or any person who is or was dependent on him and may (as well before as after he ceases to hold such office or employment) contribute to any fund and pay premiums for the purchase or provision of any such benefit.

PROCEEDINGS OF DIRECTORS

88. Subject to the provisions of the articles, the directors may regulate their proceedings as they think fit. A director may, and the secretary at the request of a director shall, call a meeting of the directors. It shall not be necessary to give notice of a meeting to a director who is absent from the United Kingdom. Questions arising at a meeting shall be decided by a majority of votes. In the case of an equality of votes, the chairman shall have a second or casting vote. A director who is also an alternate director shall be entitled in the absence of his appointor to a separate vote on behalf of his appointor in addition to his own vote.

89. The quorum for the transaction of the business of the directors may be fixed by the directors and unless so fixed at any other number shall be two. A person who holds office only as an alternate director shall, if his appointor is not present, be counted in the quorum.

90. The continuing directors or a sole continuing director may act notwithstanding any vacancies in their number but, if the number of directors is less than the number fixed as a quorum, the continuing directors or director may act only for the purpose of filling vacancies or of calling a general meeting.

91. The directors may appoint one of their number to be the chairman of the board of directors and may at any time remove him from that office. Unless he is unwilling to do so, the director so appointed shall preside at every meeting of directors at which he is present. But if there is no director holding that office, or if the director holding it is unwilling to preside or in not present within five minutes after the time appointed for the meeting, the directors present may appoint one of their number to be chairman of the meeting.

92. All acts done by a meeting of directors, or of a committee of directors, or by a person acting as a director shall, notwithstanding that it be afterwards discovered that there was a defect in the appointment of any director or that may of them were disqualified from holding office, or had vacated office, or were not entitled to vote, be as valid as if every such person had been duly appointed, and was qualified and had continued to be a director and had been entitled to vote.

93. A resolution in writing signed by all the directors entitled to receive notice of a meeting of directors or of a committee of directors shall be as valid and effectual as it if had been passed at a meeting of directors or (as the case may be) a committee of directors duly convened and held and may consist of several documents in the like form each signed by one or more directors; but a resolution signed by an alternate director need not also be

signed by his appointor and, if it is signed by a director who has appointed an alternate director, it need not be signed by the alternate director in that capacity.

94. Save as otherwise provided by the articles, a director shall not vote at a meeting of directors or of a committee of directors on any resolution concerning a matter in which he has, directly or indirectly, an interest or duty that is material and that conflicts or may conflict with the interests of the company unless his interest or duty arises only because the case falls within one or more of the following paragraphs:

(a) the resolution relates to the giving to him of a guarantee, security, or indemnity in respect of money lent to, or an obligation incurred by him for the benefit of, the company or any of its subsidiaries;

(b) the resolution relates to the giving to a third party of a guarantee, security, or indemnity in respect of an obligation of the company or any of its subsidiaries for which the director has assumed responsibility in whole or part and whether alone or jointly with others under a guarantee or indemnity or by the giving of security;

(c) his interest arises by virtue of his subscribing or agreeing to subscribe for any shares, debentures or other securities of the company or any of its subsidiaries, or by virtue of his being, or intending to become, a participant in the underwriting or sub-underwriting of an offer of any such shares, debentures, or other securities by the company or any of its subsidiaries for subscription, purchase or exchange;

(d) the resolution relates in any way to a retirement benefits scheme which has been approved, or is conditional upon approval, by the Board of Inland Revenue for taxation purposes.

For the purposes of this regulation, an interest of a person who is, for any purpose of the Act (excluding any statutory modification thereof not in force when this regulation becomes binding on the company), connected with a director shall be treated as an interest of the director and, in relation to an alternate director, an interest of his appointor shall be treated as an interest of the alternate director without prejudice to any interest which the alternate director has otherwise.

95. A director shall not be counted in the quorum present at a meeting in relation to a resolution on which he is not entitled to vote.

96. The company may by ordinary resolution suspend or relax to any extent, either generally or in respect of any particular matter, any provision of the articles prohibiting a director from voting at a meeting of directors or of a committee of directors.

97. Where proposals are under consideration concerning the appointment of two or more directors to offices or employments with the company or any body corporate in which the company is interested the proposals may be divided and considered in relation to each director separately and (provided he is not for another reason precluded from voting) each of the directors concerned shall be entitled to vote and be counted in the quorum in respect of each resolution except that concerning his own appointment.

98. If a question arises at a meeting of directors or of a committee of directors

as to the right of a director to vote, the question may, before the conclusion of the meeting, be referred to the chairman of the meeting and his ruling in relation to any director other than himself shall be final and conclusive.

SECRETARY

99. Subject to the provisions of the Act, the secretary shall be appointed by the directors for such term, at such remuneration and upon such conditions as they may think fit; and any secretary so appointed may be removed by them.

MINUTES

100. The directors shall cause minutes to be made in books kept for the purpose:
    (a) of all appointments of officers made by the directors; and
    (b) of all proceedings at meetings of the company, of the holders of any class of shares in the company, and of the directors, and of committees of directors, including the names of the directors present at each such meeting.

THE SEAL

101. The company seal shall only be used by the authority of the directors or of a committee of directors authorised by the directors. The directors may determine who shall sign any instrument to which the seal is affixed and unless otherwise so determined it shall be signed by a director and by the secretary or by a second director.

DIVIDENDS

102. Subject to the provisions of the Act, the company may by ordinary resolution declare dividends in accordance with the respective rights of the members, but no dividend shall exceed the amount recommended by the directors.

103. Subject to the provisions of the Act, the directors may pay interim dividends if it appears to them that they are justified by the profits of the company available for distribution. If the share capital is divided into different classes, the directors may pay interim dividends on shares that confer deferred or non-preferred rights with regard to dividend as well as on shares that confer preferential rights with regard to dividend, but no interim dividend shall be paid on shares carrying deferred or non-preferred rights if, at the

time of payment, any preferential dividend is in arrear. The directors may also pay at intervals settled by them any dividend payable at a fixed rate if it appears to them that the profits available for distribution justify the payment. Provided the directors act in good faith they shall not incur any liability to the holders of shares conferring preferred rights for any loss they may suffer by the lawful payment of an interim dividend on any shares having deferred or non-preferred rights.

104. Except as otherwise provided by the rights attached to shares, all dividends shall be declared and paid according to the amounts paid up on the shares on which the dividend is paid. All dividends shall be apportioned and paid proportionately to the amounts paid up on the shares during any portion or portions of the period in respect of which the dividend is paid; but, if any share is issued on terms providing that it shall rank for dividend as from a particular date, that share shall rank for dividend accordingly.

105. A general meeting declaring a dividend may, upon the recommendation of the directors, direct that it shall be satisfied wholly or partly by the distribution of assets and, where any difficulty arises in regard to the distribution, the directors may settle the same and in particular may issue fractional certificates and fix the value for distribution of any assets and may determine that cash shall be paid to any member upon the footing of the value so fixed in order to adjust the rights of members and may vest any assets in trustees.

106. Any dividend or other monies payable in respect of a share may be paid by cheque sent by post to the registered address of the person entitled to, if two or more persons are the holders of the share or are jointly entitled to it by reason of the death or bankruptcy of the holder, to the registered address of that one of those persons who is first named in the register of members or to such person and to such address as the person or persons entitled may in writing direct. Every cheque shall be made payable to the order of the person or persons entitled or to such other person as the person or persons entitled may in writing direct and payment of the cheque shall be a good discharge to the company. Any joint holder or other person jointly entitled to a share as aforesaid may give receipts for any dividend or other monies payable in respect of the share.

107. No dividend or other monies payable in respect of a share shall bear interest against the company unless otherwise provided by the rights attached to the share.

108. Any dividend which has remained unclaimed for 12 years from the date when it became due for payment shall, if the directors so resolve, be forfeited and cease to remain owing by the company.

ACCOUNTS

109. No member shall (as such) have any right of inspecting any accounting records or other book or document of the company except as conferred by statute or authorised by the directors or by ordinary resolution of the company.

CAPITALISATION OF PROFITS

110. The directors may with the authority of an ordinary resolution of the company:

(a) subject as hereinafter provided, resolve to capitalise any undivided profits of the company not required for paying any preferential dividend (whether or not they are available for distribution) or any sum standing to the credit of the company's share premium account or capital redemption reserve;

(b) appropriate the sum resolved to be capitalised to the members who would have been entitled to it if it were distributed by way of dividend and in the same proportions and apply such sum on their behalf either in or towards paying up the amounts, if any, for the time being unpaid on any shares held by them respectively, or in paying up in full unissued shares or debentures of the company or a nominal amount equal to that sum, and allot the shares or debentures credited as fully paid to those members, or as they may direct, in those proportions, or partly in one way and partly in the other; but the share premium account, the capital redemption reserve, and any profits which are not available for distribution may, for the purposes of this regulation, only be applied in paying up unissued shares to be allotted to members credited as fully paid;

(c) make such provision by the issue of fractional certificates or by payment in cash or otherwise as they determine in the case of shares or debentures becoming distributable under this regulation in fractions; and

(d) authorise any person to enter on behalf of all the members concerned into an agreement with the company providing for the allotment to them respectively, credited as fully paid, of any shares or debentures to which they are entitled upon such capitalisation, any agreement made under such authority being binding on all such members.

NOTICES

111. Any notice to be given to or by any person pursuant to the articles shall be in writing except that a notice calling a meeting of the directors need not be in writing.

112. The company may give any notice to a member either personally or by sending it by post in a prepaid envelope addressed to the member at his registered address or by leaving it at that address. In the case of joint holders of a share, all notices shall be given to the joint holder whose name stands first in the register of members in respect of the joint holding and notice so given shall be sufficient notice to all the joint holders. A member whose registered address is not within the United Kingdom and who gives to the company an address within the United Kingdom at which notices may be given to him shall be entitled to have notices given to him at that address,

but otherwise no such members shall be entitled to receive any notice from the company.

113. A member present, either in person or by proxy, at any meeting of the company or of the holders of any class of shares in the company shall be deemed to have received notice of the meeting and, where requisite, of the purposes for which it was called.

114. Every person who becomes entitled to a share shall be bound by any notice in respect of that share which, before his name is entered in the register of members, has been duly given to a person from whom he derives his title.

115. Proof that an envelope containing a notice was properly addressed, pre-paid and posted shall be conclusive evidence that the notice was given. A notice shall be deemed to be given at the expiration of 48 hours after the envelope containing it was posted.

116. A notice may be given by the company to the persons entitled to a share in consequence of the death or bankruptcy of a member by sending or delivering it, in any manner authorised by the articles for the giving of notice to a member, addressed to them by name, or by the title of representatives of the deceased, or trustee of the bankrupt or by any like description at the address, if any, within the United Kingdom supplied for that purpose by the persons claiming to be so entitled. Until such an address has been supplied, a notice may be given in any manner in which it might have been given if the death or bankruptcy had not occurred.

WINDING UP

117. If the company is wound up, the liquidator may, with the sanction of an extraordinary resolution of the company and any other sanction required by the Act, divide among the members in specie the whole or any part of the assets of the company and may, for that purpose, value any assets and determine how the division shall be carried out as between the members or different classes of members. The liquidator may, with the like sanction, vest the whole or any part of the assets in trustees upon such trusts for the benefit of the members as he with the like sanction determines, but no member shall be compelled to accept any assets upon which there is a liability.

INDEMNITY

118. Subject to the provisions of the Act but without prejudice to any indemnity to which a director may otherwise be entitled, every director or other officer or auditor of the company shall be indemnified out of the assets of the company against any liability incurred by him in defending any proceedings, whether civil or criminal, in which judgment is given in his favour or in which he is acquitted or in connection with any application in which relief is granted to him by the court from liability for negligence, default, breach of duty or breach of trust in relation to the affairs of the company.

3.2.1 Amendments to Table A Articles

The following document contains the typical additions and/or amendments contains to table A and will often, in practice, be adopted by a private company limited by shares.

THE COMPANIES ACTS, 1988 TO 1989
PRIVATE COMPANY LIMITED BY SHARES ARTICLES OF ASSOCIATION OF

Preliminary
1. (a) The Regulations contained in table A in the schedule to the Companies (tables A to F) Regulations 1985 (S.I. 1985 No. 805) as amended by the Companies (tables A to F) (Amendment) Regulations 1985 (S.I. 1985 No. 1052) (such table being hereinafter called "table A") shall apply to the company save in so far as they are excluded or varied hereby and such regulations (save as so excluded or varied) and the articles hereinafter contained shall be the regulations of the Company.
    (b) In these articles the expression "the Act" means the Companies Act 1985, but so that any reference in these articles to any provision of the act shall be deemed to include a reference to any statutory modification or re-enactment of that provision for the time being in force.

Allotment of shares
2. (a) Shares that are comprised in the authorised share capital with which the company is incorporated and that the directors propose to issue shall first be offered to the members in proportion as nearly as may be to the number of the existing shares held by them respectively unless the company in general meeting shall by special resolution otherwise direct. The offer shall be made by notice specifying the number of shares offered, and limiting a period (not being less than 14 days) within which the offer, if not accepted, will be deemed to be declined. After the expiration of that period, those shares so deemed to be declined shall be offered in the proportion aforesaid to the persons who have, within the said period, accepted all the shares offered to them; such further offer shall be made in like terms in the same manner and limited by a like period as the original offer. Any shares not accepted pursuant to such offer or further offer as aforesaid or not capable of being offered as aforesaid except by way of fractions and any shares released from the provisions of this article by any such special resolution as aforesaid shall be under the control of the directors, who may allot, grant options over or otherwise dispose of the same to such persons, on such terms, and in such manner as they think fit, provided that, in the case of shares not accepted as aforesaid, such shares shall not be disposed of on

terms that are more favourable to the subscribers therefor than the terms on which they were offered to the members. The foregoing provisions of this paragraph (b) shall have effect subject to section 80 of the Act.

(c) In accordance with section 91(1) of the Act sections 89(1) and 90(1) to (6) (inclusive) of the Act shall not apply to the company.

(d) The directors are generally and unconditionally authorised for the purposes of section 80 of the Act, to exercise any power of the company to allot and grant rights to subscribe for or convert securities into shares of the company up to the amount of the authorised share capital with which the company is incorporated at any time or times during the period of five years from the date of incorporation and the directors may, after that period, allot any shares or grant any such rights under this authority in pursuance of an offer or agreement so to do made by the company within that period. The authority hereby given may at any time (subject to the said section 80) be renewed, revoked or varied by ordinary resolution of the company in general meeting.

Shares

3. The lien conferred by Clause 8 in table A shall attach also to fully paid-up shares, and the company shall also have a first and paramount lien on all shares, whether fully paid or not, standing registered in the name of any person indebted or under liability to the company, whether he shall be the sole registered holder thereof or shall be one of two or more joint holders, for all monies presently payable by him or his estate to the company. Clause 8 in table A shall be modified accordingly.

4. The liability of any member in default in respect of a call shall be increased by the addition at the end of the first sentence of Clause 18 in table A of the words "and all expenses that may have been incurred by the Company by reason of such non-payment."

General meetings and resolutions

5.   (a) Every notice convening a general meeting shall comply with the provisions of section 372 (3) of the Act as to giving information to members in regard to their right to appoint proxies; and notices of and other communications relating to any general meeting that any member is entitled to receive shall be sent to the directors and to the auditors for the time being of the company.

(b) No business shall be transacted at any general meeting unless a quorum is present. Subject to paragraph (c) below two persons entitled to vote upon the business to be transacted, each being a member or a proxy for a member or a duly authorised representative of a corporation, shall be a quorum.

(c) If and for so long as the company has only one member, that member present in person or by proxy or if that member is a corporation by a duly authorised representative shall be a quorum.

(d) If a quorum is not present within half an hour from the time appointed for a general meeting the general meeting shall stand adjourned to the same day in the next week at the same time and place or to such other day and at such other time and place as the directors may determine; and if at the adjourned general meeting a quorum is not present within half an hour from the time appointed therefor such adjourned general meeting shall be dissolved.

(e) Clauses 40 and 41 in table A shall not apply to the company.

6.   (a) If and for so long as the company has only one member and that member takes any decision that is required to be taken in general meetings or by means of a written resolution, that decision shall be as valid and effectual as if agreed by the company in general meeting save that this paragraph shall not apply to resolutions passed pursuant to sections 303 and 391 of the Act.

(b) Any decision taken by a sole member pursuant to paragraph (a) above shall be recorded in writing and delivered by that Member to the Company for entry in the company's minute book.

Appointment of directors

7.   (a) Clause 64 in Table A shall not apply to the Company.

(b) The maximum number and minimum number respectively of the directors may be determined from time to time by ordinary resolution in general meeting of the company. Subject to and in default of any such determination there shall be no maximum number of directors and the minimum number of directors shall be one. Whensoever the minimum number of directors shall be one, a sole director shall have authority to exercise all the powers and discretions by table A and by these articles expressed to be vested in the directors generally, and clause 89 in table A shall be modified accordingly.

(c) The directors shall not be required to retire by rotation and clauses 73 to 80 (inclusive) in table A shall not apply to the company.

(d) No person shall be appointed a director at any general meeting unless either:

(i) he is recommended by the directors; or

(ii) not less than 14 nor more than 35 clear days before the date appointed for the general meeting, notice signed by a member qualified to vote at the general meeting has been given to the company of the intention to propose that person for appointment, together with notice signed by that person of his willingness to be appointed.

(e) Subject to paragraph (d) above, the company may by ordinary resolution in general Meeting appoint any person who is willing to act to be a director, either to fill a vacancy or as an additional director.

(f) The director may appoint a person who is willing to act to be a director, either to fill a vacancy or as an additional director, provided that the appointment does not cause the number of directors to exceed any number determined in accordance with paragraph (b) above as the maximum number of director and for the time being in force.

(g) In any case where as the result of death of a sole member of the company the company has no members and no directors the personal representative of such deceased member shall have the right by notice in writing to appoint a person to be a director of the company and such appointment shall be as effective as if made by the company in general meeting pursuant to paragraph (e) of this article.

Borrowing powers

8. The directors may exercise all the powers of the company to borrow money without limit as to amount and upon such terms and in such manner as they think fit and subject (in the case of any security convertible into shares) to section 80 of the Act to grant any mortgage, charge or standard security over its undertaking, property and uncalled capital, or any part thereof, and to issue debentures, debenture stock, and other securities whether outright or a security for any debt, liability or obligation of the company or of any third party.

Alternate directors

9. (a) An alternative director shall not be entitled as such to receive any remuneration from the company, save that he may be paid by the company such part (if any) of the remuneration otherwise payable to his appointor as such appointor may be notice in writing to the company from time to time direct, and the first sentence of clause 66 in table A shall be modified accordingly.

(b) A director, or any such other person as is mentioned in clause 65 in table A, may act as an alternate director to represent more than one director, and an alternate director shall be entitled at any meeting of the directors or of any committee of the directors to one vote for every director whom he represents in addition to his own vote (if any) as a director, but he shall count as only one for the purpose of determining whether a quorum is present.

Gratuities and pensions

10. (a) The directors may exercise the powers of the Company conferred by clause 3(ii)(s) of the memorandum of association of the company and shall be entitled to retain any benefits received by them or any of them by reason of the exercise of any such powers.

(b) Clause 87 in table A shall not apply to the company.

Proceedings of directors

11. (a) A director may vote, at any meeting of the directors or of any committee of the directors, on any resolution, notwithstanding that it in any way concerns or relates to a matter in which he has, directly or indirectly, any kind of interest whatsoever, and if he shall vote on any such resolution as aforesaid his vote shall be counted; and in relation to any such resolution as aforesaid he shall (whether or not he shall vote on the same) be taken into account in calculating the quorum present at the meeting.

(b) Clause 94 to 97 (inclusive) in table A shall not apply to the company.

The seal

12. (a) If the company has a seal it shall only be used with the authority of the directors or of a committee of directors. The directors may determine who shall sign any instrument to which the seal is affixed and unless otherwise so determined it shall be signed by a director and by the secretary or second director. The obligation under clause 6 of table A relating to the sealing of share certificates shall apply only if the company has a seal. Clause 101 of Table A shall not apply to the company.

(b) The company may exercise the powers conferred by section 9 of the Act with regard to having an official seal for use abroad, and such powers shall be vested in the directors.

Indemnity

13. (a) Every director or other officer or auditor of the company shall be indemnified out of the assets of the company against all losses or liabilities which he may sustain or incur in or about the execution of the duties of his office or otherwise in relation thereto, including any liability incurred by him in defending any proceedings, whether civil or criminal, or in connection with any application under section 144 or section 727 of the Act in which relief is granted to him by the Court, and no director or other officer shall be liable for any loss, damage or misfortune which may happen to or be incurred by the company in the execution of the duties of his office or in relation thereto. But this article shall only have effect in so far as its provisions are not avoided by section 310 of the Act.

(b) The directors shall have power to purchase and maintain for any director, office or auditor of the company, insurance against any such liability as is referred to in section 310(1) of the Act.

(c) Clause 118 in table A shall not apply to the company.

STANDARD TRANSFER ARTICLE (please delete if not required)

TRANSFER OF SHARES

14. The Director may, in their absolute discretion and without assigning any reason therefor, decline to register the transfer of a share, whether or not it is a fully paid share, and the first sentence of Clause 24 in Table A shall not apply to the Company.

NAMES AND ADDRESSES OF SUBSCRIBERS

Dated this
Witness to the above Signatures:

3.2.2 Transfer Articles

As has been discussed, article 24 of table A does not give the directors complete control over the *transfer* of a company's shares. In order to increase the director's powers over transfers, there are several variations of article 24. Three of those variations are referred to as type A, B, C, set out below. The other variation is the absolute discretion provision (see Appendix 3.2.1).

Type A optional transfer article

Transfer of Shares
14.   (a) the Directors shall, subject to Clause 24 in Table A, register the transfer or, as the case may be, transmission of any shares:—
   (i)   to a member of the family of a Member or deceased Member;
   (ii) to any person or persons acting in the capacity of trustee or trustees of a trust created by a Member (by deed or by Will) or, upon any change of trustees of a trust so created, to the new trustee or trustees (so that any such transfer as aforesaid shall be registered pursuant to this paragraph only if such shares are to be held upon the terms of the trust) provided that there are no persons beneficially interested under the trust other than the Member and members of his family and the voting rights conferred by any such shares are not exercisable by or subject to the consent of any person other than the trustee or trustees of the trust or the Member or members of his family and also the Directors are satisfied that the trust is and is intended to remain a trust the sole purpose of which is to benefit the Member or members of his family;
   (iii) by the trustee or trustees of a trust to which sub-paragraph (ii) above applies to any person beneficially interested under the trust being the Member or a member of his family;
   (iv) to the legal personal representatives of a deceased Member where under the provisions of his will or the laws as to intestacy the persons beneficially entitled to any such shares, whether immediately or contingently, are members of the family of the deceased Member and by the legal personal representatives of a deceased Member to a member or members of the family of the deceased Member;
   (v)   to any other Member of the Company
   (b) For the purpose of this Article:
   (i)   the word ''Member'' shall not include a person who holds shares only in the capacity of trustee, legal personal representative or trustee in bankruptcy but shall include a former member in any case where the person concerned ceased to be a Member as a result of the creation of the relevant trust; and
   (ii) the words ''a member of the family of a Member'' shall

mean the husband, wife, widow, widower, child and remoter issue (including a child by adoption), parent (including adoptive parent), brother and sister (whether of the full or half blood and including a brother or sister related by adoption), and child and remoter issue of any such brother or sister (including a child by adoption), of the Member.

(c) The directors may, in their absolute discretion without assigning any reason therefore, decline to register any transfer or transmission of a share (whether or not it is fully paid) to which paragraph (c) above does not apply.

(d) Clause 24 in table A shall be modified accordingly.

Type B optional transfer article

Transfer of Shares

14. (a) Any person (hereinafter called "the proposing transferor") proposing to transfer any shares shall give notice in writing (hereinafter called "the transfer notice") to the company that he desires to transfer the same and specifying the price per share that in his opinion constitutes the fair value thereof. The transfer notice shall constitute the company the agent of the proposing transferor for the sale of all (but not some of) the shares comprised in the transfer notice to any member or members willing to purchase the same (hereinafter called "the purchasing member") at the price specified therein or at the fair value certified in accordance with paragraph (c) below (whichever shall be the lower) A transfer notice shall not be revocable except with the sanction of the directors.

(b) The shares comprised in any transfer notice shall be offered to the members (other than the proposing transferor) as nearly as may be in proportion to the number of shares held by them respectively. Such offer shall be made by notice in writing (hereinafter called "the offer notice") within seven days after the receipt by the company of the transfer notice. The offer notice shall state the price per share specified in the transfer notice and shall limit the time in which the offer may be accepted, not being less than 2 days nor more than 42 days after the date of the offer notice, provided that if a certificate of fair value is requested under paragraph (c) below the offer shall remain open for acceptance for a period of 14 days after the date on which notice of the fair value certified in accordance with that paragraph shall have been given by the company to the members or until the expiry of the period specified in the offer notice whichever is the later. For the purpose of this article an offer shall be deemed to be accepted on the day on which the acceptance is received by the company. The offer notice shall further invite each member to state in his reply the number of additional shares (if any) in excess of his proportion that he desires to purchase and if all the members do not accept the offer in respect of their respective proportions in full he shares not so accepted shall be used to satisfy the claims for additional shares as nearly as may be in proportion to the number of shares already held by them respectively, provided that no member shall be obliged to take more shares than he shall have applied for. If any shares shall not be capable without fractions of being offered to the members in proportion to their existing holdings, the same shall be offered to the members, or some of them, in such proportions or in such manner as may be determined by lots drawn in regard thereto, and the lots shall be drawn in such manner as the directors think fit.

(c) Any member may, not later than eight days after the date of the offer notice, serve on the company a notice in writing requesting that the auditor for the time being of the company (or at the discretion of the auditor, a person nominated by the president for the time being of the Institute of Chartered Accountants in the country of the situation of its registered office) certify in writing the sum that in his opinion represents the fair value of the shares comprised in the transfer notice as at the date of the transfer notice and for the purpose of this article reference to the auditor shall include any person so nominated. Upon receipt of such notice the company shall by notice in writing inform all Members of the fair value of each share and of the price specified in the transfer notice and the fair value of each share) at which the shares comprised in the transfer notice are offered for sale. For the purpose of this article the fair value of each share comprised in the transfer notice shall be its value as a rateable proportion of the total value of all the issued shares of the company and shall not be discounted or enhanced by reference to the number of shares referred to in the transfer notice.

(d) If purchasing members shall be found for all the shares comprised in the transfer notice within the appropriate period specified in paragraph (b) above, the Company shall not later than seven days after the expiry of such appropriate period give notice in writing (hereinafter called "the sale notice") to the proposing transferor specifying the purchasing members and the proposing transferor shall be bound upon payment of the price due in respect of all the shares comprised in the transfer notice to transfer the shares to the purchasing members.

(e) If in any case the proposing transferor after having become bound as aforesaid makes default in transferring any shares the company may receive the purchase money on his behalf, and may authorise some person to execute a transfer of such shares in favour of the purchasing member. The receipt of the company for the purchase money shall be a good discharge to the purchasing members. The company shall pay the purchase money into a separate bank account.

(f) If the company shall not give a sale notice to the proposing transferor within the time specified in paragraph (d) above, he shall, during the period of 30 days next following the expiry of the time so specified, be at liberty to transfer all or any of the shares comprised in the transfer notice to any person or persons but in that event the directors may, in their absolute discretion, and without assigning any reason therefor, decline to register any such transfer and clause 24 in table A shall, for these purposes, be modified accordingly.

(g) In the application of clauses 29 to 31 (inclusive) in table A to the company:

    (i) any person becoming entitled to a share in consequence of the death or bankruptcy of a member shall give a transfer notice before he elects in respect of any share to be registered himself or to execute a transfer;

    (ii) if a person so becoming entitled shall not have given a transfer notice in respect of any share within six months of the death or bankruptcy, the directors may at any time thereafter upon resolution passed by them give notice requiring such person within 30 days of such notice to give a transfer notice in respect of all the shares to which he has so become entitled and for which he has not previously given a transfer notice and if he does not do so he shall at the end of such thirty days be deemed to have given a transfer notice pursuant to paragraph (a) of this article relating to those shares in respect of which he has still not done so;

    (iii) where a transfer notice is given or deemed to be given under this paragraph (g) and no price per share is specified therein the transfer notice shall be deemed to specify the sum which shall, on the application of the directors, be certified in writing by the auditors in accordance with paragraph (c) of this article as the fair value thereof.

(h) Whenever any member of the company who is employed by the company in any capacity (whether or not he is also a director) ceases to be employed by the company otherwise than by reason of his death the directors may at any time not later than six months after his ceasing to be employed resolve that such member do retire, and thereupon he shall (unless he has already served a transfer notice) be deemed to have served a transfer notice pursuant to paragraph (a) of this article and to have specified therein the fair value to be certified in accordance with paragraph (c) of this article. Notice of the passing of any such resolution shall forthwith be given to the member affected thereby.

Type C optional transfer article

Transfer of shares

14. (a) The directors shall subject to clause 24 in table A, register transfer or, as the case may be, transmission of any shares:

    (i) to a member of the family of a member or deceased member;

    (ii) to any person or persons acting in the capacity of trustee or trustees of a trust created by a member (by deed or by will) or, upon any change of trustees of a trust so created, to the new trustee or trustees (so that any such transfer as aforesaid shall be registered pursuant to this paragraph only if such shares are to be held upon the terms of the trust) provided that there are no persons beneficially interested under the trust other than the member or members of his family and the voting rights conferred by any such shares are not exercisable by or subject to the consent of any person other than the trustee or trustees of the trust or the member or members of his family and also the directors are satisfied that the trust is and is intended to remain a trust the sole purpose of which is to benefit the member or members of his family;

(iii) the trustee or trustees of a trust to which sub-paragraph (ii) above applies to any person beneficially interested under the trust being the member or a member of his family;

(iv) the legal personal representatives of a deceased member where under the provisions of his will or the laws as to intestacy the persons beneficially entitled to any such shares, whether immediately or contingently, are members of the family (as hereinafter defined) of the deceased member and by the legal personal representative of a deceased member to a member or members of the family of the deceased member;

(v) to any other member of the company.

(b) For the purpose of paragraphs (a) and (j) of this article but not any other paragraph:

(i) the word ımember' shall not include a person who holds shares only in that capacity of trustee, legal personal representative or trustee in bankruptcy but shall include a former member in any case where the person concerned ceased to be a member as the result of the creation of the relevant trust; and

(ii) the words "a member of the family of a member" shall mean the husband, wife, widow, widower, child and remoter issue (including a child by adoption), parent (including adoptive parent), brother and sister (whether of the full or half blood and including a brother or sister related by adoption), and child and remoter issue of any such brother or sister (including a child by adoption), of the member.

(c) Notwithstanding the provisions of this article, the directors may decline to register any transfer or transmission which would otherwise be permitted hereunder without assigning any reason therefor, if it is a transfer:

(i) of a share (whether or not it is fully paid) made pursuant to paragraph (i) below;

(ii) of a share pursuant to paragraph (a) by a member of the company who is employed by the company in any capacity provided that this restriction shall not apply to such members' legal personal representatives.

Clause 24 in Table A shall, for these purposes, be modified accordingly.

(d) Save where a transfer is made pursuant to paragraph (a) above any person (hereinafter called "the proposing transferor") proposing to transfer any shares shall give notice in writing (hereinafter called "the transfer notice") to the company that he desires to transfer the same and specifying the price per share which in his opinion constitutes the fair value thereof. The transfer notice shall constitute the company the agent of the proposing transferor for the sale of all (but not some of) the shares comprised in the transfer notice to any member or members willing to purchase the same (hereinafter called "the purchasing member") at the price specified therein or at the fair value certified in accordance with paragraph (f) below (whichever shall be the lower). A transfer notice shall not be revocable except with the sanction of the directors.

(e) The shares comprised in any transfer notice shall be offered to the members (other than the proposing transferor) as nearly as may be in proportion to the number of shares held by them respectively. Such offer shall be made by notice in writing (hereinafter called "the offer notice") within seven days after the receipt by the company of the transfer notice. The offer notice shall state the price per share specified in the transfer notice and shall limit the time in which the offer may be accepted, not being less than 21 days nor more than 42 days after the date of the offer notice, provided that if a certificate of valuation is requested under paragraph (f) below the offer shall remain open for acceptance for a period of fourteen days after the date on which notice of the fair value certified in accordance with that paragraph shall have been given by the company to the members. For the purpose of this article an offer shall be deemed to be accepted on the day on which the acceptance is received by the company. The offer notice shall further invite each member to state in his reply the number of additional shares (if any) in excess of his proportion which he desires to purchase and if all the members do not accept the offer in respect of their respective proportions in full the shares not so accepted shall be used to satisfy the claims for additional shares as nearly as may be in proportion to the number of shares already held by them respectively, provided that no member shall be obliged to take more shares than he shall have applied for. If any shares shall not be capable without fractions of being offered to the members in proportion to their existing holdings, the same shall be offered to the members, or some of them, in such proportions or in such manner as may be determined by lots drawn in regard thereto, and the lots shall be drawn in such manner as the directors may think fit.

(f) Any member may, not later than eight days after the date of the offer notice, serve on the company a notice in writing requesting that the auditor for the time being of the company (or at the discretion of the auditor, a person nominated by the president for the time being of the Institute of Chartered Accountants in the Country of the situation of its registered office) certify in writing the sum that in his opinion represents the fair value of the shares comprised in the transfer notice as at the date of the transfer notice and for the purpose of this article reference to the auditor shall include any person so nominated. Upon receipt of such notice the company shall instruct the auditor to certify as aforesaid and the costs of such valuation shall be apportioned among the proposing transferor and the purchasing members or borne by any one or more of them as the auditor in his absolute discretion shall decide. In certifying fair value as aforesaid the auditor shall be considered to be acting as an expert and not as an arbitrator or arbiter and accordingly any provisions of law or statute relating to arbitration shall not apply. Upon receipt of the certificate of the auditor, the company shall by notice in writing inform all members of the fair value of each share and of the price per share (being the lower of the price specified in the transfer notice and the fair value of each share) at which the shares comprised in the transfer notice are offered for sale. For the purpose of this article the fair value of each share comprised in the transfer notice shall be its value as a rateable proportion of the total value of all the issued shares of the company and shall not be discounted or enhanced by reference to the number of shares referred to in the transfer notice.

(g) If purchasing members shall be found for all the shares comprised in the transfer notice within the appropriate period specified in paragraph (e) above, the company shall not later than seven days after the expiry of such appropriate period give notice in writing (hereinafter called "the sale notice") to the proposing transferor specifying the purchasing members and the proposing transferor shall be bound upon payment of the price due in respect of all the shares comprised in the transfer notice to transfer the shares to the purchasing members.

(h) If in any case the proposing transferor after having become bound as aforesaid makes default in transferring any shares the company may receive the purchase money on his behalf, and may authorise some person to execute a transfer of such shares in favour of the purchasing member. The receipt of the company for the purchase money shall be a good discharge to the purchasing members. The company shall pay the purchase money into a separate bank account.

(i) If the company shall not give a sale notice to the proposing transferor within the time specified in paragraph (g) above, he shall, during the period of 30 days next following the expiry of the time so specified, be at liberty subject to paragraph (c) above to transfer all or any of the shares comprised in the transfer notice to any person or persons.

(j) In any case where any shares are held by the trustee or trustees of a trust following a transfer or transfers made pursuant to subparagraph (ii) of paragraph (a) above and it shall come to the notice of the Directors that not all the persons beneficially interested under the trust are members of the family (as herein before defined) or the member by whom the trust was created, the directors may at any time within 28 days thereafter resolve that such trustee or trustees do transfer such shares and such trustee or trustees shall thereupon be deemed to have served a transfer notice comprising such shares pursuant to paragraph (d) above and to have specified therein the fair value to be certified in accordance with paragraph (f) above and the provisions of this article shall take effect accordingly. Notice of such resolution shall forthwith be given to such trustee or trustees.

(k) In the application of clauses 29 to 31 (inclusive) in table A to the company:

    (i) save where the proposed transfer or transmission is within paragraph (a) above ("permitted transfer") any person becoming entitled to a share in consequence of the death or bankruptcy of a member shall give a transfer notice before he elects in respect of any share to be registered himself or to execute a transfer;

    (ii) if a person so becoming entitled shall not have executed a permitted transfer or given a transfer notice in respect of any share within six months of the death or bankruptcy, the directors may at any time thereafter upon resolution passed by them give notice requiring such person within 30 days to execute permitted transfers or give a transfer notice in respect of all the shares to which he has so become entitled and for which he has not previously done so and if he does not do so he shall at the end of such 30 days be deemed to have given a transfer notice pursuant to paragraph (d) of this Article relating to those shares in respect of which he has still not executed permitted transfers or given a transfer notice;

    (iii) where a transfer notice is given or deemed to be given under this paragraph (k) and no price per share is specified therein the transfer notice shall be deemed to specify the sum which shall, on the application of the directors, be certified in writing by the auditors in accordance with paragraph (f) of this article as the fair value thereof.

(l) Whenever any member of the company who is employed by the company in any capacity (whether or not he is also a director) ceases to be employed by the company otherwise than by reason of his death the directors may at any time not later than six months after his ceasing to be employed resolve that such member do retire, and thereupon he shall (unless he has already served a transfer notice) be deemed to have served a transfer notice pursuant to paragraph (d) of this article and to have specified therein the fair value to be certified in accordance with paragraph (f) of this article. Notice of the passing of any such resolution shall forthwith be given to the member affected thereby.

3.2.3 Additional Optional Articles

The following articles may also be adopted in addition to those matters set out in Appendix 3.2.1.

ENHANCED VOTING RIGHTS FOR DIRECTORS

Every director for the time being of the company shall have the following rights:

(a) if at any general meeting a poll is duly demanded on a resolution;

(b) if at any general meeting a poll is duly demanded on a resolution to delete or amend the provisions of this article, to 10 votes for each share of which he is the holder if voting against such resolution.

Clause 54 in table A shall be modified accordingly.

Casting vote

The chairman shall not, in the event of an equality of votes at any general meeting of the company, or at any meeting of the directors or of a committee of directors, have a second or casting vote. Clause 50 in table A shall not apply to the company and clauses 88 and 72 in table A shall be modified accordingly.

Associate directors

(a) The directors may at any time and from time to time appoint any employee of the company to the position of associate director.

(b) An associate director shall advise and assist the directors but shall not attend board meetings except at the invitation of the directors, and when present at the board meetings he shall not be entitled to vote, nor be counted in the quorum, but subject as aforesaid he shall as associate director have such powers, authorities and duties as the directors may in the particular case from time to time determine.

(c) An associate director shall not be deemed a member of the board, nor any committee thereof, nor shall he be a director for any of the purposes of these articles of association or (so far as provision may lawfully be made in this behalf) for any of the purposes of the Companies Act 1985.

(d) Without prejudice to any rights or claims the associate director may have under any contract with the company, any appointment as an associate director may be terminated by the directors at any time and shall, ipso facto, terminate if the associate director shall from any cause cease to be an employee of the company;

(e) An associate director may receive such remuneration (if any) in addition to the remuneration received as an employee of the company as the directors shall from time to time determine.

3.3 Other Company Documents

The documents necessary to incorporate a company (in addition to the constituent documents) are the Forms G10 and G12 (see Chapter 9) reproduced below.

3.3.1 Forms G10 and G12

Form G10
Statement of first directors and secretary and intended situation of registered office.
Company name (in full) _____

_____

_____

Registered office of the   _____
company on   _____
incorporation.   Post town_____
                               Country/Region_____
                               Postcode_____

If the memorandum is
delivered by an agent   _____
for the subscribers of
the memorandum mark   _____
"x" in the box opposite
and give the agent's
name and address.

                               _____

                               Post town_____
                               Country/Region_____
                               Postcode_____

Number of continuation   _____
sheets attached

                               _____

To whom should
Companies House direct
any enquiries about the
information shown in
this form?

_____

_____

_____Postcode_____

Telephone_____Extension_____

Company secretary
(see notes 1–5)
Name *Style/Title
    Forenames
    Surname
    *Honours, etc.
    Previous forenames
    Previous surname
Address
Usual residential
address must be given.
In the case of a
corporation, give the
registered or principal
office address.

Post town_____
Country/Region_____
Postcode_____Country_____
I consent to act as secretary of the company
named on page 1.

Consent signature   Signed_____Date_____

Directors (see notes 1–5)
Name *Style/Title
    Forenames
    Surname
    *Honours etc
    Previous forenames
    Previous surnames
Address
Usual residential address
must be given. In the
case of a corporation,
give the registered or
principal office address.

Post town_____
Country/Region_____
Postcode_____Country_____

Date of birth
Business occupation
Other directorships

_____Nationality_____

*voluntary details

I consent to act as secretary of the company
named on page 1.

Consent signature

Signed_____Date_____

Directors (continued)
(see notes 1–5)
Name *Style/Title _____
    Forenames _____
    Surname _____
    *Honours etc _____
    Previous forenames _____
      Previous surname _____

Address
Usual residential address _____
must be given. In the case _____
of a corporation, give the Postcode _____
registered or principal County/Region _____
office address Postcode _____ Country _____

      Date of birth
Business occupation _____ Nationality _____
Other directorships _____
_____

*voluntary details

I consent to act as director of the company
named on page 1

Consent signature

signed _____ Date _____

Delete if the form is
signed by the subscribers

Signature of agent on behalf of all subscribers
Delete if the form is   Date
signed by an agent on Signed _____ Date
behalf of all the
subscribers. Signed _____ Date

All the subscribers must Signed _____ Date
sign either personally or
by a person or persons Signed _____ Date
authorised to sign for
them.

Notes to Form G10
1. Show for an individual the full forenames *not initials* and surname together
with any previous forenames or surname(s).

    If the director or secretary is a corporation or Scottish firm—show the
corporate or firm name on the surname line.

    Give previous forenames or surname except that:

    (a) for a married woman, the name by which she was known before
        marriage need not be given,
    (b) names not used since the age of 18 or for at least 20 years need
        not be given.

In the case of a peer, or an individual usually known by a British title you may state instead of or in addition to the forenames and surname that that person was known before he adopted the title or succeeded to it.

Give the usual residential address. In the case of a corporation or Scottish firm give the registered or principal office.

2. Directors known by another description: a director includes any person who occupies that position even if called by a different name, for example, governor, member of council. It also includes a shadow director.

3. Director's details: show for each individual director his date of birth, business occupation and nationality.

The date of birth must be given for every individual director.

4. Other directorships: give the name of every company of which the individual concerned is a director or has been a director at any time in the past five years. You may exclude a company which either *is* or at *all times during the past five years* when the person was a director *was*:

(a) dormant;
(b) a parent company that wholly owned the company making the return;
(c) a wholly owned subsidiary of the company making the return;
(d) another wholly owned subsidiary of the same parent company.

If there is insufficient space on the form for other directorships you may use a separate sheet of paper.

5. Use photocopies of page 2 to details of joint secretaries or a directors and include the company name and number.

6. The address for companies registered in England and Wales is:
The Registrar of Companies
Companies House
Crown Way
Cardiff
CF4 3UZ
or, for companies registered in Scotland:
The Registrar of Companies
Companies House
100–102 George Street
Edinburgh
EH2 3DJ.

Form G12
Statutory declaration of compliance with requirements on application for registration of a company.

Pursuant to section 12(3) of the Companies Act 1985.
To the Registrar of Companies

Name of company

Insert full name of company

I, _____

of _____

_____

delete as appropriate# do solemnly and sincerely declare that I am a (Solicitor engaged in the formation of the company)# (person named as director or secretary of the company in the statement delivered to the registrar under section 10(2)# and that all the requirements of the above Act in respect of the registration of the above company and matters precedent and incidental to it have been compiled with,

And I make this solemn declaration conscientiously believing the same to be true and by virtue of the provisions of the Statutory Declarations Act 1835

Declared at _____

_____

the _____ day of _____

One thousand nine hundred and_____

before me _____

A Commissioner for Oaths or Notary Public or Justice of the Peace or Solicitor having the powers conferred on a Commissioner for Oaths.

_____

Precentor's name address and   For official Use
reference (if any):   Companies Section
Post room

3.3.2 Stock Transfer Form—J30

This is the document enabling the transfer of shares from one shareholder to another (together with the share certificate). See Chapter 11 on the procedural requirements regarding the transfer of shares.

Certificate lodged with the registrar

Consideration money £....................

Full name of undertaking

Full description of security

Number or amount   words   Figures
shares, stock or
other security and, in
figures column only,

number and denomi-
nation of units, if
any.

(units of)

Name(s) of registered
holder(s) should be
given in full: the
address should be
given where there is
only one holder.

In the name(s) of

If the transfer is not
made by the registered
holder(s) insert also
the name(s) and
capacity (*e.g.*
executor(s) of the
person(s) making the
transfer

I/We hereby transfer the above security out of the name(s) aforesaid to the
person(s) named below *or to the several persons named in Parts 2 of
brokers transfer forms relating to the
above security:*

Stamp of selling broker(s) or,
for transactions which are not
stock exchange transaction,
of agent(s), if any, acting for
the transferor(s).

**Delete words in italics except for
stock exchange transactions**

Signature(s) of transferor(s)

1 ....

2 ....

3 ....

4 ....

Bodies corporate should execute under their   Date....................................
common seal.

Full name(s) and full
address(es) (including
county or, if
applicable, postal
district number) of the

person(s) to whom the
security is transferred

Please state title, if
any, or whether Mr,
Mrs or Miss.

Please complete in
typewriting or in block
capitals.

I/We request that such entries be made in the register as are necessary
to give effect to this transfer.

Stamp of buying broker(s). Stamp or name and address of person (if
any) lodging this form (if other than the buying broker(s)

Form of certificate required where transfer is not liable to stamp duty
Pursuant to the Stamp Duty (Except Instruments) Regulations 1987

(1)	Delete as appropriate	(1) I/We hereby certify that this instrument falls within category (2) in the schedule so the Stamp Duty (Exempt Instruments)
(2)	Insert "A", "B" or appropriate category	Regulations 1987, set out below.
	*Signature(s)	*Description: "Transferor", "Solicitor", or state capacity of other person duly authorised to sign and giving the certificate from his known knowledge of the transactions.

Date_____19_____

Note The above certificate should be signed by (i) the transferor(s) or (ii) a
solicitor or other person (e.g. income acting as trustee or executor) having a full
knowledge of the facts. Such other person must state the capacity in which he
signs, that he as authorised so to sign and gives the certificate form this own
knowledge of the transactions.

A.   The vesting of property subject to a trust in the trustees of the trust on
the appointment of a new trustee or in the continuing trustees on the
retirement of a trustee.

B.   The conveyance or transfer of property the subject of a specific devise or legacy to the beneficiary named in the will (or his nominee).

C.   The conveyance or transfer of property which forms part of an interstate's estate to the person entitled on intestacy (or his nominee).

D.   The appropriation of properly within section 84(4) of the Finance Act 1985 (death: appropriation in satisfaction of a general legacy of money) or section 84(5) or (7) of that Act (death: appropriation in satisfaction of any interest of surviving spouse and in Scotland also of any interest of issue).

E.   The conveyance or tansfer of property which forms part of the residuary estate of a testator to a beneficiary for his nominee) entitled solely by virtue of his entitlement under the will.

F.   The conveyance or transfer of property out of a settlement in or towards satisfaction of a beneficiary's interest not being an interest acquired for money or money's worth, being a conveyance or transfer constituting a distribution of property in accordance with the provisions of the settlement.

G.   The conveyance or transfer of property on an in consideration only of marriage to a party to the marriage for his nominee) or to trustees to be held on the terms of a settlement made in consideration only of the marriage.

H.   The conveyance or transfer of property within section 83(1) of the Finance Act 1985 (transfers in connection with divorce etc.).

I.   The conveyance or transfer by the liquidator of property that formed part of the assets of the company in liquidation to a shareholder of that company (or his nominee) in or towards satisfaction of the shareholder's rights on a winding-up.

J.   The grant in fee simple of an easement in or over land for no consideration in money or money's worth.

K.   The grant of a servitude for no consideration in money or money's worth.

L.   The conveyance or transfer of property operation as a voluntary disposition *inter vivos* for no consideration in money or money's worth nor any consideration referred to in section 57 of the Stamp Act 1891 (conveyance in consideration of a debt etc).

M.   The conveyance or transfer of property by an instrument within section 84(1) of the Finance Act 1985 (deathcraying disposition).

Instructional notes

1. In order to obtain exemption from stamp duty on transaction described in the above schedule the certificate must be completed and may then be lodged for registration or otherwise acted upon. Adjudication by the stamp office is not required.

2. This form does not apply to transactions falling within categories (a) and (b) in the form of certificate required where the transfer is not liable to ad valorem stamp duty set out below. In these cases the form of certificate printed below should be used. Transactions within either of those categories require submission of the form to the stamp office and remain liable to 50p duty.

Ad valorem stamp duty

Instruments of transfer are liable to a fixed duty of 50p when the transaction falls within one of the following categories.

(a) Transfer by way of security for a loan or re-transfer to the original transferor on repayment of a loan.

(b) Transfer, not on sale and not arising under any contract of sale and where no beneficial interests in the property passes:
    (i) to a person who is a mere nominee of, and is nominated only by, the transferor;
    (ii) from a mere nominee who has at all times, held the property on behalf of the transferee;
    (iii) from one nominee to another of the same beneficial owner where the first nominee has at all times held the property on behalf of that beneficial owner.

Note This category does not include a transfer made in any of the following circumstances:

(a) by a holder of stock, etc., following the grant of an option to purchase the stock, to the person entitled to the option or his nominee as a nominee in contemplation of a contract for the sale of the stock, *etc.*, then about to be entered into;

(b) from the nominee of a vendor, who has instructed the nominee orally or by some unstamped writing to hold stock, *etc.*, in trust for a purchaser, to such a purchaser.)

(1) "I" or (1) hereby certify that the transaction in respect of which this transfer

'We" is made is one which falls within the category (2) above.

(2) Insert (3)

'a" or

'b"

(3) Here set out concisely the facts explaining the transaction Adjudication may be required *signature(s) *Description ("Transfer" "Solicitor", etc)
Date   19

Note The above certificate should be signed by (1) the transferor(s) or (2) a member of a stock exchange or a solicitor or an accredited representative of a bank acting for the transferor(s); in cases falling within (a) where the bank or its official nominee is a party to the transfer, a certificate, instead of setting out the facts, may be to the effect that "the transfer is excepted from section 74 of the Finance (1909–10) Act 1910". A certificate in other cases should be signed by a solicitor or other person (*e.g.* a bank acting as trustee or executor) having a full knowledge of the facts.

3.4 Shares and Shareholders Self-Test Questions and Answers (see Chapter 11)

SHARES AND SHAREHOLDERS SELF-TEST QUESTIONS

1.   What is meant by the expression "par value"?

2.   What is the significance of the expression "authorised share capital"?

3.   What is the difference between an "issue" and an "allotment" of shares?

4.   Can directors issue shares under table A?

5.   What is the usual distribution between "ordinary" and "preference" shares?

6.   What is a dividend?

7.   How is a dividend payment authorised?

8.   What is the document by which shares are transferred?

9.   What are pre-emption rights?

10.   What is the rule in *Foss v. Harbottle*?

11.   What tests must a person satisfy to bring a section 459 Companies Act 1985 action?

12.   How is the action in 11. commenced?

13   What remedies are available pursuant to section 459 of the Companies Act 1985?

14.   If there is a falling out between a member and the company that appears irretrievable, what is the best practical solution?

ANSWERS TO SHARES AND SHAREHOLDERS SELF-TEST QUESTIONS

1. Par value is the value attributed to the shares in the authorised share capital clause in the memorandum of association. Also called "nominal value."

2. "Authorised share capital" represents the maximum number of shares that the directors can issue and allot without increasing the authorised share capital by amending the memorandum of association.

3. The issue is the first stage—the general process of getting shares from the company to a shareholder. The allotment is the end of the process—achieved when the transferee has a right to have his name entered in the register of members.

4. No, not covered by article 70 or article 2. They must be given such a power at general meeting.

5. They are not terms of art, but differences arise as to:
    (a) the right to vote;
    (b) receive dividends; and
    (c) on a winding-up.

6. A dividend is a sum paid per share out of the company's profits.

7. It is dependent on a profit being made by the company. The directors recommend a figure and the shareholder's approve it or a lesser sum.

8. The stock transfer form.

9. Rights of first refusal given to existing members of a company or other specified groups, ahead of third parties.

10. That the company is the proper plaintiff in relation to a wrong done to the company.

11. That he has suffered "unfair prejudice", which has materially affected his shareholding.

12. By petition to the civil courts.

13. Remedies are available under section 461 of the Companies Act 1985. They include the court making an order to administer the affairs of the company; purchase the disgruntled shareholders shares, etc.

14. Probably the buy order under section 46 of the Companies Act 1985 referred to above.

3.5 Directors Self-Test Questions and Answers

Please provide cases, section numbers or specifics where you can.

1. What in general terms are the two types of duty binding a director?

2. To whom does a director owe his primary duty?

3. To whom must directors have regard in exercising their duties?

4. What is the purpose of the Section 324 Register?

5. What is:
   (a) a shadow director;
   (b) an alternate director?

6. How is a director appointed under table A?

7. What is the reason small companies delete the "retirement by rotation" provision re the directors in table A?

8. What book-keeping matters need to be attended to when a director resigns his directorship?

9. If a director receives a golden handshake of £50,000 how will it be taxed?

10. Are directors required to hold shares in the company in which they are directors?

11. Can an undischarged bankrupt be a company director?

12. Can a sole director also be the company's secretary?

STATUTORY PROVISIONS: DIRECTORS' SELF-TEST QUESTIONS
(TRUE/FALSE) (SEE CHAPTER 12)

For each question, state true or false and provide a brief explanation.

13. Any member of a company, even one holding only one share can trigger a section 303 of the Companies Act 1985 action to remove a director.

14. A director removed by section 303 of the Act can not vote at the EGM at which the resolution is voted on.

15. Removal under section 303 of the Act deprives a director from claiming compensation for wrongful dismissal.

16. Special notice is given by the members to the company.

17. A shareholder needs to hold 10 per cent of the voting rights to seek the holding of an EGM.

18. A "targeted director" under a section 303 of the Act action does not get an opportunity to put his side of the case.

19. Section 320 of the Companies Act 1985 provides that a contract concerning a car belonging to a director and worth £4,000 being sold to the company never needs the approval of the shareholders in general meeting.

20. Section 312 of the Companies Act only requires "exorbitant" gratuitous payments to directors to be authorised by the shareholders in general meeting.

21. A director can borrow any amount of money from the company if it is for the purposes of carrying out his duties.

22. The section 324 register records share and salary information concerning directors.

23. A shareholder holding 1 per cent of the voting shares can get a resolution put on at an EGM.

24. A service agreement of six years duration requires shareholder approval before being signed.

25. If a 20-year service agreement between Runrig PLC and Big Rowland was not approved by shareholders:

    (a) the contract period is void; and
    (b) instead a six-month termination period could be inserted.

26. A copy of the proposed service contract for a director has to be available for inspection by shareholders 21 days before the EGM.

27. The requirements of section 317 of the Act can be avoided by a director by inserting a provision in the articles of association of the company or in the service contract.

Answers to Directors Statutory Provisions Self-Test Questions

1. A fiduciary duty to act bona fide in the best intersts of the company as a whole/not for a secret profit and a duty of care and skill.

2. The company as a separate entity (see *Percival v. Wright*) (and not any individual shareholder).

3. Companies Act 1985, s. 309: the members; the employees.

4. A public record of the shares held by a Director in his company *and* of loans made to/by the director (whether secured or not) by/to the company.

5. A "shadow director" is a director "in fact" even if not shown on the public record *i.e.* he directs the affairs of the company from behind the scenes (see Companies Act 1985, s. 741) (this excludes those giving professional advice).

    An "alternate director" (see table A: regulations 65–69) stands in for a director when the Director is not available.

6. Articles 73–80 table A: two ways:
    Articles 76–78 (i)   recommended by Directors or proposed by the shareholders *and*
                    (ii) approved at EGM by ordinary resolution – between 28 and 7 days before EGM, members get appointee's details *OR*
    Article 79   – additional Director; vacancy *or* addition
                    – appointment by Directors until next AGM
                    – then he vacates or is confirmed at AGM.

7. So that there is "stability of management"; planning purposes, etc.

8. Delete her name from Regester of Directors: section 288 (at the registered office and at Companies House by filing Form G288) also amend the Register of Directors' Interests (section 324) and the Register of Members (if appropriate).

9. The first £30,000 is tax free; the balance is taxable as earned income (a payment for early termination).

10. No, unless required by the articles or their service agreements or a shareholders' agreement. Such shares are referred to as "qualification shares".

11. Only with the leave of the court (see Company Directors Disqualification Act 1986, s. 11).

12. No. See Companies Act 1985, s. 283 (2).

13. True. To trigger the section 303 procedure, a member must requisition a meeting and state its objects pursuant to section 368 of the Companies Act 1985. To requisition such a meeting, the member must hold not less than 1/10th of the paid-up voting capital of the company (s. 368(2). Therefore, a member holding one share can only trigger the procedure unilaterally if that share represents at least 1/10th of the paid-up voting capital. To actually remove the director under section 303 requires an ordinary resolution (a simple majority of votes cast at the meeting; deadlock is insufficient).

14.   False. A Director can attend the EGM and he can vote on the resolution *if he is a member of the company*; in such case, he may have weighted voting rights (*Bushell v. Faith*).

15.   False – see section 303(5) of the Companies Act 1985 – compensation or damages claims are unaffected.

16.   True – see section 379(1) of the Companies Act 1985 – it reverses the usual situation of notice being *initiated* by the company. **Note:** special notice is *not* notice of a meeting; this must still be given in the usual way.

17.   True – see section 368(2) of the Companies Act 1985 – a shareholder needs 1/10th of the paid up share capital that carries voting rights.

18.   False – section 304 of the Companies Act 1985 – oral and written representations are possible.

19.   False – It depends on the book value of the company assets or, if no accounts have been prepared, on the value of called-up share capital (see s. 320).

      Note: (i)   transactions under £2000 – no approval.
                  (ii) transactions between £2000 and £100,000 – approval if the transaction is worth more than 10 per cent of either the company book value and called-up share capital.
                  (iii) transactions over £100,000—approval of shareholders in all circumstances.

20.   False—section 312 covers "*any* payment" for loss of office *i.e.* any gratuitous payment. A gratuitous payment is one over and above that specified in the director's service contract.

21.   False—section 337(3) of the Companies Act 1985—the amount is limited to a loan of £20,000 for a purpose specified in section 337(1), *i.e.* for the company's purpose or to carry out his duties. EGM approval is also required. See also section 334: "any purpose" loans of less than £5000 (in aggregate) are allowed.

22.   False—It records details of share and debenture holdings.

23.   False—

      EGM: section 368(3): *10 per cent of paid-up voting capital*
      AGM: section 376(2): *5 per cent of total voting rights* can require notice of a resolution to be circulated and that it be moved at such a meeting.

24.   True—s. 319(1)—if it cannot be terminated by notice or can only be terminated by notice in specified circumstances.

25. (a) True—s. 319(6)
    (b) "Maybe"—s. 319(6)—it depends on what is reasonable notice in
        the "circumstances", *e.g.* length of service; remuneration;
        responsibilities; balance of term to run, etc.

26. False—s. 319(5)(a) 15 days.

27. False—*disclosure* of interests is required and not to do so is an offence
    (s.317(7). "Interests" include loans; substantial property transactions;
    service contracts. See *article 85 table A* for provisions on *benefiting*
    from transactions in which directors are interested. Also, *note Article
    94*—the restrictions on *voting* on matters in which directors are
    interested.

3.6 The Board Meeting Self-Test Questions and Answers (see Chapter 13)

THE BOARD MEETING SELF-TEST QUESTIONS

1. Under table A, what powers of the company can the directors exercise
   in board meetings?

2. Under table A, what is the minimum and maximum number of directors
   and what is the quorum for business to be validly transacted at board
   meetings?

3. Under table A, how and by whom may a meeting of the board of directors be called?

4. Summarise briefly the position under the Companies Act 1985 *and* table
   A in relation to a director's obligation to disclose contracts/arrange-
   ments with his company in which he has a personal interest *and* his
   ability to vote/count in a quorum in a board meeting in respect of such
   contracts/arrangements and his ability to benefit personally from the
   same.

5. Is it possible under any circumstances for the following business to be
   transacted by the board of directors without reference to the members
   where the company has adopted table A?:
   (a) appointment of an additional director;
   (b) execution of a lease/the granting of security over it;
   (c) decision to sue a major supplier of the company in tort/contract.

6. In which of the following circumstances can a director vote and count
   in the quorum at a board meeting where the company has adopted table
   A?:
   (a) approval of his service contract;

    (b) issue of new shares to him;

    (c) sale to him of property owned by the company.

7.   How are decisions made at board meetings (*i.e.* how are votes counted)?

8.   Does the chairman of the board of directors have a casting vote at board meetings under table A?

ANSWERS TO THE BOARD MEETING SELF-TEST QUESTIONS

1.   Article 70, table A: the directors exercise all the powers of the company save those reserved to the members by the Companies Acts/the memorandum and articles of association.

2.   Article 64, table A: not less than two but no maximum.
Article 89 table A: quorum is two (unless otherwise fixed by directors).

3.   Article 88, table A: Any director may call a Meeting of the directors. No particular period of notice is required, so that a meeting will be validly held if reasonable notice is given.

Note no notice need be given to directors outside the United Kingdom.

4. *Disclosure of personal interest*
Under section 317 of the Companies Act 1985 a director who is interested, directly or indirectly, in a contract (transaction/arrangement) or proposed contract with his company *must* declare the nature of his interest at a board meeting. (This duty cannot be excluded.)

Note
1. This duty is reinforced in table A (see article 85 below relating to benefits).
2. In addition to this, directors have quite *separate* duties to disclose their interests in the company's shares/debentures (Companies Act 1985, s. 324)

Ability to vote/count in quorum at the board meeting: articles 94–96, table A:
    (a) Article 94 prohibits a director from voting on any resolution concerning a matter in which he has an interest that is material and that conflicts or *may* conflict with the company's interests (subject to exceptions).
    (b) Article 95 prevents the director counting in the quorum of a meeting in relation to such a resolution.
    (c) Article 96 allows the company to suspend the operation of the above by ordinary resolution of members.

Ability to benefit personally from such contracts/arrangements
Provided he has declared the nature and extent of his interest (section 317), Article 85, table A allows a director to be a party to an interested contract/

arrangement/transaction and to retain any benefit he derives (subject always to general common law fiduciary duties not to make a secret profit and always to act bona fide in the best interests of the company as a whole).

5. (a) Article 79: directors *can* appoint additional directors.
    (b) Article 70: directors *can* commit the company to a lease and grant a lender security over it.
    (c) Article 70: directors decide whether or not the company issues proceedings (subject to derivative actions).

6. Generally, a director cannot vote in relation to a matter in which he has a personal interest (Article 94) *but* there are exceptions. The only exception that applies here relates to the issue of new shares to him (article 94 (c)). He cannot vote in respect of his service contract or the property transaction.

7. Article 88: directors regulate their proceedings as they think fit. Questions arising at the meeting shall be decided by a majority of votes (on a show of hands).

8. Article 88: in the case of equality of votes, the chairman has a second and casting vote.

3.7 The Extraordinary General Meeting Self-Test Questions and Answers (see Chapter 13)

THE EXTRAORDINARY GENERAL MEETING: SELF-TEST QUESTIONS

1. Outline briefly the different types of shareholders' meetings.

2. Outline briefly the different types of shareholders' resolutions.

3. Outline the normal notice period required to be given by the Company to shareholders for

    (a) an AGM; and
    (b) an EGM under table A.

4. What is consent to short notice and how does it operate in respect of:

    (a) an AGM; and
    (b) an EGM?

5. Outline briefly the contents of the notice of a shareholders' meeting under table A.

6. Under table A, what is the quorum required before business can be properly transacted at a shareholders' meeting?

7. Under table A, how are decisions made at shareholders' meetings (*i.e.* how are votes counted)?

8. Have you encountered to date any situation in which a shareholder is unable to vote/count in the quorum at a shareholders' meeting?

9. In what circumstances can shareholders' meetings be dispensed with?

ANSWERS TO EGM: SELF-TEST QUESTIONS

1. (a) *Annual general meetings (AGM)*. This must be held once in every calendar year and usually must be within 15 months of the last AGM.
    (b) *Extraordinary general meetings (EGM)*. This is a meeting of the members that is not an AGM. An EGM is held as and when necessary.

2. (a) *Ordinary Resolutions*. A resolution that requires a simple majority of votes in favour (*i.e.* 50 per cent plus one of votes cast). Equality of votes is not sufficient.

Note The chairman of the meeting has a casting vote in the case of equality of votes under table A article 50, *and* that chairman will ordinarily be the chairman of the board of directors (article 42) whether or not he is a shareholder entitled to vote in his own right at the members' meeting.

All business is transacted by ordinary resolution unless a special, extraordinary or elective resolution is required by the articles or Companies Act.

    (b) *Extraordinary and Special Resolutions*. Resolutions which require a three-quarter majority (*i.e.* 75 per cent flat of votes cast). Extraordinary resolutions require 14 days' notice if considered at an EGM; special resolutions require 21 days' notice if considered at an EGM.
    (c) Elective Resolutions. A resolution that requires the *unanimous* approval of all shareholders (100 per cent in favour) and 21 days' notice is required before it can be passed. Elective resolutions can be used by private companies to simplify internal management.

3. (a) *AGM*: 21 clear days' notice is required (article 38);
    (b) *EGM*: 14 clear days' notice is required (article 38) *unless* a special resolution is to be proposed *or* an ordinary resolution appointing a director is to be proposed *or* an elective resolution is proposed, when the period is 21 clear days.

4. Section 369(3) of the Companies Act 1985 and article 38 table A provide that it is possible to have a shorter notice period than normally required (see answer 3 above) if:

    (a) in the case of an *AGM*; *all* members entitled to attend and vote agree;

(b) in the case of an *EGM*; a majority *in number* (*e.g.*, three members out of five but *not* two members out of five) owning together at least 95 per cent of voting shares agree.

This operates to reduce the notice required to potentially zero days provided that no other procedural requirement of the Companies Act or articles of association insists that a certain notice period is required.

5. (a) date, time, place of meeting;
    (b) general nature of business to be transacted;
    (c) special/elective/extraordinary resolutions must be set out verbatim;
    (d) member entitled to appoint proxy who need not be a member to attend and vote.

Note Err on the side of caution; include as much as possible (article 38, table 4 Companies Act 1985, s. 372)

6. Article 40: two members (or their proxies) entitled to vote constitutes a quorum.

7. Article 46: first, a resolution put to the vote is decided on a show of hands (*i.e.* number of shares held are *not* counted and each member has one vote (Article 54)). However, before this vote or once the result is known, a *poll* can be demanded (see article 46 for by whom); on a poll every member shall have one vote for every share of which he is the holder (article 54). A proxy *cannot* vote on a show of hands but only on a poll (a proxy has the same rights to call for a poll as does a member).

Note Remember the chairman's casting vote in the case of an equality of votes on a show of hands/poll (article 50, table A).

8. You may *not* have encountered any situation in which a member *cannot* vote/count in the quorum at a shareholders' meeting. Remember, it is *directors* at board meetings who are subject to section 317 of the Companies Act 1985 and, perhaps, articles 94–96 table A regarding disclosure of interests and restrictions on voting/counting in the quorum. Shareholders own the company and can vote for quite selfish interests (subject to threat of minority or derivative action).

9. Instead of holding meetings, members can pass written resolutions under section 381A of the Companies Act 1985. To be valid, they must be signed by *all* members entitled to attend/vote at a meeting. The written resolution can consist of one or several documents. The written resolution procedure *cannot* be used to remove a director from office under *section 303 of the Act* nor to remove an auditor under section 391. In practice, this is the most common way of transacting business.

Note Directors can pass written resolutions instead of holding board meetings under article 93, table A.

3.8 Basic Company Finance Self-Test Questions and Answers (see Chapter 14)

BASIC COMPANY FINANCE SELF-TEST QUESTIONS

1. Outline briefly the *two* major sources of finance available to a private limited company.

2. Explain what is meant by the nominal or par value of shares.

3. Explain what is meant by the market value of shares.

4. What are preference shares?

5. Why are preference shares sometimes said to blur the distinction between "equity" and "debt"?

6. Outline briefly the statutory framework to consider when a private limited company wishes to raise money through the issue of shares.

7. Who exercises the company's power to borrow?

8. Outline the different types of loans that are available to private limited companies.

9. Outline briefly the requirements of the Companies Act 1985 in respect of the registration of charges over company property. What is the effect of no or late registration?

10. What remedy is most likely to be taken by a debenture holder when a company defaults on loan repayments due to it?

11. What is meant by "financial assistance"? Give two examples.

12. Under what circumstances can a private limited company give "financial assistance"?

13. How can a private limited company finance a buy-back of its shares?

ANSWERS TO BASIC COMPANY FINANCE SELF-TEST QUESTIONS

1. A company can raise money either in the form of an investment by shareholders or in the form of loans.

    Investment by shareholders is referred to as "equity" or "risk capital" (*e.g.* ordinary shares); the shareholders own the company and vote at meetings of the members in respect of their shareholdings.

    Loans (by banks and other financial institutions and indeed private individuals) are referred to as "debt"; the benefit of which is held by creditors of the company; the creditor has no share in the ownership of the company but is merely owed money by it. The debt can be evidenced in a loan instrument (or loan note or debenture) and often security over the assets of the company is taken by the lender in the form of a variety of charges or mortgages. The loan agreement is a contract like any other agreement.

2. This is the value of the shares set out in the capital clause of the memorandum; it is simply a classification and says very little about the true value of the company's shares.

3. This is the true value of the shares, which fluctuates according to the success of the company. Shares may even be worth less than the par value but companies cannot issue new shares at a discount to par value (Companies Act 1985, s. 100).

4. Preference shares are shares which carry a fixed rate dividend; such dividends to be paid out in priority to anything paid out to ordinary shareholders. Usually, this situation is compensated for by restricting the right of preference shareholders to vote (*i.e.* preference shares carry no entitlement to vote save in respect of matters affecting preference shareholders as a class of members). The dividend that the holder of a preference share is entitled to may be a fixed sum/at a fixed rate each year and if no profits are available for distribution in any given year the entitlement may be carried forward for payment when profits become available (in this latter situation, preference shares are expressed to be "cumulative").

5. Preference shares often carry an entitlement to a fixed income (*i.e.* like interest under a loan agreement); they usually carry no entitlement to vote (*i.e.* like debenture/loan stock). Capital is returned to preference shareholders in priority to ordinary shareholders in the event of an insolvent liquidation (*i.e.* like debt, although preference shareholders rank *after* secured and unsecured creditors in an insolvency).

6. Companies Act 1985, s. 121 Increase in authorised share capital (if required).
   Companies Act 1985, s. 80 Power of directors to allot relevant securities.
   Companies Act 1985, s. 89 Pre-emption rights exist on the issue of equity securities wholly for cash.

7. Usually, the directors (see article 70, table A, if adopted); some articles of association impose restrictions on the exercise of the power to borrow.

8. *Secured Loans.* A loan agreement/loan note/loan stock instrument/ debenture document will evidence indebtedness and create security in

the form of fixed and/or floating charges over the assets of the company (the creditor will be able to enforce such security by appointing a receiver/administrative receiver to sell company assets or the company business as a going concern in accordance with the terms of the debenture contract if the company defaults in repayment).

Unsecured Loans. Contractual debts with no security for the creditor (*i.e.* the creditor is said to be an unsecured creditor).

Loans with quasi-security. E.g. the contractual debt is guaranteed by company directors.

Note Banks often require security *and* personal guarantees.

9.   Where a company creates a charge (of the type listed in the Companies Act 1985, s. 396) it must deliver the document creating the charge *and* prescribed particulars (currently form 395) to the registrar of companies within 21 days.

Note Charges over land may also be subject to additional registration.

If particulars are *not* registered, the company and every officer is liable to a fine and the charge created is void against an administrator or liquidator of the company appointed after its creation. The charge is also void against any person who acquires an interest in/right over the property subject to the charge (*e.g* a subsequent chargee).

The Companies Act does contain a procedure for late registration in certain circumstances (see Companies Act 1985, s. 404).

10.   The debenture is likely to contain an express power of sale and a power to appoint a receiver/administrative receiver. The receiver is appointed to realise the security of the debenture holder (he will sell company assets to enforce the security).

11.   *Section 151(1) of the Companies Act 1985* makes financial assistance, direct or indirect, by a company for the acquisition of its own shares prima facie unlawful (see also Companies Act 1985, s. 151(2)).

Financial assistance can be given by a company in a number of ways (see Companies Act 1985, s. 152), *e.g.*:

Gift. ABC Ltd makes a gift of £500 to X who uses the money to buy shares in ABC Ltd.

Loan. ABC Ltd. lends X £500 who uses the money to buy shares in ABC Ltd. (or more commonly, X borrows £500 from a bank, ABC Ltd. discharges the loan on X's behalf and X uses the advance to buy shares in ABC Ltd.).

12.   There are two exceptions to the general prohibition on the giving of financial assistance:

(a) *Companies Act 1985, s. 153(1). All* companies can make use of the principal and incidental purpose exceptions. This exception should be treated cautiously given uncertain judicial pronouncement (*Brady* v. *Brady* [1989] A.C. 785 H.L.).

(b) *Companies Act 1985, s. 155. This allows private* companies to give all kinds of financial assistance provided a strict procedure is adhered to (see *section 155* generally) *and* net assets are not reduced (or assistance is given out of profits available for dividend).

13. Generally, the company must pay for the shares to be bought back out of profits available for distribution *or* the proceeds of a fresh issue of shares but private companies have the power to make the payment out of capital provided it is authorised by its articles (see wording of article 35 of table A).

Strict procedures must be followed by companies buying back shares.

3.9 Sale of a Private Limited Company Self-Test Questions and Answers (see Chapter 17)

1. Explain the difference between a share sale agreement and an asset sale agreement.

2. Explain what is meant by deferred consideration.

3. What is a warranty?

4. What are the functions of warranties?

5. What are the usual remedies available to a purchaser for breach of warranty?

6. What is the function of the disclosure letter?

7. What is a conditional contract in the context of share sale agreements?

8. Give two examples of conditions often found in share sale agreements.

ANSWERS TO SALE OF A PRIVATE LIMITED COMPANY SELF-TEST QUESTIONS

1. A share sale agreement is a contract for the sale or transfer of the entire issued share capital of the company and is often referred to as a company sale/disposal. The contract is between selling and buying shareholders. The target company remains a distinct legal entity separate from its members but control over its affairs has passed from selling shareholders (or vendors) to purchasing shareholders (or purchasers).

An asset sale agreement is a contract for the sale of specific assets owned by a company or the entire business of a company as a going concern. Here, control of the company owning the assets in question remains in the hands of the original shareholders; the company as vendor simply sells or transfers assets (its business to purchasers).

2. In a share sale agreement, not all of the consideration to be paid by a purchaser to selling shareholders in return for the transfer of the shares may be paid at the signing of the agreement or the completion of the stock transfer forms. Instead, payment of some of the consideration may be delayed until some time in the future pending, for example, the future profit performance of the target company or the expiration of the time period during which warranty claims can be brought by the purchaser. Consideration can be adjusted if, for example, profits are not as expected by both parties or a warranty claim surfaces.

3. Warranties are found in the share sale agreement. They are a series of statements about the financial and commercial status of the target company made by the vendors.

4. Warranties serve two functions:

   (a) They elicit information about the target company and allow the purchaser to plan its future obligations.

   (b) They allocate risk for the pre-completion state of the target company to the vendors. Normally, *caveat emptor* applies to a share sale agreement and the purchaser takes the target company as he finds it. The warranties alter this situation and give the purchaser a right of legal action against the vendors if the target company is not as represented to them.

   The remedies available to a purchaser for breach of warranty are:

5. (a) A claim for loss of bargain as a result of breach of contractual term (the warranties are terms of the contract). Damages will amount to the difference between the market value of the shares and their value as they would have been if the warranty had been true (*i.e.* to put the purchaser in to the position he would have been in if the contract had been properly performed).

   (b) A claim in misrepresentation; namely, the warranty is a false statement of fact that induced the contract. Damages sought under Section 2(1) of the Misrepresentation Act 1967 are assessed in the tort of deceit with, arguably, all the benefits of a fraud action but note that in tort damages will amount to the difference between the market value of the shares and the price paid (*i.e.* to put the purchaser in to the position he would have been in if the tort had not been committed).

   (c) The contract itself may provide for indemnity damages (*i.e.* the vendors will pay £1 for £1 the amount necessary to put the company into the position which would have existed if the warranties had been true). Vendors resist this strongly.

Note Rescission is probably *not* feasible after transfer of the shares although it is possible in a conditional agreement between signing and completion of the share transfers.

6. The disclosure letter is a list of qualifications to the warranties provided by the vendors. Here, the vendors are given the opportunity to restrict the effectiveness of the warranties in the share sale agreement. The disclosures affect risk allocation and are the source of much negotiation. Vendors will want to disclose as much information as possible in order not to be accountable for anything relating to it; purchasers will want to restrict disclosed materials. Alternatively, purchasers may accept disclosures and seek a reduction in purchaser price or if what is revealed is too terrible to contemplate, they may pull out of the deal and not proceed to signing and completion.

7. A conditional contract is one where there is a gap between the signing of the agreement for the transfer of the shares and legal completion of the share transfers (*i.e.* by execution of stock transfer forms). The gap exists to allow any condition to be fulfilled prior to completion.

8. Two examples of conditions often found in share sale agreements:

   (a) If the target company is subject to the rules of a regulatory body (*e.g.* a Lloyds' Broking firm in subject to Lloyds' rules) then it may be a condition that the consent of the regulatory body to the transfer of the shares is obtained prior to completion.
   (b) The share transfers may require the approval of the shaerholders of the purchaser (*e.g.* Companies Act 1985, s. 320: vendor of shares in target company is a director of the purchasing company and so the transaction constitutes a transaction with a director of requisite value). In this case, the agreement is conditional on approval being obtained.

Appendix 4 Tax and Insolvency

4.1 Taxation Terms, Definitions and Legislation

LEGISLATION TO CONSIDER

Inheritance Tax Act 1984
Income and Corporation Taxes Act 1988
Capital Allowances Act 1990
Taxation of Chargeable Gains Act 1992
Finance Act 1994

DEFINITIONS TO CONSIDER WITH TAXATION

Advance corporation tax (ACT)	is a prepayment of mainstream corporation tax (MCT) made by a company when it pays dividends to shareholders. In that instance the company pays the dividend to the shareholder and an amount of tax (ACT) to the revenue as part of an early payment of MCT.
Associate	means a relative, trustee, etc., of a "participator" as defined in section 417(2) of the Income and Corporation Taxes Act 1988. See also "associated company" defined in section 416.
Benefit in kind	a benefit in kind is a non-cash emolument paid as part of the consideration in a service agreement. For example, a company director may receive the use of a car in addition to a salary component. The car represents a benefit in kind, the salary is a cash benefit. Benefits in kind are also referred to as fringe benefits or non-cash perquisites.
Capital allowances	"writing off" for tax purposes the value of a capital asset so as to reduce taxable income. For example, buildings and plant and machinery may be written down or depreciated at rates set by the Taxation of Capital Gains Act 1988.
Capital gain	the increase in value of a chargeable asset as defined by the Taxation of Capital Gains Act 1988 over and above the increase for the period in question of the inflation index.
Capital Gains Tax (CGT)	the tax payable as a result of a capital gain having been made.

396

Cash benefit	see ''benefit in kind''.
Close company	a company defined by section 414(1) of the Income and Corporation Taxes Act 1988 where there is a degree of overlap between those people who own the company (the shareholders) and those people who manage it (the directors). It is a company under the control of five or fewer ''participators,'' or of participators who are directors (see participators).
Corporation tax	see ''mainstream corporation tax''.
Deductible expenses	those expenses that may, in accordance with tax legislation be used to reduce income profits and therefore, the taxation liability (see expenses).
Direct tax	paid directly by the taxpayer.
Dividend	an amount of profit made by the company payable in respect of certain of its shares to shareholders after recommendation by the directors and approval by the members.
Donee	The recipient of a gift or undervalue transaction (see donor).
Donor	the person or entity making a gift or giving an asset away for less than its market value, *i.e.* where there is a ''gratuitous intent''; otherwise known as an ''undervalue transaction''.
Election	an election is a choice offered to either the taxpayer (and sometimes the Revenue) under various areas of the tax legislation; to enable more efficient tax planning. Examples of elections are as follows:

    (a) with a gift or undervalue transaction the donor and donee can elect to ''hold-over'' (delay) any capital gain payment.

    (b) the ''old'' partnership rules allowed the taxpayer to make an ''actual income basis'' election. (See Chapter 6.)

    (c) the ''old'' partnership rules allowed the Revenue to make a similar election in respect of the closing years of a business (see Chapter 6).

Emoluments	see perquisites.
Expenses	those items incurred in making income profits. See deductible expenses.
Franked dividend	a dividend on which tax (ACT) has already been paid by the company to the Revenue allowing the taxpayer a tax credit, with the pos-

sibility, depending on the taxpayer's marginal rate, of the taxpayer paying no further tax.

Fringe benefit   see benefit in kind.

Golden handshake   is a bonus paid to an employee upon that employee leaving the business, *i.e.* an amount over and above contractual entitlements.

Gratuitous Intent   see donor.

Indirect tax   borne by the taxpayer but paid by a third party to the Revenue, *e.g.* sales tax.

Income profits   receipts that fall under one or other of the various schedules. As such, income is subject to the payment of income tax (in the case of an office, a partner or sole trader) or corporation tax (in the case of a company).

Interest   for tax purposes, the cost of borrowing, *e.g.* the interest rate on a mortgage debenture is a sum calculated against the capital amount borrowed and is payable borrower (mortgagor) to the lender (mortgagee) at periodic intervals (usually monthly) in accordance with the terms of the mortgage debenture.

Losses   amounts that may be used to reduce income profits under the schedules.

Mainstream   corporation tax (MCT) the tax paid by a company on its income profits, *i.e.* equivalent to income tax payable by an individual taxpayer.

Marginal rate   a taxpayer's top rate of income tax.

Non-cash benefit   see benefit in kind.

Offices   includes employees, company directors and the like (see Income and Corporation Taxes Act 1988, s. 19). It is not statutorily defined but has been held by case law to refer to a "subsisting, permanent, substantive position filled in succession by successive holders."

Participator   is defined in section 417(1) of the Income and Corporation Taxes Act 1988 as a person having a share or interest in the capital or income of the "close" company and includes someone entitled to acquire share capital or voting rights in the company and lenders (other than banks lending to the company in the normal course of its business).

Perquisites   refers to all benefits, whether cash or non-cash paid pursuant to a service agreement.

Personal allowances   those tax-free portions of a person's income profits.

Qualifying distribution   a term of some technicality defined for the purposes of the Income and Corporation Taxes Act 1988 to refer to amounts that the taxpayer is

	bound to pay to a third party and are, therefore, excluded from forming part of the income profits for the purpose of the Schedules.
Relief	refers to concessions to the full rigour of the rules concerning the payment of income tax and CGT.

For example:

(a) reliefs, such as the personal relief, reduce the taxpayer's taxable income profits;

(b) hold-over relief and roll-over relief *delay* the payment of CGT.

(c) retirement relief *reduces* rather than delays the payment of CGT.

(d) incorporation relief *reduces* the payment of CGT

Schedules	refers to the various income tax schedules under which income profits are allocated under the Income and Corporation Taxes Act 1988.
Small companies rate	the rate of MCT that applies to those companies whose profits fall below a specified amount pursuant to section 13 of the Income and Corporation Taxes Act 1988.
Standard rate	the MCT rate that applies in a particular year.
Tapering relief	a form of tax relief that applies to that section of profits that falls between the rate amount of small and standard companies.
Tax credit	no further tax may be payable by the taxpayer as tax has already been paid and credited as paid. If for example, a 40 per cent taxpayer has a tax credit of 25 per cent he will have a further 15 per cent tax to pay. If the taxpayer is a 25 per cent taxpayer he will have no further tax to pay.

4.2 Insolvency Terms, Definitions and Legislation

LEGISLATION TO CONSIDER

Bankruptcy Act 1914
Companies Act 1985
Insolvency Act 1986

DEFINITIONS TO CONSIDER WITH INSOLVENCY

Administration order	an administration order is an order made by a

court placing a company that if, or is likely to become, insolvent under the control of an administrator, following the presentation of a petition by the company, its directors or a creditor of the company. The aim of the order is to seek to preserve the company's business as going concern; to allow a reorganisation of the company, or to ensure the most advantageous realisation of its assets whilst protecting it from further court action by its creditors.

Administrative receiver   an administrative receiver is the duly qualified insolvency practitioner appointed by a secured creditor holding a registered charge over the whole (or substantially the whole) of a company's assets, in order to recover the money due to the secured creditor. Amongst other things he can carry on the company's business and sell the business and other assets secured by the charge.

Administrator   an administrator is the duly qualified insolvency practitioner appointed by the court to manage a company that is subject to an administration order to achieve the purposes set out in the order.

Bankrupt   a bankrupt is an individual against whom a court has made a bankruptcy order as the result of the bankrupt failing to pay a statutory demand or to satisfy execution of a court judgment. On the making of the order, the bankrupt's property vests by operation of law in the trustee in bankruptcy.

Bankruptcy   bankruptcy is the process by which the trustee in bankruptcy deals with the estate of a bankrupt.

Compulsory liquidation   a compulsory liquidation of a company is a liquidation initiated by court order. This is usually as a result of a petition presented to the court by a creditor and is the only method by which a creditor can bring about a liquidation of its debtor company.

Creditor's committee   a creditors' committee is formed to represent the interests of all creditors in supervising the activities of an administrator or trustee in bankruptcy, or receiving reports from an administrative receiver.

Creditors' voluntary liquidation   a creditors' voluntary liquidation relates to an insolvent company. It is commenced by resolution of the shareholders, but is under the effective control of creditors, who can choose the liquidator.

Demand

a statutory demand is a formal demand issued by a creditor, requiring the debtor to pay a debt within three weeks. Failure to pay is evidence of insolvency and is one of the grounds upon which a creditor may present a petition to the court of the compulsory liquidation on bankruptcy of the debtor.

Extortionate credit transaction

an extortionate credit transaction is a transaction by which credit is provided on terms that, on an objective basis, are exorbitant or grossly unfair compared with the risk accepted by the creditor. Such a transaction may be challenged by an administrator, a liquidator or a trustee in bankruptcy.

Fixed assets

assets intended for continuing use by the business typically land, fixed plant, machinery, buildings.

Fixed charge

A fixed charge is a form of security granted over specific assets typically "fixed assets" preventing the debtor dealing with those assets without the consent of the secured creditor. It gives the secured creditor a first claim on the proceeds of sale and the creditor can usually appoint a receiver to realise the assets in the event of default.

Fixed and floating charge

a combination of a fixed and floating charge over substantially the whole of the assets of a compound, typically providing for the appointment of an administrative receiver.

Floating charge

a floating charge is a form of security granted to a creditor over general assets or a company that which may change from time to time in the normal course of business (*e.g.* stock). The company can continue to use the assets in its business until an event of default occurs and the charge crystallises. If this happens, the secured creditor can realise the assets to recover his debt, usually be appointing an administrative receiver and obtain the net proceeds of sale, subject to the prior claims of the preferential creditors.

Fraudulent trading

fraudulent trading (Insolvency Act 1986, s. 203) applies to a company in liquidation where the company had carried on business with intent to defraud creditors, or for any fraudulent purpose. It is a criminal offence and those

	involved can be made personally liable for the the company's liabilities.
Insolvency	insolvency refers to the financial problems encountered by companies from time to time when assets are outweighed by liabilities, *i.e.* on a balance sheet test, the company is technically not in a position to carry on business. Winding up may be either on an insolvent basis or a solvent basis (where the shareholders choose to end the company's activities).
Insolvency practitioner	the Insolvency rules 1986 (as amended) provide the detailed working procedures for the provisions of the Insolvency Act 1986.
Insolvent	insolvent, in the case of both a company and an individual, may be defined as the inability to meet liabilities as they fall due. A company may also be described as insolvent if the value of its assets is less than the amount of its liabilities.
Insolvent liquidation	a company goes into insolvent liquidation if its goes into liquidation at a time when its assets are insufficient for the payment of its debts and other liabilities and the expenses of liquidation, etc.
Interim order	an individual who intends to propose voluntary arrangement to his creditors may apply to the court for an interim order that, if granted, precludes bankruptcy and other legal proceedings whilst the order is in force, etc.
Lien	a lien is right of possession over goods or property belonging to another, with a right to retain possession until debts due to the possessor are paid.
Liquidation	a liquidation is the process of realising a company's assets and distributing the proceeds to satisfy its liabilities and to repay its shareholders. The term "winding up" is also used.
Liquidation committee	a liquidation committee is formed to represent the interests of all creditors in order to supervise the activities of a liquidator in a compulsory or creditors' voluntary liquidation.
Liquidator	a liquidator is the duly qualified insolvency practitioner responsible for dealing with the liquidation of a company.
Members' voluntary liquidation	a member's voluntary liquidation relates to a company that is able to settle all its debts in full within a period of 12 months of being placed into liquidation.
Nominee	a nominee is the insolvency practitioner who

	acts in the preliminary stages of a voluntary arrangement and considers whether proposals should be put to creditors.
Official receiver	an official receiver is a civil servant who is an officer of the court. He deals with the administration of compulsory liquidations and bankruptcies, either as liquidator or trustee in bankruptcy, or overseeing an insolvency practitioner acting as such. There is an official receiver attached to each court that deals with insolvency matters.
Onerous property	the term "onerous property" in the context of a liquidation or bankruptcy, applies to unprofitable contracts and to property that is unsaleable or not easily saleable or that might give rise to a continuing bankruptcy. Such property can be disclaimed by a liquidator or a trustee in bankruptcy.
Preference	preference (Insolvency Act 1986, s. 239) is any transaction that has the effect of putting a creditor of a company (or an individual) in a better position than would have been the case in the event of a subsequent liquidation or bankruptcy and where there was a desire to produce this effect. In certain circumstances a preference can be challenged by an administrator, a liquidator or a trustee in bankruptcy.
Preferential creditors	preferential creditors must be paid in priority to the holders of floating charges and in priority to unsecured creditors. These include PAYE, NIC, VAT and employees' remuneration up to certain limits.
Proof of debt	a proof of debt (Insolvency Rules 1986, rule 6.37) is the document by which a creditor seeks to establish its claim against a debtor in a liquidation or bankruptcy.
Provisional liquidator	a provisional liquidator is an insolvency practitioner appointed by the court to protect the assets of a company after a winding-up petition has been presented, but before a liquidator is appointed.
Proxy	a proxy is an authority given by a creditor to a person to attend a meeting and speak and vote as that creditor's representative.
Receiver	a receiver is the person appointed by a secured creditor holding a fixed charge over specific assets of a company in order to take control of those assets for the benefit of the secured creditor. The term can also be used generally to

	describe any person appointed by a secured creditor (see also Administrative receiver).
Receivership	receivership is the general term applied when an administrative receiver or a receiver is appointed.
Recognised professional bodies	recognised professional bodies are those approved by the Secretary of State as being able to authorise their members to act as insolvency practitioners.
Retention of title clause (Romalpa clause)	a clause in a sale agreement in which the vendor retains ownership in the goods until they are completely paid for even if the possession of the goods rests with the purchaser.
Secured creditor	a secured creditor is a creditor that holds a charge (sometimes also referred to as a mortgage or a debenture) granted by a debtor over the debtor's assets. As a result, the creditor has a right of priority for the repayment of its debt although the exact priority depends on the type of charge. (See Fixed charge and Floating charge.)
Shadow director	a shadow director (Companies Act 1985, s. 741) is a person who is not formally appointed as a director but in accordance with those directions or instructions the directors of a company are accustomed to act. However, a person is not a shadow director merely because the directors act on advice given by him in a professional capacity.
Special manager	a special manager is a person appointed by the court in compulsory liquidation to assist the liquidator or provisional liquidator in managing the company's business. A special manager may also be appointed in a bankruptcy.
Statutory demand	a statutory demand is a formal demand issued by a creditor requiring the debtor to pay a debt within three weeks. Failure to pay is evidence of insolvency and is one of the grounds upon which a creditor may present a petition to the court of the compulsory liquidation or bankruptcy of the debtor.
Supervisor	a supervisor is the insolvency practitioner appointed by creditor to supervise the implementation of an approved voluntary arrangement.
Transaction at an undervalue	a transaction at an undervalue (Insolvency Act 1986, s. 238) can describe either a gift or a transaction in which the consideration received is significantly less than that given. In certain

circumstances, such a transaction can be challenged by an administrator, a liquidator or a trustee in bankruptcy.

Trustee in bankruptcy a trustee in bankruptcy is the person who administers and realises the assets of a bankrupt and distributes the proceeds for the benefit of the bankrupt's creditors.

Unsecured creditor an unsecured creditor is a creditor whose claim has no secured prior right, whether in relation to a company in liquidation, or a bankruptcy.

Voluntary arrangement company a voluntary arrangement for a company is a procedure whereby a scheme of arrangement usually involving delayed or reduced payments of debt is put forward to creditors and shareholders. There is a limited involvement by the court and the scheme is under the control of a supervisor.

Voluntary arrangement individual (IVA) a voluntary arrangement for an individual is a procedure whereby a scheme of arrangement, usually involving delayed or reduced payments of debts, is put forward to creditors. Such a scheme requires the approval of the court and is under the control of a supervisor.

Voluntary liquidation see Creditor's voluntary liquidation and Member's voluntary liquidation.

Winding up see liquidation.

Winding-up petition a winding-up petition is a petition presented to the court seeking an order that a company be put into compulsory liquidation.

Wrongful trading applies where a director of a company in liquidation allowed the company to continue trading in circumstances where he should have concluded that there was no reasonable prospect that the company would avoid going into insolvent liquidation. Any director involved may be made liable to make a contribution from his personal assets to the company's assets.

4.3 Tax Self-Test Questions and Answers

TAX SELF-TEST QUESTIONS

1. What forms on tax relief *delay* the payment of capital gains tax?

2. What forms of tax relief *reduce* the amount of capital gains tax to be paid?

3. What is the purpose of the income schedules?

4. When will provision by the employer for the living accommodation of the employee not be treated as a taxable emolument in the hands of the employee?

5. What is an emolument?

6. When will "living accommodation" not be treated as a taxable emolument?

7. When Wendy retired form Delta Electronics Ltd, she received a termination payment of £100,000. How is it taxed?

8. What is Advance Corporation Tax and what purpose does it serve?

9. What is a close company?

10. What is meant by the expression "gratuitous intent"?

ANSWERS TO TAX SELF-TEST QUESTIONS

1. Rollover relief (replacement of business assets)
   Holdover relief (gift or under value sale relief).

2. Retirement relief and Indexation allowance.

3. The means by which the various sources of income are categorised under the Income and Corporation Taxes Act 1988.

4. It is the basis by which so-called old partnership businesses, *i.e.* those established prior to April 6, 1994, are assessed to tax. The tax payable is based on the income that is made in the accounting period which ends in the previous tax year.

5. A cash or non-cash receipt received by an employee, which is generally subject to tax.

6. When the tax payer can demonstrate to the Revenue that it is necessary for his safety or the proper performance of his duties.

7. The first £30,000 is tax free; the balance is taxed at Wendy's marginal rate.

8. A prepayment of Mainstream Corporation Tax; payable by a company to the Revenue in respect of "qualifying distributions", *e.g.* when the company pays dividends.

9. A "close" company is defined for tax purposes as one where there are overlaps between management (directors) and owners (shareholders). It

is a company where there are five or fewer participators or of participators who are directors. See Income and Corporation Taxes Act 1988, s. 414.

10. A transaction at less than market value, *i.e.* there is not full consideration paid.

4.4 Personal Insolvency Self-Test Questions and Answers

INSOLVENCY SELF-TEST QUESTIONS

Reference should be made to the Insolvency Act 1986.

1. Can Bob, the subject of an IVA, act as a Director?

2. What is a statutory demand?

3. What happens to a bankrupt's property on the making of a bankruptcy order?

4. What is "onerous property"?

5. Can a trustee in bankruptcy sell the bankrupt's family home?

6. What is a preference?

7. Bob gives his home to his brother Simon in 1990. Bob is made bankrupt in 1994. Could the trustee in bankruptcy set aside such a transaction?

8. What is the significance of a "Romalpa Clause" for a vendor?

9. What are preferred debts?

10. Ian who has been bankrupted in 1980 is bankrupted again in 1994. How long will the 1994 bankruptcy last?

ANSWERS TO PERSONAL INSOLVENCY SELF-TEST QUESTIONS

1. Yes, an IVA does not bar Bob from directorship unlike a formal bankruptcy order.

2. A written demand that complies with the Insolvency Act 1986 and rules served on a debtor by a creditor with the view of seeking a bankruptcy order if it is not paid within 21 days.

3. It vests by operation of law in the trustee in bankruptcy.

4. Property that is literally "more trouble than it is worth", *i.e.* because of excessive maintenance costs, etc., it is disclaimed by the trustee in bankruptcy and thereafter, does not form part of a bankrupt's property (see section 315 of the Insolvency Act 1986).

5. He must first get the court's approval if there is a spouse or children in residence (at least in the first 12 months of bankruptcy) because such rights are regarded as a charge on the property (see section 336 of the Insolvency Act 1986).

6. A "preference" refers to a transaction made by a bankrupt which puts the interests of one creditor ahead of another creditor in contravention of the order of creditors determined by the Insolvency Act 1986 (see s. 340). The trustee in bankruptcy can seek to set aside such transactions.

7. Simon is an "associate" of Bob pursuant to section 435(2) of the Insolvency Act 1986, which includes a "relative". As the transaction is at an under value, the Trustee in Bankruptcy can seek to set it aside if made not more than two years before the bankruptcy, *i.e.* 1992. It appears therefore that the trustee could not set it aside as an under value transaction. If the transaction were fraudulent and made within five years of the bankruptcy order, Bob would commit an offence under section 357 of the Insolvency Act 1986. If it is a transaction defrauding creditors pursuant to section 423 of the Insolvency Act 1986, it could be set aside at any time later.

8. The vendor retained ownership of goods until the buyer completes payment, even though the buyer has possession of the goods.

9. Debts covered by statute payable on a bankruptcy or winding-up, *e.g.* tax, VAT, wages (see section 386 of the Insolvency Act 1986).

10. Section 279(1)(a) of the Insolvency Act 1986 provides that an individual adjudged bankrupt at any time in the previous 15 years requires a court order under s. 279(3) before being discharged from the bankruptcy order.

4.5 Corporate Insolvency Self-Test Questions and Answers (see Chapter 15)

Corporate Insolvency Self-Test Questions

1. In what circumstances is a company said to be "technically insolvent"?

2. Briefly describe an "administration."

3. What are the consequences of the grant of an administration order?

4.   Briefly describe an "administrative receivership."

5.   What is the relationship between an administration *and* an administrative receivership?

6.   Briefly outline the different types of liquidation.

7.   What is the function of an administrator?

8.   What is the function of an administrative receiver?

9.   What is the function of a liquidator?

10.   Briefly outline the constituent elements of "wrongful trading."

11.   Briefly outline the constituent elements of a preference.

ANSWERS TO CORPORATE INSOLVENCY: QUESTIONS

1.   A private limited company is said to be technically insolvent when it is unable to pay its debts in accordance with sections 122 and 123 of the Insolvency Act 1986.
    Section 123 states that a company is unable to pay its debts as they fall due if either:

   (a) a creditor owed more than £750 has served a statutory demand at the company's registered office and the debt has not been paid for three weeks thereafter; or
   (b) execution of a judgment or other court order is returned unsatisfied.

   Note (a) & (b) are the so called "cash flow" tests of solvency.
   or
   (c) it is proved that the value of the company's assets is less than the amount of its liabilities, taking into account its contingent and prospective liabilities.

   Note (c) is the so called "balance sheet" test of solvency.

2.   Administration is an alternative to winding up (or liquidation). It is designed with the aim of saving all or part of the business concerned or obtaining more for the business (*i.e.* by selling it as a going concern) than what could be obtained by a liquidator who sells off assets individually and distributes the proceeds to those entitled in accordance with the Insolvency Act 1986.
    An administration order will only be granted by the court if the company is technically insolvent (*i.e.* unable to pay its debts) *and* it is likely to achieve one or more of three things (survival of company, approval of a voluntary arrangement, a more advantageous realisation of company assets than on liquidation).

3.   The granting of an administration order results in a *moratorium*

(a) No creditor can take any steps to enforce any security over company property.

Note Between presentation of the petition and grant of the order, a floating-charge holder may appoint an administrative receiver and effectively block the grant of the order.

(b) No creditor can repossess goods in the company's possession under a hire-purchase agreement, a conditional sale agreement, a chattel leasing agreement or a retention of title agreement.

(c) No creditor can commence or continue legal proceedings against the company.

(d) No creditor can levy distress on company property.

4.   A creditor who takes security over a company's assets in the form of a *floating charge* is entitled to appoint an administrative receiver over the whole of the company's property in accordance with the contractual terms of the loan agreement/debenture document (usually on the occurrence of an event of default; namely, non-payment of monies due when demanded). Such a creditor is usually a bank.

Once appointed the administrative receiver effectively replaces the directors in the management of the company. He is given wide powers (see Schedule 1 of the Insolvency Act 1986 and the actual loan agreement itself) *and* is subject to statutory duties for the benefit of all creditors/shareholders.

The primary aim of the administrative receiver is to realise the security of the debenture holder who appointed him (*i.e.* the bank). He may well attempt to sell the business of the company as a going concern in order to maximise the return to his appointee. Before accounting to the Bank, he must pay certain preferential creditor (*i.e.* tax authorities/employees) and he will also discharge his fee and costs from the amount realised.

Note The bank may very well also have a fixed charge over specific assets capable of sustaining a legal charge or mortgage, such as freehold land and premises. The holder of a fixed charge is entitled to appoint a *receiver* over the specific assets concerned when a power of sale arises and such charge holder is entitled to the proceeds realised from the sale of such specific assets in priority to *everyone*.

5.   The two are mutually exclusive. When a petition for an administration order is presented, notice must be given to any person who has appointed or is entitled to appoint an administrative receiver (*i.e.* a floating-charge holder). An administration order *cannot* be made if, by the time of the hearing, an administrative receiver has been appointed.

Once an administration order has been made, no appointment of an administrative receiver is possible.

In effect, the bank with a floating charge has a right to veto an administration.

6. *Compulsory winding-up.* This is initiated by a petition to the court; usually by an unsecured creditor on the ground that the company is unable to pay its debts (see Insolvency Act 1986, ss. 122, 123).

Voluntary winding-up

(a) *Members' voluntary winding-up.* The *members* pass a special resolution to wind up the company and the directors (or a majority thereof) make a statutory declaration to the effect that they are of the opinion that the company will be able to pay its debts in full within 12 months of the commencement of the winding up.

Note The company must be solvent; this is *not* an insolvency procedure.

(b) *Creditors' voluntary winding-up.* The *members* pass an extraordinary resolution to the effect that the company should be wound up as it cannot continue in business because of its debts (*i.e.* it is insolvent). A meeting of creditors is called and they may nominate a liquidator to carry out the liquidation.

7. An administrator is appointed to run the company and its business with a view to saving the viable parts of the business or with a view to obtaining approval for a voluntary scheme or with a view to advantageous realisation (selling) of assets. He must be an insolvency practitioner. He has wide ranging powers under section 14 of the Insolvency Act 1986 and Schedule 1 to the Insolvency Act 1986.

8. An administrative receiver is appointed by the holder of a floating charge to realise the security of his appointee (*i.e.* to sell the property that is the subject of the charge; given that this will ordinarily be the whole of the undertaking of the company, he may attempt a sale of the business as a going concern). He must be an insolvency practitioner. Again, he has wide ranging powers contained in Schedule 1 to the Insolvency Act 1986 and the terms of the loan agreement itself.

9. A liquidator is appointed to collect in the assets of the company and to pay their value to those creditors who are entitled according to the statutory order for payment. His job is to bring the life of the company to an end and he has wide ranging powers contained in sections 165 and 167 of the Insolvency Act 1986.

10. Section 214 of the Insolvency Act 1986 provides that a director is liable for wrongful trading if the company goes into liquidation *and* he knew or ought to have concluded (at some time *before* the commencement of winding up) that there was no *reasonable* prospect that the company would avoid going into insolvent liquidation.

There is only *one* defence; namely, that he took *every* step with a view to minimising the potential loss to the company's creditors as he *ought* to have taken.

Note

(1) Directors found liable may be made to contribute to the assets of the company as the court thinks fit.
(2) Applications are made to the court by the liquidator. The cost of litigation means relatively few cases are brought to court.

11. Section 239 of the Insolvency Act 1986 provides that a preference is given by a company if it does anything or suffers anything to be done that puts a creditor into a better position on liquidation than he would have been in if that thing had not been done (*e.g.* payment in full of an unsecured trade creditor who would have received nothing on liquidation because secured creditors rank above him and would have taken all assets of the company on enforcement of their security).

Note

(1) The company must be influenced by a desire to put that person into better position. This influence is *presumed* if the person is a connected person (*e.g.* director). The company may *not* be so influenced if it is responding to the threat of proceedings or other commercial pressure from an unconnected trade creditor.
(2) Applications are made to the court by the liquidator (on a liquidation) or administrator (on an administration) and the transaction can be set aside if made at the *relevant time* (*i.e.* within six months before commencement of a winding up or presentation of the administration petition or within two years of such a date where the preference is given to a connected person such as a director).

Appendix 5   Glossary

This Glossary is an amalgam of the specialist subject glossaries, *i.e.* it includes definitions in relation to Sole Traders, Taxation, Partnerships, Companies and Insolvency.

Active partners
are active in the day-to-day management and business of the partnership.

Administration order
an administration order is an order made by a court placing a company that is, or is likely to become, insolvent under the control of an administrator, following the presentation of a petition by the company, it's directors or a creditor of the company. The aim of the order is to seek to preserve the company's business as a going concern; to allow a reorganisation of the company, or to ensure the most advantageous realisation/sale of it's assets whilst protecting it from further court action by it's creditors.

Administrative receiver
an administrative receiver is the duly qualified insolvency practitioner appointed by a secured creditor holding a registered charge over the whole (or substantially the whole) of a company's assets, in order to recover the money due to the secured creditor. Amongst other things he can carry on the company's business and sell the business and sell the business and the other assets secured by the charge.

Administrator
an administrator is the duly qualified insolvency practitioner appointed by the court to manage a company that is subject to an administration order to achieve the purposes set out in the order.

Advance corporation tax (ACT)
is a prepayment of mainstream corporation tax (MCT) made by a company when it pays dividends to shareholders. In that instance the company pays the dividend to the shareholder and an amount of tax (ACT) to the revenue as part of an early payment of MCT.

Allotment
the unconditional right for a would-be shareholder to have his name registered in the company's register of members.

413

Alternate director	a director who stands in for the usual director, whilst they are away or unable to act.
Annual general meeting (AGM)	a meeting of shareholders of the company generally held once a year.
Annual return	a financial return made by the company to the registrar of companies each year.
Articles of association	a company's internal regulations of a contractual nature between the company and the shareholder "inter se" (see Table A).
Articles of partnership	See "Partnership deed".
Associate	means a relative, trustee, etc., of a "participator" as defined in section 417(2) of the Income and Corporation Taxes Act 1988. See also "sssociated company" defined in s. 416.
Auditor	a person who audits and confirms the accuracy of the accounts of a company.
Bankrupt	a bankrupt is an individual against whom a court has made a bankruptcy order as a result of the bankrupt failing to pay a statutory demand or to satisfy execution of a court judgment. On the making of the order the bankrupts property vests by operation of the law in the trustee in bankruptcy.
Bankruptcy	bankruptcy is the process by which the trustee in the bankruptcy deals with the estate of a bankrupt.
Benefit in kind	a benefit in kind is a non-cash emolument paid as part of the consideration in a service agreement. For example, a company director may receive the use of a car in addition to a salary component. The car represents a benefit in kind, the salary a ıbenefit in cash', or a cash benefit. Benefits in kind are also referred to as fringe benefits or non-cash requisites.
Board of Directors	collectively the managers of a company.
Bonus Share	a share issued by the company to a member usually in proportion to his existing holding.
Business names	a name adopted by a business that complies with the Business Names Act 1985.
Call	a written demand made on a member of a company (through the directors) to pay up the amount remaining or part of the amount unpaid on his shares.
Capital	(capital contribution) the permanent investment whether in assets, money or in kind made by a partner into the partnership.
Capital allowances	writing off for tax purposes the value of a capital asset so as to reduce taxable income. For example, buildings and plant and machinery

	may be written down or depreciated at rates set by the Taxation of Capital Gains Act 1988.
Capital gain	the increase in value of a chargeable asset as defined by the Taxation of Capital Gains Act 1992 over and above the increase for the period in question of the inflation index.
Capital gains tax (CGT)	the tax payable as a result of a capital gain having been made.
Capital partner	a partner entitled to share in the profits of the partnership in accordance with the terms of the partnership agreement. A capital partner will usually receive income in addition to a share of the profits.
Cash benefit	see ''Benefit in kind''.
Certificate of incorporation	a document issued by the registrar of companies to confirm the formation of the company.
Close company	a company defined by section 414(1) of the Income and Corporation Taxes Act 1988 where there is a degree of overlap between those people who own the company and those who manage it. It is a company under the control of five or fewer participators or of participators who are directors.
Company limited by guarantee	a company, the liability of whose members is limited by reference to guarantee amount.
Company limited by shares	a company, the liability of whose members is limited by reference shares.
Compulsory liquidation	a compulsory liquidation of a company is a liquidation initiated by court order. This is usually as a result of a petition presented to the court by a creditor and is the only method by which a creditor can bring about a liquidation of it's debtor company.
Corporation tax	see ''Mainstream corporation tax''.
Creditor's committee	a creditor's committee is formed to represent the interests of all creditors in supervising the activities of an administrator or trustee in bankruptcy, or receiving reports from an administrative receiver.
Creditors' voluntary liquidation	a creditor's voluntary liquidation relates to an insolvent company. It is commenced by the resolution of shareholders but is under the effective control of the creditors, who can choose the liquidator.
Debenture	a document acknowledging the indebtedness of A to B.
Deductible expenses	those expenses that may, in accordance with tax legislation be used to reduce income profits and therefore the taxation liability.

Demand	a statutory demand is a formal demand issued by a creditor, requiring the debtor to pay a debt within three weeks. Failure to pay is evidence of insolvency and is one of the grounds upon which a creditor may present a petition to the court of the compulsory liquidation on bankruptcy of the debtor.
Director	(a) an officer of the company, along with the secretary;
	(b) principally concerned with the management of the company;
	(c) may be "alternate", *i.e.* a stand-in director whilst the usual director is unable to act;
	(d) shadow, *i.e.* someone who exercises de facto control of the company behind the scenes;
	(e) a matter of public record when appointed, removed or resign, *i.e.* details sent to registrar.
Direct tax	paid directly by the taxpayer.
Dividend	a distribution paid of a company's profits to the shareholder in proportion to his shares and in accordance with the rights attaching to his shares.
Donee	the recipient of a gift or undervalue transaction.
Donor	the person or entity making a gift or giving something away for less than market value, i.e. where there is a "gratuitous intent".
Election	an election is a choice offered to the taxpayer and sometimes the revenue under various areas of the tax legislation; to enable more efficient tax planning. Examples of elections are as follows —
	(a) with a gift or undervalue transaction the donor and donee can elect to "holdover" (delay) any capital gain payment.
	(b) the old partnership rules allowed the taxpayer to make an actual income basis election.
	(c) the old partnership rules allowed the revenue to make a similar election in respect of the closing years of a business.
Elective resolutions	resolutions made by private companies to relax procedural requirements under the Companies Act 1985—see s. 379A.
Emoluments	see "Perquisites".
Execution of a judgment	the process of recovery of a judgment sum once judgment has been given by the court.

Executive director	a director who is working full-time for the company or under an obligation to devote a substantial amount of his time to the management of the company.
Expenses	those items incurred in making income profits.
Extraordinary general meeting (EGM)	a meeting of shareholders of the company other than the AGM, held whenever required by the Companies Act 1985 or if the directors feel it is appropriate.
Extraordinary resolution	a resolution passed by a majority of not less than three quarters of the shareholders voting in person or by proxy at a general meeting.
Extortionate credit transaction	an extortionate credit transaction is a transaction by which credit is provided on terms that, on an objective basis, are exorbitant or grossly unfair compared with the risk accepted by the creditor. Such a transaction may be challenged by an administrator, a liquidator or a trustee in bankruptcy.
Firm	in law, a business organisation, usually a partnership.
Fixed assets	assets intended for continuing use, *e.g.* land and machinery.
Fixed charge	a fixed charge is a form of security granted over specific assets typically ''fixed'' assets, preventing the debtor dealing with those assets without the consent of the secured creditor. It gives the secured creditor a first claim on the proceeds of sale and the creditor can usually appoint a receiver to realise the assets in the event of default.
Fixed and floating charge	a combination of a fixed and floating charge over substantially the whole of the assets of a compound, typically providing for the appointment of an administrative receiver.
Floating charge	a floating charge is a form of security granted to a creditor over general assets or a company which may change from time to time in the normal course of a business. The company can continue to use the assets in it's business until an event of default occurs and the charge crystallises. If this happens, the secured creditor can realise the assets to recover his debt, usually be appointing an administrative receiver and obtain the net proceeds of sale, subject to the prior reference claims of the preferential creditors.
Franked dividend	a dividend on which tax (ACT) has already been paid by the company to the revenue

allowing the taxpayer a tax credit, with the possibility, depending upon the taxpayer's marginal rate, of the taxpayer paying no further tax.

Fraudulent trading applies to a company in liquidation where the company had carried on business with intent to defraud creditors, or for any fraudulent purpose. It is a criminal offence and those involved can be made personally liable for the company's liabilities.

Fringe benefit see "Benefit in kind".

General meeting a meeting of the members of the company.

Golden handshake is a bonus paid to an employee upon that employee leaving the business, i.e. an amount over and above contractual entitlements.

Gratuitous intent See "donor".

Income partner a partner entitled only to receive an income from the partnership and not to share in the profits.

Income profits receipts that fall under one or other of the various schedules. As such income is subject to the payment of income tax or corporation tax.

Indirect tax borne by the taxpayer but paid by a third party to the Revenue, e.g. sales tax.

Insolvency insolvency refers to the financial problems encountered by companies from time to time when assets are outweighed by liabilities, *i.e.* on a balance sheet test, the company is technically not in a position to carry on business. Winding up may be either on an insolvent basis or a solvent basis (where the shareholders choose to end the company's activities).

Insolvency practitioner the Insolvency Rules 1986 (as amended) provide the detailed working procedures for the provisions of the Insolvency Act 1986.

Insolvent in the case of both a company and an individual, may be defined as the inability to meet liabilities as they fall due. A company may also be described as insolvent if the value of it's assets is less than the amount of it's liabilities.

Insolvent liquidation a company goes into insolvent liquidation if it goes into liquidation at a time when it's assets are insufficient for the payment of it's debts and other liabilities and the expenses of liquidation etc.

Interest for tax purposes, the cost of borrowing, e.g. the interest rate on a mortgage debenture is a sum calculated against the capital amount borrowed and is payable borrower to the lender at peri-

	odic intervals in accordance with the terms of the mortgage debenture.
Interim order	an individual who intends to propose a voluntary arrangement to his creditors may apply to the court for an interim order which, if granted, precludes bankruptcy and other legal proceedings whilst the order is in force.
Joint liability	where liabilities rather than being shared between two or more people are theoretically able to be imposed on one of those people alone. For example A, B, C and D in partnership have joint liability, for a debt of £100,000 and B, C and D are bankrupt, A will be liable for the whole £100,000 debt.
Joint and several liability	a combination of joint and several liability. For example, if A,B,C and D have joint and several liability in respect of a debt of £100,000, A may be held liable by the creditor for either £25,000 (several liability) or the whole £100,000 (joint liability).
Lien	a lien is right of possession over goods or property belonging to another, with a right to retain possession until debts doe to the possessor are paid.
Limited partnership	a partnership governed by the Limited Partnerships Act 1907 whereby the partners will have limited liability rather than unlimited liability as is the usual case. Note, however, that at least one of the partners in a limited partnership must bear unlimited liability. Section 717 of the Companies Act 1985 and section 4 of the Limited Partnership Act 1907 limits the number of partners in a limited partnership to no more than 20.
Liquidation	liquidation is the process of realising a company's assets and distributing the proceeds to satisfy it's liabilities and to repay it's shareholders.
Liquidation committee	a liquidation committee is formed to represent the interests of all creditors in order to supervise the activities of a liquidator in a compulsory or creditors voluntary liquidation.
Liquidator	a liquidator is the duly qualified insolvency practitioner responsible for dealing with the liquidation of a company.
Listed securities	those securities listed on a recognised stock exchange.
Losses	amounts that may be used to reduce income profits under the schedules.

Mainstream corporation tax (MCT)	the tax paid by a company on it's income profits, i.e. equivalent to income tax payable by an individual taxpayer.
Managing director	a director appointed to oversee the day-to-day running of the company.
Marginal rate	a taxpayer's top rate of income tax.
Meetings	a company usually conducts its business through meeting procedure, unless it adopts written resolution procedure.
	refer either to a director's meeting or a shareholder's meeting which may be AGMs, EGMs.
Member/shareholder	interchangeable terms, i.e someone who holds at least one share in a company in own name or as a bare trustee or nominee on behalf of someone else.
Member's voluntary liquidation	a member's voluntary liquidation relates to a company that is able to settle all it's debts in full within a period of 12 months of being placed into liquidation.
Memorandum of association	contains key information about the company, *e.g.* business aims.
Nominal capital	the amount up to which the company can issue shares.
Nominee	the insolvency practitioner who acts in the preliminary stages of a voluntary arrangement and considers whether proposals should be put to creditors.
Nominee shareholder	a shareholder who holds shares as a nominee for another person.
Non-cash benefit	see "Benefit in kind".
Non-executive director	usually a director who is not under an obligation to devote whole, or substantially whole, time to the company.
Offices	includes employees, company directors and the like.
Officer	a broad term including managers, directors and secretaries.
Official receiver	an official receiver is a civil servant who is an officer of the court. He deals with the administration of compulsory liquidations and bankruptcies, either as liquidator or trustee in bankruptcy, or overseeing an insolvency practitioner acting as such. There is an official receiver attached to each court that deals with insolvency matters.
Onerous property	in the context of a liquidation or a bankruptcy applies to the unprofitable contracts and to property that is unsaleable or not easily saleable

or that might give rise to a continuing bankruptcy.

Ordinary resolution	a resolution passed by a simple majority of members at a general meeting.
Ordinary share	a share entitling it's holder to receive a dividend after dividends paid on preference shares.
Par value	authorised or nominal value of a share.
Participator	person having a share or interest in the capital or income of the close company and includes someone entitled to acquire share capital or voting rights in the company and lenders (Income and Corporation Taxes Act 1988 s. 417).
Partnership	a relation between two persons carrying on a business with the same aim of profit.
Partnership deed or agreement	the document governing the relationship between partners that complements and/or replaces the Partnership Act 1890.
Perquisites	refers to all benefits, whether cash or non-cash paid pursuant to a service agreement in contract of employment.
Personal allowances	those tax free portions of a persons income profits.
Poll	a method of voting enabling each member vote for or against a resolution according to the number of shares held.
Pre-emption	a right of first refusal given to shareholders to purchase the shares of any member wishing to sell shares. The term is used also to refer to the right of certain shareholders to subscribe for further shares on a new issue.
Preference	any transaction that has the effect of putting a creditor of a company (or an individual) in a better position than would have been the case in the event of a subsequent liquidation or bankruptcy and where there was a desire to produce this effect.
Preference shares	a share giving it's holder preferential rights in respect of dividends, and-or return of share capital on a solvent winding up. Such shares usually have limited voting rights.
Preferential creditors	preferential creditors must be paid in priority to the holders of floating charges and in priority to unsecured creditors. These include PAYE and VAT.
Pre-incorporation contract	a contract entered into before a company has been incorporated.
Private company	a company that is not a public company.
Professional partnership	not a term of art but a partnership comprised

	of professionally qualified groups, such as solicitors.
Promoter, subscriber, founder	a person who takes steps to form a company or set it in motion.
Proof of debt	the document by which a creditor seeks to establish it's claim against a debtor in a liquidation or bankruptcy.
Prospectus	an invitation to the public to subscribe for shares or debentures of a company.
Provisional liquidator	a provisional liquidator is an insolvency practitioner appointed by the court to protect the assets of a company after a winding-up petition has been presented, but before a liquidator is appointed.
Proxy	a proxy is an authority given by a creditor to a person to attend a meeting and speak and vote os their representative.
Qualifying distribution	a term of some technicality defined for the purposes of the Income and Corporation Taxes Act 1988 to refer to amounts that the taxpayer is bound to pay to a third party and are, therefore, excluded from forming part of the income profits for the purpose of the Schedules.
Quorum	the minimum number of persons necessary to constitute a valid shareholder's meeting.
Receiver	a receiver is the person appointed by a secured creditor holding a fixed charge over specific assets of a company in order to take control of those assets for the benefit of the secured creditor. The term can also be used generally to describe any person appointed by a secured creditor.
Receivership	the general term applied when an administrative receiver or receiver is appointed.
Recognised professional bodies	those approved by the Secretary of State as being able top authorise their members to act as insolvency practitioners.
Redeemable shares	shares of a company that can be redeemed by the company.
Register of members	a register kept by the company of membership of the company.
Registered office	the office where the company is required to keep certain documents and records as required by the Companies Act 1985.
Registrar	the person with whom a company must file it's public records.
Regulations	the articles of association.
Relief	concessions to the full rigour of the rules concerning the payment of income tax and capital

gains tax, e.g. retirement relief reduces rather than delays the payment of capital gains tax.

Resolution
a formal decision by a majority of the members of the company of the Board of directors.

Retention of title clause
(Romalpa clause) a clause in a sale agreement in which the vendor retains ownership in the goods until they are completely paid for regardless of who has possession.

Rights issue
a right given to an existing shareholder to subscribe for further shares in the company.

Schedules
refers to the various income tax schedules under which income profits are allocated.

Secured creditor
a creditor that holds a charge granted by a debtor over the debtor's assets. As a result the creditor has the right of priority for the repayment of it's debt, although the exact priority depends upon the type of charge.

Several liability
where liabilities are shared between two or more people. For example, if A, B, C and D are in partnership and have equal several liability and a debt of £100,000, they will each be responsible for £25,000 only.

Shadow director
a person who is not formally appointed as a director but in accordance with those directions or instructions the directors of a company are accustomed to act. However, if a person is not a shadow director merely because the directors acts on advice given by him in a professional capacity.

Share
unit of ownership of a company. Different rights are attached to different types of shares. Rights are set out in the contract of allotment when the member is issued and allocated the shares.

Sleeping partners
are partners who have contributed "capital", *i.e.* "permanent investment" in the partnership but they are not active in the management of the business.

Small companies
rate of MCT that applies to those companies whose profits fall below a specified amount.

Special manager
a special manager is a person appointed by the court in a compulsory liquidation to assist the liquidator or provisional liquidator in managing the company's business. A special manager may also be appointed in a bankruptcy.

Special resolution
a resolution passed by a majority of not less than three quarters of members voting at a general meeting of the company of which not less than 21 days notice is given.

Standard rate	the MCT that applies in a particular year.
Statutory demand	a formal demand issued by a creditor requiring the debtor to pay a debt within three weeks. Failure to pay is evidence of insolvency and is one of the grounds upon which a creditor may present a petition to the court of the compulsory liquidation or bankruptcy of the debtor.
Stock exchange	an exchange that provides markets for the buying and selling of securities.
Subscriber of memorandum	a person who signs the memorandum of association.
Supervisor	the insolvency practitioner appointed by creditors to supervise the implementation of an approved voluntary agreement.
Table A	a model set of articles of association.
Tapering relief	a form of tax relief that applies to that section of profits that falls between the small companies rate amount and the standard companies rate amount.
Tax credit	no further tax may be payable by the taxpayer as tax has already been paid and credited as paid. If for example, a 40 per cent taxpayer has a tax credit of 25 per cent he will have a further 15 per cent tax to pay. If the taxpayer is a 25 per cent taxpayer he will have no further tax to pay.
Third party	a generic term referring to a party existing and operating outside the business.
A trading company	not defined in the Companies Act 1985. An active as opposed to a ''dormant'' company (see Companies Act 1985, s. 250). ''dormant'' is defined in this context as no significant accounting transaction occurring for a period of time.
Trading partnerships	as distinct from professional partnerships; they are comprised of members other than those listed in section 716 of the Companies Act 85. Limited in size to no more than 20 partners: (a) management, or (b) decision-making.
Transaction at an undervalue	can describe either a gift or a transaction in which the consideration received is significantly less that given.
Transfer of shares	(a) transfer of the legal and beneficial ownership in the shares; (b) sale or gift.
Transmission of shares	similar to a transfer of shares in its effect. A vesting by operation of law of a shareholder's shares in another person on death.

Trustee in bankruptcy	the person who administers and realises the assets of a bankrupt and distributes the proceeds for the benefit of the bankrupt's creditors.
Unlimited liability	where the owner of the business is solely responsible to pay the debts incurred by the business.
Unsecured creditor	a creditor whose claim has no secured prior right, whether in relation to a company in liquidation, a bankruptcy.
Ultra vires	a company acting in excess of its object or powers as set out in its memorandum or articles.
VAT registration	registering under the Value Added Tax Act (1985) which is necessary depending on the turnover of the business.
Voluntary arrangement company	procedure whereby a scheme of arrangement usually involving delayed or reduced payments of debt, is put forward to creditors and shareholders. There is a limited involvement by the court and scheme is under the control of a supervisor.
Voluntary arrangement individual (IVA)	a voluntary arrangement for an individual is a procedure whereby a scheme of arrangement, usually involving delayed or reduced payments of debts, is put forward to creditors. Such a scheme requires the approval of the court and is under the control of a supervisor.
Voluntary liquidation	voluntary liquidation and members voluntary liquidation.
Winding-up	see "liquidation".
Winding-up petition	a winding-up petition is one presented to the court seeking an order that a company be put into compulsory liquidation.
Written resolutions	a resolution in written form signed by each shareholder replaces the need to hold meetings of shareholders (see section 381A of the Companies Act 1985). Written resolutions can be used for all company matters except the removal of.
Wrongful trading	applies where a director of a company in liquidation allowed the company to continue trading in circumstances where he should have concluded that there was no reasonable prospect that the company would avoid going into insolvent liquidation. Any director involved may be made liable to make a contribution to the company's assets.

Appendix 6   Ready Reckoner Regarding Fees, Percentages and Sterling Amounts Referred to in this Guide

VAT (see Chapter 1)

Registration threshold—£46,000 anticipated in respect of sales for the business the next 12 months or on the basis of the previous month's sales. In the Budget of November 1995 plans were announced to increase the registration amount to £47,000.

Standard VAT rate—17.5 per cent.

Bankruptcy (see Chapter 5)

Threshold—£750 unsecured debt Insolvency Act 1986, s. 267(4).

Companies (see Chapters 9, 10 and 12)

FEES

Change of name fee £20.
Incorporation fee—usually £20; expedited, *i.e.* same day registration is £200.

OTHER MATTERS

Substantial property transactions (s. 320):
—require shareholder approval by ordinary resolution at general meeting if:
   over £100,000 in value; or
   if over £2,000 in value and over 10 per cent of the company's net assets (based on the balance sheet) or if no balance sheet available, based on the called up capital.

Loans to directors:
—generally prohibited by s. 330.
—the exceptions are as follows:

426

s. 334 a loan for any purpose, up to £5,000
s. 335 a loan in the ordinary course of business, up to £10,000
s. 337 a loan to enable a director to meet expenditure for the company's purposes or to enable him to perform his duties and repaid within 6 months, up to £20,000

Insolvency threshold:
£750 unsecured debt.

Taxation (see Chapters 6 and 16)

INDIVIDUALS

Personal allowance—the first £3,765 is exempt from tax

Rates of Tax:
20 per cent on income band £3,766 to £7.665
24 per cent on income band £7,666 to £29,265
40 per cent on income above £29,265
Married couples allowance £1,790

Redundancy:
The first £30,000 is received free of tax.

Capital Gains Tax:
Applicable rate: at the taxpayer's marginal rate
Annual exemption: £6,300

Retirement relief:
The qualifying age is 50 years of age.
100 per cent relief on business assets up to £250,000
50 per cent relief on business assets between £250,000 and £1,000,000.

Inheritance Tax:
Applies to estates worth in excess of £200,000 from April 6, 1996 (before then it is £154,000)
Annual exemption: £3,000
Small gifts: £250
Chargeable transfers:
Include all shareholdings in unquoted companies.
Applicable rate: 40 per cent.

CORPORATIONS TAX

Small companies rate (applies to companies with profits less than £300,000 annually)—24 per cent.
Mainstream corporation rate (applies to all companies with profits in excess of £1,500,000 annually)—33 per cent.

For companies with profits in excess of £300,000 but less than £1.5 million, a sliding scale applies.

Advance Corporation Tax is I/100–I, where I is the lower tax rate of 20 per cent. ACT = 20/100–20 = 20/80 = 1/4 of the dividend or 1/5 of the grossed up amount.

Stamp Duty (Stamp Act 1891, Schedule 1) (see Chapter 11)

For the transfer of shares: the rate is 1/2 per cent of market value, *i.e.* 50p per £100 or part of £100—see Chapter 11.

For the transfer of other property: the rate is 1 per cent unless the consideration does not exceed £60,000 and the instrument contains a certificate of value to that effect, in which case it is nil.

E.C. law (see Chapters 20 and 21)

The ECU (European currency unit)—worth approximately 85 pence as at March 1996.

Competition law (Article 85 E.C.) (see Chapter 21)

Agreements of minor importance: the threshold is 5 per cent of market share or 300 million ECU businesses.

Index